A Companion to the Works of Hugo von Hofmannsthal

Studies in German Literature, Linguistics, and Culture

Edited by James Hardin
(South Carolina)

The Camden House Companions provide well-informed and up-to-date critical commentary on the most significant aspects of major literary works, periods, or figures. The Companions may be read profitably by the reader with a general interest in the subject. For the benefit of student and scholar, quotations are provided in the original language.

Hugo von Hofmannsthal

A COMPANION TO THE WORKS OF

Hugo von Hofmannsthal

EDITED BY
THOMAS A. KOVACH

CAMDEN HOUSE

First published 2002
by Camden House

Camden House is an imprint of Boydell & Brewer Inc.
PO Box 41026, Rochester, NY 14604–4126 USA
and of Boydell & Brewer Limited
PO Box 9, Woodbridge, Suffolk IP12 3DF, UK

ISBN: 1–57113–215–5

Library of Congress Cataloging-in-Publication Data

A companion to the works of Hugo von Hofmannsthal / edited by Thomas A.
Kovach.
    p. cm. – (Studies in German literature, linguistics, and culture)
Includes bibliographical references and index.
ISBN 1–57113–215–5 (alk. paper)
1. Hofmannsthal, Hugo von, 1874–1929 — Criticism and interpretation.
I. Kovach, Thomas A., 1949–   II. Studies in German literature, linguistics, and
culture (Unnumbered)

PT2617.047 Z37543 2002
831'.912—dc21
                                                                  2001059853

A catalogue record for this title is available from the British Library.

This publication is printed on acid-free paper.
Printed in the United States of America

For my wife

Contents

Acknowledgments   xi

References to the Works of Hugo von Hofmannsthal   xiii

List of Principal Works of Hugo von Hofmannsthal   xv

Introduction: Hofmannsthal Today   1
Thomas A. Kovach

CONTEXTS

Hofmannsthal and *Wiener Moderne*:
The Cultural Context   25
Hinrich C. Seeba

THE WRITINGS

Hofmannsthal's Poems and Lyric Dramas   47
Andreas Thomasberger

Hofmannsthal's Narrative Prose:
The Problem of Individuation   65
Ellen Ritter

Hofmannsthal's "Ein Brief": Chandos and His Crisis   85
Thomas A. Kovach

Hofmannsthal's Theater of Adaptation   97
Benjamin K. Bennett

The Hofmannsthal-Strauss Collaboration   117
Joanna Bottenberg

Hofmannsthal's Comedies   139
W. E. Yates

Hofmannsthal and the Salzburg Festival   159
Judith Beniston

Hofmannsthal's Essays: Conservation as Revolution   181
Katherine Arens

THE LEGACY

Hugo von Hofmannsthal's Political Vision   205
Nina Berman

Hofmannsthal Reception in the Twentieth Century   227
Douglas A. Joyce

Notes on Contributors   251

Index   253

Acknowledgments

A S THIS VOLUME SEES THE LIGHT OF DAY, there are a number of individuals and groups whose help I would like to acknowledge. First of all, my thanks to Dr. James Hardin, General Editor of the Camden House *Studies in German Literature, Linguistics, and Culture*, for inviting me to undertake this project and for his exacting and helpful support throughout my work. Then (of course!) to my contributors, who have made it possible to present a multifaceted view of Hugo von Hofmannsthal in this volume, one which, it is hoped, will do justice to this multifaceted writer.

I want to thank my colleagues in the Department of German Studies, whose collegiality has made my job as Department Head sufficiently manageable to complete this project on schedule. I'd also like to thank my university, the University of Arizona, for granting me a much-needed semester of sabbatical leave, and my colleague Professor Renate Schulz for giving me the peace of mind of knowing that the department would be well led in my absence.

I'd like to thank Camden House Managing Editor James Walker for his calm and able support in the final stages of getting the manuscript ready to print.

And finally, I want to thank my wife Candy Siegel, to whom this volume is dedicated, for her patience, love and support.

References to the Works of Hugo von Hofmannsthal

THERE ARE THREE editions of the collected works of Hofmannsthal: the *Gesammelte Werke in Einzelausgaben*, edited by Herbert Steiner and published by Fischer-Verlag in Frankfurt am Main and Stockholm from 1946 through 1959, with reprinted volumes appearing as late as 1973; a ten volume paperback *Gesammelte Werke*, edited by Bernd Schoeller in consultation with Rudolf Hirsch and published by Fischer Taschenbuch Verlag in Frankfurt am Main from 1979 through 1980; and the *Kritische Ausgabe Sämtlicher Werke*, edited by Rudolf Hirsch and others, published by Fischer-Verlag and appearing from 1975 onward. For the sake of convenience, references in this volume will be to the easily accessible paperback *Gesammelte Werke*, and will be abbreviated as follows:

GDI = *Gedichte • Dramen 1: 1891–1898. 1979.*
DII = *Dramen II: 1892–1905. 1979.*
DIII = *Dramen III: 1893–1927. 1979.*
DIV= *Dramen IV: Lustspiele. 1979.*
DV = *Dramen V: Operndichtungen. 1979.*
DVI = *Dramen VI: Ballette, Pantomimen, Bearbeitungen,*
      Übersetzungen. 1979.
Erz = *Erzählungen, Erfundene Gespräche und Briefe, Reisen. 1979.*
RAI = *Reden und Aufsätze I: 1891–1913. 1979.*
RAII = *Reden und Aufsätze II: 1914–1924. 1979.*
RAIII = *Reden und Aufsätze III: 1925–1929. Aufzeichnungen. 1980.*
   (*Aufzeichnungen* were co-edited by Ingeborg Beyer-Ahlert.)

Passages not contained in this edition will be cited from the *Kritische Ausgabe Sämtlicher Werke* by volume number: *SW1, SW18*, etc.

Principal Works of Hugo von Hofmannsthal

Listed by year of first appearance. When available in translation, English title and date of appearance are given.

1892   *Der Tod des Tizian,* lyric drama
        "Vorfrühling," "Erlebnis" ("An Experience," 1961), poems
        "Südfranzösische Eindrücke," travel account
        Essays on Swinburne, Ibsen, Eleonora Duse

1893   "Idylle" ("Idyll," 1961), lyric drama
        Der Tor und der Tod ("Death and the Fool," 1961), lyric drama
        Essay on D'Annunzio (I)

1894   "Terzinen I–IV" ("Stanzas in Terza Rima," 1961),
            "Weltgeheimnis," poems
        Essays on Pater, D'Annunzio (II), "Über moderne englische
            Malerei" (on Pre-Raphaelites), "Philosophie des Meta-
            phorischen"

1895   "Das Märchen der 672. Nacht," story
        "Ballade des äusseren Lebens," "Manche freilich," "Ein
            Traum von großer Magie" ("Ballad of the Outer Life,"
            "Many Truly," "A Dream of Great Magic," 1961), poems
        Essays on D'Annunzio (III), Francis Vielé-Griffin

1896   "Die Beiden," "Lebenslied" ("Song of Life," 1961), poems
        "Poesie und Leben," speech
        Essay on Stefan George

1897   "Der Kaiser von China spricht" ("The Emperor of China
            Speaks," 1961), poem
        Das kleine Welttheater, Der weiße Fächer, "Der Kaiser und
            die Hexe" ("The Little Theatre of the World,"
            "The Emperor and the Witch," 1961), lyric dramas

1898   "Reiselied" ("Traveler's Song," 1961), poem
        "Reitergeschichte" ("A Tale of the Cavalry," 1952), story

1899   *Das Bergwerk zu Falun* ("The Mine at Falun" [Act I only],
        1961), drama

1900   "Erlebnis des Marschalls von Bassompierre" ("An Episode in
        the Life of the Marshal de Bassompierre," 1952), story

1901   *Studie über die Entwickelung* [*sic*] *des Dichters Victor Hugo*
        (Habilitationsschrift)

1902   "Ein Brief" ("The Letter of Lord Chandos," 1952), fictional
        letter

1903   *Elektra* (*Electra*, 1908), drama
        "Das Gespräch über Gedichte" (fictional dialogue)
        Essays on Duse (III), "Die Bühne als Traumbild"

1904   *Das gerettete Venedig* (*Venice Preserved*, 1915), drama

1905   *Ödipus und die Sphinx* (drama)
        "Sebastian Melmoth" (translated 1952), essay on Oscar
        Wilde

1906   "Der Dichter und diese Zeit," speech

1907   "Vor Tag," poem
        "Die Briefe des Zurückgekehrten," fictional letters

1908   Essay on Balzac (trans. 1961)

1909   *Elektra* ("Electra," 1963), opera

1910   "Verse zum Gedächtnis des Schauspielers Josef Kainz," poem
        Cristinas Heimreise (drama)

1911   *Jedermann* (*Everyman*, 1917), drama
        Der Rosenkavalier ("The Cavalier of the Rose," 1963), opera
        "Das alte Spiel von Jedermann," "Das Spiel vor der Menge,"
        essays

1916   *Ariadne auf Naxos,* final version of opera

1919   *Die Frau ohne Schatten,* opera
        Die Frau ohne Schatten (*The Woman Without a Shadow,*
            1993), prose narrative
        "Deutsche Festspiele zu Salzburg," "Die Salzburger Fest-
            spiele," essays

1921   *Der Schwierige* ("The Difficult Man," 1963), comedy
        Buch der Freunde, aphorisms

1922   *Das Salzburger große Welttheater* (*The Salzburg Great Theatre
            of the World,* 1963), drama

1923   *Der Unbestechliche,* comedy

1925   "Reise im nördlichen Afrika," (portion translated as "Journey
            in Northern Africa: Fez," 1952), travel account

1927   *Der Turm* ("The Tower," 1966), final version of drama
        "Das Schrifttum als geistiger Raum der Nation," speech

1928   *Die ägyptische Helena,* opera
        "Das Publikum der Salzburger Festspiele," "Zum Programm
            der Salzburger Festspiele 1929," essays

1929   "Einige Worte als Vorrede zu St.-J. Perse 'Anabasis,'" essay

1930   *Ad me ipsum* [*To Myself*], notes toward a self-interpretation;
            first complete publication in book form 1959

1932   *Andreas* (portion translated 1952), first book edition of novel
            fragment

1933   *Arabella* (translated 1963), opera

View of the Oberes Belvedere (Upper Belvedere) from the south.
Photograph by Thomas A. Kovach.

THOMAS A. KOVACH

Introduction: Hofmannsthal Today

SINCE GOETHE, there have been few if any writers in the German language who created masterpieces in every major genre: lyric poetry and verse drama, stage tragedy and comedy, narrative prose, and essays. One such writer, and arguably the first since Goethe himself, is Hugo von Hofmannsthal (1874–1929). One of the towering figures of German literature in the first decades of the twentieth century, Hofmannsthal is the author of some of the most beloved and anthologized poems of the German language, some written while he was still in his teens; he is arguably the greatest writer of comedies in the German language; he is the author of several short works of narrative prose which are among the richest and most haunting ever written; he is the author of a number of dramas and tragedies in which masterworks of European tradition are adapted to create new works that are both modern and original; he is one of the most prolific and perceptive essayists in the German language; and last but not least, in his collaboration with the composer Richard Strauss, he is the author of six opera libretti that raised the opera libretto to a level of literary refinement never before and never since achieved.

Hofmannsthal was born on February 1, 1874, in Vienna, Austria, the city which was to be his home throughout his life. His parents' home was on Salesianergasse, in the immediate vicinity of those glories of Baroque architecture, the Upper and Lower Belvedere, and it is here that he was raised in an atmosphere of upper middle-class comfort and refinement. He was the only son of Hugo August Peter von Hofmannsthal, a lawyer in the employ of one of Vienna's leading banks, and Anna Maria Josefa née Fohleutner, whose family came to Vienna from the Sudetenland via Bavaria. His paternal grandfather Augustin Emil von Hofmannsthal, who had inherited the silk and manufacturing industry from his father, had married a woman from an aristocratic Italian family. And thus Hugo von Hofmannsthal, the great-grandson of the Jewish merchant Isaak Löw Hofmann, to whose services on behalf of the House of Habsburg the family owed the patent of nobility represented by the name "von Hofmannsthal," belonged to the third generation of Catholic Hofmannsthals. Nevertheless, as we shall see later on, his Jewish origins were by no means a non-issue in the highly charged atmosphere of *fin-de-siècle* Vienna.

Hofmannsthal's biographer Werner Volke quotes a revealing comment by the writer Hermann Bahr about the Hofmannsthal family: "sie fühlten sich in der Provinz nie wohl, dort wehe die Wirklichkeit zu stark und deshalb hätten sie sich in Wien angesiedelt" (8). Descriptions of Hofmannsthal's youth almost always evoke this sense of a young man protected from reality, raised in an atmosphere of aesthetic refinement and shielded from all reminders of a harsher world outside. Hermann Broch in his pioneering study *Hofmannsthal und seine Zeit* (1955) contrasted the poet's upbringing with that of young Mozart, pointing out that while Leopold Mozart trained his son from an early age in the family profession of music, August von Hofmannsthal concentrated "auf die Vermittlung von 'Bildung,' von 'Schaufähigkeit,' also auf die Entwicklung von Fähigkeiten, durch welche die Mußestunden des Bürgers zu 'edlem Genuß' verwandelt werden"(112). And yet the forces of reality were not really absent. Although young Hofmannsthal was largely protected from the immediate consequences of his family's financial losses in the market crash of 1873, this economic crisis, which Carl E. Schorske has shown to be the event that precipitated the demise of political liberalism in Vienna, was to have significant consequences for the city's aesthetic culture in the *fin-de-siècle*.[1]

At the age of ten, Hofmannsthal entered the *Akademisches Gymnasium*, one of Vienna's leading secondary schools. Other writers from the circle soon to be known as *Junges Wien*, such as Arthur Schnitzler (1862–1931) and Richard Beer-Hofmann (1866–1945), had already graduated from the school by the time he entered in 1884. Fellow pupils recalled him as animated in speech and gesture, yet fundamentally solitary. But as early as 1890, at the age of sixteen, Hofmannsthal's first poems and essays — published under the pseudonym "Loris" since his school forbade its students to publish — attracted the attention of the writers and artists congregating in the famous Café Griensteidl, and Hofmannsthal was brought into their midst in the same year. The young man astonished his older colleagues with his vast and discerning knowledge of European literature, with his fluency in several languages, and above all with the apparently effortless mastery he displayed in both his verse and prose writings. In fact, the outpouring of works published in the following years was to cement his reputation as the *Wunderkind* of German literature: poems such as "Vorfrühling" and "Erlebnis" (both 1892), "Weltgeheimnis" and "Terzinen" (1894), "Ballade des äusseren Lebens," "Ein Traum von großer Magie," and "Manche freilich" (1895), lyric dramas *Der Tod des Tizian* (1892), *Idylle* (1893), and *Der Tor und der Tod* (1894), the story "Das Märchen der 672. Nacht" (1895), and a number of essays on contemporary artists and writers had all been completed by 1895, when he turned twenty-one. Apart from the writers and artists of *Junges Wien*, a significant encounter took place in December 1891, when the young man met Stefan George (1868–1933), prominent German poet, leader of a select literary circle, and editor of the literary journal *Blätter für die Kunst*. George was the first poet of world rank whom the young man had met, and through George he had his first real encounter with the poetry and theory of French Symbolism, which was to have a decisive influence on his own writing. Though the relationship was a stormy one — an early misunderstanding nearly led to a duel, and their correspondence was terminated for good in 1906 — Hofmannsthal later acknowledged the importance of this encounter, both in confirming his own poetic calling, and, more practically, in leading to the publication of several of his early poems and verse plays in the pages of *Blätter für die Kunst*.

In October 1894, Hofmannsthal began his year of military service, most of which was spent in the small Moravian town of Göding, only about sixty-five miles northeast of Vienna, but worlds away in atmosphere from the cultivated environment in which he had lived up to that time. In his first encounter with the province and (recalling Bahr's remark quoted earlier) the dose of reality it represented, Hofmannsthal suffered from depression and illness. During a visit home, a significant choice was made in consultation with his parents: abandoning the legal studies he had begun in deference to his father's wishes, he decided to pursue an academic career in Romance Languages, and began his university studies in this field on his return to Vienna in the fall of 1895. In addition to his study in Romance literature, he attended lectures by the classical philologist Alfred von Berger, the philosophers Franz Brentano and Friedrich Jodl, and the scientist-philosopher Ernst Mach; the latter in particular was to exert a significant impact on his world view and writings. His military obligations called him twice more to the provinces: in May 1896 to Tlumacz, in July 1898 to Czortkow, both towns in East Galicia. He completed his dissertation on the use of language by the poets of the French *Pléiade*, and received his doctorate in March of 1899. In May of 1901, he turned in his *Habilitationsschrift*, a dissertation intended for publication, on Victor Hugo, but after several months' wait he withdrew his application for an academic position. He pled a nervous disorder, but in a letter to Theodor Gomperz he spoke of the impossibility of leading "eine solche innere Doppelexistenz" (*Briefe 1890–1901* 338), meaning the attempt to carry on simultaneously an academic and a literary career. For the remainder of his life, he would devote himself exclusively to literature in the broadest sense.

In June of 1901, Hofmannsthal was married in Vienna's Schotten-kirche to Gerty (Gertrud) Schlesinger, the daughter of a banker, and the offspring of a Jewish family whose assimilation was more recent than that of Hofmannsthal's own. Prior to the wedding, they had picked out the residence where they would spend their married life: the "Fuchsschlössel" (named after a tutor of the Empress Maria Theresa who had received the house as a gift) in Rodaun, then a village on the outskirts of Vienna, not far from Schönbrunn Palace. On the surface, the decision regarding his future career and his marriage and settling into a new home, all of which occurred within the course of a couple of months, would seem to signal a kind of resolution of personal uncertainty. Beneath the surface, though, the writer Hofmannsthal was undergoing a crisis that, in 1902, led to the creation of one of his most famous works, the so-called "Chandos Letter" ("Ein Brief," *Erz* 461–72). Although the earlier view of this work as an entirely autobiographical document has rightly been refuted by recent scholarship, there is no question that the crisis of language and cognition expressed by the fictional Lord Chandos reflects Hofmannsthal's own experience of the limits of language as a tool to express reality, of the problematic nature of the external world and of the self.

Nor is there any question that Hofmannsthal's later career was to take a very different shape from his earlier career. Although he had continued to produce major works of lyric poetry and drama in the 1890s (the poems "Die Beiden" and "Lebenslied" in 1896, the lyric dramas *Das kleine Welttheater*, *Der weiße Fächer*, and *Der Kaiser und die Hexe* in 1897), after 1899 he wrote no more lyric dramas, and only a small handful of poems. There are few instances in all literature of a writer abandoning the forms that had gained him fame, but Hofmannsthal did just that. Having recognized and criticized the alienation from life characterizing the Aestheticism that constituted the milieu of his earlier life and work, he was concerned henceforth to find what he called a "Weg zum Sozialen" in his writing. This new approach would take a number of different forms. One was his collaboration with the composer Richard Strauss in the creation of six operas, *Elektra* (1908, based on his drama of the same name from 1903), *Der Rosenkavalier* (1910), *Ariadne auf Naxos* (1913), *Die Frau ohne Schatten* (1915), *Die Ägyptische Helena* (1928), and *Arabella* (1933; the opera was completed and first performed after Hofmannsthal's death). Another was a less happy choice in the view of many: his activity as an active supporter and propagandist for the Austrian war effort during the years

1914 to 1918, reflected in a series of essays (e.g. "Die Bejahung Öster-reichs" [1915], "Die österreichische Idee" [1917]). Finally, in response to the calamitous defeat in the World War, which brought about the end of the Habsburg Monarchy to which he had been devoted, he was instrumental in the founding of the Salzburg Festival, which he envisioned as a way of recreating a cultural milieu destroyed in the war.

Yet the lasting accomplishments of these years were not limited to the opera stage. His essay production continued unabated, and those that were not primarily propagandizing efforts retained the high critical and stylistic level of his earlier works in the genre. He made his breakthrough in the field of comedy (which he himself described as "Das erreichte Soziale") with two comic masterpieces of the 1920s, *Der Schwierige* (1920, first publication in book form 1921) and *Der Unbestechliche* (1923, first book edition 1956). He wrote a series of dramas, which at first glance seem to be adaptations of standard works, but which on closer examination prove to be extraordinarily challenging responses to the crises of both the inner and the outer worlds in his time. In particular, the second version of *Der Turm* (1927), in its depiction of a coming political order of ruthless manipulation, seems in retrospect to be frighteningly prophetic of events that occurred in the next decade.

These events, perhaps mercifully, Hofmannsthal did not live to see. Apart from his activity for the war effort and the inevitable visibility associated with productions of his works, especially the Strauss operas, he lived a relatively quiet existence in Rodaun with his wife and three children, Christiane (1902–1987), Franz (1903–1929), and Raimund (1906–1974). His home life was enriched by regular visits from friends and associates among the leading writers, artists, and intellectuals of the German-speaking world. On July 13, 1929, his son Franz committed suicide; leaving the house for his son's funeral two days later, Hugo von Hofmannsthal was felled by a massive stroke and died that same day.

* * *

When one thinks of those writers who have achieved a secure place in the literary pantheon, it seems that with few exceptions, they have helped their cause by some obvious form of unity linking their works, either as to genre (even Shakespeare is known primarily for his plays), style, or subject matter. In this respect, Hugo von Hofmannsthal has presented posterity with a challenge. Whether one surveys his works by genre — they encompass lyric poetry and drama, stage tragedy and comedy, narrative prose, essay, opera libretto, and numerous combinations of the above categories — or by setting — ranging from classical

antiquity to Renaissance Europe to the anomie of the modern city —
this *oeuvre* displays a bewildering variety to the casual observer, one
which unfortunately has made it difficult for some to classify him and
thus guarantee him a secure place on Parnassus.

And yet, as Hofmannsthal scholars and critics have pointed out in
the last few decades, the earlier notion that his career underwent a radical split around the turn of the century, with his abandonment of lyric
poetry, must be discarded; Hofmannsthal's own claim that his work
taken as a whole displays a "formidable Einheit" (*RAIII* 620) has
largely been vindicated by the repeated demonstration of themes that
run through his works from the earliest years to his death, crossing generic boundaries in the process.

The question of the writer and his audience, one which occupied
Hofmannsthal himself in several of his essays and other works, is inevitably raised when we consider his work from the vantage point one
hundred years after the *Jahrhundertwende* with which he is associated.
Hofmannsthal, in large part through his association with the Aestheticist circle of George and its journal *Blätter für die Kunst* (1892–1919),
in which several of his most famous poems and lyric dramas first appeared, early on acquired the reputation of an aesthete, one who
scorned the general public and wrote only for an elite of the aesthetically refined. The somewhat condescending tone of some of his early
essays and lectures (for example, "Poesie und Leben," 1896) certainly
did their part in confirming this impression. Even Theodor W. Adorno,
writing in 1939, ten years after Hofmannsthal's death, spoke of "die
von George und Hofmannsthal urgierte Entfremdung der Kunst vom
Leben, die die Kunst zu erhöhen gedenkt" (278), as if there were no
distinction to be made between the two poets in this respect.

But ever since the critical writings of Richard Alewyn in the 1940s
and fifties, this view has had to be revised. Alewyn showed that whatever connection Hofmannsthal may have had with Aestheticism and its
tendency to place art above life (in all senses of the word, embracing
both the social and the biological), he was also, from the outset, one of
the most incisive critics of Aestheticism as an artistic movement and
aestheticism (which he sometimes referred to as "Ästhetismus" in his
notebooks) as a way of life. Criticism of the movement can be found
especially in his essays of the 1890s on writers and artists such as Wilde,
Swinburne, Pater, and the Pre-Raphaelites. The critique of the aestheticist lifestyle can be found in the early lyric dramas, most notably in *Der
Tor und der Tod* (1893). In this work Hofmannsthal explicitly condemns a way of life devoted entirely to *objets d'art*; this is associated
with an inability to form human ties, with estrangement from life, and

finally with a barren and empty existence. The terms that appear repeatedly in Hofmannsthal's works in the 1890s and later — Fruchtbarkeit, unfruchtbar, etc. — show most distinctly where Hofmannsthal left Aestheticism and its legacy behind. The sterile virginal goddess, or the destroying, sexualized *femme fatale* (to which the virginal goddess might be seen as an antidote), represented the only options in Aestheticism. For these artists, human, and especially female, sexuality was feared, and the processes of life associated with sexuality were rejected.[2] Here Hofmannsthal's path diverges emphatically from that of Aestheticism, as can be seen most clearly in *Die Frau ohne Schatten*, both the opera text (1915) and the prose narrative (1919), in which humanity and a fulfilled human existence, for both man and woman, are explicitly associated with fertility.[3] Along with this affirmation of life in the biological sense is also an affirmation of life in the social sense: rejecting the Aestheticist model of the artist hopelessly estranged from the general public, Hofmannsthal sought, especially in his operatic collaboration with Strauss and his role in co-founding and providing dramatic repertoire for the Salzburg Festival, to break out of this artistic isolation and reach a larger public.

But in one respect Adorno came closer to the mark than did many of the critics who followed in Alewyn's path: Adorno recognized that both George and Hofmannsthal were working in the tradition of French Symbolism, whereas some major Hofmannsthal scholars of the 1950s and sixties were prone to deny or minimize this influence, or to dismiss it as merely a matter of technique. I will return shortly to examine the factors that conditioned both Adorno's insistence on this relationship, and the reluctance of other critics to acknowledge it, but first it is important to grasp the significance of this relationship in literary history. As has now been established by three monographs of recent decades,[4] Hofmannsthal's encounter with the work of the French Symbolist masters Baudelaire, Verlaine, and Mallarmé was perhaps the decisive aesthetic experience of his early years, one that shaped his approach to art for the rest of his career. He belongs to that group of major European poets who exemplify and partake in what C. M. Bowra called "the heritage of Symbolism" in his book of the same title. Although Bowra does not treat Hofmannsthal in his volume, T. S. Eliot placed Hofmannsthal in the Symbolist tradition, grouping him with Yeats and Claudel as the writers who did the most to revive verse drama in the twentieth century (Eliot xii). This influence manifests itself on many levels: one can see it in the use of metaphor as a structuring principle, almost like a musical leitmotif, in poems such as "Vorfrühling" (1892), in the increasing turn to dramatic form in the poems, and in the view of language as something problematic, unstable, arbitrary. In all these ways, Hofmannsthal's writing, and his poetry in particular, shows a marked departure from the tradition of *Innerlichkeit* stemming from German Romanticism. To insist on his belonging to Symbolism is not to stress Hofmannsthal's indebtedness to the past, however; quite the contrary, it is the hallmark of his modernity. As has been pointed out by both Edmund Wilson (in *Axël's Castle*) and Hugo Friedrich (in *Die Struktur der modernen Lyrik*), it is Symbolism that sets the stage for the Modernism of the 1920s.

There are other, broader contexts in which Hofmannsthal's work can be viewed. It was Hermann Broch, in his groundbreaking study *Hofmannsthal und seine Zeit* (1955, translated as *Hugo von Hofmannsthal and His Time: The European Imagination, 1860–1920,* 1984), who pointed the way to an examination of Hofmannsthal's work in the context of the "fröhliche Apokalypse" (Broch's term) of late Habsburg Vienna. For Broch, *fin-de-siècle* Vienna was anything but an object of fond nostalgia; he spoke scathingly of the "Unstil" that characterized the art and design of the period, and the "Potemkin city" character of the Ringstraße facades, all of which embodied what he called the "Wert-Vakuum," the loss of any shared aesthetic or ethical value system. In considering Hofmannsthal as the exemplary figure of the epoch, Broch by no means identified him with this artistic and moral vacuum. Rather, he used this context to emphasize Hofmannsthal's enormous accomplishment:

> Sein Leben war Symbol, edles Symbol eines verschwindenden Österreichs, eines verschwindenden Adels, eines verschwindenden Theaters —, Symbol im Vakuum, doch nicht des Vakuums.
>
> Allein, ungeachtet des Vakuums, ungeachtet des Zusammenbruchs des alten Wertsystems, das Stück um Stück sich auflöste und vom Vakuum verschlungen wurde [. . .], es ist die Selbstbehauptung eines wahren Schicksals geblieben, Hofmannsthals Dasein, sein hoher Stil und seine hohe Kunst. (149)

Carl E. Schorske, whose less apocalyptic but broader analysis in *Fin-de-siècle Vienna: Politics and Culture* shaped what was to become a fascination with the culture of *fin-de-siècle* Vienna in the 1980s and 1990s, likewise treated Hofmannsthal as a key figure in the generation that experienced the demise of political liberalism in the wake of the 1873 stock-market crash, and that probed the depths of the unconscious and the irrational in search of cultural models to replace the presumed rationality of their parent's generation. In the 1980s and 1990s, Jacques Le Rider and others such as Jens Rieckmann and Sander Gilman have viewed Hofmannsthal in the context of Vienna *fin-de-siècle* crises of identity.

But as soon as identity issues in Vienna Modernism are mentioned, we are faced with another important factor in our view of Hofmannsthal: that of his Jewishness. Here too, Broch's work was groundbreaking. Referring to the poet's paternal great-grandfather Isaak Löw Hofmann, a Jewish silk and textile merchant who was granted a charter of nobility by the Austrian emperor in 1827 in recognition of his services to the Imperial Army, Broch views the Hofmannsthal family history as "Geschichte einer Assimilation," and presents the concept of assimilation as crucial in grasping the import of Hofmannsthal's lifework. Indeed, Broch speaks of the young Hofmannsthal's "zweite Assimilation": having rejected the accomplished assimilation into the Viennese bourgeoisie represented by his father and grandfather, Hofmannsthal sought to achieve through his art a kind of mystical assimilation into the aristocracy of an imagined Austria. Due obviously in part to the sensitivity of Jewish-related topics in the post-Shoah German-speaking world, this aspect of Hofmannsthal was not pursued to any significant extent in Hofmannsthal scholarship until the recent work of Jens Rieckmann.

On the face of it, even to discuss the Jewishness of Hugo von Hofmannsthal, whose mother and grandmother were both Gentile, who was raised as a Catholic and chose to be buried in monastic garb, and several of whose texts display an explicitly Christian worldview, might seem at first glance to validate National Socialist definitions of Jewishness; clearly, Hofmannsthal was not a Jew either by Jewish law or by self-definition. And yet, the matter is not as simple as this. Hofmannsthal was a key member of the group which became known as *Junges Wien* and which formed the core of what is now regarded as *Wiener Moderne* or Vienna Modernism, and this group was regarded by contemporaries, with partial justification, as a largely Jewish phenomenon. Hofmannsthal was close to Arthur Schnitzler (1862–1931), who, despite his own ambivalence about his Jewishness, treated Jewish themes in two major texts (*Der Weg ins Freie* [1908] and *Professor Bernhardi* [1912]), and to Richard Beer-Hofmann, who made no secret of his Jewishness in his life or his work. Likewise, the critics of *Junges Wien*, notably Ottokar Stauf von der March, often framed their attacks in explicitly antisemitic terms. The rise of antisemitism in Austria after the 1873 crash, which gave rise to the proto-Nazi German nationalist movement led by Georg von Schönerer and to the milder but far more successful Christian Socialism of Karl Lueger (who was mayor of Vienna from 1897 to 1910, thus during a significant portion of Hofmannsthal's adult life) caused a good deal of anguish among Jews and those, like Hofmannsthal, who were publicly identified with Jewish circles. It also did not escape notice that Hofmannsthal's claim to nobility was derived from a Jewish ancestor. As Rieckmann points out, even colleagues in *Junges Wien* such as Leopold von Andrian believed they could detect "Jewish" mannerisms in Hofmannsthal's speech and behavior (472). Ironically, as Sander Gilman notes, Andrian himself was more "Jewish" than Hofmannsthal, being the grandson of the famed German-Jewish composer Giacomo Meyerbeer who, unlike Hofmannsthal's grandfather, had never converted. Rieckmann shows that although Hofmannsthal as a teenager had displayed some signs of sympathetic identification with the Jewish past, he increasingly internalized antisemitic stereotypes of the sterile, cerebral, essentially non-creative Jew, alternately fearing this "racial" element in his own make-up and externalizing this aversion in ugly comments about the "Wiener Judenmilieu."

Connected to what Broch called his attempt at a "zweite Assimilation" into an idealized Austrian aristocracy, and to his increasingly pronounced striving to repress all traces of his Jewish descent — flying into a rage, for instance, when his friend Willy Haas wrote a chapter on Hofmannsthal for the collection *Juden in der deutschen Literatur* in which he analyzed his friend's literary career through 1920 in terms of his Jewishness (Rieckmann 470) — are the political statements, both implicit and explicit, of his later years. More than any other factor, it is this aspect of his career which has done the most to problematize our view of Hofmannsthal today. Although his early work, especially the lyric dramas and stories, was marked by a self-proclaimed *Weg zum Sozialen* and a critique of the isolated aesthetic existence, some critics detect a fear of the underclass and of women even in some of these early texts. During the First World War, he promoted the Austro-German cause in a series of essays, some of which are embarrassing even to his admirers today. In the post-war era, his close association (Volke 150–52) with the notorious *völkisch* literary historian Josef Nadler is viewed by many with dismay. His involvement with the Salzburg festival is rightly seen as stemming from a radical cultural conservatism, an attempt to recreate an idealized prewar order in the postwar era. Specifically, his play *Das Salzburger große Welttheater* (1922; *The Salzburg Great Theatre of the World*, 1963), in its revival of the Spanish Baroque topos of the world theater created by God in which we must all play our assigned part, is legitimately viewed as Hofmannsthal's response to Bolshevism: we should not complain about the role we are assigned in life, since it is not who or what we are in life, but rather how we play our part, that makes the difference. In the words of the Marschallin from *Der Rosenkavalier*, the most famous and beloved of all Hofmannsthal's dramatic creations: "Und in dem 'Wie' da liegt der ganze

Unterschied" (*DV* 39). His 1926 speech "Das Schrifttum als geistiger Raum der Nation," delivered in Munich three years after Hitler's putsch attempt in the same city, with its famous motto of "konservative Revolution," is widely seen as prefiguring the radical right-wing revolution which was to sweep the German-speaking world in the following decade, after the poet's death. Some, like Adorno in his 1939 essay, have even viewed Hofmannsthal as deliberately courting those elements which would later be responsible for National Socialism:

> Der Flügel der deutschen Rechten, mit dem Hofmannsthal sympathisiert, ist zum Nationalsozialismus übergangen, soweit man es ihr erlaubt hat [. . .]. Sie dienen der Propaganda auf eigene Weise: ihr besonnenes Maßhalten dementiert das maßlose Grauen. 1914 begnügte sich die äußerste Gemeinheit mit den Reimen, zu denen freilich auch Hofmannsthal beitrug. Im Zeitalter der Konzentrationslager haben die Skribenten das verschlossene Schweigen, die herbe Rede und die nachsommerliche Fülle gelernt. (244–45).

During the Nazi years, Hofmannsthal's works were grudgingly approved for publication and distribution by the *Reichsschrifttumkammer* based on the fact that only one of his grandparents was Jewish, but he was not a favored author. On the other hand, due to his cultural and political conservatism and his aristocratic pretensions, his work was largely scorned or ignored by German and Austrian exile writers. Ironically, this repeated a pattern earlier in his career: initially celebrated by the aesthetic elite as the "Wunderkind" of *Junges Wien*, his turn to a more public or social art after 1900 lost him much of his following from this elite, but his elusive and difficult style made it difficult for him to gain a following in the general public.

And now we may return to the question posed earlier: given the rich and distinguished heritage of Symbolism (writers discussed by Bowra, for instance, include Rilke, Yeats, and Valéry, and might well have included Pound and Eliot as well), why is it that Adorno, whose view of Hofmannsthal is extremely critical, is more inclined to acknowledge Hofmannsthal's ties to this movement than are more sympathetic and, on the whole, more knowledgeable scholars of Hofmannsthal's work? The answer is plain in Adorno's essay, and in the critique of aesthetic culture associated with the Frankfurt School. That is, Aestheticism, which had previously been viewed as at worst irresponsible and elitist, came to be seen as a precursor of Fascism in its indifference to social welfare, just as Fascism is widely viewed as representing an "aestheticization" of politics. Thus the association of Symbolism with Aestheticism confirms Adorno in his negative view of Hofmannsthal, whereas those critics of the post-1945 era who wished to rehabilitate

Hofmannsthal instinctively downplayed his ties to Symbolism and thus to Aestheticism.

With this example — the acknowledgement or denial of Hofmannsthal's ties to Symbolism — we can see how political factors have skewed perceptions of this writer. As is apparent from the Adorno quotation above, in the era of concentration camps, and especially in the years since, during which the knowledge of Auschwitz has seared our consciousness of the past, it has been difficult for thoughtful intellectuals to embrace writers without any regard to their politics, though ironically some more clearly "tainted" artistic or intellectual figures such as Gottfried Benn or Martin Heidegger have actually fared better than Hofmannsthal. In the 1970s, it was still largely true in the English-speaking world that the trend was to judge writers irrespective of their politics; thus a predominantly left-of-center academic literary culture could lionize a T. S. Eliot, or even an Ezra Pound. Dwight MacDonald's essays of the 1940s and 1950s, including one acclaiming the award of the prestigious Bollingen Prize to Ezra Pound, provided an eloquent defense of this position.[5] However, in the intervening years the ground has shifted even in the United States. Eliot's politics and his antisemitism have justifiably become the objects of considerable critical scrutiny. The case of Richard Wagner illustrates the situation; whereas his admirers long argued (and some still do) that his music dramas were unsullied by his execrable antisemitic views, recent scholars such as Marc Weiner (1995) have suggested that these "sublime" works of art are in fact inscribed with antisemitic subtexts.

So where does all this leave us in the case of Hofmannsthal? Even if one defends him — as I would — against Adorno's charges that Hofmannsthal concealed a kind of bloodthirstiness behind a veneer of aristocratic restraint, and that he courted right-wing elements, there are few of us who are comfortable with the conservative or even reactionary political stance which Hofmannsthal assumed in his later years. The question, then, is how central a role do his political sentiments play in his literary texts? And here, I would suggest, with few exceptions (*Das Salzburger große Welttheater* comes to mind), the answer is: not that great a role. To say that Hofmannsthal was politically naïve, especially in light of developments in the years following his death, seems to be stating the obvious.[6] If one seeks a clear-sighted analysis of social or political dynamics, informed by contemporary theory and a commitment to a liberal democratic political order, Hofmannsthal is probably not the first writer to whom one should turn. But is this really all one can or should seek from works of literature?

And thus we must finally turn to what is after all the essence of Hugo von Hofmannsthal, and the reason that his name is still spoken and contested in the twenty-first century: the astonishing array of literary texts which he has left to us. It is to this body of work that the greater part of this volume is dedicated. I would like to single out some examples of this legacy, which will serve to illustrate why Hofmannsthal remains among the major writers of the *fin de siècle* and the early twentieth century.

Almost inevitably, we must begin with the poetry. In spite of the strange anomaly that this supremely gifted lyric poet wrote few poems during the last three decades of his life, in spite of the fact that (as in Rilke's case) some of the poems of his early years are quite forgettable, Hofmannsthal has left us with a small handful of some of the most often quoted and anthologized poems of the German language. The term language magic, "Sprachmagie," has been applied to Hofmannsthal's work so often that it has become almost a cliché. And yet, how else can one speak of the spell cast by lines like these, from "Ballade des äusseren Lebens" (1895; *GDI* 23):

> Und Kinder wachsen auf mit tiefen Augen
> Die von nichts wissen, wachsen auf und sterben,
> Und alle Menschen gehen ihre Wege.
>
> Und süße Früchte werden aus den herben
> Und fallen nachts wie tote Vögel nieder
> Und liegen wenig Tage und verderben.
>
> Und immer weht der Wind, und immer wieder
> Vernehmen wir und reden viele Worte
> Und spüren Lust und Müdigkeit der Glieder.
>
> Und Straßen laufen durch das Gras, und Orte
> Sind da und dort, voll Fackeln, Bäumen, Teiche
> Und drohende, und totenhaft verdorrte . . .

The incantatory quality of the language, which seems to transport us to an elevation from which we view our lives as if for the first time, in a way that is both melancholy and clear-sighted, does not exhaust the art of the poem. For following these lines, the poet turns to question the vision he has just evoked.

> Wozu sind diese aufgebaut? und gleichen
> Einander nie? Und sind unzählig viele?
> Was wechselt Lachen, Weinen und Erbleichen?

> Was frommt das alles uns und diese Spiele,
> Die wir doch groß und ewig einsam sind
> Und wandernd nimmer suchen irgend Ziele?

> Was frommts, dergleichen viel gesehen haben?

As much as the ability to evoke these visions, this questioning, this search for the underlying meaning, characterizes Hofmannsthal's writing from the start. And, as in all of Hofmannsthal's best work, no simple answer is either given or available:

> Und dennoch sagt der viel, der "Abend" sagt,
> Ein Wort, daraus Tiefsinn und Trauer rinnt
> Wie schwerer Honig aus den hohlen Waben.

The discussion of the meaning of these final lines is voluminous, but what is beyond dispute is that Hofmannsthal deliberately withholds any easy answer; instead he leaves us with a heavily laden word ("Abend") and a vivid image ("schwerer Honig aus den hohlen Waben"). What is the significance here of the saying of the word "evening"? Evening is at once the time when the pure externality of our lives, to which the poem's title refers, fades away in favor of dream, of inward reflection. Evening is also a metaphor for decline, for the inevitable transience of life as described in the first two stanzas. If we read both of these senses — the "Tiefsinn" and the "Trauer" — at the same time, we arrive at a sense of life's frailty which at the same time awakens a sense of its beauty — thus it might well be claimed that this word "says much." Another way of approaching these lines is from the vantage point of language: it is the poet's speaking of the word "Abend" which creates both the "Tiefsinn" and the "Trauer," and thus the poem can be read in part as a tribute to the power of language and the poet as purveyor of meaning amidst the sheer externality of our existence, the bee (to follow the metaphor) who creates the honey of deepened experience. The musical quality of this verse is obvious, but its philosophical content is equally clear: philosophical in the sense that fundamental questions of human existence are addressed, but answered only in the language of poetry — image and metaphor — rather than that of philosophical abstraction.

The lyric dramas, which like the poetry are a product of the 1890s, display many of the same themes and stylistic features as the poems. In particular, the critique of the aesthetic existence is a central feature of plays such as *Der Tod des Tizian* (1892) and *Der Tor und der Tod* (1893). In *Der Tod des Tizian* Hofmannsthal presents the disciples of the dying Italian master, who have allowed their devotion to his art to

alienate them from life; the young disciple Gianino, in whom this alienation has not yet taken place, and who still sees a vision of the wholeness
of being, is admired and envied by the other disciples, who are frozen
into a mask of contempt as they contemplate the city below. In *Der Tor
und der Tod*, the critique of aestheticism as a way of life is most explicit.
Claudio, the fool of the title, has failed at all human contact, trying to
lead a vicarious existence through works of art, and the advent of death
awakens him, all too late, to the emptiness of his existence. In *Das kleine
Welttheater* (1897), a progression of human types is presented on stage:
a poet overwhelmed by the multiplicity of existence and groping to find
his place within it, a "gardener" who reveals himself to be a former ruler
and reflects on the essential sameness of his former realm and his current
one (the garden), a young gentleman who reflects the joys of youth, a
"stranger" who reveals himself to be an artist struggling to give a shape
to the ever-changing forms of reality, a young girl whose wish for a song
is granted by a balladeer, whom she then dismisses, and finally the servant and physician who attend on the madman who brings the play to an
end. The play is characterized throughout by the same lyric intensity as
in the best of the poems, and delves into the same themes of temporality
and transience, of the tenuous nature of our identity and our attempts to
give meaning to our existence, culminating in the madman's impatience
with all earthly signification:

> Was aber sind Paläste und die Gedichte:
> Traumhaftes Abbild des Wirklichen!
> Das Wirkliche fängt kein Gewebe ein:
> Den *ganzen* Reigen anzuführen,
> Den wirklichen, begreift ihr dieses Amt? (*GDI* 386)

The narrative prose works of these years display very similar themes:
the quest for identity unites them all, but ties them to the later work as
well, especially *Die Frau ohne Schatten* and the never finished novel
Andreas. Stories such as "Das Märchen der 672. Nacht," "Erlebnis des
Marschalls von Bassompierre," and "Reitergeschichte" are among the
most inexhaustible German fictional texts. In "Das Märchen der 672.
Nacht," a merchant's son whose isolated existence is reminiscent of
Claudio's in *Der Tor und der Tod* is summoned into the city under
mysterious circumstances and dies a wretched death that is as remote as
could be imagined from the protected existence he has led until that
time. The dreamlike character of the narrative is unmistakable, as is the
renewed concern with the perils of the aesthetic existence. In "Erlebnis
des Marschalls von Bassompierre," the protagonist, who narrates the
tale in retrospect, reflects on an enigmatic experience involving sexual-

ity, death from the plague, and possible political intrigue. "Reiter-geschichte," which reflects some of the desolation of Hofmannsthal's period of military service, tells the story of a soldier in the 1848 Austrian campaign in Italy whose enigmatic moment of defiance costs him his life. These texts and others have had radically divergent readings, even within the pages of this volume.

About the Chandos Letter ("Ein Brief," 1902), which must be included among the fictional texts, there has never been any doubt that it is one of the founding texts of Modernism. And the prose narrative of *Die Frau ohne Schatten*, though sometimes overshadowed by the libretto, is a literary masterpiece that signals a major milestone in Hofmannsthal's career and in the history of twentieth-century Modernism: in this work he manages to affirm the metaphoric power exemplified in the tradition of Symbolism, while rejecting the denial of life which inhered in that same tradition and eloquently pleading the value of human life.

Hofmannsthal's essays by themselves constitute a major claim to a leading position in the literature of the early twentieth century. This claim is justified both by their artistry of language and form, and by the way in which they address and attempt to resolve the shifting cultural dilemmas of Hofmannsthal's career, from the 1890s through the 1920s. As one example of many, consider this passage from the essay "Sebastian Melmoth," written on the occasion of Oscar Wilde's death (1905):

> Man muß das Leben nicht banalisieren, indem man das Wesen und das Schicksal auseinanderzerrt und sein Unglück abseitsstellt von seinem Glück. Man darf nicht alles sondern. Es ist alles überall. Es ist Tragisches in den oberflächlichen Dingen und Albernes in den tragischen. Es ist etwas würgend Unheimliches in dem, was man Vergnügen nennt. [. . .] Man kann kein Ding ausschließen und keines für so niedrig nehmen, daß es nicht eine sehr große Macht sei. (*RAI* 344)

Here, a reflection on the fate of one man who is at the same time an emblematic figure of his age opens out into a reflection on the human condition.

If one looks at Hofmannsthal's dramas as a group, excluding lyric dramas, opera texts, and comedies, we are left with what might well be regarded as a series of adaptations. And yet, even here, this is hardly a sign of the failure of original vision; rather, it is precisely the radical nature of his vision of the fragility of human language and the theater that seeks to perform that language which drives him to these adaptations. *Das Salzburger große Welttheater*, viewed by most as a fundamental document of Hofmannsthal's cultural and political conservatism, may also be interpreted as a sort of manifesto of Hofmannsthal's theater of adaptation. And finally, *Der Turm*, especially its final version (1927), is at once a haunting summation of all the major themes of Hofmannsthal's earlier work and a frightening prophecy of the descent of Europe into political atavism.

Hofmannsthal's two masterpieces of stage comedy, *Der Schwierige* and *Der Unbestechliche*, are the final fruit of a long and arduous process, but these two by themselves allow one to claim for Hofmannsthal the status as arguably the greatest writer of comedy in the German language. *Der Schwierige* in particular is a transcendent work, funny as only a work that exposes the painful limits of human existence and the tragedies of history can be. The difficulties and failures of communication and of human contact, shown in such varied earlier texts as the poem "Die Beiden" (1896) and "Ein Brief" (1902), make up the core of this comedy, and the eventual union of the "difficult" couple Hans-Karl Bühl and Helene Altenwyl gives the audience a "happy ending" that is both convincing and entirely irrelevant, since the play makes painfully clear that the world they represent is vanishing.

And finally, there are the opera texts, the main source of Hofmannsthal's fame among a wider audience today. What can be said about *Der Rosenkavalier*, for instance, that has not already been said? It is likely the most popular and most-performed opera in the German language. It combines humor of all levels from the crude comedy associated with Ochs to the delicate ironies of the Marschallin's exchanges with Octavian, with the wisdom of years confronting the impetuous and oblivious fervor of youth. And in the Marschallin's famous monologue, her discourse on time to Octavian, and the transcendently beautiful final duet (all the more poignant since the Marschallin's blessing and exit remind us of the transience of all happiness in this life), the language of opera enters a realm where it had never before existed, and never has since. The two artists' relationship was in many respects a difficult one, and unquestionably Hofmannsthal learned a great deal from the composer about the demands of the musical stage. Nevertheless, in his language and in his creation of characters like the Marschallin, Hofmannsthal expanded the possibilities of the genre for the future. As was suggested earlier, underlying the Marschallin's world-weary wisdom is the same notion of accepting the lot given to one and bearing it with grace that is the central theme of *Das Salzburger große Welttheater*; but while the latter play might put one off due to its obviously political message, it is hard not to be won over by the Marschallin's "Und in dem Wie. . . ."

It is only when we consider the poet's accomplishments in all these varied fields that his true greatness emerges. And a careful view of all these texts also serves to convince us of their modernity. Here again,

his political conservatism has been partly responsible for the still pervasive belief that Hofmannsthal is an "old-fashioned," essentially nineteenth-century writer. With Brecht as the archetypal literary Modernist,
in the German-speaking world literary and political progressivism are
more often assumed to go hand-in-hand than is the case in the English-
speaking world. But it is not only the political conservatism; the Hofmannsthal of the early years of the century, the author of the Chandos
letter and *Elektra*, both indisputably "avant garde" texts, seemed on
the surface to retreat to a more traditional mode in works such as *Der
Rosenkavalier* or *Jedermann*, just as his collaborator Strauss seemed to
revert to more traditional tonalities in his later works. And yet, in the
case of Hofmannsthal at least, this "traditionalism" is not what it
seems. The reflections of the Marschallin on the passing of time and the
shifting boundaries of the self reflect the cognitive crisis expressed in
the Chandos letter as well, and the apparent cultural conservatism of
the Salzburg dramas can also be viewed as radical attempts to cope with
the problematic nature of artistic representation. Even Hofmannsthal's
propaganda on behalf of the Salzburg festival, which could be seen as
conclusive proof of his traditionalism, may be viewed as an attempt to
reconstitute a cultural configuration which no longer exists, in a world
which is no longer conducive to this culture; the political gesture may
well be conservative or even reactionary, but the notion might also be
viewed as radically modern, in the sense that T. S. Eliot's views on tradition might be seen as constitutive of modernity in the English-
speaking world.[7]

* * *

The essays presented in this volume fall into three categories. The first,
consisting of the essay by Hinrich Seeba, provides a broader view of the
cultural context of *Wiener Moderne*. The second and largest group is a
series of essays devoted to Hofmannsthal's works, divided by genre:
Andreas Thomasberger on the poems and lyric dramas, Ellen Ritter on
the narrative prose, myself on the Chandos letter, Benjamin Bennett on
the dramas viewed as a "theater of adaptation," Joanna Bottenberg on
the collaboration with Richard Strauss, W. E. Yates on the comedies,
Judith Beniston on the Salzburg festival and dramas, and Katherine
Arens on the essays. Finally, two essays seek to examine Hofmannsthal's
legacy: Nina Berman deals with the political legacy, particularly as
manifested in the early works, and Douglas Joyce surveys the tides of
Hofmannsthal reception in the twentieth century. It is my hope that
the excellence of these individual contributions will provide a richness

of perspective on the work of this multifaceted artist that no mono-graph could achieve.

Thus, in presenting this collection of essays on the Austrian poet, dramatist, essayist, prose writer, and librettist Hugo von Hofmannsthal, it is hoped that Hofmannsthal's legacy as a crucial writer of the twenti-eth-century will be made plain — a writer who created works of art that live on because of their beauty, their modernity, and their inexhaustible richness.

A Note on Editions and Resources for Further Research

Not counting a very incomplete edition that appeared during the poet's lifetime, there are three editions of Hofmannsthal's works which are referred to in the secondary literature. The first was the fifteen-volume *Gesammelte Werke in Einzelausgaben*, edited by Herbert Steiner, pub-lished by S. Fischer Verlag beginning in Stockholm in 1945 and con-tinuing in Frankfurt from 1947 onward. The set was completed in 1959. This was the edition cited in all Hofmannsthal secondary litera-ture until the late 1970s. Though it has been superseded for the most part by subsequent editions, it is still widely available in libraries.

The second was the ten-volume paperback *Gesammelte Werke* edited by Bernd Schoeller in consultation with Rudolf Hirsch; the *Aufzeich-nungen* contained in the last volume are edited by Ingeborg Beyer-Ahlert. This edition was published in Frankfurt am Main by the Fischer Taschenbuch Verlag in 1979 and 1980. Though it has been criticized by some for preserving some errors from the Steiner edition and adding some new ones of its own, it does include new material which was not available at the time of the Steiner edition, and it is relatively inexpensive and widely available. For these reasons, citations from Hofmannsthal's works in this volume will be from this edition wherever possible.

Finally, there is the *Sämtlicher Werke Kritische Ausgabe*, edited by Rudolf Hirsch, Clemens Köttelwesch, Christoph Perels, Heinz Rölleke, and Ernst Zinn, published in Frankfurt am Main by Fischer Verlag starting in 1975 and still ongoing. Clearly this is the "gold standard" in Hofmannsthal texts, but it is not yet complete, the volumes are expen-sive and found primarily in large research libraries.

Hofmannsthal was an avid writer of letters, and there are far too many volumes of correspondence to be listed here; Mathias Mayer's *Sammlung Metzler* volume lists around 40 volumes in print as of 1993, and several volumes have appeared since then. These include entire volumes devoted to his correspondence with fellow writers (in alphabetical order) Leopold von Andrian, Richard Beer-Hofmann, Stefan George, Rainer Maria Rilke, and Arthur Schnitzler, and the correspondence with his collaborator, the composer Richard Strauss. This latter, translated as *A Working Friendship* (New York: Random House, 1961), is of special interest, since the two men seldom met in person, and thus one has a unique opportunity to observe their creative process in these letters.

In terms of bibliographies, there are two for the primary texts, including translations: Horst Weber, *Hugo von Hofmannsthal. Bibliographie: Werke, Briefe, Gespräche, Übersetzungen, Vertonungen* (Berlin/New York: De Gruyter, 1972), and Hans-Albrecht and Uta Koch, *Hugo von Hofmannsthal. Bibliographie: 1964–76 (Hofmannsthal-Forschungen 4)* (Freiburg i. Br.: Deutsches Seminar der Universität, 1976). For secondary literature, there is Horst Weber, *Hugo von Hofmannsthal: Bibliographie des Schrifttums 1892–1963* (Berlin: De Gruyter, 1966). Supplements for both primary and secondary literature for later years, edited by Hans-Albrecht and Uta Koch, and after 1980 by Clemens Köttelwesch, can be found in the pages of the journal *Hofmannsthal-Blätter*. There are several *Forschungsberichte* listed in Mayer 183–84. Then there is the above-mentioned journal *Hofmannsthal-Blätter*, issued since 1968 by the Hugo von Hofmannsthal-Gesellschaft. Finally, there is the series *Hofmannsthal-Forschungen*, commissioned by the Hofmannsthal-Gesellschaft from 1971 onward, often containing the proceedings from symposia organized by the Gesellschaft on a variety of themes.

In terms of archival materials, the two principle collections are in the Freies Deutsches Hochstift in Frankfurt am Main, and in the Houghton Library of Harvard University in Cambridge, Massachusetts.

Notes

[1] See especially the essay "Politics and the Psyche: Schnitzler and Hofmannsthal" in *Fin-de-siècle Vienna: Politics and Culture*, 3–23 (See *Works Cited*).

[2] See, for instance, Mario Praz, *The Romantic Agony*, trans. Angus Davison (London: Oxford UP, 1933).

[3] I present this argument in greater detail in "*Die Frau ohne Schatten*: Hofmannsthal's Response to the Symbolist Dilemma," *The German Quarterly* 57, No. 3 (Summer 1984), 377–91.

[4] Sondrup's of 1976, Kovach's of 1985, and Vilain's of 2000; see *Works Cited*.

[5] See, for instance, "*Kulturbolshewismus* & Mr. Van Wyck Brooks" (1941) and "Homage to Twelve Judges" (1949), reprinted in DM, *Memoirs of a Revolutionist* (New York: Farrar, Straus and Cudahy, 1957), 203–14, 215–18.

[6] Although one could argue, as I have elsewhere ("'Acheronta movebo': A New Light on the Figure of the Physician in Hofmannsthal's *Turm*," *Focus on Vienna 1900: Change and Continuity in Literature, Art and Intellectual History*, ed. Erika Nielsen. [Munich: Wilhelm Fink Verlag, 1982], 77–83), that the figure of Olivier in his final drama *Der Turm*, especially the final version of 1927, is a frightening premonition of the Nazi rise to power.

[7] I make this argument in greater detail in "Traditionalist Modernism or Modernist Traditionalism: The Case of Hugo von Hofmannsthal," *Philological Papers* 39 (1993), 57–61.

Works Cited

Adorno, Theodor W. "George und Hofmannsthal. Zum Briefwechsel." *Prismen: Kulturkritik und Gesellschaft*. Frankfurt: Suhrkamp, 1955. 232–82.

Alewyn, Richard. *Über Hugo von Hofmannsthal*. Göttingen: Vandenhoeck & Ruprecht, 1963.

Bowra, C. M. *The Heritage of Symbolism*. London, Macmillan & Co. Ltd., 1943.

Broch, Hermann. "Hofmannsthal und seine Zeit. Eine Studie." *Dichten und Erkennen. Essays Band I*. Zürich: Rhein-Verlag, 1955.

Eliot, T. S. "Preface." Hugo von Hofmannsthal, *Poems and Verse Plays*. Ed. and intro. Michael Hamburger. Bollingen Series XXXIII/2. New York: Panthcon, 1961. xi–xii.

Friedrich, Hugo. *Die Struktur der modernen Lyrik*. Hamburg: Rowohlt, 1956.

Gilman, Sander. "Smart Jews in Fin-de-siècle Vienna: 'Hybrids' and the Anxiety about Jewish Superior Intelligence — Hofmannsthal and Wittgenstein." *Modernism/Modernity* 3, No. 2 (1996), 45–48.

Hofmannsthal, Hugo von. *Briefe 1890–1901*. Berlin: S. Fischer, 1935.

Kovach, Thomas A. *Hofmannsthal and Symbolism: Art and Life in the Work of a Modern Poet*. New York/Bern/Frankfurt am Main: Peter Lang, 1985.

Le Rider, Jacques. *Modernity and Crises of Identity: Culture and Society in Fin-de-siècle Vienna*. Trans. Rosemary Morris. Cambridge, Eng.: Polity Press, 1993. [Original French ed. 1990].

Mayer, Mathias. *Hugo von Hofmannsthal*. Stuttgart/Weimar: J. B. Metzler, 1993.

Rieckmann, Jens. "Zwischen Bewußtsein und Verdrängung: Hofmannsthals jüdisches Erbe." *Deutsche Vierteljahrsschrift* 67 (1993). 466–83.

Schorske, Carl E. *Fin-de-siècle Vienna: Politics and Culture.* New York: Random House, 1981.

Sondrup, Steven P. *Hofmannsthal and the French Symbolist Tradition.* Bern/Frankfurt am Main: Herbert Lang, 1976.

Vilain, Robert. *The Poetry of Hugo von Hofmannsthal and French Symbolism.* New York: Oxford University Press, 2000.

Volke, Werner. *Hugo von Hofmannsthal in Selbstzeugnissen und Bilddokumenten.* Reinbek bei Hamburg: Rowohlt, 1967,

Weiner, Marc. *Richard Wagner and the Anti-Semitic Imagination.* Lincoln: University of Nebraska Press, 1995.

Wilson, Edmund. *Axël's Castle.* New York: Scribner & Sons, 1931.

Contexts

HINRICH C. SEEBA

Hofmannsthal and *Wiener Moderne*: The Cultural Context

WHILE FOR SOME TIME the turn of a century has been an emotionally fraught marker of change — the time for taking stock of the
passing of generations, ages and epochs — the recent turn of the millen-
nium offers a rare opportunity to look at such turning points and their
cultural significance more historically, even in terms of historiography.[1]
For each of the recent turns of the century have served to promote the
concept of modernity. The end of the seventeenth century, with fading
memories of the Thirty Years' War, had paved the way for the *querelle
des anciens et des modernes* to question the timeless validity of the classical
canon, and the end of the eighteenth century, with constant reminders
of the French Revolution, had paved the way for the Romantics to question the claims of Classicism. Be it Charles Perrault in 1697 or Friedrich
Schlegel in 1797, in both cases it was the experience of historical change
that brought about a sense of temporal difference and, subsequently,
new versions of the concept of modernity. While Perrault was the first to
claim the modern individual as different from but equal to the Greeks
("c'est nous qui sommes les Anciens" [Jauss, 29]), Schlegel in his essay
on Greek poetry defined as characteristically modern the excess of individuality: "Nichts kann die Künstlichkeit der modernen ästhetischen Bildung besser erläutern und bestätigen, als das große Übergewicht des
Individuellen, Charakteristischen und Philosophischen in der ganzen
Masse der modernen Poesie" (Schlegel 140). But not before the end of
the nineteenth century, literally in the *fin de siècle*, was there a new, more
existential sense of time and temporality, one which would throw excessive individuality into a very modern crisis of identity.

The *Wiener Moderne*, that is, the period roughly from 1890 to
1910, has been identified with the experience of temporality, of short-
lived sensation, of dream-like intuitions of the ethereal, of elusive time.
The sensitivity of the nerves to titillating stimuli, as it is traced in the so-
called "Nervenkunst" (Worbs *passim*), favors the selective perception of
the momentary in tentative sketches. But in the ever-present tradition of

baroque dualism, Vienna's impressionism of seizing the moment (*carpe diem*) apparently was always mindful of its existential counterpart, *memento mori*. The concept of *Leben*, this philosophical mantra with shades of Friedrich Nietzsche and Wilhelm Dilthey, could not be separated from *Tod*. According to Hermann Broch (1886–1951), who in his *Hofmannsthal und seine Zeit* (1955) offered the most incisive analysis of Vienna's "fröhliche Apokalypse" (Broch 49), the celebration of amoral hedonism was also a dance of death, a performative reminder that the fluid quality of time will eventually be arrested in irreversible termination. Not incidentally, death figures prominently in Hugo von Hofmannsthal's dramas from *Der Tod des Tizian* (1892) and *Der Tor und der Tod* (1893) to *Jedermann* (1911). By assigning to the powerful character of death the task of grounding the intangible, Hofmannsthal only reinforced the impressionistic sense that life is transitory and that the experience of rushing time implies its opposite, the finality of death. Following the literary tradition of the dance of death and its moral message, *respice finem* (consider the end), Hofmannsthal used the notion of *finis saeculi*, the *fin de siècle*, to impart a sense of responsibility and thus to balance the aesthetic with the ethical: Claudio, the aestheticist main character of *Der Tor und der Tod*, who thrives on beauty in form rather than in function, is confronted with his own death, when the personified figure of death reminds him of his irresponsibility in living his life as if the flow of time would never stop.

The sense of fleeting time, which is so symptomatic of the end of the century, is most poignantly expressed — and questioned — in the famous aria of the Marschallin in *Der Rosenkavalier*, Richard Strauss's opera of 1910, which, based on Hofmannsthal's libretto, staged the experience of the late nineteenth century in the costumes of the late eighteenth century:

> Die Zeit, die ist ein sonderbares Ding
> Wenn man so hinlebt, ist sie rein gar nichts.
> Aber dann auf einmal,
> da spürt man nichts als sie:
> sie ist um uns herum, sie ist auch in uns drinnen.
> In den Gesichtern rieselt sie, im Spiegel da rieselt sie,
> in meinen Schläfen fließt sie.
> Und zwischen mir und dir da fließt sie wieder.
> Lautlos, wie eine Sanduhr.
> O Quin-quin!
> Manchmal hör ich sie fließen unaufhaltsam.
> Manchmal steh ich auf, mitten in der Nacht,
> und laß die Uhren alle stehen. (*DV* 42)

Reading these simple sensations of passing time, one cannot fail to hear the transcendental musicality of the aria, which transformed the dubiously precious poetry of the lines. Reified into a strangely sensual "thing," time drips and flows like water and runs down the face like sand in an hourglass, the symbol of declining strength and eventually death. The repeated metaphor of flowing water, reminiscent of Heraclitus who was among the first to imagine time as a river, underlines the age-old notion that everything is in flux (*panta rhei*) and that there is nothing left to hold onto. While the eighteenth-century sense of time was based on the concept of progress "in aufsteigender Linie," the *fin-de-siècle* sense of time reflects only the melancholy of decline, with the despair of imminent end lurking in the wings. As time is no longer immaterial, the gaze into the mirror is fixed on its opaque materiality. The metonymic time frame has become the picture itself. No longer a mere window, it resembles the — of course, beautifully — painted glass that separates us from the reality called *Leben*. Like the Marschallin, we realize that what existed yesterday no longer does today and that therefore what is now is irreversibly doomed. In this musical juxtaposition of rise and fall, "Glück und Ende" (as in Grillparzer's play of King Ottokar's demise of 1825), ascent and its opposite, decadence, we can find the master narrative of Aristotelian poetics, with *peripeteia* being the turning point that brings about the reversal of the upward movement and turns the dramatic action downward into the final catastrophe. Thus, when the Marschallin sometimes gets up at night to stop all clocks, she not only tries to halt the process of aging, which is about to make her the loser in the competition for Octavian's love, she also tries to stem the tide of decline, the experience of loneliness, alienation and eventual loss of identity. Her desperate nocturnal move tragically suggests what it tries to prevent, it foreshadows the non-poetic catastrophe that already looms on the political horizon. The twilight of the imperial rococo world which the Marschallin represents prefigures the anticipated twilight of the Austrian Empire. What the Marschallin fears is the predetermined loss of authenticity that was envisioned in the nineteenth-century concept of *Epigonentum*, for example in Karl Immermann's novel *Die Epigonen* (1835), and epitomized at the beginning of the twentieth century in Thomas Mann's novel *Buddenbrooks: Verfall einer Familie* (1901); it is the "Glück und Ende" of a social class, including the aristocrat as a bourgeois in disguise, at the ominous turning point of its aesthetic self-representation. Hofmannsthal was hardly nineteen when he assumed the attitude of the epigone: "Man hat manchmal die Empfindung, als hätten uns unsere Väter, die Zeitgenossen des jüngeren Offenbach, und unsere Großväter, die Zeitgenossen

Leopardis, und alle die unzähligen Generationen vor ihnen, als hätten sie uns, den Spätgeborenen, nur zwei Dinge hinterlassen: hübsche Möbel und überfeine Nerven" (*RAI* 174). Suffering from this heritage, which furnished the delicate psyche with pretty objects, became the fashionable attitude of the day.

The end of the century constitutes also the end of an epoch. The tendencies of the time — Symbolism, Aestheticism, Decadence — mark a period which carries in its name the very end it both fears and celebrates. The *fin de siècle* is one of the few period concepts in historiography determined not by style (like baroque, rococo, classicism, Biedermeier, to name but a few) but by the calendar, in this case by the end of a century and the sense of imminent change it generated. But while the *Vormärz*, another temporally defined period of originally Austrian literature, was understood as anticipating — and its often politically inspired literature as leading up to — the things to come, that is, the revolution of March 1848, the *fin de siècle* could be seen as looking back to the century — and the social system it represents — that was coming to an end. While the former was conceived of as progressive, the latter was marked by a conservative, nostalgic sense of imminent loss of trust and purpose to the acceleration of time, historical fluctuation and political uncertainty. While the former was eminently political in the active promotion of change, the latter, with its aesthetic foundation in *l'art pour l'art*, was curiously apolitical even in its passive anticipation of change. Against this background of a perceived threat to the established social order, its more sensitive representatives (including those from the recently ennobled bourgeoisie, as in Hofmannsthal's case) both warned against and proclaimed the cultural change that would eventually hasten the downfall of Vienna's waning grandeur. The political *status quo*, which had been upheld by Metternich against all oppositional turmoil, but which was already being undermined by subversive tendencies in the Austrian *Vormärz*, had turned into an economic and social *status quo* adopted by the rising middle classes. It had created a stagnant cultural milieu, in which the passing of time, as experienced on the eve of the new century, generated an ever more urgent sense of temporality and looming upheaval couched in images of beautiful death.

Aestheticism and the celebration of fragile beauty in treasured *objets d'art* and delicate poetry were not limited to *fin-de-siècle* Vienna. It was a European phenomenon. Oscar Wilde (1856–1900) in England, Arthur Rimbaud (1854–1891) and Joris-Karl Huysmans (1848–1907) in France, Maurice Maeterlinck (1862–1949) in Belgium, Gabriele D'Annunzio (1863–1938) in Italy, Anton Chekhov (1860–1904) in Russia and, within German literature, Stefan George (1868–1933) and

Rainer Maria Rilke (1875–1926) — all of these writers belonged to a generation of hypersensitive "Spätgeborene" who, in spite of their youth, thrived on their weary perception of decline. All of them show some affinity to the refined, somewhat jaded and blasé dandy anticipated by Lord Byron and best personified, in the eyes of contemporary critics, by the character des Esseintes in Huysmans's novel *À rebours* (1884), a hypochondriac aristocrat living in a totally secluded dream world of precious sensations. While Berlin, capital of the recently-founded German Reich, with its thriving economy, was a bustling place looking to the future and little inclined to melancholy and morbid beauty, Vienna, always nostalgic for past glory, was ideally suited to foster a culture of decline. The cultural difference between socially determined objectives in Berlin and psychologically inspired concerns in Vienna is best reflected in the different ways the same author, Henrik Ibsen (1828–1906), whose psychological treatment of delicate characters had served as an inspiration for many young writers throughout Europe, was perceived in two historic performances of his works. While Berlin's advocates of naturalism had taken their cues from a performance of Ibsen's *Ghosts* (1881, in German *Gespenster*) in Otto Brahm's *Freie Bühne* on September 29, 1889, in Vienna it was after a performance of Ibsen's *Pretenders* (1863, in German *Die Kronprätendenten*) on April 11, 1891 that the writers of *Junges Wien*, who would usually meet in the famed Café Griensteidl, made their first public appearance, in the presence of Ibsen. Hofmannsthal, who was barely seventeen at the time, was among those in the audience who celebrated Ibsen as a Symbolist. Young Hofmannsthal, who used the pen name Loris because as a high school student he was not allowed to publish under his real name, wrote critical essays on Algernon Charles Swinburne, D'Annunzio, and Walter Pater as well as Ibsen, trying to capture the narcissism of their characters ("Sie denken übers Denken, fühlen sich fühlen und treiben Autopsychologie" [*RAI* 150]), as if he wanted to inscribe himself into the European annals of Symbolism, Aestheticism, and Decadence, into a culture of *l'art pour l'art*, which seemed to ignore cultural differences in Paris, London, Rome, or Vienna. At the same time, he began to distance himself from excesses of the aesthetic lifestyle, as it could be pursued anywhere, thus calling attention to the particularities of Vienna culture that are of historiographic interest.

In accounts of Hofmannsthal and his time most critics today seem to prefer the historical term *fin de siècle*[2] to competing concepts such as: Symbolism, a poetological movement of non-mimetic aesthetics associated with French writers such as Charles Baudelaire (1821–1867), Stéphane Mallarmé (1842–1898), Paul Verlaine (1844–1896), Rimbaud and other opponents of positivism and naturalism; *Decadence*, which is a disparaging, often ideologically tainted label for some kind of depravity, used by Théophile Gautier (1811–1872) around 1860 to characterize Baudelaire, by Friedrich Nietzsche (1844–1900) in 1888 to blame Richard Wagner (1813–1883) for his impact on French Symbolism (Nietzsche 912), and finally, in its most ominous form, by Max Nordau (1849–1923), in his comprehensive invective *Entartung* (1892–93), to indict most modern artists as degenerates;[3] Impressionism, which signifies a tentative, mainly painterly style of intuition of atmosphere and surface phenomena in perpetually changing shades of light;[4] Neo-Romanticism, which indicates a mere predilection for the Romantics' fondness of fantasy, dreams and hallucinations; and Aestheticism, which means a mental and emotional obsession with beauty and with stylizing one's own life into a work of art. None of these concepts, which are often used interchangeably as if they were referring to the same phenomena, are specific in terms of time and place. Decadence was first developed as a historiographic category by Edward Gibbon for his *History of the Decline and Fall of the Roman Empire* (1788) and made famous as a lifestyle by Oscar Wilde and his portrayal of decaying beauty in *The Picture of Dorian Gray* (1891). Impressionism as a category of art history never quite accomplished the disciplinary crossover from visual to verbal representation and from a specific art style to a general cultural paradigm. Neo-Romanticism, while used already by contemporaries,[5] is only another historiographic label in the long series of revivals from neoclassicism to Neue Subjektivität and New Historicism and can be applied to many periods. Finally, Aestheticism was a dominant, though not exclusive, movement of the time and in pronounced opposition to the social concerns of concurrent naturalism, but it was questioned and eventually rejected by Hofmannsthal, ever since he staged a death sentence for the basically asocial aesthetic man in *Der Tor und der Tod.*[6] Obviously, none of the concepts used for historiographic groupings could appropriately define the particularly Viennese situation around 1900. Therefore, most English-speaking critics have opted for *fin-de-siècle* Vienna, with *Wiener Moderne* becoming the favored German equivalent.[7]

Hermann Bahr (1863–1934), who was the critical mentor of *Wiener Moderne*, took its name from the journal *Moderne Dichtung*, which, edited by Eduard Michael Kafka (1868–1893) and Jacques Joachim (1868–1925), appeared in Brünn since January 1, 1890. To the editors, who were only twenty-one years old when the first issue appeared, being *jung* and *modern* were the same, just as the terms *Wiener Moderne* and *Junges Wien* would become interchangeable. One year later, after the journal was renamed *Moderne Rundschau* and moved to Vienna, the two editors demonstrated their youthful determination by arranging a splendid reception in the Hotel Kaiserhof to honor Ibsen following the premiere of his *Pretenders*, i.e., the very event which would become the founding moment of the entire movement. The first issue of *Moderne Dichtung* (1890) carried Bahr's programmatic essay "Die Moderne," in which he characteristically encouraged the "Spätgeborene" to seize the moment: "Wir wollen die faule Vergangenheit von uns abschütteln, die, lange verblüht, unsere Seelen in fahlem Laube erstickt. Gegenwart wollen wir sein" (Wunberg 1, 31). Consequently, Bahr always heralded the latest "present" of the time and never failed to be a few steps ahead of the next trend. Long before he would become one of the first advocates of expressionism, he even had some roots in antisemitic circles, turning from nationalist to socialist and from socialist to aestheticist. Berlin, where he had been exposed to nationalism, and Paris, where he had been confronted with Symbolism, served as the backdrop for his crusade to rejuvenate Austrian literature, to make Vienna the center of a new movement, the literature of the "young" and the "modern." *Wiener Moderne* thus became the label of a movement that made the senses the exclusive vehicle of perception, and psychological analysis of the nerves the favored approach. Since Bahr could not deliver in literary works what he demanded in his critical proclamations, he sponsored young writers such as Hofmannsthal and his friend Leopold von Andrian-Werburg (1875–1951) to spread the message, especially since slightly older colleagues such as Peter Altenberg (1859–1919) and Arthur Schnitzler (1862–1931) kept more of a distance. When Bahr (at age twenty-seven) met the seventeen-year-old Hofmannsthal, who had just published a positive review of Bahr's drama *Die Mutter* (1891) in *Moderne Rundschau*, just a few days after the historic reception for Ibsen, he immediately adopted the young critic into his circle: "Man sieht es auf den ersten Blick, man hört es an jedem Worte, daß er der Moderne angehört. [. . .] Ich werde einen zuversichtlichen Instinct nicht los, daß mit ihm die zweite Periode der Moderne beginnt, die das Experimentieren überwinden und uns, an denen sich die erste entwickelt hat, ihrerseits nun als die 'Alten' behandeln wird" (Fiechtner 42–43). The rapid passing of generations, with young rebels becoming guardians of the old before they turn thirty, only confirms the increasing role of time, urban acceleration, historical transition, and uncontrollable change in the cultural process. The easy, mostly vague and often even tautological references to "Moderne" betray a certain uneasiness, not unlike that of the Marschallin, at the experience of *tempus fugit*.

Nowhere, it seems, do anthropological and sociological considerations converge as much as in the analysis of the special mentality, the kind of aesthetic *Lebensgefühl* that permeated the culture of Vienna around the turn of the century. The experience of temporality and transitoriness is central to the culture of social change. It was most of all the crash of the Vienna stock market on May 9, 1873, the "Black Friday," that had effectively undermined any sense of security and permanently shattered the trust in the staying power of financial values — or ethical values, for that matter — to such a degree that Broch's term "Wert-Vakuum" became synonymous with criticism of *fin de siècle* (Broch 39). Following Austria's military defeat of 1867, which put an end to restrictive monetary policies, Vienna had experienced excessive speculation. The resulting construction boom created the eclectic palatial architecture of the Ringstraße, this empty claim to nobility in mere facades, which in 1898 reminded Vienna's forerunner of architectural Modernism, Adolf Loos (1870–1933), of Potemkin's deception (Wunberg 2, 870–72) and which ten years later would trigger Hitler's megalomaniac dreams of architecture for his world capital Germania. "Mit Sittensprüchen baut man keine Eisenbahn" was an infamously cynical maxim of the new society, which, through overspending, rushed into the crisis of 1873, with 230 insolvencies in just two days and with all but eight of the seventy banks that had been founded in Vienna between 1868 and 1873 collapsing within just one decade.[8] The famous lines from Johann Strauss's operetta of 1872, *Die Fledermaus,* "Glücklich ist, wer vergißt, / was doch nicht zu ändern ist," took on special significance only now, when living in the moment became the preferred strategy for repressing the debacle, and when the experience of fleeting time meant forgetting the recent misfortune. For today's good fortune could be tomorrow's bankruptcy, and vice versa. What was shunned today could be celebrated tomorrow, and vice versa. And yesterday, as we learn from Hofmannsthal's dramolet *Gestern* (1891), was ages ago: "Ein Abgrund scheint von gestern mich zu trennen, / Und fremd steh ich mir selber gegenüber. . . ." Even though Hofmannsthal, speaking through Andrea, tries to correct the dominant view of his time by saying, "Dies Gestern ist so eins mit deinem Sein, / Du kannst es nicht verwischen, nicht vergessen: / Es *ist*, so lang wir wissen, daß es *war*" (*GDI*, 242), the notion of continuity has become questionable as much as the concept of identity based on it; for the *Ich* of yesterday can no longer be trusted to be the same today and tomorrow. "Das Ich ist unrettbar": this statement by the Vienna philosopher Ernst Mach (1838–1916), in his *Beiträge zur Analyse der Empfindungen* (1886; Mach, 20), became the slogan of the time, undermining any claim to sustained personal identity and, at the same time, feeding into the continued mourning of its loss. The resulting crisis of identity is one obvious reason for the growing popularity of psychology and the development of psychoanalysis by Sigmund Freud (1856–1939) in *fin-de-siècle* Vienna. Arthur Schnitzler, whose works parallel some of Freud's issues most closely,[9] lets the main character in *Liebelei* (1894), Christine, despair because her lover was just killed in a duel for another woman: "Und ich . . . was bin denn ich? Was bin denn ich ihm gewesen . . .? [. . .] Und ich — ?. . . Was bin denn ich? [. . .] Was bin denn ich — ?" (Schnitzler 65, 67). Where love without continuity is nothing but a fleeting affair, a "Liebelei," there is no room for *Ich*, and everyone can be replaced by anyone in the never-ending circle of rapid pursuits (as in *Reigen*, 1896).

What is striking in Hofmannsthal's and Schnitzler's dramatic accounts of the new sense of time is the individualist, potentially psychological, and implicitly moralistic interpretation of a primarily cultural crisis. Their characters are faulted because they failed to meet their moral responsibilities. Their lack of commitment over time is seen as an individual flaw and not as a reflection of a much larger unsettling of values, the social destabilization that followed the financial and political demise of liberalism, a crisis that eventually gave rise to antisemitism and the ascent to political prominence of Karl Lueger (1844–1910), the militantly antisemitic lord mayor of Vienna from 1897. Sigmund Freud, Gustav Mahler, Arnold Schönberg, Richard Beer-Hofmann, Peter Altenberg, Arthur Schnitzler, Felix Salten, Karl Kraus — an entire culture of modernity was threatened by increasing discrimination. But Hofmannsthal and many of his contemporaries, who considered themselves members of the cultural elite, if not the ruling class, seemed to live in denial of the alarming signs of what was in store for them. As if his great-grandfather had not been the Jewish merchant Isaak Löw (1761–1849), who came to Vienna from Bohemia in 1794 to develop the silk industry and who was ennobled by Austrian Emperor Franz I in 1827 to become *Edler von Hofmannsthal*, and as if his own father — like the fathers of Freud and Schnitzler — had not lost a fortune in the stock market crash of 1873, Hofmannsthal (who, incidentally, was born exactly nine months after the crash, on February 1, 1874) enjoyed living the spoiled life of an aristocrat, cultivating the sense of elitism that marked both his social attitudes and much of his subtle poetry. When he, at age nineteen in the essay on Gabriele D'Annunzio, emphatically spoke of "Wir! Wir!," he meant the European elite of "ein paar tausend Menschen, in den großen europäischen Städten verstreut," praising "das Privilegium dieser geistigen Freimaurerei" and their "besondere Empfindlichkeit" which clearly set them apart (*RAI* 175). From early on, Hofmannsthal and his contemporaries cultivated a delicately nervous hypersensitivity of the happy few as the treasured sign of creative nobility.

Hofmannsthal's precocious role in the aesthetic culture of post-crash Vienna was symptomatic of its social texture. Emerging from an economic event of grave consequences, the aesthetic paradigm of the time, which was often associated with *l'art pour l'art* in its refusal to consider the social context of the arts, was determined to exclude from its consideration all social responsibility and to adopt the kind of brash "Sozial-gleichgültigkeit" that Broch found so disgusting among the artists of Hofmannsthal's time (Broch 21–22). Clearly, Hofmannsthal had good reason to distance himself from the social ignorance of his formative years and eventually to introduce into his program of literature ethical principles through what he called "das Soziale." He did so in a moral exhortation addressed to himself, *Ad me ipsum* (published posthumously in 1930), long before he acknowledged in a letter of April 1912 to Eberhard von Bodenhausen: "Wir gehen einer dunklen Zeit entgegen, das fühlt jeder Mensch, können von Schritt zu Schritt alles verlieren — und — das ist das Schlimmste, auch wo wir siegen nichts Rechtes gewinnen, als nur Verlegenheit" (Fiechtner 18). Again, the apocalyptic vision of the future with its political dimension is quickly reduced to the individualist response to loss, presumably of both material possessions and social position, and the embarrassment this loss would generate. There is no other response to the worst-case scenario ("das Schlimmste") but embarrassment, as it is usually caused merely by a violation of the social decorum. Maintaining this kind of *countenance*, even in the face of destruction and dissolution, would later become the studied attitude of Kari Bühl in Hofmannsthal's *Der Schwierige* (1921). A count by title, this "difficult" man, who does not fit the schemes made on him, remains the noble bourgeois who is as much embarrassed by the horrors of the war as by any breach of etiquette, including the intrusive telephone, which for him is nothing but an "indiskrete Maschine." Kari Bühl's gentle gesture of melancholy and resignation at the vulgarity of modern times is the strongest comment on former "Kakania" before Robert Musil's *Mann ohne Eigenschaften* (1930–43).

Obviously, the culture of *fin-de-siècle* Vienna lends itself to the cultural approach that has become the hallmark of German Studies in the last two decades; but it did not have to wait for the culturalists' newly found interest in the interaction of verbal and visual representation to become an ideal example of the ensemble of literary movement (Hermann Bahr's *Junges Wien*) and journalism (Karl Kraus) on the one hand, and modernist architecture (Adolf Loos), art (Gustav Klimt, Egon Schiele), music (Gustav Mahler, Arnold Schönberg), and psychoanalysis (Sigmund Freud) on the other. While Berlin, the legendary *Metropolis* of the "Golden Twenties" and beyond, clearly moved into the center of German Studies and affiliated film programs, especially when Berlin's need to reinvent itself as the capital of united Germany after 1990 coincided with the emerging urban discourse in interdisciplinary culture studies, *fin-de-siècle* Vienna had been the dominant reference point ever since a whole generation of Austrian emigrants, who had escaped to the United States since 1938, began to play a prominent role in the German departments of American universities. Still rooted in the Vienna of the turn of the century, exiled intellectuals — such as Franz H. Mauthner, Heinz Politzer, Walter Sokel, Hans Eichner, Harry Zohn, Egon Schwarz, Peter Heller, Dorrit Cohn — had kept the memory of their birthplace alive. While Berlin was shunned as the center of fascism and was disappearing from the cultural map as the site of terror, destruction and ideological division, Vienna remained a supreme point of reference. The unabashed gesture of melancholy, so typical of the Viennese physiognomy long before the forced exodus, consistently marked the exiles' nostalgic account of Vienna culture, especially of the *fin de siècle*. Exploring the superb achievements in the cultural ensemble of design, architecture, music, theater, literature, philosophy, and psychology called for no other but an interdisciplinary approach *avant la lettre*, with literature playing an important but no longer the exclusive role in representing cultural change. Thus, the exiles from Vienna arguably became the forerunners of the cultural turn in German Studies. As most of them were too young to be trained Germanists at the time of their escape, they never saw themselves merely as teaching scholars of German literature, but as witnesses, recorders, and advocates of an entire, largely Jewish culture that was threatened by extinction. They tried to preserve a critical memory of the past, covering all and often very diverse aspects of Vienna culture, long before the culture of memory was discovered as a hot topic in cultural studies. In fact, most of the exiled Viennese had already entered retirement age when the cultural turn took effect in the early 1980s, with the "successor generation," i.e., American-trained and American-born scholars of German culture, adopting positions of critical distance and cultural theory, which largely differed from that of their immigrant mentors. With the passing of this generation of Viennese exiles, the number of college courses dealing with particularly Austrian issues has dwindled. Institutionally, Austrian Studies, if they ever existed in the curriculum of American colleges and universities, have definitely taken a backseat to German Studies. With courses on "Weimar Berlin" taking the place of "*fin-de-siècle* Vienna," Schnitzler, Kraus, and Hofmannsthal are no longer household names among American undergraduates, if they ever were. Like their predecessors Raimund, Nestroy, and even Grillparzer, *fin-de-siècle* authors have all but disappeared from the curriculum. Beyond the ever popular *Sound of Music*, which rendered Julie Andrews and Christopher Plummer honorary Austrians, there is little left to remind the average American of Austrian culture. Even the fact that the popular TV series of the 1970s, *Upstairs Downstairs*, resembled Nestroy's play *Zu ebener Erde und erster Stock*, that John Irving's novel of 1976, *The World According to Garp*, played on Grillparzer's name, that the libretti of most of Richard Strauss's increasingly popular operas were written by Hofmannsthal and, most recently, that Stanley Kubrick's last film *Eyes Wide Shut* (1998) was based on Schnitzler's *Traumnovelle*, has not saved Austrian literature from obvious neglect in the public arena.

In academic discourse, however, the issue of Jewish Modernism, which is easily associated with *Wiener Moderne*, has raised interest in this period far beyond the small circle of scholars of Austrian literature. It is the anti-Modernism of Nazi ideology that directed the attention toward the role of Jews in Vienna Modernism. "Die Wiener Moderne galt als jüdisch," Brigitte Hamann states in her recent book *Hitlers Wien: Lehrjahre eines Diktators* (1998; *Hitler's Vienna: A Dictator's Apprenticeship*, 1999) which traces the roots of Hitler's antisemitism: "die Abwehr des Judentums stand im antisemitisch regierten Wien im Mittelpunkt des Kulturkampfes" (Hamann 112–13). After the Liberals were excluded from the government of Eduard von Taaffe (1833–1895) in 1879, the defeat of liberalism opened the gates for radical movements whose first victims were going to be Jews. In 1885 the radically antisemitic Georg von Schönerer (1842–1921), who in his demand for special laws to separate Jews from the Christian majority stopped just short of calling for their internment, founded the Deutschnationale Partei; and in 1897 the new coalition of Christians, socialists, nationalists etc., who were united in their opposition to the liberal upper middle class and its ties to Jewish intellectuals and artists, made Karl Lueger the lord mayor of Vienna.

These ideological currents were a response as much to dramatic demographic changes in Vienna's population as to the liberal legislation that had made them possible. In 1867 a new state law had granted Jews equal rights, among them acquisition of real estate, choice of residence, access to the civil service and to the university. With these changes, Vienna attracted huge waves of immigrants, mostly from the provinces in the east, from Hungary, Galicia, and Bukowina. The Jewish population grew from 6,200 in 1860 (2.2 percent) to 72,600 in 1880 (10.1 percent) and 147,000 in 1900 (with a constant share of 8.7 percent after incorporation of the outskirts).[10] As most of these immigrants were more ambitious and more mobile than the complacent members of bureaucracy and traditional lower and middle classes, they quickly succeeded in taking their places in the emerging modernization of the stagnant society (Beller). The success was most obvious in education: in the period from 1898 to 1902, 24.5 percent of the Jews living in Vienna attended the university, compared to only 5.3 percent of non-Jews, with one third of all students being Jewish. Since at the same time Russian Jews, who escaped the pogroms following the assassination of Tsar Alexander II in 1881, moved to Vienna to compete economically with the underprivileged, the antisemitic backlash spanned all social levels. In turn, the surge of antisemitism caused another radical reaction, Zionism, as it was propagated in the manifesto *Der Judenstaat* (1896) by Theodor Herzl (1860–1914), a journalist who had just returned from a four-year stint as correspondent in Paris to become editor of the feuilleton of Vienna's leading newspaper, *Neue Freie Presse*. It was the first time that assimilation, the ambition of most Jews drawn to Vienna's cultural blend, was effectively questioned in a separatist response to the public antisemitic campaign against those who seemed to have made it into the cultural elite, regardless of whether they were observant Jews or not. The Dreyfus affair of 1894, in which a French colonel was wrongly accused of spying for the Germans because he was Jewish, was a turning point. In view of such strident antisemitism, Herzl, who had covered the Paris trial as a correspondent, decided to renounce all hopes for assimilation, while others like Kraus (who converted to Catholicism in 1911), Peter Altenberg (who converted in 1900), Hofmannsthal (who was raised Catholic) and, in an extreme case of self-denial, Otto Weininger (1880–1903), belittled their Jewish heritage and, to different degrees, joined the campaign. Karl Kraus (1874–1936) wrote one of the most virulent attacks on Zionism (Kraus, "Eine Krone für Zion"), and Weininger proclaimed in his widely read book *Geschlecht und Charakter* (1903): "was dem echten Juden in aller Ewigkeit unzugänglich ist: das unmittelbare Sein, das Gottesgnadentum, der Eichbaum, die Trompete, das Siegfriedmotiv, die Schöpfung seiner selbst, das Wort, ich bin" (Weininger 445). If the *Ich* cannot be "saved" (to borrow Ernst Mach's terminology), it is because Jews have no access to Wagnerian redemption, because they forever lack the depth of primary Germanic genius. Weininger's argument was used in the Third Reich even against Hofmannsthal. In 1937 Franz Koch, who held the prestigious chair of German literature at the university of Berlin, positioned him "zwischen den Rassen" only to declare him racially incapable of overcoming aestheticism: "Es bedarf rassisch ungebrochener Persönlichkeiten und ursprünglich dichterischer Wesenheit [. . ,.], um diesen Ästhetizismus zu überwinden und zu wesentlichen Schöpfungen aufzusteigen" (Koch 287).

In order to show that the modern identity crisis is merely a problem of Jewish nerves, antisemitic critics resorted to old stereotypes that could be applied as much to Jews as to the literary avant-garde. One of the earliest critics of "Dekadent Loris," Ottokar Stauf von der March (actually Ottokar F. Chalupka, 1868–1941), was also among the first to suggest an easy explanation for "die hektisch-neuralgische Poesie der Hermaphroditen, in deren literarischem Organismus anstatt Blut eine Mischung von Morphium und odeur de femmes fließt" (529): "Die meisten Dekadenten sind Semiten." The rhetoric of blood did not bode well for the future of what in antisemitic stereotyping is the feminized Jew: "Die Zukunft wird die Dekadenten vom Horizont fegen [. . .]. Dem Charakter der Zukunft wird nur eine starke, gesunde, männliche Poesie entsprechen" (533). The feminization of the Jew, which is an old cliché, parallels the feminization of *Wiener Moderne*. The anti-Modernist sentiment of those who were left behind economically, socially, and culturally gained momentum once it could be associated with the emotional impact of the racist argument. For example, in 1902 Rudolf Lothar (actually Rudolf Spitzer, 1865–1943), who had written for the feuilleton of *Neue Freie Presse* since 1889 and become better known through his book *Kritische Studien zur Psychologie der Literatur* (1895), says of Richard Beer-Hofmann (1866–1945), who was very open about his Jewish identity and would later unequivocally defend it against Hofmannsthal:[11] "Mit Bahr und Hofmannsthal verbindet ihn auch das feminine Wesen, der Mangel jener Kraft, die in straffer Komposition sich ausspricht" (Wunberg 2, 1175–76). Such gendering of aesthetic principles is symptomatic of critics who felt threatened by non-gender-specific sensitivities. It flourished in the frustrated milieu from which Hitler would soon emerge after he failed as an aspiring artist in Vienna in 1908. Antisemitic critics of *Junges Wien* could easily have borrowed from what Wolfgang Menzel said half a century earlier about *Junges Deutschland*, which he saw embodied by Heinrich Heine: "Die Physiognomie des jungen Deutschland war die eines aus Paris kommenden, nach der neuesten Mode gekleideten, aber gänzlich blasierten, durch Lüderlichkeit entnervten Judenjünglings mit spezifischem Moschus- und Knoblauchgeruch" (Hermand 337–38). Odeur de femmes and the smell of garlic combine to denigrate the same outsider, the gaunt dandy who may be a virtuoso of the form but never a real artist of substance. In terms of the most frequently used cliché, there is no "Schöpferkraft," no creative originality. It is only the ephemeral, the technical perfection, that the Jewish artist was allowed to display, from Menzel to the propagandist of the Third Reich, Alfred Rosenberg: "Man schaue auf das Massenhaft-Übertriebene des Theaterzirkus Reinhardt-Goldmann, man prüfe die jüdischen Wunderkinder am Klavier, an der Geige, auf den Brettern: Talmi, Technik, Mache, Effekt, Quantität, Virtuosität, alles was man will, nur keine Genialität, keine Schöpferkraft" (Rosenberg 365). It was Heine more than anyone else who had come to personify these secondary features of a virtuoso who only could play tricks. In a strange twist, Heine — or rather, journalists like Bahr or Herzl trying to write in the tradition of Heine — was presented in a similar light, with shades of antisemitic sentiments about Jewish brilliance in style, when Karl Kraus in his famous article "Heine und die Folgen" (1911) indicted the feuilletonism of his time, employing some of the very stereotypes that were used against "the Jewish press." In this context Kraus, who was an articulate opponent of Hermann Bahr and his circle of Modernists (*Die demolirte Literatur*, 1896), wrote one of his famous lines, in accordance with Adolf Loos's anti-ornamental Modernist stance: "Ein Feuilleton schreiben heißt auf einer Glatze Locken drehen" (Kraus, "Heine," 293). Making an ornament out of nothing, splash without substance, virtuosity without genius, intellectual sophistication without genuine feeling — that is the loaded discourse of antisemitic "aesthetics" developed in reaction to *Wiener Moderne*.

Karl Kraus's crusade against pretensions and the corruption of language as social degeneration shifted the emphasis from physiological markers of decadence to stylistics. Where Max Nordau, following Cesare Lombroso's medical studies on the madness of genius (*Genio et Folia*, 1864), had portrayed decadents as genetic cripples, Kraus turns them into linguistic criminals who, by corrupting both good style and accurate thought, destroy character. The emphasis on style, be it caustic in the moral indictments by Kraus or polished into poetic beauty by Hofmannsthal, resulted from a new critical awareness of language, which was fostered in the increasingly multilingual culture of *fin-de-siècle* Vienna, where Hungarian, Czech, Polish, Italian, Croatian, Serbian, Romanian, and Bulgarian were as common as the Yiddish of recent immigrants. While it may be tempting to transform Jewish alienation into a trope of Modernism, the heightened awareness of, and frequent reflection on, language cannot be essentialized as genuinely Jewish. But it can be better understood against the background of the Jewish experience. As Jews were forced in the early nineteenth century to pay a very high price for their social emancipation, by giving up their

Hebrew names[12] and their Yiddish language, Jewish identity formation within the mainstream culture was bound — often more subconsciously than not — to an adaptation of the enforced German by forming and, at the same time, overcoming an idiom of their own. In developing a special sensitivity to linguistic nuances they made opaque, visible, material and thematic the very language that most people were using naively as a mere window opening up to the real, that is, linguistically untainted world. The resistance of language that can no longer be taken for granted became a creative challenge. Anxious to be indistinguishably German, many Jews doubled their efforts to perfect their proficiency in German style when there was a question as to whether Jews, however assimilated they might be socially, could ever lose their linguistic markers as outsiders. As attention to language was central to educational aspirations, it comes as no surprise that Jewish writers contributed substantially to the refinement of the German language, with overwhelming evidence in twentieth-century German literature. The belief in this inherent linguistic difference was so pervasive, among Jews as well as non-Jews, that the special sensitivity to linguistic nuances these writers cultivated around the turn of the century could even be interpreted as a compensation for "Jewish self-hatred."[13]

If the reflection on language, be it literary as in Hofmannsthal's "Ein Brief" (1902), critical as in the invectives of Karl Kraus's journal *Die Fackel,* or philosophical as in Ludwig Wittgenstein's *Tractatus logico-philosophicus* (1921), is indeed the acclaimed cornerstone of *Wiener Moderne,* it is undoubtedly involved in the kind of identity crisis that was experienced, recognized and often suffered more by Jewish modernists than by their non-Jewish contemporaries. One year after Fritz Mauthner (1849–1923), who had turned away from his Jewish origins in Prague and moved to Berlin, published his *Beiträge zur Kritik der Sprache* (1901), arguing for language as an epistemological tool, Chandos's lament, "Es ist mir völlig die Fähigkeit abhanden gekommen, über irgend etwas zusammenhängend zu denken oder zu sprechen" (*Erz* 465), was to become synonymous with the modern *Sprachkrise,* which was later reinterpreted as the Modernist renunciation of the mimetic and redemptive power of language. In Vienna, living between the languages may not have been as obvious a struggle as in Prague, where Kafka, to name only the most obvious example, had lost the language of his Jewish background and replaced it with German, the adopted language of both Austrian bureaucracy (which he served in an insurance company) and German literature (which he served by breaking entirely new ground). But in Vienna, too, the dominance of German increasingly proved a challenge for the waves of immigrants from the eastern provinces. Generations later Elias Canetti, who was born in Rustschuk, Bulgaria in 1905, and Paul Celan, who was born in Czernowitz, Bukowina in 1920, best represent Jewish writers who moved to Vienna and, by holding on to the language of their persecutors, created new levels of linguistic reflection and poetic perfection in German.

In conclusion, a direct line could be drawn from the emphasis among writers of *fin-de-siècle* Vienna on the inability of language to express adequately the sensitivities of the young Modernists and the post-Auschwitz position that the horrors of the Holocaust cannot — and should not — be co-opted in language. What originally was an affected position by those who, like Hofmannsthal, paradoxically resorted to the most beautiful language to proclaim the crisis of mimetic language, later became a measure of authenticity: On the one hand, the gravity of unspeakable experience (Adorno argued in his famous dictum that writing poetry after Auschwitz would be barbaric)[14] precludes any representation; and on the other, Paul Celan's famous poem "Todesfuge" (1948) refuted such a comprehensive ban on language. When Celan, in his Bremen speech of 1958, defended his decision to remain within his native tongue by saying that the German language first "had to pass through its own answerlessness, pass through a frightful falling mute, pass through the thousand darknesses of death-bringing speech" before it would be possible again to write poems in German,[15] he clearly spoke from the tradition of writers in *fin-de-siècle* Vienna, many of them Jews, for whom language became thematic because it could no longer be taken for granted. The crisis of language around 1900, which affected only a relatively small circle, was only the precursor to the other crisis after 1945 when the horrifying fact that the Holocaust was prepared and executed in German, and in the name of what the German language supposedly stands for, could no longer be denied.

Against this background and with the historical and cultural difference of a full century in mind, we can appreciate the extent to which the experience of volatile time and temporality, while caused by social change, seemed to further destabilize social structures and psychological patterns, turning upside down an entire world whose loss was mourned long before it collapsed. And we can accept reflection on the possibilities and limitations of language in this rapidly changing and culturally ever more diversified world as one important legacy of *fin-de-siècle* Vienna — in terms of current interest in both, theoretically, the concept of non-mimetic language and, practically, the role of language in intercultural studies.[16]

Notes

[1] Cf. Arndt Brendecke, *Die Jahrhundertwenden: Eine Geschichte ihrer Wahrnehmung und Wirkung* (Frankfurt/New York, 1999).

[2] Cf. *Fin de siècle: Zur Literatur und Kunst der Jahrhundertwende,* ed. Roger Bauer (Frankfurt am Main, 1977); Jens Malte Fischer, *Fin de siècle: Kommentar zu einer Epoche* (Munich, 1978); Carl E. Schorske, *Fin-de-siècle Vienna: Politics and Culture* (1980); Gisa Briese-Neumann, *Ästhet — Dilettant — Narziss: Untersuchungen zur Reflexion der fin de siècle-Phänomene im Frühwerk Hofmannsthals,* Tübinger Studien zur deutschen Literatur vol. 10 (Frankfurt am Main, Bern, New York: Verlag Peter Lang, 1985).

[3] Cf. Richard Gilman, *Decadence: The Strange Life of an Epithet* (New York: Farrar, Straus and Giroux, 1979). Characteristically, Jacques Barzun had to emphasize in his historiographic account of the Western World from 1517 to the present — *From Dawn to Decadence* (Harper Collins, 2000) — that he used the term "decadence" not as a slur but as a technical label to signify the fourth and last of the great periods, postmodernism.

[4] Cf. Richard Hamann & Jost Hermand, *Impressionismus in Leben und Kunst* (Munich: Nymphenburger, 1972); Wolfgang Nehring, "Hofmannsthal und der Wiener Impressionismus," in: *Zeitschrift für deutsche Philologie* 94, 4 (1975), 481–98.

[5] Cf. Ludwig Coellen, "Ästheten/Dekadenten und Mystiker," in: *Neuromantik* (Jena, 1906), 69–77.

[6] Cf. Richard Alewyn, "Der Tod des Ästheten," in: Alewyn, *Über Hofmannsthal* (Göttingen: Vandenhoeck & Ruprecht, [2]1960), 64–77; Hinrich C. Seeba, *Kritik des ästhetischen Menschen: Hermeneutik und Moral in Hofmannsthals "Der Tor und der Tod"* (Bad Homburg v. d. H., Berlin, Zürich: Gehlen, 1970).

[7] Cf. *Das Junge Wien,* ed. Gotthart Wunberg, 2 vols.; Dagmar Lorenz, *Wiener Moderne,* Sammlung Metzler 290 (Stuttgart: Metzler, 1998).

[8] Roman Sandgruber, "Der große Krach," in: *Traum und Wirklichkeit — Wien 1870–1930.* Catalogue of the exhibit at Historisches Museum der Stadt Wien, from March 28 to October 6, 1985 (Eigenverlag der Museen der Stadt Wien, 1985), 68–75, here p. 69 f.

[9] Cf. Rolf-Peter Janz/Klaus Laermann, *Arthur Schnitzler: Zur Diagnose des Wiener Bürgertums im Fin de siècle* (Stuttgart: Metzler, 1977).

[10] For these and the following statistics cf. Hamann 467 ff.

[11] Cf. *Hugo von Hofmannsthal — Richard Beer-Hofmann. Briefwechsel,* ed. Eugene Weber (Frankfurt am Main 1972), 167; on this exchange see Stefan Scherer, *Richard Beer-Hofmann und die Wiener Moderne* (Tübingen, 1993), 404–10.

[12] Cf. Dietz Bering, *Der Name als Stigma: Antisemitismus im deutschen Alltag 1812–1933* (Stuttgart: Klett-Cotta, 1987).

[13] Cf. Sander Gilman, *Jewish Self-Hatred: Antisemitism and the Hidden Language of the Jews* (Baltimore and London: The Johns Hopkins University Press, 1986), esp. 209–308. Gilman refers to Theodor Billroth, the famous surgeon at the university of Vienna, who in 1876 argued for excluding Jewish students from the university by saying: "They often understand so little German that they can grasp neither the language nor the sense of the questions, and they are quite incapable of expressing their thoughts, either in German or in any other tongue" (quoted 215).

[14] Theodor W. Adorno, "Kulturkritik und Gesellschaft" (1951), in: Adorno, *Prismen: Kulturkritik und Gesellschaft* (Munich: dtv, 1963), 7–26, 26: "Kulturkritik findet sich der letzten Stufe der Dialektik von Kultur und Barbarei gegenüber: nach Auschwitz ein Gedicht zu schreiben, ist barbarisch, und das frißt auch die Erkenntnis an, die ausspricht, warum es unmöglich ward, heute Gedichte zu schreiben."

[15] In John Felstiner's translation, quoted from John Felstiner, "Translating Celan's Poem," in *The American Poetry Review* (July/August 1982), 23.

[16] With regard to present concerns, the conclusion parallels what Allan Janik & Stephen Toulmin (*Wittgenstein's Vienna* [New York: Simon and Schuster/A Touchstone Book 1973]) presented as their "central hypothesis about Viennese culture — namely, that to be a fin-de-siècle Viennese artist or intellectual, conscious of the social realities of Kakania, one had to face the problem of the nature and limits of language, expression and communication" (117).

Works Cited

Beller, Steven. "Who made Vienna 1900 a capital of modern culture?" *Kreatives Milieu: Wien um 1900.* Ed. Emil Brix and Allan Janik. Vienna: Verlag für Geschichte und Politik, 1993. 175–80.

Broch, Hermann. *Hofmannsthal und seine Zeit: Ein Versuch.* Mit einem Nachwort von Hannah Arendt. Munich: R. Piper, 1964.

Fiechtner, Helmut, ed. *Hugo von Hofmannsthal: Der Dichter im Spiegel der Freunde.* Bern: Francke, 1963. 39–43.

Hermand, Jost, ed. *Das Junge Deutschland: Texte und Dokumente.* Stuttgart: Reclam, 1966.

Jauss, Hans Robert. "Literarische Tradition und gegenwärtiges Bewußtsein der Modernität." *Literaturgeschichte als Provokation*. Frankfurt am Main: Suhrkamp, 1970. 11–66.

Koch, Franz. *Geschichte deutscher Dichtung*. Hamburg: Hanseatische Verlagsanstalt, 1942.

Kraus, Karl. "Heine und die Folgen" (1910). *Ausgewählte Werke*. Ed. Dietrich Simon. Vol. 1: *Grimassen. 1902–1914*. Munich: Kösel, n.d. 290–312.

———. "Eine Krone für Zion." *Frühe Schriften, 1892–1900*. Ed. Johannes J. Braakenburg, 2 vols. Munich: Kösel, 1979. Vol. 2, 298–314.

Mach, Ernst. *Die Analyse der Empfindungen und das Verhältnis des Physischen zum Psychischen*. Jena: Verlag von Gustav Fischer, 1922.

Nietzsche, Friedrich. "Der Fall Wagner." *Werke in drei Bänden*. Ed. Karl Schlechta. Vol. 2. Munich: Carl Hanser Verlag, 1966. 901–27.

Rosenberg, Alfred. *Der Mythos des zwanzigsten Jahrhunderts: Eine Wertung der seelisch-geistigen Gestaltenkämpfe unserer Zeit*. Munich: Hoheneichen-Verlag, 1933.

Schlegel, Friedrich. *Über das Studium der griechischen Poesie* (1797). *Kritische Schriften*. Ed. Wolfdietrich Rasch. Munich: Carl Hanser, 1964. 113–230.

Schnitzler, Arthur. "Liebelei." *Liebelei / Reigen*. Frankfurt am Main: Fischer Bücherei, 1960. 5–68.

Stauf von der March, Ottokar. "Décadence." *Die Gesellschaft* (April 1894) 526–33.

Weininger, Otto. *Geschlecht und Charakter: Eine prinzipielle Untersuchung*. Vienna, Leipzig: Wilhelm Braumüller, 1907.

Worbs, Michael. *Nervenkunst: Literatur und Psychoanalyse im Wien der Jahrhundertwende*. Frankfurt am Main, 1983.

Wunberg, Gotthart, ed. *Das Junge Wien: Österreichische Literatur- und Kunstkritik 1887–1902*. 2 vols. Tübingen: Max Niemeyer Verlag, 1976. 30–33.

The Writings

ANDREAS THOMASBERGER

Hofmannsthal's Poems and Lyric Dramas

Wer bin ich denn, welch eine Welt ist dies,
In der so Kleines hat so viel Gewalt!
Kein Festes nirgends! Droben nur die Wolken,
Dazwischen, ewig wechselnd, weiche Buchten
Mit unruhvollen Sternen angefüllt . . .
Und hier die Erde, angefüllt mit Rauschen
Der Flüsse, die nichts hält: des Lebens Kronen
Wie Kugeln rollend, bis ein Mutiger drauf
Mit beiden Füßen springt; Gelegenheit,
Das große Wort; wir selber nur der Raum,
Drin Tausende von Träumen buntes Spiel
So treiben wie im Springbrunn Myriaden
Von immer neuen, immer fremden Tropfen;
All unsre Einheit nur ein bunter Schein,
Ich selbst mit meinem eignen Selbst von früher,
Von einer Stunde früher grad so nah,
Vielmehr so fern verwandt, als mit dem Vogel,
Der dort hinflattert.
Sie schaudert Weh, in dieser Welt
Allein zu sein, ist übermaßen furchtbar. (*GDI* 473–74)

T HESE WORDS SPOKEN by Miranda in Hofmannsthal's lyric drama *Der weiße Fächer* (1897) contain practically all of the themes which were to take artistic shape during the first decade of the poet's work. As is well known, most of Hofmannsthal's lyric poetry and lyric dramas were written in this decade. It is no coincidence that a dramatic figure such as Miranda should give a summation of this kind, for Hofmannsthal's writing points from the start to dramatic form, and an unsparing reflection on his own situation is an integral part of the poet's writing at all times.

The locus of this reflection — which is simultaneously criticism of one's epoch and self-criticism — is the lyrical dramas. In these works, the problematic issues raised by such characteristic clichés of the day as decadence, aestheticism, or dilettantism are made visible, especially through the self-questioning of a figure such as Claudio in the lyric drama *Der Tor und der Tod* (1893). It is the fact of death, and this alone, that allows the limits set for the play of imagination to appear; death allows us to recognize our failures and the guilt we have incurred in and toward life. Hofmannsthal as poet lives up to this thoroughly moral standard inasmuch as he constantly, and ever anew, works on finding a language which might do justice to the particular constellation of things. Dead words should not distort reality; rather, the living word, which is the poet's task, should convey meaning. To this extent, his concern is always with the social function of language as well — even the rather monologic stance of the lyric poetry is ever mindful of the fact that it is always participating in a conversation. In the development of the poet's work, this brings about a logical development from lyric poetry to drama; in the author's own life, the development is from a solitary writer to one who participates in collaborations of various kinds.

What Hofmannsthal was able to say through the mask of Miranda in 1897 was based on more than seven years of literary creation. The superficial popular fascination with the fact that the author was then only twenty-three years old fades into the background when one considers the extent and the variety of the poet's creations up to that time. As early as 1891 he had already written ninety lyric texts, almost a quarter of his total output. Since it was characteristic of Hofmannsthal's approach to writing that he used the same images, motifs, and turns of phrase several times, irrespective of traditional generic boundaries, whenever they were suited to express an insight important to him, it is difficult clearly to distinguish lyric and dramatic sketches from narrative or essayistic ones. The governing principle is that language is always used in light of its figurativeness [Bildlichkeit], and that Hofmannsthal never attempts to formulate a thought without an image, a metaphor, or a comparison of some sort. It is with this background in mind that the poetry and lyrical dramas of the 1890s reveal their particular qualities.

If, on account of Hofmannsthal's extreme reluctance to publish his poems, the public impression arose that he effortlessly produced a unique masterpiece in every major lyric genre on his first attempt, a glance at the manuscripts still unpublished at the time of the poet's death reveals a different story. Precisely the voluminous poetic output of the year 1890 shows to what an extent the poet kept on revising texts he had already produced. Here we see not only cycles of sonnets and ghasels which relate formally to nineteenth-century poets such as Lenau, Rückert, and Platen; above all, we see that from the start the situation of the epigone is thematized and reflected on, and that the question is raised with the utmost intensity as to how it is possible to create a poem at all in view of the enormous weight of literary tradition.

The poem "Siehst du die Stadt" (1890) raises the question by means of personification; the poem asks whether and how something can be seen and how it is possible to give artistic form to what has been seen. Here the text allows us to see that the problem named in the verses quoted at the beginning of this essay — "All unsre Einheit nur ein bunter Schein" — motivates but at the same time calls into question the poet's writing.[1] The condition of poetic speech — what the poet calls "Schweben" — is made explicit. This "hovering" language of the poem moves within the paradox of having to be dynamic and fixed at the same time, without losing itself in uncertainty on the one hand or rigidity on the other. Later, for instance in the poem "Lebenslied," the poet uses the images of "Welle" and "Schwelle" to express this condition.

"Siehst du die Stadt" may serve as a good example as well for the migration of texts within the entire context of the poet's work. These lines were incorporated in modified form into Desiderio's monologue in the lyric drama *Der Tod des Tizian* (1892), where they receive a new, expanded meaning in the context of the drama. It may be said in general that the lyric poetry and the lyric dramas of the early 1890s are most closely connected, as may be seen from the numerous adoptions of lines from the poetry into the lyric dramas. It remains the task of Hofmannsthal scholars to give an exact account of this wealth of self-referentiality in the poet's texts, one in which the context of the new text must be considered equally with that of the earlier text from which the element is borrowed, but in which attention must be paid above all to the changes of meaning in each specific context.

Even Hofmannsthal's early texts thematize the question of influencing and being influenced. Thus we can see from the linguistic variations in the different versions of the poem "Wolken" (1892) what problems arise in perceiving, in "grasping" something external, something dynamic, specifically as a symbol of one's own inner life. The context of French Symbolism, which Hofmannsthal came to know through Stefan George, can be seen here.[2] Before his meeting with George in December 1891, Hofmannsthal had given conventional form to the theme, following the language of the German Romantic poet Eichendorff; stimulated by the linguistic constructions of the French Symbolist master Mallarmé, the syntax and diction change completely. At the same time, the text thematizes the question as to the ability of a symbol to contain a dynamic element, and allows one to observe through the development from version to version how, by way of concentrating on an ever-smaller number of stanzas, the poet discovers the appropriate form for the poem's theme. This formal gain through reduction and condensation can be observed throughout Hofmannsthal's poetry.

But the wealth of vocabulary and quotation in many of these texts seems to contradict the above observation. Hofmannsthal's early works were admired for a long time for their virtuosic handling of language and culture; readers observed a wealth of diverse costumes and an indifference to the historicity of whatever is being quoted in each particular instance. This phenomenon is sometimes pejoratively referred to as flaunting one's vocabulary. However, a glance at these texts allows us to recognize, quite apart from either fascination or aversion, that there is a complementarity appropriate to the subject, from which one can in each instance infer the theme. In this way a poem like "Leben" (1892) speaks volubly, taking up Symbolist images and others stemming from Dionysian mythology, but it does so in the extraordinarily strict strophic form of the Italian stanza. In this way it can lend the poem's content, which verges on disintegration, a modicum of formal structure. The relation between nature and art in the poem "Mein Garten" (1891) is given an analogous structure: here too, the rigid realm of fixating artificiality is evoked in lines of free verse, whereas the "other garden" of lively uncertainty is conveyed in strict form. Finally, the two halves of the poem "Erlebnis" (1892) correspond to one another, in this case primarily on the level of content: the tendency toward dissolution in the element of death, presented in colors and sounds, is corrected by way of the homesickness for a life which can still be glimpsed, in which, rather than choosing random colors, the poet is fully conscious of the iconographic implications of each color choice. Moreover, "Erlebnis" belongs to that series of texts which present the problem of self-knowledge ("Ich selbst mit meinem eignen Selbst von früher"). If here it is the child in which "einer" sees "sich selbst," in another place this child which one once was can be compared to a "Hund unheimlich stumm und fremd" ("Terzinen: Über Vergänglichkeit," 1894), or — later — the same child may appear in the mirror as a "blasse[r], übermächtige[r] Fremde[r]" ("Vor Tag," 1907).

What is common to all of these scenes of self-encounter is the extreme displeasure which always arises when the ego observes itself in a particular outer form. If this points on the one hand to the fact that the continuity of past and present is not simply a given, and that the question of near and far can not be decided according to conventional standards, it also points to the fact that while these texts intend to offer a kind of self-knowledge, this knowledge will not be of a comforting nature. Instead, the poet's aim is to allow the reader to recognize "Binden mit dem Schattenbande" beyond any real-life ties, in other words, constellations and explanations which allow one to experience both the most remote correspondences as well as unexpected dimensions. The effect of a poem conceived in this way is described in the following lines from "Wo ich nahe, wo ich lande . . ." (1894):

> Daß sie mit verhaltnem Grauen
> An sich selber niederschauen,
> Von Geheimnis ganz durchwoben
> Fühlen sich emporgehoben
> Und den Himmel dunkler blauen! (*GDI* 168)

This programmatic statement — Hofmannsthal used the first stanza of the poem "Wo ich nahe, wo ich lande" as a motto for the volume *Die Gedichte und Kleinen Dramen* (1911) — is actually formulated in the corresponding lyric genre of the epigram in the poem titled "Inschrift" (1896):

> Entzieh dich nicht dem einzigen Geschäfte!
> Vor dem dich schaudert, dieses ist das deine:
> Nicht anders sagt das Leben, was es meine,
> Und schnell verwirft das Chaos deine Kräfte. (176)

Rational planning and classification, which distorts reality with derivative words, is confronted again and again with intuition; the poet repeatedly describes moments in which an insight emerges unexpectedly. "Solche Dinge *begreift* man nicht: man weiß sie plötzlich" (*Erz* 36), it is said in the story "Das Glück am Weg" (1893) with reference to the woman who rides by totally unexpected and who appears to the protagonist with absolute certainty as the fulfillment of all his secret wishes: "in ihrer Gegenwart lag etwas, das allem einen Sinn gab, etwas unsäglich Beruhigendes, Befriedigendes, Krönendes" (36). As an authority which mediates such intuitions, even what is small has "so viel Gewalt" (as in the words of Miranda quoted at the beginning of the essay). This might be something as insignificant as a diving beetle in the poem "Der goldene Apfel" (1897), but it might also be the word of the poem, which becomes alive when it is understood not in its everyday character, but as something completely new.

One of the most revealing treatments of this theme is the poem "Weltgeheimnis" (1894), which in its carefully constructed ambiguity describes precisely the possibility of conveying the incomprehensible secret of the world. The stanza before the last, which was added later, states this explicitly:

> In unsern Worten liegt es drin
> So tritt des Bettlers Fuß den Kies,
> Der eines Edelsteins Verlies. (*GDI* 20)

The final stanza speaks of the apparently past but at the same time continuously present condition of "Einst," which accompanies the real present as its paradoxical foundation, and of which it may be said: "Nun zuckt im Kreis ein Traum herum." In this poem Hofmannsthal uses the levels of meaning inherent in language in several ways: the continuity of the poem's stanzas, which is deceivingly suggested, in reality does not exist, the realm of the mystery is consistently named by the word "es," and the possibilities of conveying meaning metaphorically are by comparison given a traditional name taken from Romantic lyric: "Zauberworte" (Eichendorff).

Quotes of this kind never appear in Hofmannsthal's textual constructions without intertextual marking, in this case through the formulation in the form of a comparison ("Wie Zauberworte . . ."), in other cases as a phrase that is taken up literally (for example, "Cherub und hoher Herr ist unser Geist" [*GDI* 25] in "Ein Traum von großer Magie," 1895) and that through its character as a quote (from Paracelsus in this case) allows us to recognize that an original personal statement as to what "unser Geist" really is may not be possible, but that a statement might nevertheless be attempted experimentally by means of the quote, thus by a traditional turn of phrase amounting to a kind of historical solution.

In his lyric poetry, Hofmannsthal gives form to this paradoxical situation of intuitive knowledge by means of the linguistic elements of mysticism, mediated through the lyric of Goethe (as in "Ich lösch das Licht," 1893), but also by way of apparently simple nature imagery ("Leise Tratest . . .," 1894, and "Hier lieg ich," 1896) which through their context and rhythm express a happy sense of being borne aloft, and yet which in their very simplicity seem totally unrealistic, as in "Ich ging hernieder . . ." (1893): "Die Winde liefen und die Vögel sangen" (*GDI* 150).

If in the lyric drama *Der Tor und der Tod* a life which had previously been missed out on is not illuminated until death appears (*Adstante morte nitebit vita* — "When Death stands near, Life shines more brightly" — is the Latin motto in Hofmannsthal's manuscript), this is a transformation of a perception which previously had been mired in the everyday. Transformations of this kind are likewise given shape throughout the first part of *Die Frau im Fenster* (1897; *Madonna Dianora*, 1916), as Madame Dianora sees reality with the eyes of love, and also in the first part of the poem "Der Jüngling und die Spinne" (1897), where it is the recognition "Sie liebt mich!" which produces a feeling of more than earthly power, as well as the fancy that all reality is related to one's own, thus elevated ego. In "Ein Traum von grosser Magie" this condition of "hovering" is ascribed to the magician:

Dann warf er sich mit leichtem Schwung der Lenden —
Wie nur aus Stolz — der nächsten Klippe zu;
An ihm sah ich die Macht der Schwere enden. (*GDI* 24)

To be sure, also integral to the statement implicit in Hofmannsthal's lyrical texts is the insight that a weightlessness of this kind does indeed necessarily make intuition possible, but in its unarticulated exuberance it is a hybrid phenomenon with respect to human life. Thus the nurse's warning in "Die Frau im Fenster," with which she opposes humility to pride ("Wenn uns der liebe Gott das Leben schenkt" [*GDI* 352]) and in "Der Jüngling und die Spinne" (1897) the reversal in the youth's mood in face of the deadly spider ("Welch eine Angst ist hier, welch eine Not") which leads him to final insight:

Nun spür ich schaudernd etwas mich umgeben,
Es türmt sich auf bis an die hohen Sterne,
Und seinen Namen weiß ich nun: das Leben. (*GDI* 49)

The apparently diffuse talk about "life" in Hofmannsthal's works must be viewed with care, as critics have long since demonstrated.[3] The concepts "existence" and "preexistence," which were brought into play by the poet himself in his self-interpretation *Ad me ipsum* (1916 f.), are being applied by critics directly to his lyrical language, although the texts themselves make it clear that a language of "preexistence" cannot exist. This condition of undivided unity is a necessary presupposition for the understanding of Hofmannsthal's work, but "preexistence" is inevitably a liminal concept which can at best point to a reality beyond words. Thus the first half of the poem "Ein Knabe" (1896) points to this time "Eh er gebändigt war für sein Geschick," but, as would follow from the above, it can do so only in the past tense: "Lang *kannte* er die Muscheln nicht für schön" (Emphasis added; *GDI* 46).[4]

On the other hand, agents of mediation appear again and again in the lyric texts. The most famous of these is probably the spring wind in the poem "Vorfrühling" (1892), which brings "strange things" in its capacity as a medium between the here and now on the one hand, and an enticing distance which seems rich in promise. Twenty years later, Hofmannsthal tried once more to give artistic expression to this activity of mediation between the realms of distance and the past, with their rich multidimensionality, and the present moment in time; this can be seen in the lyrical fragment "Vox et praeterea nihil" ("A voice and nothing besides") (1912). The title, borrowed presumably from Keats — in Robert Burton's *Anatomy of Melancholy*, the wording *vox es praeterea nihil* ("thou art a voice and nothing besides") is applied to the nightingale — describes exactly the impossibility of placing the voice's origin on a continuum of time or space, but indicates at the same time the voice's status as one which takes in a variety of elements. It is precisely this voice which may become the language of the poems, as is made explicit in the famous penultimate stanza of the poem "Manche freilich . . ." (1895), to which we will now turn our attention.

> Manche freilich müssen drunten sterben
> Wo die schweren Ruder der Schiffe streifen,
> Andre wohnen bei dem Steuer droben,
> Kennen Vogelflug und die Länder der Sterne
>
> Manche liegen immer mit schweren Gliedern
> Bei den Wurzeln des verworrenen Lebens,
> Andern sind die Stühle gerichtet
> Bei den Sibyllen, den Königinnen,
> Und da sitzen sie wie zu Hause,
> Leichten Hauptes und leichter Hände.
>
> Doch ein Schatten fällt von jenem Leben
> In die andern Leben hinüber,
> Und die leichten sind an die schweren
> Wie an Luft und Erde gebunden:
>
> Ganz vergessener Völker Müdigkeiten
> Kann ich nicht abtun von meinen Lidern,
> Noch weghalten von der erschrockenen Seele
> Stummes Niederfallen ferner Sterne.
>
> Viele Geschicke weben neben dem meinen,
> Durcheinander spielt sie alle das Dasein,
> Und mein Teil ist mehr als dieses Lebens
> Schlanke Flamme oder schmale Leier. (*GDI* 26)

Hofmannsthal considered "Manche freilich . . ." to be one of his seven or eight best poems, as he wrote in a letter to Rilke on February 28, 1902 (*HvH-Rilke Bw* 42–43). This poem displays a number of the thematic emphases which characterize all of his lyric poetry, and it is likewise composed in the form which appears most frequently in his poetry, namely blank verse. Through this relatively simple verse form with its unrhymed stanzas, it awakes the appearance of an everyday communication, perhaps a letter. "Manche freilich . . ." in fact shows manifold correspondences with the contexts in which Hofmannsthal's lyric work was created.

The poem was probably composed in two phases; the first four stanzas possibly in the summer of 1895, the conclusion at a later time, perhaps the beginning of 1896. On February 7, 1896 the author sent this poem, together with three others ("Weltgeheimnis," "Dein Antlitz . . . ," and "Gesellschaft"), to Stefan George. His expressed wish not to see these poems published separately was fulfilled; the group of poems, augmented by "Über Vergänglichkeit" (= "Terzinen I"), appeared in March 1896 in George's *Blätter für die Kunst.*

Considering "Manche freilich . . ." by itself, we can observe that here once again the connections that exist between things which seem far apart are thematized: first in the image of the ancient ship, then in the realms of the "Wurzeln des verworrenen Lebens" and that of the sibyls and queens. The lower realm of heaviness, as a diffuse everyday domain, is characterized especially by the fact that life here is "verworren." Opposed to this, but not entirely separated from it, is the lightness and clarity of that life which has connections and far-reaching perspectives within its view: the life of the royal artist, who is "wie zu Hause" among the prophetic sibyls.

Hofmannsthal was stimulated to use these images by Michelangelo's portrayal of the sibyls in the Vatican's Sistine Chapel. He saw these frescos depicted in Knackfuß's Michelangelo monograph from the year 1895, which preoccupied him during the summer of that year. Here we can see in concrete form the importance of the visual arts to his poetic creation.

In the poem's first draft, the bond between the "light" and the "heavy" life was an "echo," an acoustic phenomenon, which he eventually replaced by the optical image of the shadow. The genesis of lines 15 to 21 is particularly revealing. Here is the original version:

> Wenn ich meine große Harfe schlage
> Tönen die Harfen verlorener Völker wieder
> Viele Geschicke weben neben dem meinen
> Und ich trage mehr als dieses Leben. (*SW1* 260)

The association with harp-playing King David can be strengthened by a reading of the Michelangelo monograph mentioned above, where, à propos of the Sistine frescos, it is pointed out that in the church hymn "Dies Irae" the sibyls are named along with David as witnesses of the coming Day of Judgment ("teste David cum Sibylla") (Knackfuß 40). The connections between things most remote in time and space and their effect on the poet's "(Augen-) Lider" and "Seele" are placed beside the "Geschicke" of the others as connected, and yet somehow removed. Line 21 states explicitly: "Und mein Teil ist mehr als dieses Lebens . . .," a line which in the original version reads "Und ich trage mehr als dieses Leben." And in this first version, this is how the poem ended. The poem's last line — "Schlanke Flamme oder schmale Leier" — was not added until the beginning of 1896. Hofmannsthal apparently was not sure about this addition; the manuscript shows how it was crossed out and then added once more. This may have something to do with the enigmatic nature of the line; perhaps it is also related to the fact that the line shows the strong influence of Stefan George. In the latter's book *Die Bücher der Hirten und Preisgedichte. Der Sagen und Sänge und der hängenden Gärten*, which Hofmannsthal received from George in December 1895, the following line appears in the poem "An Phaon": "an den schmalen flüssen. Schlanken bäumen deiner gegend" (38). Hofmannsthal quoted this line by George in his essay "Gedichte von Stefan George," which he was working on at the end of January 1896, and which in at least one passage is also reminiscent of "Manche freilich . . .": "Diese Menschen scheinen freier, leichten Hauptes und leichter Hände, behender und lautloser ihr Atem, minderes Gewicht auf ihren Augenlidern." Nevertheless, it was precisely this last line of the poem which was to become famous. One way this can be shown is the fact that Rilke asks in the third of his *Sonette an Orpheus*: "Ein Gott vermags. Wie aber, sag mir, soll / ein Mann ihm folgen durch die schmale Leier?"

What Hofmannsthal thematizes in "Manche freilich . . ." is his concept of the poet, whose work must receive and preserve far more than perceptions of "verworrenen" everyday life. The portion ("Teil") of destiny which the poet must bear is more than "dieses Lebens / Schlanke Flamme oder schmale Leier." To be sure, this concluding image does not allow us to identify the "schlanke Flamme" and "schmale Leier" entirely with the life which is "schwer" and "verworren"; instead, through the images of the slender flame and narrow lyre, it elevates this life into the sphere of art — just as the whole poem does the same thing by naming that which is absorbed and effective within itself.

Furthermore, Hofmannsthal's lyric texts reflect also the hermeneutic situation of reception. The early version of the poem "Dein Antlitz . . ." (1896) provides evidence that this is not a merely academic matter, but rather one which takes in the whole person, especially in a bodily sense:

> Und die Himbeeren deren Duft im Dunkel Essen
> Mitwisser aus uns macht von fürchterlichen
> Geheimnissen, uralter Königshäuser
> Mit denen wir im Blute sehr verwandt. (*SW1 267*)

This notion may also be found in the text "Gedichte," which was written around the same time, and in which it is said: "Wir wollen ihren Ursprung nicht vergessen" (*GDI 180*). This is also true, albeit on a simpler level, for the origin of the language one uses, and generally for the taking up of what already exists, as is shown by the dedicatory poem "In ein Exemplar von Gestern" (1892):

> Gedanken sind Äpfel am Baume,
> Für keinen Bestimmten bestimmt,
> Und doch gehören sie schließlich
> Dem einen, der sie nimmt. (137)

This high degree of reflexivity, and the thoughts which are often given explicit expression, although never without an image (e.g. "Gedanken sind Äpfel am Baume"), are the reasons for the first part of the title which Hofmannsthal had intended for an edition of his poetry which was to have been published in 1898 but never appeared: *Die Betrachtungen, die geschnittenen Steine und die redenden Masken*. Under the rubric "redende Masken," monologues from the lyric dramas, especially *Das kleine Welt-theater* (1897) were to have been included; under the rubric "Betrach-tungen," reflective lyrical poems ("Ballade des äußeren Lebens," "Weltgeheimnis," "Terzinen") were to have appeared; and the rubric "Geschnittene Steine" was to have included several more of the most prominent poems, on the model of gems from antiquity (among others, "Erlebnis," "Vorfrühling," and "Reiselied").

It can be seen from this metaphor taken from the visual arts, and from the examples he had chosen, that in these poems a high formal standard and at the same time a diversity of possible forms was intended by the poet. "Erlebnis" may represent the considerable number of po-ems that are written in blank verse and that make use of the unassuming form of a letter. Song stanzas likewise appear with frequency (e.g. "Vor-frühling"), especially in those poems which display fairy-tale motifs (e.g. "Ballade von einem kranken Kinde," 1892) — this extends to his adap-tations from Arnim and Brentano's collection of folk poetry *Des Knaben Wunderhorn* (1805–1808) from the year 1899 (e.g. "Das Wort"), which seem to abjure any claim to original creation, since they only slightly al-ter the original poems. After blank verse, the next most commonly used meter in Hofmannsthal's verse is Spanish trochees, as in the "Prolog" (1893) for *Der Tor und der Tod*, "In dem alten Wien mit Türmen . . ." (301–6); this poem has the additional peculiarity that the meter is dis-cernible only when the text is read with an Austrian accent, with the rolled "r which seems to include a "d" sound as well: "Über der Sankt-Kar(d)ls-Kuppel."

With this great attention to form, we come to a theme to which Hofmannsthal gave expression in "Idylle" (1893), after he had already alluded to it as early as 1890 in the poem "Gedankenspuk":

Wir tragen im Innern
Leuchtend die Charis,
Die strahlende Ahnung der Kunst.
Aber die Götter haben sie tückisch
Mit dem Hephästos vermählt:
Dem schmierigen Handwerk,
Der hinkenden Plage,
der humpelnden, keuchenden Unzulänglichkeit. (97)

The never-ending conflict between artistic freedom and the discipline and concentration of the craftsman, both equally necessary for the creative artist, are shown in "Idylle" through the masks of the centaur and the smith.

Beyond the dichotomy between formal craftsmanship and artistic intuition, this paradox may also be seen in a number of pairs of antitheses that likewise appear in the poet's work: unity and separation, eternity and transitoriness, endurance and transience. All these conditions of human existence, which are at the same time necessary and in conflict, form essential themes of both the poems and lyric dramas; at the same time, it can always be seen that there is a relationship of complementarity between these apparent antitheses.

This intuitively gained knowledge (as in the lines "Und dieses wußt ich, / Obgleich ichs nicht begreife, doch ich wußt es" [19] from "Erlebnis") can of course be contrasted with the confusion that reigns when the connection with a living totality is not evident. Thus the admonitory speech which "[der] Herr, der liebe Gott" addresses to humanity in the poem "Bild spricht" (1893) contains these lines: "Wie sie verworren stehen gehen / Sich selber und Leben nicht verstehen" (160). On the other hand, eternity and transitoriness are two dimensions of time which may be viewed as constituting a harmonious antithesis. Hofmannsthal gave most concise expression to this theme in his original translation of Coleridge's "Inscription for a Time-Piece" (1902):

Nun, und vorbei! Die Stunden gleiten hin
verthan, verhaucht, in Sehnsucht hingehetzt:
Doch jede, scheidend, senkt in deinen Sinn
Daß es dort wohne — ein unsterblich Jetzt. (202)

The most significant of Hofmannsthal's poems written after 1900, "Vor Tag" (1907), unfolds a moment in time which is repeatedly named with the word "Nun," and illustrates the content of this most pregnant moment in which time seems to stand still, but which is followed by the event that brings release: "Nun geht die Stallthür. Und nun ist auch Tag" (40).

A further theme is the question of continuity, which was already touched on in the reference to the problem of identifying with the child which one supposedly once was. Hofmannsthal speaks of "physischer Kontinuität," in contrast to which such ideal constructions as unity and enduring connection seem not to be tenable, at least when they take their provisional reality to be real existence. The "bunte Schein . . . all unsre(r) Einheit" of which Miranda spoke is at the same time indispensable. Hofmannsthal formulates this once more with a reference to Goethe: "Am farbigen Abglanz haben wir das Leben" ("Brief an Lili," 1893/94; *SW2* 97–98). The danger which this insight also contains is nevertheless embodied, using the same image of the fountain used in Miranda's monologue, in the essay "Englischer Stil" (1896): "Wer das Starre sucht und das Gegebene, wird immer ins Leere greifen. [. . .] Mit den Augen, die uns den Springbrunnen vorlügen, müssen wir das Leben der Menschen anschauen" (*RAI* 572). The apparent shape viewed by our eyes is always in danger of being a lie. For this reason, every connection formed by our consciousness must be questioned as to whether it corresponds to reality; judgment in this matter must be left to the cultivated feeling, for which an overly-confident certainty is almost surely a lie. A clear formulation of this theme, in a moral context, may be found in the lyric drama "Der Kaiser und die Hexe" (1897; "The Emperor and the Witch," 1961), particularly in the emperor's words to the chamberlain:

> Sag nie mehr, bei deiner Seele!
> Als du spürst. Bei deiner Seele!
> Tu nicht eines Halms Gewicht
> Mit verstelltem Mund hinzu. (*GDI* 487)

Here we can see what Hofmannsthal means in viewing speech "als soziales Element, als *das* soziale Element": it is the result of the first seven years of his literary career, and one which was to remain true for the rest of his life.

And yet, in tension with this endeavor to remain mindful of both the social character and the visual character of language is the so-called "Chiffren-Sprache" or coded language which develops in Hofmannsthal's lyric texts of the 1890s. It is characteristic of these "Chiffren" (such as a garden, a fountain, a tower) to possess exclusively individual significance, and thereby for the most part to abandon any social or historical reference. These "Chiffren" developed by Hofmannsthal become interpretable in the context of his entire literary output, which only the study of his unpublished works has allowed critics to decode. One can therefore understand why the poet's contemporaries didn't know what to make of a poem such as "Lebens-lied."[5] This enigmatic character characterizes Hofmannsthal's lyric pro-duction as hermetic in part, but at the same time, an interpretation based on the context of his entire literary production brings productive insights into the complexity of these "encoded" images.

Thus Hofmannsthal expresses this paradox of being reflected, and at the same time seeing through the object, in the image of the "dark mir-ror," which is likewise a traditional image in the field of religious knowl-edge ("For now we see through a glass, darkly," Corinthians I 13:12), but which takes on progressively more layers of meaning since its first appearance in Hofmannsthal's work, in the poem "Weltgeheimnis" ("ein Lied — / Auf dessen dunklen Spiegel"). This may be explained not least by the fact that this "dark mirror" stands as a "chiffre" for the poem. It is precisely this paradox of self-reflection cast back upon itself and survey-ing that which is tangible which the "dark mirror" of the poem is to make possible. And thereby Hofmannsthal's "Chiffrensprache" is in fact not removed from the social character of speech, but instead it confirms this character inasmuch as it draws our attention to and poses problems that seem in principle to be insoluble as a challenge for discussion, rather than simply confirming our ordinary perceptions.

But this can only take place with a due consideration of what is past; this can be seen in the emphatic inclusion of traditional cultural ele-ments, but also in the fundamental importance accorded to memory. In contrast to the anticipatory fantasy by means of which Claudio in *Der Tor und der Tod* has held himself apart from reality, the poet's glance is directed backward in time, and is able to take in and "in sich . . . fort tragen" ("Glückliches Haus," 1900, *GDI* 38) both temporal and spatial dimensions. This backward glance of remembrance also conditions the form of past tense in which numerous texts are composed. The depic-tion of a morning in the mountains, which Hofmannsthal borrowed from the letter of a woman friend[6] for the opening of *Der Tor und der Tod*, is with consistency situated in the evening: "Die letzten Berge lie-gen nun im Glanz . . ." (281). And thereby we may clearly see the sym-bolic character of various times of day of which Hofmannsthal speaks, borrowing from the German Romantic poet Novalis. This situating of backward-looking remembrance in the evening is explicitly referred to in line 20 of "Ballade des äußeren Lebens" (1895): "Und dennoch sagt der viel, der 'Abend' sagt" (23). In "Glückliches Haus," the constitu-ents of this retrospection are differentiated: here, the succession of gen-erations ("ein Greise" [an archaic singular form], "Enkel") are explicitly named, as is the wordless communication ("Ein Zittern") and the poet's position as outsider ("der Wandrer"), who is just glancing behind himself and carrying with him "entschwebend" the image of his memory. A poem of this kind contains the self-reflexivity of its essential conditions in the complexity of its imagery, through which the language carefully avoids any false sense of immediacy.

In his lyric poems and dramas, Hofmannsthal developed techniques of linguistic creation which correspond to the interplay of lyric and drama. Among these are the speaker roles which appear in the poems as well as the dramas (e.g. "Gesellschaft," 1896, "Großmutter und Enkel," 1899), the descriptive imagery which plays an important role in *Der Tod des Tizian* but which appears to be present in "Die Beiden" (1896) as well, although the text's ecphrasis (OED: "a plain declaration or interpretation of a thing") is not related here to any previously identifiable image. In addition to the dramatic monologue, there are a number of dramatic situations evident in other poems, such as that between the "Ich" and the "Du" in "Siehst Du die Stadt?" (1890), in which to be sure one must not imagine a "Du" existing outside the text, but rather it is the hypothetical poem itself which is addressed. The ecphrasis is related not only to real ("Mit Handschuhen für Leopold Andrian," 1894) or potential works of art, but rather it appears also as a kind of landscape description, in which landscape is evoked as a stage set, for example in the dialogue between the bride and the child in the small lyric drama "Was die Braut geträumt hat" (1896). The artificiality of even those works, which were unquestionably intended for a real stage, can finally be seen again and again in the years between 1892 and 1897 in the idea that the work could be performed as a shadow play or a puppet theater. Hofmannsthal expresses this idea in relation to the "verse proverb" *Gestern* as well as to the "Verse für ein durch Wasser getriebenes Puppenspiel," to *Das kleine Welttheater*, and *Der weiße Fächer*. He makes it explicit in the "Prolog" to *Die Frau im Fenster* (1897):

> Es wär mir beinah lieber, wenn nicht Menschen
> dies spielen würden, sondern große Puppen,
> von einem der's versteht gelenkt an Drähten. (*GDI* 339)

The social element in language, which is not excluded from the lyric poems even though they are "aus Einsamkeit geboren" ("Für Eberhard von Bodenhausen," 1911, 206), receives through these techniques the corrective reminder that this social speech is at the same time a form of art. In contrast to the supposed directness of social speech, Hofmannsthal's art of indirect representation stands as a *narrative art*, as can be seen in the epigram "Kunst des Erzählens" from the year 1898:

Schildern willst du den Mord? So zeig mir den Hund auf dem Hofe:
Zeig mir im Aug von dem Hund gleichfalls den Schatten der Tat. (192)

It is this art that Hofmannsthal developed in his early lyric composi-
tions, and which he refined in later texts such as *Elektra*. Thus his
themes cannot be unlocked only by way of what is explicitly said; instead they reveal their wealth of signification only when one takes into
consideration that "in jedem Gedichte auch die Dinge mitspielen, die
nicht in ihm vorkommen, indem sie rings um das Ganze ihre Schatten
legen" ("Shakespeares Könige und grosse Herren," 1905, *RAI* 37).
The multiplicity of shadows cast allows the lyric poetry and drama to
become increasingly rich and more concrete; the mediating and thus
lively language is constantly in the state of crisis to which he later gave
virtuosic expression in the famous "Chandos Letter" ("Ein Brief,"
1902). But his language overcomes this crisis with each successful
poem.

Translated by Thomas A. Kovach

Notes

[1] Detailed interpretations of this poem, as well as others mentioned in the fol-
lowing examples, may be found in Andreas Thomasberger, *Verwandlungen in
Hofmannsthals Lyrik — Zur sprachlichen Bedeutung von Genese und Gestalt*
(Tübingen: M. Niemeyer, 1994).

[2] Cf. Thomas A. Kovach, *Hofmannsthal and Symbolism: Art and Life in the
Work of a Modern Poet* (New York, Bern, Frankfurt am Main: Peter Lang Verlag, 1985), esp. 63–74.

[3] Cf. Karl Pestalozzi, *Sprachskepsis und Sprachmagie im Werk des jungen Hof-
mannsthal* (Zurich: Atlantis Verlag, 1958); Andrew O. Jaszi, "Die Idee des
Lebens in Hofmannsthals Jugendwerk 1890–1900," *Germanic Review* 24,
No. 2 (1961), 69–95; Steven P. Sondrup, "The Contexts and Concepts of
'Leben' in the Poetry of Hugo von Hofmannsthal," *Colloquia Germanica* 11
(1978), 289–97.

[4] Cf. Peter Szondi, "Intention und Gehalt. Hofmannsthal ad se ipsum,"
Schriften II (Frankfurt am Main: Suhrkamp, 1978), 272.

[5] Cf. Richard Exner, *Hugo von Hofmannsthals "Lebenslied": Eine Studie*. Heidelberg: C. Winter Verlag, 1964), especially 21–22.

[6] Cf. Andreas Thomasberger, "Eine Anregung zum Eingangsmonolog von
'Der Tor und der Tod,'" *Hofmannsthal-Blätter* 29 (1984), 42–44.

Works Cited

Hofmannsthal, Hugo von and Rainer Maria Rilke. *Briefwechsel 1899–1925.* Ed. Rudolf Hirsch and Ingeborg Schnack. Frankfurt am Main: Insel Verlag, 1978.

George, Stefan. *Die Bücher der Hirten und Preisgedichte. Der Sagen und Sänge und der hängenden Gärten.* Berlin: G. Bondi, 1896.

Knackfuß, Hermann. *Micholangelo.* Bielefeld: Velhagen & Klasing, 1926.

ELLEN RITTER

Hofmannsthal's Narrative Prose:
The Problem of Individuation

DEPENDING ON ONE'S point of view, the scope of Hofmannsthal's works in the area of narrative prose can be viewed as either small or quite ample. If one looks only at what may be described as stories in the strictest sense of the word, there are five titles to be named: "Das Märchen der 672. Nacht" (1895), "Reitergeschichte" (1898), "Erlebnis des Marschalls von Bassompierre" (1900), "Lucidor" (1910) and "Die Frau ohne Schatten" (1919). Apart from these works, Hofmannsthal's narrative prose is either fragmentary (like the novel *Andreas*, which Hofmannsthal worked on from 1906 until his death), or of a generic character not easily determined, a characteristic of Hofmannsthal's narrative works which will be discussed extensively in what follows. In this essay, I will review the significant narrative works and fragments and trace a theme — the problem of individuation — that binds them together.

On July 22, 1889, the fifteen-year-old Hugo von Hofmannsthal wrote his first story (as far as we know), "Der Geiger vom Traunsee" (*Erz* 13–18). This text contains the description of an afternoon's dream encounter with the Austrian lyric poet Nikolaus Lenau (1802–1850) at the resort of Traunsee, where the young Hofmannsthal was just spending his vacation. Still awkward in style, it is a youthful fantasy about a poet whom he was to admire until the end of his life. The encounter with Lenau, who appears in the text as a mad fiddle player, creates associations with Franz Grillparzer's masterful novella "Der Arme Spielmann" (1848; "The Poor Fiddler," 1967), a text with which, however, it cannot bear comparison. But as early as two years later, the story "Age of Innocence" (original title in English), a partly fragmentary text, displays an astonishing talent in its description of psychological states. The self-observation of the pubescent youth and the "Stationen der Entwicklung" are recorded in a modern psychological style that shows the influence of Danish Naturalist writer Jens Peter Jacobsen (1847–1885). Because of its fragmentary character, the story was rejected by the editors of the *Freie Bühne für modernes Leben*, to whom he had sent the first part of the text. Hofmannsthal took up similar psychological studies in "Knabengeschichte" (*SW29*; no translation), a text on which he worked in the years 1906 to 1912 but which also remained a fragment. His attempt at a "Soldatengeschichte" (*Erz* 67; no translation) from the years 1895 to 1896 also belongs in this series of psychological sketches with strongly autobiographical character, of which, however, none were ever finished or published during the poet's lifetime.

As early as 1895, though, in his first published story, the poet produces a masterpiece: "Das Märchen der 672. Nacht" (1895). In its title and setting it suggests an oriental fairy tale, in particular one from *Thousand and One Nights*, but it is so enigmatic in content and artful in construction that its ambiguity has not been exhausted to this day by its numerous interpreters; the concept of "unausdeutbaren Deutbarkeit," which Hofmannsthal in his *Buch der Freunde* applies to an object (*RAIII* 263), may apply to the poet's text as well.

The external action is relatively simple. A merchant's son, heir to a great fortune, lives with his four servants in a summer palace in the mountains. When he receives a mysterious letter accusing one of the servants of an offense, the merchant's son decides to settle the matter and makes his way to the city. Since he does not find the servant's former masters as he had hoped, he wanders around aimlessly, until in the evening he comes by a barracks where soldiers are looking after their horses. He comes too close to a horse and is struck by its hoof in such an unfortunate manner that he dies from the injury.

The apparently random path taken by the merchant's son through the city, along with its various stations, symbolizes the path of his life. The mysterious letter drives him out of the isolation and protection of his palace into the world of human beings, and in the process he is confronted with a life he has never known or even suspected. For this reality with which he is suddenly confronted did not appear in the books which shaped his previous picture of the world, and which told of brilliant battles and victories. Enclosed in his palace, which he inherited from his father, in self-chosen isolation, he had for company only himself and the unreal stories in his books of fairy tales. For his four servants are nothing other than distorted mirror images of his own self, and in the books he thinks he sees a mirror of his future life. This life is still an unwritten book. Until now, the merchant's son has been one with his environment. He has not experienced anything that could distinguish him from his environment and thus enable him to become an individual, and yet an indeterminate longing, personified in the younger maidservant, has already taken hold of him. He has not yet dared to become active, when the letter causes him to leave his house. He makes his way to the city where he owns a house, which however is closed to him now, during the summer season. Since from the start his undertaking is not turning out the way he had imagined, he is compelled to search in his home town "wie ein Fremder" (*Erz* 53) for a place to spend the night. The surroundings in which he wanders aimlessly seem to him alien and at the same time familiar. The path he takes leads him to various stations which always in some way evoke memories of his four servants. Involuntarily he lets himself be drawn on by an indeterminate flow and does not once attempt to become active. When he asks wearily for a bed, it doesn't occur to him to ask for an inn. He continues his mindless wandering and comes to the barracks, where his final destiny overtakes him. He dies in a lonely room in the barracks, having been robbed by the soldiers: "Er haßte seinen vorzeitigen Tod so sehr, daß er sein Leben haßte, weil es ihn dahin geführt hatte" (*Erz* 62–63).

Thus, his destiny is fulfilled in the evening in a manner entirely different from that which he had imagined in the morning. He had gone out to save his life, which he felt was threatened, and instead he loses his life through ignorance and by rigidly holding on to the images of his fantasy. He perceives the external world as if it were only a dream. He does not really enter into anything that he encounters, and thus he demonstrates his incapacity for life. He does not recognize the signs that might help him onward. Communication never occurs, neither with the servants whom he meets at the Persian Embassy, nor with the jeweler, nor with the child in the greenhouse, nor with the soldiers, nor with any other human being. Like a modern-day Parzival he wanders back and forth, mute and unperceiving. In a world which he seeks to ward off because he does not understand it, he reaps only hatred, until in the end he hates his own life.

The path of Sergeant Anton Lerch in "Reitergeschichte" (1898) ends just as fatefully as that of the merchant's son. Just as the latter is one with his palace, so Lerch forms a unity with his squadron. Within it, he shares in the military victories, the fame and the glory. Outside it, he is nothing. His whole existence is defined by being a soldier. He too pursues a path of incredible linearity, from the chance meeting with a woman in Milan, whom he recognizes from earlier days, to the ride through an abandoned village, to the battle which follows immediately afterward, to his insubordination and consequent execution. Like the merchant's son, he encounters various mirrorings of his self. In the man whom he meets at the woman's house, he sees the possibility of his future life reflected. He identifies himself with him, but at the same time his fantasy shows the man to him as a future servant, friend, and blackmailer. Stimulated by his encounter in the house in Milan, for the first time he imagines a life outside the military, a comfortable "Zivil-atmosphäre" with "angenehmer Gewalttätigkeit" (*Erz* 124–25). A desire for possessions and sexuality gradually takes hold of all his thoughts. The abandoned village into which he is driven by this newly awakened desire for plunder symbolizes the condition of his psyche, which is dominated by sexual desire and mute fantasies of power and violence. The village's squalor corresponds to his squalid thoughts, and when he wants to leave the village by way of a bridge, as a warning and a reminder to him his own double appears to him in his former unsullied form. In the battle that follows immediately, his bottled-up aggressions are released. How differently this battle is described than that at the beginning of the story! Readers are drawn this time into the bloody details, which they were spared the first time. The sergeant's mood spreads to the reader. An uncanny feeling remains, even during the rest that follows after the battle. The red color of blood predominates, and it cannot be determined if it is a remnant of the preceding brutality of the battlefield or the reflection of the setting sun. In this manner, the reader is prepared for the ending, which is astonishing but consistent with what has come before. Still vaguely caught up in his dream world, the sergeant is unable to respond to the captain's command. It is for this reason alone that the shot strikes him unexpectedly, since it had been signaled for some time by a series of symbols and warnings. Unlike the merchant's son, the sergeant has no more time for reflection. The moment he falls, his comrades release their horses. Order has been restored, the atmosphere purified. Author and reader alike withdraw from the event, which represents only a small, insignificant occurrence amid the general course of the military campaign.

Critics have ascribed an autobiographical character to both stories, and with good reason. In 1894 Hofmannsthal began his one year of military service, which took him in 1895 to the Moravian city of Göding. For the first time in his life, he left behind the extremely protected upper middle-class environment in which he had been raised in Vienna, and the contrast with the decrepit village in which he now found himself could not have been greater. In addition to this, he was dissatisfied with the legal studies, which he had chosen just to please his parents, and the first stage of which he had just completed. And to top it all off, the newspapers reported in May 1895 the sentencing of Oscar Wilde, the chief protagonist of European Aestheticism, to five years' hard labor following his conviction for sodomy. Suddenly, Hofmannsthal saw his entire previous existence called into question. He responded at first with illness and depression. Around Easter he suffered from a bad case of influenza and a state of exhaustion such that a suspension of his military service was seriously considered. During his convalescence he stayed with his parents in Vienna. In his long period of recovery he took frequent walks with his father in the course of which he confided in his father his plans for the future. He felt drawn to be a professional writer, but his father insisted on a profession with a secure income. Finally they agreed that he would study Romance Languages with the goal of achieving an academic career. In the mood generated by these radical changes in the course of his life, he wrote in a few days the "Märchen der 672. Nacht," into which Hofmannsthal inscribed the anxieties of his psyche. The "Reitergeschichte," written three years later, shows more distance from the poet's own experiences. His military service serves mainly as a source of props and scenery for the story's setting. Unlike the "Märchen der 672. Nacht," "Reitergeschichte" has no confessional character. His period of coming to terms with the problematic legacy of Aestheticism had also come to an end by the time he wrote the later story. A few plans for stories taken from the military milieu which have been preserved, dating from the years 1895 and 1896 — "Soldatengeschichte," "Geschichte des Cadet Offizlersstellvertreters," "Geschichte eines österreichischen Officiers" (none translated) — bear witness to Hofmannsthal's further attempts to come to terms with his period of military service. Much later, in *Die Frau ohne Schatten* (1919; *The Woman Without a Shadow*, 1993),[1] he falls back on his Göding experiences once more in his description of the milieu of the dyer's house. But now they are worked through in literary fashion and adapted to the strict form of the narrative. In the same way, Hofmannsthal's reliance on the tales from the *Arabian Nights* progresses through the sketches for "Amgiad und Assad" (1895) and "Der goldene Apfel" (1897, neither text translated), likewise culminating in *Die Frau ohne Schatten*.

"Lucidor, Figuren zu einer ungeschriebenen Komödie" is the title of a narrative text from the year 1910. It is the story of a man caught between two women whom he believes to be the same person, because one of them, disguised throughout the day as a young man, at night pretends to be the other, whom he thinks he loves. Both women embody various facets of his own personality, which in the course of the action become entangled and then untangled. When the true identity of his nocturnal lover is revealed, by committing himself to her, he finds his own identity as well. Thus the inner and outer action run strictly parallel in this story. At first glance, "Lucidor" seems to have nothing in common in its content with the two stories discussed previously. Nevertheless, the hermaphroditic character of the main figure Lucidor/Lucile, which is reflected in the doubleness of the lover Vladimir, reveals a different view. Here too, the protagonists are alienated from themselves. In the case of Lucile, this is true in an external sense, through the compulsion of her disguise. But Vladimir becomes aware of the split in his own personality only through what he believes to be the split in Arabella. This awareness, to be sure, distinguishes him from the merchant's son and the sergeant. Presumably it is this too that leads him on the path to life, rather than to death as in the case of the two earlier protagonists. And when Lucile finds a way to incorporate Lucidor into her future life, this means that the eventual union with Vladimir will also turn out well. But the reader learns nothing more of this. In any event, Vladimir is the first figure in Hofmannsthal's narrative fictions who succeeds in shedding his illusions and who profits from this success.

The motif of gender reversal has enjoyed great popularity in world literature, from antiquity to Virginia Woolf and beyond. Even in his earliest youth, Hofmannsthal was attracted to what he called "das Knaben-mädchenhafte." He values this quality in his friend Georg von Franckenstein, in the English women dancers, the Barrisons, who gave a guest performance in Vienna in 1895, and in the innkeeper's daughter Romana Gasperl from Aussee, who was to provide a model for the figure of Romana in the novel *Andreas*. This quality is seen as synonymous with a person who is unfinished, still without a destiny. In the 1894 essay "Über moderne englische Malerei" he writes of "Psyche, die jüngling-mädchenhafte, die nichts erlebt hat als ihr eigenes rätselhaftes Auf-der-Welt-Sein, die aus unergründlichen Augen bange schaut" (*RAI* 547). About the figure of Paula in the "Geschichte der beiden Liebespaare" it is said that she had a "knaben-mädchenhafte[s] Gesicht" with a "ruhigen forschenden Blick, in dem nichts lag als Jugend" (*Erz* 83). In later works, this doubleness achieves consciousness through the reversal of clothing and thus of gender as well. In the "Gespräch über Gedichte," that poem in the *Griechische Anthologie* is praised "wo sie die Gewänder tauschen und einander aufs neue fester umschlingen" (*Erz* 505). Here the exchange occurs for the sake of increased pleasure. This is true also for Vladimir, but in his case the issue is not exclusively sexual pleasure. In discovering the second half of his self, he gains a dimension and thereby expands his personality. Hofmannsthal takes up this motif in various forms again and again, most clearly in *Der Rosenkavalier* (1911), where it once more plays a central role.

The expression "Doppelnatur" is used explicitly in "Lucidor" (*Erz*, 180). In 1907, Hofmannsthal became acquainted with a work which gave a scientific explanation to much of what he had previously experienced and expressed in his prose fictions: the book by Morton Prince, *The Dissociation of a Personality*, which had appeared in 1906. To the Princess Marie von Taxis, who had brought the book to his attention, he wrote an enthusiastic letter of thanks: "Nicht als ob mich diese Möglichkeiten des menschlichen Innern ganz ahnungslos überraschten — im Gegenteil, sie kommen wie gerufen, um Ahnungen zu bestätigen und mein dunkles Gefühl von diesem dunkelsten Mechanismus zu bereichern und zu ermutigen" *(SW18* 538). The encounter with Prince's book gives rise to two projects: a drama *Dominic Heintls letzte Nacht* (1906/7, 1912; *SW18*), and the novel *Andreas* (first published 1932). In both works, the dual nature of the protagonist is played out in concrete fashion. It is no longer a question of two sides of a person, instead one person actually split into two different persons, who operate with and against one another. The double is no longer a vision, he is actually materialized. But the author's task remains the same: to combine these dividing parts into one person. This explains the programmatic title of the novel, chosen in 1913: *Andreas, oder die Vereinigten*. The constellation Andreas-Maria/Mariquita is the same as Vladimir-Lucidor/Lucile. It almost seems as though Hofmannsthal wanted provisionally to display this problem, the solution of which he never completed within the novel, in a light and playful manner in "Lucidor," perhaps to attain clarity for himself in this simplified construction.

By grappling with the various aspects and possibilities within a single person, Hofmannsthal promotes the process of self-realization, as we would call it today. For him, destiny is character. He formulates this quite clearly in the 1905 essay "Sebastian Melmoth" which discusses Oscar Wilde's *De Profundis* (1905): "Es hat gar keinen Sinn so zu sprechen, als ob Oscar Wildes Schicksal und Oskar Wildes Wesen zweierlei gewesen wären und als ob das Schicksal ihn so angefallen hätte wie ein bissiger Köter ein ahnungsloses Bauernkind, das einen Korb mit Eiern auf dem Kopf trägt. [. . .] Oscar Wildes Wesen und Oscar Wildes Schicksal sind ganz und gar dasselbe" (*RAI* 342). It is for this reason that it is so important for a person to know oneself and to exert influence on one's own being. For the deed which determines one's life must follow from self-knowledge. One must act and determine one's destiny in a sovereign fashion, if one does not want to share the lot of the merchant's son, or that of the fool in the lyric drama *Der Tor und der Tod* (1893).

In Sergeant Anton Lerch, we found the beginnings of such activity, but in his case they necessarily remained unsuccessful, since they took place not in a conscious, reflective fashion, but instead on a dreamlike plane far removed from reality. With the figure of the grocer woman in the "Erlebnis des Marschalls von Bassompierre," Hofmannsthal develops a counter-image to these earlier figures, the example of a successfully developed personality. The action of this story may be related briefly: the glorious Marshal of Bassompierre, making a brief stop in a city afflicted by the plague, is invited by a pretty grocer woman to spend the night with her. The Marshal enters into the adventure. They agree to a second rendezvous, at which time he finds his lover dead from the plague, at the side of her dead husband. This is the extent of the external action. The real events of the story take place within the two protagonists, in their encounter and in the change in their personalities which follows from this encounter.

Without question it is the extraordinary situation created by the plague that facilitates the grocer woman's remarkable action. But the way in which she acts, the self-assured posture with which she encounters the Marshal in every situation, displays her strong personality. Here the reversal of gender takes place not merely through costume; instead it is the conventional gender roles that are exchanged. The grocer woman takes over the masculine role, she challenges her partner to a sexual encounter, and she even determines the place and the way in which it is to occur. Even in their erotic play she takes the leading role, and relegates the Marshal, who is so experienced in warfare, to a minor role. "Gewalt" and "Stärke" (*Erz* 137) are her epithets. The Marshal is so astonished and fascinated by her that she seizes control of his thoughts, not only in the brief time of their encounter, but even long thereafter, so that he is driven many years later to record the story in order to share it with posterity. With her deed, the grocer woman transforms not only herself but also the Marshal of Bassompierre, who all at once comes to know a completely new side of his self. He, the warrior and realist who always stood with his two feet firmly planted on the ground, suddenly becomes a dreamer. He spends the time between their first night of love and the expected second night in an attempt to track her down, to seek an encounter with her. When he does not succeed, his imagination is preoccupied with her. The closer the time of the second encounter comes, the stronger his imagination becomes. Finally she has taken hold of him to such an extent that he confuses phantasms with reality, only to awaken all the more terribly with the grim reality of his discovery. To be sure, the grocer woman is dead, but how different is her view of her past life from that of the merchant's son. "Je n'ai rien négligé" [I have not missed out on anything], the last words of the painter Poussin which Hofmannsthal places at the end of his *Buch der Freunde* and which were always a motto for him, apply in a most particular fashion to the figure of the grocer woman.

The motif of doubleness and of mutual transformation was to be handled extensively, among other works, in the grandly conceived novel *Andreas*. This plan for a novel of development, modeled equally on Goethe's *Wilhelm Meisters Lehrjahre* (1795; *Wilhelm Meister's Apprenticeship*, 1823) and Arnim's *Die Kronenwächter* (1817; no translation), had its origin in a series of fictive letters, originally planned as a work of considerable scope, but then reduced to a small number with the title "Die Briefe des Zurückgekehrten" (1907; no translation). "Das venezianische Erlebnis des Herrn v S." and "Die Ehe des Herrn von Ferschengelder mit Fräulein della Spina" were planned as novellas within "Briefe des Zurückgekehrten." They are the germ cells of Andreas, in that they were realized only after the original plan was abandoned (see *SW30* 303–4). This original plan was to involve a coming to terms with the modern world, with contemporary Austria and Germany, seen through the eyes of "one who had returned," a man who has lived for decades overseas and has earned a fortune, and who now wants to settle again in his old homeland of Austria. He ascertains that in the meantime everything has changed there. He views the homeland which has become alien to him with critical eyes, comparing it to the other part of the world with which he now seems to be more familiar than with the land of his fathers. Only a single artistic experience, his chance acquaintance with the pictures of the Dutch painter Van Gogh, reconciles him with the present. Here the transformation takes place through the medium of art, through the discovery of a kindred personality that is revealed to the protagonist through the works produced by that personality. The "Briefe" end with this fundamental artistic experience.

In the novel *Andreas*, Hofmannsthal draws back from the present day and enters the world of the eighteenth century. From a distance of one hundred years, he is able to gain a better oversight on the development of his protagonist. For here, for the first time in his narrative production, the action is not restricted to a short span of time. A novel of development, as *Andreas* was planned to be, presents an entire life, embedded in the events of its age. In a note on the manuscript, Hofmannsthal formulates the motto for the work: "Lerne zu leben!" (*SW30* 118).

As stated earlier, the plan for this novel is closely connected with Hofmannsthal's acquaintance with Morton Prince's case studies. As early as the third note to *Andreas*, the two women Maria and Mariquita appear; later, in imitation of Prince, they are also called M_1 and M_2. In

them "[ist] die Zweiheit Person geworden" (*SW30* 145). In addition
to this, there is talk of their "Astralleib," a concept derived from
Paracelsus "bestehend aus ihren Gedanken, Ängsten, Aspirationen" (9).
While the grave and pious Christian Maria suffers from inner conflicts
and attempts to attain a state of wholeness, the "coquette" and pagan
Mariquita sees her whole existence threatened by Maria's attempt, and
hates her for that reason. She does everything she can to reinforce the
split. Like Vladimir in "Lucidor," Andreas finds himself drawn to both
women. In the course of the action, his love is intended to establish
unity. However, from the fragment that Hofmannsthal completed, it is
impossible to get even an inkling of how this could happen. In any
event, according to Hofmannsthal's philosophy this would have to
happen through mutual transformation of all persons involved. The
Maltese man, another leading figure in the novel, is also caught up in
this constellation. "Die Vereinigten — auch auf die Subiecte selbst be-
zogen: Andreas — Maria — der Malteser für jeden geht es um das
Eins-werden mit sich selber" (*SW30* 119). The Maltese man also has
his double,[2] his second self; at one point there is even talk of "Seelen-
wanderung" (144). For him the saying applies: "Beständige Wiederge-
burt aus sich selber, Bestand durch Verwandlung" (148).

Transformation in a most concrete sense is the theme of *Die Frau
ohne Schatten*. In this work, the fairy-tale form serves as a means to
visualization and presentation of the thesis that Hofmannsthal had repeatedly taken up since the "Märchen der 672. Nacht," namely that life
consists in transformation, more specifically in mutual transformation.
Anyone who fails to recognize this becomes inflexible and turns to
stone, as does the emperor, or forfeits her life, like the dyer's wife. Life
is a continual process of transformation. Hofmannsthal knows this and
has propagated it ever since his turn away from Aestheticism in 1894;
here he wishes to convey this message in allegorical form. The empress
has to become one with her shadow. As a mere spirit being she has the
advantage of not knowing death, but neither does she have any acquaintance with human life. When she gets a sense of what this is, it
seems to her so valuable that she is willing to accept the price: filth,
humiliations, servitude, and finally mortality. And with this, the content
of this story has been told. What constitutes the importance of the
work in literary history, though, is the manner in which the form is
fully congruent with the content, indeed that the content is portrayed
equally through the form of the narrative as through the action itself, as
will be shown in more detail below.

Now that the themes of doubleness, dissociation, transmigration of
souls, and unification in Hofmannsthal's narrative works have been dis-

cussed in some detail, we can see the actual point which is the poet's central concern in all these variants: the process of individuation. All the figures in the works previously discussed are concerned with one thing above all: constituting themselves as individuals in order to find a stable place in the world. This process of development is presented in short episodes, in longer periods of time, or in an overview of an entire lifespan, in its failures and successes. In the end these protagonists receive what Hofmannsthal calls their "Schicksal." On some of them it is forced, because they did not recognize or comprehend the signs, challenges, and opportunities. The others choose and determine the course of this process through conscious action. Of course, none can escape death in its biological form. But those who participate actively in their destiny have a chance of surviving at least ideally, either by continuing the chain of generations (like the two couples in *Frau ohne Schatten* and probably Vladimir and Lucile in "Lucidor") or by living on in history (like the grocer woman in "Erlebnis des Marschalls von Bassompierre"). Her deed leads her out of temporality in that she enters literary history: via the memoirs of the Marshal and Goethe's narrative into the novella by Hofmannsthal.

At this point it is necessary to discuss Hofmannsthal's *Ad me ipsum*, the notes in which he attempted a self-interpretation (1930; no translation). The poet began writing this in 1916; the immediate cause was *Die Frau ohne Schatten* — the libretto, not the prose version — the content of which he wished to explain to the public, assuming quite rightly that the poet's intention could be misunderstood. Simultaneously he was working on the prose version, the form of which was intended to contribute to general understanding. Even his earliest notes on the project were not limited to the opera; rather, Hofmannsthal surveyed his entire previous *oeuvre* and attempted to show development and connections among the individual works. When the literary scholar Walther Brecht was to write a book about the poet Hugo von Hofmannsthal, which was the latter's special wish (Brecht 41), the notes constituting *Ad me ipsum* were taken up once more and expanded in order to serve as a basis for this book. In later years, Hofmannsthal added further notes. Taken together, they constitute a testament to his effort to give his work a unified character in retrospect, one which was in harmony with his own personality, and to display a continuous linear development. In doing so he created or borrowed concepts — such as "Introversion," "Präexistenz," "Existenz," "Totalität," "Verschuldung," "Läuterung," "Erlösung," "Opfer," "das Allomatische," "Schicksal" — which he filled with a content that was particularly applicable to his work and still enigmatic. After its posthumous publication edited by

Walther Brecht in the *Jahrbuch des Freien Deutschen Hochstifts* of 1930, *Ad me ipsum* was seized on enthusiastically by critics who thought they now possessed a key to the interpretation of Hofmannsthal's works. This was true only in part, since Hofmannsthal stylizes himself and constructs a connection among his works which did not exist in that form at the time of their creation. He thus develops a myth of his own creative legacy. It is true that certain lines that run through his entire creative work are clarified thereby, but these lines can be recognized without the aid of Hofmannsthal's interpretation.

As was shown above based on the example of his prose fiction, the poet's main concern is the individuation of his protagonists, what he also calls "Zu-sich-selber kommen" (*RAIII* 601). In *Ad me ipsum* he names two paths toward this goal: the mystical and the social path. I have already addressed the latter path, which may be achieved in three different ways: through one's deed, through one's work, and through one's child (602). An example for the deed is "Erlebnis des Marschalls von Bassompierre"; for the child, *Die Frau ohne Schatten*. There is no example in the narrative fiction of the social path accomplished through one's work. One might mention in this context the path of Vittoria in the comedy "Der Abenteurer und die Sängerin" (1899, *GDI* 509–88; no translation); this would be the path of the artist, in this case, a singer. The mystical path is that of introversion (601). Hofmannsthal borrows this concept from a book by Herbert Silberer, *Probleme der Mystik und ihrer Symbolik* (Vienna, 1914). It designates a retreat from the world, after one has known it and lived in it, into one's own self, just as the mystic does. As an example, Hofmannsthal himself cites Lord Chandos from his famous fictional letter "Ein Brief" (1902, *Erz* 461–72). This Lord Chandos is a successful writer known for his brilliant literary style, who turns mute at the height of his career. He explains the reasons for this in a letter to his best friend, Lord Francis Bacon. It is the last thing he will ever write, since he has lost his grasp of language. According to Hofmannsthal's *Ad me ipsum*, this is the consequential path of individual development. "[Die] magische Herrschaft über das Wort das Bild das Zeichen darf nicht aus der Prae-existenz in die Existenz hinübergenommen werden" (*RAIII* 601). Preexistence is the existence prior to individuation, the existence of early childhood or at most of adolescence, in which a human being is connected as if by an umbilical cord with everything past and future. Everything that has ever been done or thought previously is known to one in this condition in a dreamlike fashion, and in dreamlike fashion likewise the individual follows his path until he comes to a fork in the road where he must decide if he wants to hold on stubbornly to his previous "magical" form of life (like the merchant's son) or whether he will transform himself and thereby make the transition to existence, like the Empress in *Frau ohne Schatten*. Lord Chandos decided to withdraw from public life. What Hofmannsthal at the time he wrote the "Brief" called the "halbwegs Pathologische" (to be sure, with the qualification: "aber welches Geistige, welches Gesteigerte, welches Phänomen der Seele überhaupt wäre nicht pathologisch, vom König Lear, ja von den Evangelien angefangen" — (*HvH-Salm* 48) he interprets in *Ad me ipsum* as the mystical path. This applies to the fictive figure from the seventeenth century (Lord Chandos), but not to Chandos's creator. Admittedly, the "Brief" has some autobiographical features, as regards the experience of the insufficiency of language, but the conclusion drawn from this by Hofmannsthal is different from that of Chandos. One could borrow the title of an etching by the Leipzig painter, sketch artist, and sculptor Max Klinger to describe Hofmannsthal's resolve: "Und doch!" Hofmannsthal continues to write, but he no longer relies only on words; instead he makes use of other means of expression as well. In his dramatic works these means are dance, pantomime, and music, and later film. In his narrative works it is the literary form itself: the constellation formed by the various fictional figures in their relation to one another, the description of their gestures and movements, their glances, their suggestions, the images, the symbols, the synesthesias, the weaving together of sentences, sayings, and quotes. Hofmannsthal creates for himself moreover certain stereotypical images and formulas which occur again and again in order to convey certain situations and feelings: for instance, glances, mirrors, dogs, birds, the baring of teeth, in drama for example the casting off of an overcoat. All of these occur over and over in various works and thus take on a dynamic all their own.

By means of all these above-named techniques, a distanced mode of expression arises, a language of mediacy. The immediate expression through the word is, according to Hofmannsthal's thesis, possible only in very rare cases, in reality only in the case of the complete union of two people, something he planned to depict in the drama *Jupiter und Semele*. At the point in which two people meet each other completely and find themselves in a state of complete harmony, in which they become almost one and the same person, in this ecstatic moment they find the words: "Du — Ich" (*SW18* 155). When it is a union of god and human (as in the case of Jupiter and Semele), this moment cannot be endured; Semele becomes insane. It is different, though, in the relation of one human being to another. And thus the solution is phrased thusly in *Andreas*: "worin liegt Vereinigung mit einem Wesen? im Erkennen? im Besitz? Im *Ansprechen*" (*SW30* 144). Nevertheless, this immediacy is the exception, not the rule, and it is entirely denied to the poet. He must make do by associating rather than defining, intimating rather than conceptualizing, approximating rather than stating.

What specific extra-linguistic means does Hofmannsthal employ in his narrative works? The first point was hinted at in the preceding sentence, when I speak not of Hofmannsthal's stories but of his narrative works. For it is very difficult to separate genres from one another among Hofmannsthal's narrative writings. Thus every anthology, as long as it is not limited to those few titles that unmistakably belong to the genres of short story or novella, will have a different content, depending on how narrowly or how widely one construes these generic categories. The multiplicity of forms is noticeable even with those completed stories that may clearly be assigned to a generic category. For instance, there are some fairy tales which resemble the *Arabian Nights* (such as "Das Märchen der 672. Nacht," "Amgiad und Assad," "Der goldene Apfel," *Die Frau ohne Schatten*) and others which seem closer to the literary fairy tales of German Romanticism (such as "Das Märchen von der verschleierten Frau" [1900], "Die junge Frau und die Nixe im Baum" [1900, 1912/13, 1918], "Siebenbrüder" [1912], "Das Paar im Berg" [1912, 1918/19], "Prinzessin auf dem verzauberten Berg" [1912], et al.; none translated). Then there are stories that seem to conform to the generic norms of the novella, such as "Reitergeschichte," "Erlebnis des Marschalls von Bassompierre," and "Lucidor," as well as several manuscripts left unpublished at the poet's death with notes on various planned works, from as early as 1893 up through 1928, which are labeled only by the title "Novelle." In addition, there are plans for stories in a genre that cannot be more exactly defined, such as the actually completed "Geschichte der beiden Liebespaare" (1896), "Die Verwandten" (1898), et al. Then there are psychological narratives: "Age of Innocence," "Knabengeschichte," and probably also "Soldatengeschichte" had it ever been completed. "Gerechtigkeit" (*Erz* 30–32) should probably be classified as one of the prose poems, which were so popular at the end of the nineteenth century, of which Hofmannsthal composed a whole series and which alternate between lyric and narrative. "Die Wege und die Begegnungen" should be regarded as a story, since it is more a narrated dream than an essay, though in the *Kritische Ausgabe* it appears in the volume *Reden und Aufsätze* (*SW33*). One could classify "Das Dorf im Gebirge" (1896) as a feuilletonistic story, "Das Glück am Weg" (1893) as an impressionistic study; Hofmannsthal himself called the latter an "allegorische Novellette," but refers to it on the title page as a "Prosagedicht." Somewhere in between these two examples is the "Erinnerung schöner

Tage" (1908; "A Memory of Beautiful Days," 1952), a mood-portrait of Venice written during the composition of "Der Abenteurer und die Sängerin." "Hebbels Eiland" (1903) is a fragment conceived for the 100th anniversary of the birth of the writer Friedrich Hebbel (1813–1863), which tries to convey something of that writer's personality in narrative form. Similarly situated between essayistic and narrative prose are the travel accounts "Augenblicke in Griechenland" (1908, 1917; *Erz* 603–28) and "Reise im nördlichen Afrika (1925; *Erz* 641–57). Those works that were defined by Hofmannsthal as "Erfundene Briefe" (*SW31*) — especially "Ein Brief" (the famous "Letter of Lord Chandos"), "Der Brief des letzten Contarin" (1902; *Erz* 473–77), "Die Briefe des Zurückgekehrten" (1907; *Erz* 544–71), as well as several fragments — should also be regarded as part of the narrative work, as long as one does not conceive of them as constituting a separate genre. Then in addition there is the novel *Andreas*, next to which the two biographical fragments *Der Herzog von Reichstadt* (1927 onward) and *Philipp II. und Don Juan d'Austria* (1929, both in *SW30*) are of lesser importance, since they hardly got beyond the stage of collecting materials.

Things become still more confusing when one considers that Hofmannsthal in several cases treats the same subject matter in different genres. *Die Frau ohne Schatten* exists as an opera libretto and as a prose narrative. "Lucidor," whose original sub-title is "Figuren zu einer ungeschriebenen Komödie," finally turned into the opera libretto *Arabella*, after further attempts to revise the text as a comedy, vaudeville, and screenplay. Manuscripts containing the groundwork for a prose version of "Der Kaiser und die Hexe" (1897; "The Emperor and the Witch," 1961) have been preserved, which were written after the completion of the drama. After he broke off his work on the dramatic version of *Bergwerk zu Falun* (1900; *DII* 83–174), Hofmannsthal began to treat the same material in narrative form in "Märchen von der verschleierten Frau," but soon abandoned this plan as well.

As I have already hinted, the form in which Hofmannsthal frames his material is of essential importance to the particular work. This form is of equal importance to the material and to the language. To prevent misunderstanding, Hofmannsthal emphasized, contrary to his own better knowledge, that he had begun work on the prose version of *Frau ohne Schatten* "als die Gestaltung für Musik u. Bühne fertig da lag" (*SW28* 424), as he wrote to the critic Raoul Auernheimer. He expressed his indignation in a further letter to the same recipient at the fact "daß Sie in Ihrem Brief diese zwei Gebilde, die Oper u. die Erzählung, einer Art von Vergleichung unterziehen," and he continues:

> die Würdigung einer vor Ihnen liegenden Erzählung, mit einer the-
> matischen Vergleichung dieser Erzählung mit einer Oper, verbinden
> zu wollen — käme mir, verzeihen Sie, so sonderbar vor, als wollten Sie
> ausreiten und dabei zugleich mit dem einen aus dem Steigbügel gelö-
> sten Fuß spazierengehen.

Thereupon he develops what seems to him the most important point:

> Eine Erzählung und ein Drama sind doch jedes für sich, wofern sie auf
> den Namen Poesie Anspruch haben und von einem ernst zu nehmen-
> den Kopf hevorgebracht werden, in sich geschlossene Gebilde, ja ge-
> schlossene magische Welten. Wenn sie das Geringste miteinander zu
> schaffen hätten, im geringsten von einander Ergänzung oder Belich-
> tung borgen müßten, was für ein unbegreiflicher Mensch wäre ich
> dann wenn ich — den Schrank voll Scenarien und den Kopf voll Figu-
> ren neun Jahre an die Ausarbeitung der zweiten Form gewandt hät-
> te — wäre sie nicht ein völlig Neues. (*SW28* 426)

What is new is precisely the fairy-tale form, "wo die Psychologie ganz
subordiniert ist einem magischen, alle Kräfte vergestaltenden, eben
märchenhaften Geschehen." Here everything is symbolic: the characters, the setting, the action. The powers, by which he means the hidden
longings and wishes of the characters, take on a variety of forms: for example the unborn children, the fishes cooked by the nurse, the children
who wait on the emperor, and at the same time the red falcon. Symbolic actions, such as the dyer's wife throwing a slipper over her shoul-
der, are of decisive importance. In the fairy tale, language serves only to
create images and symbols that stand for themselves. It is not language
that explains, rather it is the image that evokes new images in the
reader, different ones depending on the reader's experience and education. In connection with the plot, the development of the action and
the ordering of its individual elements, with a kind of diction and syntax that again awaken associations and memories, the work comes into
being ever anew in the mind of the reader. As early as 1902, Hofmannsthal had written in reference to encounters with works of visual
art: "Hier scheinen wir etwa in Gefahr, uns selber zu verlieren: grosser
Irrthum! Hier werden wir erst geweckt, uns selber zu besitzen. Denn
wir schaffen ja unsterblichen Inhalt dieser Gebilde, indem wir sie leben-
dig nachfühlen" (Hirsch 30). Effacing of boundaries, indeterminacy,
polyvalence — all these are employed consciously by Hofmannsthal as
means of representation in order to create a living work.

Nevertheless, *Die Frau ohne Schatten* has a strict construction. What
one notices first is its symmetrical structure. The story consists of seven
chapters — a mystical number, as one might expect in this work. The
first chapter is set in the emperor's palace, thus in the human world,

but on a higher level, into which the empress (who belongs to the world of spirits) has penetrated. This chapter corresponds to the seventh and last chapter, which takes place in the spirit world, into which the dyer and his wife have penetrated. The second and third chapters, as well as the fifth and sixth chapters, take place in the human city, on a lowly level. It is here that the empress is slowly transformed into a human woman. She learns to walk the path leading from egoism to empathy and compassion with other people. At the end of the sixth chapter she identifies with the dyer's wife and thus cannot help but refuse the shadow that is offered to her at the expense of the other woman. The seventh chapter takes place in the spirit world, and elevates the entire action onto a mystical level. At the conclusion, the characters have redeemed one another. This corresponds to the many mirrorings. The imperial couple is reflected in the dyer and his wife, the parents in their respective children. The whole story is reflected in the carpet that is presented to the emperor in the middle of the story. The process of its production corresponds to that of the tale's author. This is explained by the weaver: "Ich sehe nicht was ist, und nicht was nicht ist, sondern was immer ist, und danach webe ich" (*Erz* 384).

The story is intended to be nothing less than a picture of the cosmos in which the worlds of spirits and human beings encounter each other and eventually mix. At the end, all of the characters submit to the rules of eternal becoming and perishing. They arrange themselves into the chain of generations, in which individuation is necessary as the prerequisite for living on in one's posterity. Through the attainment of a shadow, the empress becomes a human individual. Only as such can she bear children and thus live on into the future. The dyer's wife, who at first wishes to withdraw from this chain, must confront her mother at the latter's grave, for along with her shadow she would lose her past as well, and, conversely, she would make the further life of her posterity impossible. This connection of various worlds, or, to put it more precisely, living spaces, was intended to occur in *Andreas* as well. In the novel, the pure, primal existence of the Carinthian peasants is juxtaposed with the decadent society of Venice. In the figure of the Maltesian man, the distant world of the Orient joins the constellation. As is suggested already at the beginning by the entrance of evil in the figure of the servant Gotthelf, the isolation of these two worlds, so separate from one another, is to be eliminated in the course of the action.

Just as everything is finally subordinated to the cosmic principle and continues the chain of ancestors, Hofmannsthal accomplishes this on a formal level as well in literary history. The multiplicity of literary sources, backgrounds, and references characterizes his entire literary *oeuvre*. But nowhere else are they as concentrated as in *Die Frau ohne Schatten*. There are so many of them that they can scarcely all be listed, and new ones are constantly being discovered. Even in the text, Hofmannsthal does not limit himself to references; sometimes he actually interpolates literal quotations from other authors, Dostoyevsky for example. Thereby he places himself quite consciously within literary tradition. He draws from world literature as if from a well, and thus unites the most varied times and places. "Der starke Reiz für mich ist, vergangene Zeiten nicht ganz tot sein zu lassen, oder fernes Fremdes als nah verwandt spüren zu machen," he writes to Leopold von Andrian (*Briefwechsel* 161).

This is the case in all of Hofmannsthal's works, if not always to the extent it is in *Die Frau ohne Schatten*. In the short stories he actually goes so far as to approximate closely the language of the story's literary model in many cases. This is true of the "Märchen der 672. Nacht," which is executed in the linguistic manner of an almost exactly contemporaneous story by his friend Leopold von Andrian, *Der Garten der Erkenntnis* (1895; no trans.). In "Reitergeschichte" Hofmannsthal imitates the diction of Heinrich von Kleist. "Lucidor" follows rather closely the language of Goethe's story "Wer ist der Verräter" from the novel *Wilhelm Meisters Wanderjahre* (1821; *Wilhelm Meister's Travels*, 1890). In the "Erlebnis des Marschalls von Bassompierre" the linguistic approximation to its model goes so far that the Goethean text is taken over almost completely word for word. Here there is not only an approximation, but rather a virtual melting together of the two texts, and, at least as far as the language is concerned, it is difficult to say where Goethe's text ends and Hofmannsthal's begins. It is his great accomplishment that this "union" with Goethe succeeds perfectly, and it shows his enormous virtuosity in his handling of language. In spite of all his language skepticism he succeeds in creating masterpieces of language, of which precisely the one which deals with the crisis of language and the impossibility of expressing oneself adequately — the "Brief" of Lord Chandos — is the most brilliant of all. It is regrettable that Hofmannsthal was unable to complete his *Andreas*. Perhaps this novel, the theme of which is after all unification, would have been on the same linguistic plane in its mirroring of form and content, and would have become the high point of his literary creation.

Taking his narrative works as the example, I have attempted to demonstrate a basic trait of Hofmannsthal's artistic creation. His main concern is the human being as such, the development of the individual personality and the determination of its position in the world, i.e. within its social and historical connectedness. Turning away from an

Aestheticism that he too had identified with at the beginning of his career, he is equally concerned with determining, again and again, the place of art within life. "Künste neigen sich einander zu, entfernen sich vom Publicum, verderben schwächere Talente, welche die Emotion beim Genießen zum Nachproducieren treibt," notes Hofmannsthal in 1895, a commentary on his own day. And he concludes from this:

> Wenn die Denkenden sich so verträumen, empfängt die Menge nichts, denn das Raffinement dringt nicht nieder, es bleibt nichts davon übrig. Hinter solchen Generationen folgen ganz leere Generationen, hinter großen efforts, grosse innere Sicherheit, leicht herb und ablehnend, starke (tragische) Atmosphäre. (*RAIII* 404)

Hofmannsthal would like to give something to the general public, he renounces refinement and develops his own aesthetic, one which no longer relies on language alone, but which regards it as one instrument among others. With this, especially in his prose fiction, he creates a dense atmosphere that takes the reader captive. In the age when psychoanalysis was beginning, the unconscious and its influence over people's actions is familiar to him. Thus he can "an Dinge erinnern, die heimlich in uns sind."[3] All the senses are involved in this process. For example, a smell ("Märchen der 672. Nacht," *Erz* 61–62) or a voice ("Age of Innocence," *Erz* 27) can call forth an experience. With the new insights of psychoanalysis, dreams too take on an entirely different meaning than they had (for example) in German Romanticism, in which dreams also played a large part. He comes forth from the profoundest depths of the psyche and brings things to the surface of which the dreamer in a waking state claims to know nothing. Hofmannsthal makes immediate aesthetic use of this knowledge and thus creates the narrative form of the dream. It is this, for instance, that determines large sections of "Reitergeschichte." Arthur Schnitzler recognized similar traits on a first reading of "Märchen der 672. Nacht" (*SW28* 208).

Through the inclusion of these psychological insights on the one hand, and the demands of the present and future on the other, Hofmannsthal gains entirely new dimensions for his characters. Seldom before had the concept of individuality been so broadly conceived. Hofmannsthal's problem consists in not losing sight of the boundaries of the individual in spite of this expansion, as happened (in Hofmannsthal's own view) in his dramas set in antiquity (*SW18* 379). His narrative texts show the alternative: the constitution of a new concept of the individual, which no longer possesses a strictly bounded character. Over and over again, his protagonists redefine themselves anew (Hofmannsthal says they transform themselves) through their conscious contact with other individuals and through conscious action: in his own terminology, by taking their destiny upon themselves, not by surrendering to it and allowing it to propel them, but by themselves grasping the rudder and thereby determining the course of their own life. The prerequisite for this, though, is self-knowledge. Only one who knows oneself, that is, who has found oneself, can remain true to oneself. Individuation consists precisely in this fidelity to oneself. Hofmannsthal describes this process again and again in his narrative fictions, each time anew. He shows its failure and its success. Above it all might stand the motto, taken from Strindberg's *Ghost Sonata*, which Hofmannsthal had intended for *Die Frau ohne Schatten*: "Mein ganzes Leben ist wie ein Märchenbuch, Herr, und obwohl die Märchen verschieden sind, so hängen sie mit einem Faden zusammen, und das Leitmotiv kehrt regelmäßig wieder" (*SW28* 271).

Translated by Thomas A. Kovach

Notes

[1] Unless otherwise stated, all references to *Die Frau ohne Schatten* in this essay will indicate the prose work by that name, not the opera text.

[2] *SW30* 141. Cf. also p. 147: "Malteser sortir de soi-même."

[3] "Age of Innocence," *Erz* 27. See also the poem "Einem, der vorübergeht" ("To one passing by), *GDI* 121.

Works Cited

Brecht, Erika. *Erinnerungen an Hofmannsthal.* Innsbruck: Österreichische Verlagsanstalt, 1946.

Briefwechsel von Hugo von Hofmannsthal und Leopold von Andrian. Ed. Walter H. Perl. Frankfurt am Main: S. Fischer, 1968. (Abbrev. as *Briefwechsel*)

Hirsch, Rudolf. "Drei Vorträge im Jahre 1902" in Hirsch, *Beiträge zum Verständnis Hugo von Hofmannsthals.* Frankfurt am Main 1995. 29–44.

Hugo von Hofmannsthal — Christiane Thun-Salm. Briefwechsel. Ed. Renate Moering. Frankfurt am Main: S. Fischer, 1999. (Abbrev. as *HvH-Salm*)

Prince, Morton. *The Dissociation of a Personality.* New York, London, Bombay: Longmans, Green, 1906.

Silberer, Herbert. *Probleme der Mystik und ihrer Symbolik.* Vienna, Leipzig: Heller, 1914.

THOMAS A. KOVACH

Hofmannsthal's "Ein Brief": Chandos and His Crisis

IN THE HISTORY of early twentieth-century European Modernism, the name Hugo von Hofmannsthal is associated above all with the crisis of language that, it is widely supposed, afflicted many writers of the epoch, and that found its classic expression in Hofmannsthal's fictional letter of Lord Chandos, which bears the unassuming title "Ein Brief" (1902). Although much has been written on this text, much of it insightful and even brilliant,[1] there has also been considerable confusion regarding it. What I offer here is not a radically new reading of the letter, but an attempt to synthesize what seem to me the most valuable conclusions reached by various commentators into a coherent view of the letter as literary text, and to suggest some ways of placing it in various larger contexts: within Hofmannsthal's work as a whole, within literary history, and within the crises of language and cognition which found such abundant expression in the twentieth century.

Before turning to the text of the letter, one misunderstanding should be cleared up right away, though this particular one characterized earlier commentaries to a greater extent than the more recent ones. That is, though it may seem obvious, the letter is a work of *fiction*. A twenty-eight-year-old Viennese writer in 1902 composes a letter in German, purportedly written by an English gentleman writer in the year 1603 to his patron, the philosopher of science Francis Bacon; on the face of it, this would appear to be a work of fiction. If there were any doubt as to how Hofmannsthal viewed the text, he first published it in book form in a collection of prose fiction. Finally, the fact that this classic expression of a writer's inability to write is in fact written by that writer in elegant prose, however one accounts for the anomaly (and we shall return to this question later), at least serves to underline the text's fictionality.

So why have so many critics viewed it as an autobiographical document? Again, the answer is not difficult to find. The composition of the letter coincides with a significant caesura in Hofmannsthal's career: the writer who had achieved fame throughout the German-speaking world by the age of twenty-five for his lyric poems was to abandon the genre almost entirely for the remainder of his career. Thus Hofmannsthal the lyric poet "fell silent" just as did Chandos. (Of course, the portrayal of Hofmannsthal's "abandonment" of lyric poetry is an exaggeration; he wrote several poems, including "Vor Tag," one of his finest, in the years after 1902.) In addition, there is biographical evidence (see Kobel 142–43) to suggest that Hofmannsthal around the time of writing the letter had had experiences which bore some similarity to those described in the letter. Finally, the text appeared in the volume *Prosa II* (1951) of the Steiner edition of Hofmannsthal's works, the volume containing the essays of the same period, rather than in the volume *Erzählungen* (1945). The inclusion of the work in the volume of the *Gesammelte Werke* edition entitled *Erzählungen, Erfundene Gespräche und Briefe, Reisen* (1979) signals a welcome recognition of its generic status. Of course, to say that the letter is a work of fiction is not to say that it is totally without autobiographical elements, any more than the autobiographical elements in the work of any great novelist disqualify those novels from fictional status. We will return later to the significance of the letter in the poet's life and career.

The letter is introduced by a sentence, apparently the statement of an editor, identifying the text as a letter written to Francis Bacon by Philipp Lord Chandos, younger son of the Earl of Bath, "um sich bei diesem Freunde wegen des gänzlichen Verzichtes auf literarische Betätigung zu entschuldigen" (*Erz* 461). Chandos addresses Bacon, who had apparently expressed concern about Chandos' mental state in a previous letter. Chandos acknowledges the concern as directed to the author of two successful works which had brought the young writer fame, and to the man who previously had confided in his friend Bacon several ambitious future projects which, as Bacon correctly feared, were not being realized. Chandos asks if he is really still the same person, a question reminiscent of the well-known lines from "Terzinen: Über Vergänglichkeit," "Und daß mein eignes Ich, durch nichts gehemmt, / Herüberglitt aus einem kleinen Kind / Mir wie ein Hund unheimlich stumm und fremd" (*GDI* 21). But with the next breath he dismisses the question as mere rhetoric, thus apparently acknowledging a continuity of some sort.

After outlining the future projects he had envisioned, he describes the state of youthful intoxication in which such plans were conceived:

Mir erschien damals in einer Art von andauernder Trunkenheit das ganze
Dasein als eine große Einheit: geistige und körperliche Welt schien mir
keinen Gegensatz zu bilden, ebensowenig höfisches und tierisches Wesen, Kunst und Unkunst, Einsamkeit und Gesellschaft; in allem fühlte ich
Natur, [. . .] und in aller Natur fühlte ich mich selber. (463–64)

This condition has been associated with the state of "Präexistenz" described by Hofmannsthal in the later notebooks in which he attempts a
self-interpretation, *Ad me ipsum* (written in 1916 to 1929, first published 1930). After elaborating further on the dimensions of this state
of youthful omnipotence, Chandos announces the crisis in a famous
passage of shocking terseness: "Es ist mir völlig die Fähigkeit abhanden
gekommen, über irgend etwas zusammenhängend zu denken oder zu
sprechen" (465). He then describes the stages that have led to his current predicament. First, the language of philosophical and moral abstraction becomes problematic; he becomes tongue-tied even when
trying to explain to his four-year-old daughter why she must always tell
the truth. But even the everyday sort of judgments made in casual conversation (so and so is a good or bad person, a family is doing well or
poorly) become impossible for him to make or even grasp. He describes how everything in such conversations appears as if in a magni-
fying glass, so that he can no longer survey them or view them in
context: "Es gelang mir nicht mehr, [die Menschen und ihre Handlun-
gen] mit dem vereinfachenden Blick der Gewohnheit zu erfassen"
(466). He tries to "rescue" himself by studying the works of classic
authors, but it is to no avail.

The remainder of the letter is devoted to describing his present
condition, one which, viewed from the outside, is scarcely distinguish-
able from his earlier life or even that of his neighbors, but which
amounts to a total negation of the creative and self-confident writer
who had attracted the attention of Francis Bacon. He describes his life
as one of "kaum glaublicher Leere" and speaks of the "Starre [seines]
Innern" (470). And yet, most of the space in these final pages is occupied by a description of certain "freudige und belebende Augenblicke"
in which he escapes his usual emptiness. These are moments of intense
communion with animals or even inanimate objects he encounters,
sometimes only in thought. He relates an anecdote about the Roman
orator Crassus who was mocked for having wept at the death of a fa-
vorite fish, and who turned the tables on his mocker by saying that this
was more than that person had done at the deaths of either of his wives.
Yet, Chandos hastens to add, it was not the witty repartee, but solely
the thought of his intense bond with the fish which is relevant to his
own situation.

He concludes the letter by referring once more to Bacon's concerns, and stating definitively that he will write no more books, neither in English nor in Latin,

> . . . weil die Sprache, in welcher nicht nur zu schreiben, sondern auch zu denken mir vielleicht gegeben wäre, weder die lateinische noch die englische noch die italienische und spanische ist, sondern eine Sprache, von deren Worten mir auch nicht eines bekannt ist, eine Sprache, in welcher die stummen Dinge zu mir sprechen. (472)

Even this brief summary raises some of the central questions posed by the text. First of all, what are we to make of this strange crisis? What has brought it on within the realm of the letter's fiction, and how may we understand it in the broader contexts of Hofmannsthal's literary career, and of the cultural trends of his epoch?

To begin with the last question, one may offer several answers. As I have argued elsewhere (Kovach 1985), the aesthetics of Symbolism, which Hofmannsthal absorbed in the 1890s through his encounter with Stefan George and his readings in the work of the French Symbolist masters, proved to be the most decisive aesthetic experience of his early career, but one which brought with it a dilemma. Specifically, the Symbolist striving to divorce the language of the poem from everyday language, to make of poetic language an element more comparable to musical tones than to language used as a tool of communication — one which Hofmannsthal endorses in such texts as "Poesie und Leben" (1896) — must be seen in retrospect as a dangerous enterprise, for language is ultimately a social invention and derives its meaning from a social context. It is no accident that Hofmannsthal's "post-Chandos" career involved a turn to more public forms such as drama and even opera libretto, since he clearly recognized, in a critique of Aestheticist and Symbolist values which is both explicit and implicit, that the poet has a social function to perform, and while he remains attuned to the incantatory powers of language (in fact, he makes his most explicit affirmation of Symbolist aesthetics in "Das Gespräch über Gedichte," 1903), he henceforth will remain committed to the writer's social mission and responsibility. Obviously, Chandos is not a Symbolist poet, so this problematic cannot be applied directly to his case; nevertheless, as Morton has argued and as I will suggest below, Chandos's writings as described in the text, both finished and planned, suggest some similar issues.

It is important to emphasize at this point that this crisis of language is also one of cognition. As the quotation above suggests, the inability to speak coherently is preceded by the inability to think coherently. What is at issue, in other words, is not simply the difficulty of communicating an unquestioned reality, but also the obstacle facing an individual in grasping that reality, indeed the difficulty in ascertaining whether there is any universal reality that might serve as the basis for communication. In fact, the problem is still more radical than this: not only is there a question as to the tenability of our notion of reality, there is at least as much of a question regarding the notion of the self. Here we must reflect on the context in which this text is written. The impact of Ernst Mach's *Beiträge zur Analyse der Empfindungen* (1886) on Hofmannsthal and other Viennese writers of his generation has often been noted: Mach's systematic dissolution of the boundary between inside and outside, the self and the world, in favor of a mass of elements of perception, his refusal to view the self as anything other than an "ideelle denkökonomische, keine reelle Einheit" (18) is reflected in this and other texts by Hofmannsthal. The choice of Francis Bacon as recipient of the letter is of course not without significance; as Jacques Le Rider points out (49), Bacon as the founder of English empiricism is the forebear of Ernst Mach. Thus, the problem of organizing sense data into a structured reality by means of linguistic concepts, a problem that underlies Mach's work as well as "Ein Brief," is immediately placed in the foreground. Freud's *Traumdeutung* (1900), which appeared two years before the letter and which Hofmannsthal knew, was the first major statement of a view of the human psyche that likewise served to undermine traditional notions of the self, and that proved to be far more wide-reaching in its impact. Ludwig Wittgenstein's investigations of language and its relation to reality, the work of a Viennese-born philosopher who was to revolutionize twentieth-century thought, deal with similar issues.

But these larger contexts still cannot provide us with an answer to the question as to the nature and causes of Chandos's crisis as represented within the fictional world of the text. Morton points out that the dilemma is apparent already in the passage in which Chandos describes his youthful state of intoxication, even in the alternation between the nominative "ich" and the dative "mir," signaling the tension between the self as a willful, controlling subject and the self as merely part of a cosmic unity. It is the self's quest to achieve this unity, and yet it seeks to achieve it in a way that undermines unity: by purposeful individual striving. This clearly emerges in the passage that follows shortly after the one quoted above in which he describes his earlier sense of the unity of all things:

> . . . überall war ich mitten drinnen, wurde nie ein Scheinhaftes gewahr: Oder es ahnte mir, alles wäre Gleichnis und jede Kreatur ein Schlüssel der andern, und ich fühlte mich wohl den, der imstande wäre, eine nach der andern bei der Krone zu packen und mit ihr so viele der andern aufzusperren, als sie aufsperren könnte. (464)

The words "Oder es ahnte mir" mark the transition, and the tension, between the self which is part of the cosmic unity and the artistic subjectivity which oversees and depicts this unity from the outside (Morton 518–19).

As Morton goes on to show, this tension is evoked also in Hofmannsthal's descriptions of his writings, both completed and planned. The three early "Schäferspiele" are characterized by the unrestricted play of the author's imagination and mastery of evocative language, on the one hand, and by the total unreality of the subject matter on the other (*Erz* 461). The second is described as a "tractatus" with no title or subject matter supplied, although we may perhaps infer that it is the architectural monuments in Venice that he mentions in the description. What is interesting to note here is that although the genre — a tractatus — would signal a turn to the depiction of "reality" in contrast to the earlier "Schäferspiele," his own description of the work, with his emphasis on its mastery of classical literary forms and the absence of any explicit reference to the subject matter, suggests that despite the more "real" basis of the work, the writer's subjectivity is once again paramount. In fact, it is even more so than before, for now it is the "geistiger Grundriß und Aufbau" of the treatise, those aspects which point to his intentionality in the formal design of the work, which for him is the most moving part of the work (Morton 521–23).

As Morton points out, this tendency is fulfilled in the sense that the remaining works are nothing but intentionality, that is, they are plans that are never brought to realization. The first of these, which Chandos calls his "Lieblingsplan" (*Erz* 462), was to be a history of the early years of the reign of King Henry VIII — for an Englishman writing in 1603, as "real" a topic as might be imagined. But even here, it is the imaginative, super-real element that seems to predominate ("ein Ding, herrlich wie Musik und Algebra"). Chandos imagines the work as "Dichtung und Wahrheit zugleich" — for the German reader, a reference to an author (Goethe) and an age (Weimar Classicism) in which it was still possible to imagine poetry and truth coexisting in one artistic creation. In another project, he wishes to return to the classical mythology which provided the material for his Schäferspiele, but this time in an attempt to unlock the "hieroglyphics" of a higher wisdom he now sees to be contained within them. The words "[ich] sehnte mich," "ich wollte" are repeated several times as he describes this and his final plan, which is simply to be a collection, "Apophthegmata," of sayings from antiquity to the present. Though here the author's self disappears entirely in one sense, since he is using exclusively the words of others, in another sense it has become paramount: the work's title is to be *Nosce te ipsum*, "Know Thyself." And thus Morton demonstrates how Chandos's project founders on a two-fold dilemma. On one hand, there is the tension between the self as observing subject and creative portrayer of reality, and the self as object, as itself part of a cosmic unity; on the other hand, there is the tension inherent in a language which tends to lose all connection with discernible reality in its celebration of itself, whether this takes the form of words savored for their musicality with little regard to content (as in the "Schäferspiele"), language as the building blocks for a construction of such formal perfection that it surpasses that physical architecture it purports to describe (as in the "Traktat"), or language which somehow is to evoke a truth which exists beyond language and beyond ordinary perception (as in the unrealized works). But, as I suggested earlier, this latter aspect, the elusive nature of the literary artist's language, relates directly to the "Symbolist dilemma" of a language that has lost its connection with lived reality.

Thus we have gained some understanding of the background causes and the nature of Chandos's crisis, both in terms of the fictional letter and within the larger personal and cultural contexts in which the letter was composed. It remains to address the question as to how we are to view the outcome of the crisis, for Chandos, for the writer Hofmannsthal, and for the moment in European culture in which the letter arises. As part of this question, we must also suggest some answers to the anomaly that this letter, which depicts a failure of language, a lapse into total silence, in fact makes most eloquent use of the very language it purports to renounce.

One clue is offered at the end of the letter, one apparently so trivial and even silly that it has apparently been beneath the dignity of previous interpreters to make note of it: namely, Chandos not once but twice makes reference to the impossibility of writing any further in English or Latin, the second time adding Italian and Spanish for good measure. The letter is of course written in German, so technically speaking Chandos has not in fact violated his pledge in the writing of the letter. The fact that the reference to these other languages occurs twice makes it difficult to see this as accidental. Yet surely this is not intended as a kind of joke, as a way of acquitting Chandos on a "technicality?" For one thing, as suggested earlier, the language discrepancy serves once again to underline the fictionality of the text. Together with the opening sentence, which suggests the presence of an editor who is presenting the text for publication, one might view the text we have as a translation from an original text which, alas, does not exist. However one views it, this conundrum reinforces not only the fictionality of this text, but the elusiveness of *any* text, the precariousness of the entire enterprise of writing which seeks to encompass a reality outside itself. A parallel to the apparently "bad joke" regarding the language in which the letter is written is the recounting of Crassus's reply to his tormentor; though Chandos assures his reader that it is not for the sake of that repartee that he recounts the story of the Roman orator's attachment to a fish, the reader nevertheless takes note of the way Crassus uses wit, which after all involves language, to deflect attention from a state of being he either cannot or would prefer not to speak of. Thus we are seemingly caught in a bind from which there is no escape: any attempt to show the inadequacy of language necessarily will involve the use of this very language.

For Chandos himself, it is clear that his "lapse into silence" is a purely literary one; by his own account, he continues to converse with his wife and family, the workers on his estate, his neighbors, and other individuals whom he encounters in his daily life, however solitary we may imagine that life to be. His language may be considered to suffice for this letter of personal communication with a friend and well wisher, although he says that this letter will probably be his last or at least the last he will write to Bacon. Such a lapse into silence may be viewed as a kind of poetic justice, a punishment for the hubris of his belief that he could encompass truth and reality through his own magical command of the word, a reminder that language begins and ends as a means of communication. Chandos himself speculates that his present state is a kind of divine punishment for his earlier "Anmaßung." Without explicitly rejecting the suggestion, he intimates that such religious conceptions have no more power over him: "Mir haben die Geheimnisse des Glaubens zu einer erhabenen Allegorie verdichtet," and this allegory is further called a rainbow which would recede from any attempt he should make to come close to it. At this point it would be useful to recall Hofmannsthal's own later characterization, in *Ad me ipsum*, of Chandos's predicament as that of a "Mystiker . . . ohne Mystik" (*RAIII*, 601). That is, he is "ohne Mystik" in the sense that the religious faith on which traditional Christian mysticism is based is lacking for Chandos. Nevertheless, the "freudige und belebende Augenblicke" which he describes in the final pages of the letter have almost invariably and rightfully been described as mystical. The intense sense of communion with the most apparently mundane object or creature is one that he claims he cannot communicate (though some readers would claim otherwise).

In describing this state, he says the following:

> . . . das Ganze ist eine Art fieberisches Denken, aber Denken in einem Material, das unmittelbarer, flüssiger, glühender ist als Worte. Es sind gleichfalls Wirbel, aber solche, die nicht wie die Wirbel der Sprache ins

Bodenlose zu führen scheinen, sondern irgendwie in mich selber und in den tiefsten Schoß des Friedens. (471)

This is a most revealing passage. To begin with, we are reminded once more of how inextricably linked the language crisis is with a crisis of cognition. The silent communion with objects and creatures is here called a kind of feverish thinking, a mode of thought carried out in a kind of substance which is "flüssiger, glühender als Worte." And this kind of thought, just like thought involving language, brings with it the "Wirbel" or dizzying eddies which are part of everyone's experience in making sense of their reality, but these "Wirbel," unlike those of language, lead not into some bottomless abyss, but rather back into his own psyche, which is simultaneously "den tiefsten Schoß des Friedens."

How finally can we sum up the state in which Chandos takes his leave of his readers? On the one hand, as the above passage suggests, this "Mystiker ohne Mystik" has achieved a sort of nirvana, a peace which comes from his wordless communion with objects, both seen and imagined, of the world around him. And yet, not only is this fulfillment found only in isolation, it itself actually compels a kind of isolation, since the only valued moments of his existence are ones he cannot share with others. These moments must therefore be seen as essentially a form of compensation for a loss of meaningful connection with his human environment.[7] His immersion in the most ordinary and banal elements of existence might ultimately be viewed as a kind of cosmic retribution for the artistic narcissism of the state he describes in the first portion of his letter.

As we leave Chandos the fictional character behind, we must then ask: what is the significance of this resolution for the real-life author of the letter, and for the culture and society in which and about which he wrote? For Hofmannsthal himself, there is no question that this text is the marker of a crisis which, though particularly acute around the turn of the century, actually runs throughout his career (Kobel 145). The turn away from lyric poetry as his primary means of expression signals, as already observed, the recognition that language becomes meaningful only in a social context. Though this development can be observed within the lyric poetry itself, as a progressive movement toward dramatic form, it is most clearly manifest in his post-Chandos turn to more public and less hermetic forms of expression. More broadly, the necessity to acknowledge the social nature of language further implies the way in which language is implicated in our construction of a social identity. Recalling Mach's notion of "das unrettbare Ich," Chandos's experience serves as a reminder to us that it is through language that we not only establish contact with a reality outside ourselves, but it is through it also that we define ourselves as part of that reality.

And finally, Chandos's crisis points to what was to become a central philosophical preoccupation of the twentieth century, reflected in the philosophy of Ludwig Wittgenstein as well as in more recent developments such as Jacques Derrida's deconstruction: namely, the demonstration that language can no longer be relied on as a valid signifier of a reality which exists outside itself, and in fact that we cannot ever experience a "reality" which is not already mediated by our language. The implications of this proposition are ones we still wrestle with in the twenty-first century, and they have never been given more eloquent expression than they were by Hugo von Hofmannsthal at the beginning of the twentieth.

Notes

[1] I am indebted especially to the article by Michael Morton, "Chandos and His Plans" (See Works Cited).

[2] A different view is taken by Benjamin Bennett in an article entitled "Chandos and his Neighbors," *Deutsche Vierteljahrsschrift für Literaturwissenschaft und Geistesgeschichte* 49 (1975), 315–31. Bennett urges us to take literally the passage in which Chandos tells Bacon that his existence cannot be distinguished from that of his neighbors, and argues that Chandos has made an ethical choice to abandon the language of philosophical abstraction which is Bacon's domain, and thus addresses Bacon in a letter which must be read ironically. Though the argument is brilliant and not easily dismissed, still it is difficult to reconcile Bennett's view that Chandos has actually achieved a fairly contented existence with Chandos's own reference to "ein Leben von kaum glaublicher Leere" (470). Likewise, Bennett's view of Chandos as well-integrated into the (non-intellectual) society of his neighbors is problematic in light of Chandos's description of how even the judgments which form the content of everyday conversation have become problematic for him.

Works Cited

Kobel, Erwin. "Der Brief des Lord Chandos." *Hugo von Hofmannsthal.* Berlin: Walter de Gruyter & Co., 1970. 142–56.

Kovach, Thomas A. *Hofmannsthal and Symbolism: Art and Life in the Work of a Modern Poet.* American University Studies: Series III (Comparative Literature), Vol. 18. New York/Bern/Frankfurt am Main: Peter Lang Verlag, 1985.

Le Rider, Jacques. *Modernity and Crises of Identity: Culture and Society in Fin-de-siècle Vienna.* Trans. Rosemary Morris. Cambridge, England: Polity Press, 1993.

Morton, Michael. "Chandos and His Plans." *Deutsche Vierteljahrsschrift für Literatur und Geistesgeschichte* 62, No. 3 (1988) 514–39.

Sheppard, Richard. "The Crisis of Language." *Modernism 1890–1930.* Ed. Malcolm Bradbury and James McFarlane. Pelican Guides to European Literature. Harmondsworth, Middlesex (England): Penguin Books, 1976, rpt. 1978. 323–36.

BENJAMIN K. BENNETT

Hofmannsthal's Theater of Adaptation

IN THE PLAN of the present volume, we are meant to discuss Hofmannsthal's dramas in a sense of the term that excludes the opera libretti, the comedies and the early "lyrical" plays; and this definition by exclusion appears to put us in danger of having to plod text by text through a connectionless jumble of material. But if we look at the actual list of major works that fall, seemingly by accident, into our territory — *Elektra* (1903), *Das gerettete Venedig* (1904), *Ödipus und die Sphinx* (1905), *König Ödipus* (1906), *Jedermann* (1911), *Das Salzburger Große Welttheater* (1922) and *Der Turm* (1923-1927) — we find that we have, in effect, been assigned the topic of *dramatic adaptation*. The range covered by this idea is still considerable. *König Ödipus* is close to a simple translation of Sophocles, albeit with much of the choral material omitted, whereas the connection of *Der Turm* to Calderón's *La vida es sueño* is extremely tenuous; and *Ödipus und die Sphinx* fits the pattern only by suggesting interpretive perspectives upon Sophocles. But still, the question we must ask is: precisely how, and with what end in view, does Hofmannsthal adapt dramatic works of the past for the modern theater?

Adaptation, Interpretation, Performance

"Tradition" is not the defining issue here. Like any writer, Hofmannsthal both receives and develops tradition with every stroke of his pen. And he himself, in the short essay "Das Spiel vor der Menge" (1911), which is meant mainly to justify his and Reinhardt's *Jedermann*, indicates clearly that a principal question in dealing with his adaptations is that of *theatricality*. It is here, accordingly, that I intend to establish the focus for the rest of this essay, except that the idea of theatricality I will work with — in the process of ascribing it to Hofmannsthal — is radically structural, practically geometric in nature, and lacks entirely the emotional-ideological slipperiness of phrases like "das Geheimnis deutschen Wesens" (*DIII* 105), which seem to me more a response to Reinhardt than an expression of Hofmannsthal's own professional thinking. In the case of adaptations, namely, the interpretive relation of theatrical performance to its text is repeated in the relation of the text itself to the earlier dramatic text it supposedly represents. As spectators in the theater, we are thus presented with the interpretation of an interpretation; and the question of where the poetic *meaning* of the work resides now becomes difficult. We are compelled to worry about where the *original* is to be found, upon which these layers of interpretation are constructed.

It is not enough to say that the original is the earlier dramatic work of which the present text is an adaptation, and that the meaning conveyed by the performance is the meaning of that original work in a form adapted to our present cultural situation. For the obvious structural parallel connecting interpretation in the forms of adaptation and performance foregrounds the quality of *unreliability*. Theatrical performance considered as interpretation is not only empirically but also inherently questionable, imprecise, groping, because it is, above all, *mute*. It has no words of its own, no rational-verbal leverage upon its object; the only words available to it are exactly the words of the text it is supposed to interpret. And the structural parallel in the theater we are talking about therefore calls our attention strongly to the unreliability of *adaptation* considered as interpretation. For the very existence of an adaptation, assuming such a thing is needed, presupposes the *inaccessibility* of the work being adapted, at least from the point of view of the present reader or audience. After all, if it were accessible to this reader, why would he or she use an adaptation? And this reader or audience, in turn, has no basis on which to judge the adequacy of the adapter's work. There is even a problem here at the level of the adaptation's *writing*. If the adapter is attempting to do nothing but translate the language, then it follows that he or she is deliberately *concealing* any interpretive bias in the process; if the adapter makes substantial changes, then the question arises as to how an "interpretation" that alters its object can be trusted. In every possible case, we are faced again with a complete lack of certainty or reliability in the interpretive process.

What we find ourselves involved in, in this theater of adaptation, is therefore a complex interpretive and performative procedure that has no semiotic center, no original source of meaning — or at least no such source that is accessible to us. Of course the text of the adaptation can be interpreted more or less on its own terms, and can thus have a meaning ascribed to it. But precisely by being an adaptation, the text itself constantly undermines any such interpretation by deferring to its absent original; and we are left, in the end, with a work that strictly speaking *has no meaning*, a work in relation to which the hermeneutic process cannot imagine itself as goal-directed. (If we ask for the meaning of the adaptation, our attention is directed to the original, as the object of its interpretive work. But for reasons noted above, the original is inaccessible, at least for this purpose.) Or to put the matter in different terms, we find ourselves involved in a theatrical event which, since it cannot be reduced to the expression of a meaning, assumes the character of absolute or radical or intransitive performance, performance subordinated to no higher category, performance without the question of "performance of . . ." The theater of adaptation, in this sense, would be something approaching the strictly non-literary theater imagined by Artaud.

The application of these ideas to Hofmannsthal is justified in part by the "Vorspiel für ein Puppentheater" of 1906 (*DIII* 485–90),[1] which apparently was not written for an actual puppet-theater (it was published in the *Neue Rundschau*) and can therefore be taken as making a point about dramatic form. The first character who appears in this little text, "Der Dichter," begins by imagining that he is on the verge of experiencing an ecstatic union with nature itself. But what then actually emerges out of the forest is a comic but ugly old woman with a bundle of dried twigs and an urban Viennese accent; and after a quickly aborted attempt to unveil the supposed "angel" hidden in this mask, the Poet resigns himself to "reality" and to the recognition that his is a fundamentally human world, that nature as such is beyond his reach. Thus, it appears, the transition from lyrical mysticism to the more social and realistic art of theatrical drama is negotiated; and the Poet, accordingly, now becomes aware of specific human "Gestalten und Figuren" taking shape in his imagination, as it were in his blood.

At this point, however, the text becomes problematic. The Poet turns and speaks "Ad spectatores"; if we are following a supposed transition from the lyrical to the dramatic we expect him to promise that the human figures in his imagination, perhaps somehow combined with the real people he is now determined to live among, will soon appear on the stage before us. But what he actually promises is completely different: not newly imagined characters, and not "real" characters, but rather precisely those *stock* figures ("Kaspar Hauser . . . die Pfalzgräfin Genofeva . . . Leda . . . Doktor Faust") that are required by the genre of the theater in question, here the puppet theater. The secret of theatrical drama, in other words, is that whereas from the point of view of the dramatic author himself, his work may have meaning, may be the product of strong personal vision, still, what actually appears on the stage, what is actually made available to the audience, *has no manifest connection with that meaning*. This is the condition, the old hag of "reality," that every dramatic author must come to terms with: that the knowledge and vision that have driven him to write do not survive as communicable meaning in the theater; that whatever is understood publicly as the "meaning" of drama is as arbitrary, as inherently questionable, as the theatrical performance that supposedly interprets it; that in effect, theatrical drama has no meaning (unless one is willing to admit the possibility of non-communicable meaning, which would be a contradiction in terms). And I contend that Hofmannsthal's way of coming to terms with this condition, or one of his ways of doing so, is to anticipate it by the structural attenuation of meaning in dramatic adaptation.

The author of drama, like the Poet of the "Vorspiel für ein Puppentheater," always speaks with two voices: a personal voice that arises, so to speak, in his blood, and is never available for us to hear directly; and a public voice whose whole sound and content is determined by circumstances. But if we can only really hear the second of these two voices — as we have heard Hofmannsthal himself, in Reinhardt's vicinity, speaking of "das Geheimnis deutschen Wesens" — then how can we have any knowledge whatever of this dichotomy or disjunction of voices in theatrical drama?

Contingency, Negativity, Performance

It must be understood, first, that if this argument has any claim to validity, its range cannot be restricted to the field of drama. It must be true that the content of personal poetic vision is never, in any genre, successfully transformed into communicable meaning.[2] And the uniqueness of drama, then, is that it offers special possibilities for disrupting the otherwise practically unavoidable *illusion* of communicated meaning, the possibility, in particular, of representing structurally the inherent radical unreliability of its own communicative procedure. It is only in this way, only indirectly, only negatively, that the operation of an absent voice can be suggested.

But if the business of drama for Hofmannsthal is to bring to light in the theater an otherwise automatically self-obscured linguistic or communicative problematics, then exactly what type of drama will we expect to find him cultivating? We have already begun to answer this question in discussing certain general features of the theater of adaptation, especially the tendency of that theater in the direction of pure performance, ungoverned by any original source of meaning. And now, in addition, we find ourselves in a position to account in part for Hofmannsthal's choice of texts for that theater. At least in the case of Sophocles' *Electra*, Otway's *Venice Preserved*, and Calderón's *La vida es sueño*, we recognize plots and motifs that serve as *allegories* of the the-atrical situation by placing in the foreground the qualities of disorder, disconnection, contingency, lack of satisfying resolution: qualities that resonate with the general centerlessness of the theater of adaptation.

In Sophocles' play there is a definite sense of incompleteness, of loose ends. Orestes does finally return and complete the needful act of revenge; but with regard to Electra, who stands in the work's focus, that act has also become pointless, since it arrives too late to make any difference in her existence, too late to restore the possibility of marriage and children. Nowhere, moreover, are we offered any explanation of why it has taken Orestes as long as it has to embark upon his mission, even though there are clear suggestions in the text that he and Electra had long been in contact, that he had already promised a number of times that he would soon return (lines 164–73, 303–6, 319). And to this unsettled situation Hofmannsthal adds not only the vertiginous and lacerating psychological depths for which his text is famous, but also the motif of Electra's failure to provide Orestes with the fatal weapon she has saved for him, and the unfulfilment of her prophetic dream of being present at Clytemnestra's death.

The same sort of fundamental disorder obviously characterizes Ot-way's play, which is the story of a plot entered into for trivial reasons and betrayed for trivial reasons. And again, as with Sophocles, Hofmannsthal outdoes his model, most strikingly by eliminating the final heroic recon-ciliation between Jaffier and Pierre. Even *La vida es sueño* fits this pat-tern, for its main action is the *failure* of a prophetically established structure of fate to be realized. Prince Segismundo is banned because of a prophecy, at his birth, that he would violently overthrow his father; but in the very midst of fulfilling the prophecy, he achieves enlightenment and conquers his prophetically given nature. To be sure, Hofmannsthal's relation to his model here is problematic. When *Der Turm* is at last completed in 1925, the Calderonian emphasis on a successful ethical avoidance of fate has been almost entirely lost. But *Der Turm* is a prob-lem for other reasons as well, and we will come back to it below.

For now, let us return to our main concepts and note that it is theo-retically all but impossible, in any literary form, to convey a genuine sense of chance, disorder, contingency, negativity. Hofmannsthal's Ödipus, after defeating the Sphinx, can say to Kreon, "auf mir liegt das Chaos und / zernagt mich" (*DII* 476). But no sooner do we read or hear that word "chaos" than we attempt to interpret it, to make sense of it, to submit it to a larger order; and chaos itself (whatever that might be) is no longer strictly what we understand. Hence, again, the impor-tance of the theater of adaptation. For the automatic ordering process that informs our reception of poetry, or of literature in general, presupposes as its object a coherent ordering impulse behind the text it is confronted with, the impulse, precisely, that makes it this particular text. And in the case of an adaptation — given the necessary inaccessibility of any "original" — the dependent or contingent quality of what is actually presented us is sufficient to disrupt that presupposition and perhaps, so to speak, to permit "chaos" to mean something a bit closer to chaos after all. Only in the theater of adaptation, therefore, can the disorderly elements of plays like *Elektra* and *Das gerettete Venedig* actually *be* disorderly or discontinuous enough to function as allegorical reflections of a larger rhetorical situation.

But again, why is the theater of adaptation, in this sense, important to Hofmannsthal, why is it important to him to create a theater in which something like *actual* accidentalness or contingency operates, not merely the regulated fictional image of these qualities? Clearly the answer to this question must involve more than just the interpretation of the seven or so dramatic texts from which we started out. A reasonable hypothesis, in fact, would be that the theater of adaptation is meant as a guiding image of what *theater in general* should become. Of course it is impossible — even in the case of improvisational theater (we recall Hofmannsthal's oft-attested interest in the *commedia dell' arte*) — for theater ever to become in the strictest sense what we have called "absolute or radical performance," with no regulating or ordering framework whatever. But Hofmannsthal, in his dramatic adaptations, appears to be suggesting the possibility of a theater in which the semiotic organizing power of the literary text is at least *reduced* vis-à-vis the contingency, the arbitrariness, the unpredictability, the freedom, of what might conceivably happen in performance. And if we recall the "Vorspiel für ein Puppentheater," we can at least speculate on the reason for this suggestion. For if poetic vision as such (assuming it exists) can never survive as communicable meaning, then it follows that what is imposed upon us (or what we are in the habit of expecting) as the focused or unitary meaning of a poetic work, in particular a drama, is always some form of delusion or deception or, at best, confusion. In the theater as Hofmannsthal imagines it, therefore, to the extent that the imposition or expectation of poetic meaning is reduced in relative importance, the truthfulness or honesty of the theater as an institution (in a sense we have yet to specify) would be increased.

What is at stake here, to be precise, is not the theater in what we would normally regard as its objective aspects: not the shape of the stage, not the way sets are constructed, not methods or conventions of acting. For the quality of contingency, or its opposite, is not a function of these matters. Everything that happens in the real theater, by comparison with what happens entirely within the poetic imagination, is strictly contingent simply by virtue of being real; but at the same time, if it is regarded (with perfect legitimacy) as a direct expression of the poetic imagination, its accidentalness evaporates. What matters, therefore, is the institution of the theater as a whole, including its actual and potential audiences, and the manner in which this institution (in all the individuals composing it) regards itself. And what Hofmannsthal envisages, what is implied by his theater of adaptation, is a theater characterized (in its own view of itself) not by the authoritative organization of realities into a system of meaning, but by *balance* or *tension* between an unavoidable systematic tendency and the unbroken uncontrollability and contingency of its material elements.

Still, if this is Hofmannsthal's view of the theater, one might ask, then why did he not himself produce a theoretical exposition of it? In fact he did, except that the work in question does not look like a theoretical work. I mean *Das Salzburger Große Welttheater,* Hofmannsthal's adaptation of Calderón's *El gran teatro del mundo,* in which human life is allegorically represented as a stage play acted before God. For the relation, here, between the authority of Der Meister and the strict freedom of his creatures is a clear and precise allegory of the theater Hofmannsthal has in mind — an allegory that even calls itself a "theater," thus making no secret of its representative function. Normally we treat Hofmannsthal's world-theater play exactly as we treat Calderón's; we read the given structure of the theater as a metaphor for the true character of the world. And while this reading is not invalid, still, I think we have understood enough about Hofmannsthal's practice of dramatic adaptation to recognize that we must also read the *Großes Welttheater* the other way round, that the given structure of a Christian idea of the human world, as at once both determined and free, both systematic and contingent, here operates as a metaphor for the true character of the theater, of a theater, perhaps, that in its modern version has been corrupted by an excessively literary quality and must now be restored with the aid of the theater of adaptation.

Once we accept the possibility of viewing Hofmannsthal's text in this way, a number of its features make rather more sense than they would have otherwise. For example, when the play is performed, it turns out that the actors and actresses assigned to the inner play (the human figures whose lives unfold) are not playing "parts" at all, in the sense that the part is distinct from the playing of it. The actor who plays the Beggar, for instance, is not simply playing a beggar; rather, he is playing an actor playing a beggar, and the distinction between the role he is playing and what he is simply actually doing vanishes. (The one character in Calderón for whom a formulation of this type would have been questionable, the *Niño* or stillborn child, is omitted by Hofmannsthal.) To look at it differently, the actor playing the Beggar cannot possibly get his part wrong, since no matter how incompetently he speaks or gestures, he is still exactly representing an actor playing a beggar; and by the same token, he cannot get his part significantly right either. His "part," as an element of meaning, a literary or imaginary object against which his acting might be measured, is in effect simply not there; and what we have, in the inner play, is something very like an instance of the notion of absolute performance that is associated with the theater of adaptation.[3]

As with contingency, moreover, there is no place within the thoroughly intentional structure of poetic vision or meaning for negativity in a strict sense of the term. There may be oppositions or tensions or conflicts; but to the extent that these things have meaning, they contribute positively to an encompassing order. And yet, in the case of the *Großes Welttheater*, negation is an unavoidable issue. One of the characters Hofmannsthal adds is precisely the Negator, the Widersacher, who asks the God-figure how he can possibly be entertained by a play he himself has predetermined (*DIII* 112). Or to shift the question slightly: how can this play claim theological accuracy when, by its very nature as poetry, it cannot include the element of genuinely possible negativity that is required by the idea of human freedom to sin? That this is a matter of concern to Hofmannsthal is clear, for example, in his treatment of the Rich Man, whose abrupt dismissal at the end, with the two words "Nicht ihm!" (163), stands in stark, maximally negative contrast to the scene (absent in Calderón) of brotherly affection between him and the Beggar (159–61).

But more important is the scene in which the Beggar refrains from striking, with the Peasant's axe, a blow that the text suggests would destroy the very fabric of the world (145). This motif, which parallels the Kaiserin's "Ich — will — nicht!" (*DV* 374) in *Die Frau ohne Schatten*, sidesteps the inherent opposition between poetic vision and negativity by positing an act of negation that is necessary to *uphold* the poetically imagined "world." Left to itself, the world, or the poetic vision, provides material for reasonable trains of thought that would lead ultimately to its destruction, especially in the Beggar's arguments against the very notion of "order" (*DIII* 134–35). Therefore an act of simple radical negation is required by the very existence of that orderly vision, and negativity thus establishes itself even in the apparent domain of poetry, in the literary theater, after all.

This argument perhaps appears to be mainly a play with words, but only until we recognize that it reflects an entirely palpable state of affairs in the theater. For as we sit in the theater, we are presented with two different objects, whose modes of existence are entirely incommensurable: first, the poetic work as such, the system of signs, considered purely as a mental or intentional or imaginative entity; and second, the vehicle, the accidental collection of physical objects (including people) by which, tonight, that system happens to be represented. And the system, the work as such, the "world" as the work imagines it, cannot be said to attain its own coherent existence except by virtue, somewhere, of a move of strict negation with respect to the arbitrary physical vehicle that has brought it to us, which move is then itself represented quite transparently in the scene where the Beggar refrains from striking. Indeed, if we recall that the Beggar's acting is in the strict sense not regulated by a distinct "part" belonging to the work as system, so that his speeches turn out to be characterized by an arbitrariness not fundamentally different from that of the performance's physical vehicle, then it might even be said that his refusal to strike, his rescue of the poetic order, constitutes a kind of uniquely concentrated *self*-negation.

Two points must be borne in mind here. First, arguments like this one on the *Großes Welttheater* do not need to be interpretively complete, or even central, with respect to their texts. Their function is solely to support our main argument about the theater of adaptation by showing how works that Hofmannsthal chooses for this theater resonate with its tendency to foreshadow a renewal of theater in general, a readjustment of the balance of its systematic and contingent elements. And second, this main argument in turn concerns not the theater in any objective sense, but rather the manner in which the theater, by way of its audience, understands itself. By saying this, I do not mean to diminish the matter. The nature of theater, or of a particular theater — to the extent that such a "nature" can be spoken of — certainly has more to do with how that theater is regarded than with any catalogue of objective features. But it remains true nonetheless that the ground of our inquiry (and of Hofmannsthal's project) tends to shift, and that our concepts and arguments therefore require constant reinspection.

Jedermann, in fact, seems to me a fairly clear instance of the kind of danger or difficulty that besets our endeavor and Hofmannsthal's. The theater of adaptation, we have said, brings to light a failure of communication. But is this bringing to light not itself a *form* of communication? And if so, then communication on what level, by way of what medium — assuming that what has been brought to light is the inevitable failure of communication among individuals, communication of anything like the *Puppentheater* Poet's vision of natural truth? From here it is not very far to the idea of some type of slumbering collectivity within which the failure of individual communication assumes positive value as a raising and articulating of collective consciousness. Ideas like "das Volk," or "das Geheimnis deutschen Wesens," begin to suggest themselves; and if we can believe "Das Spiel vor der Menge," it is in this spirit that Hofmannsthal prepares *Jedermann* for the theater of adaptation. But as I have suggested, such a grasping for the positive is in truth a perversion of that theater, a danger to be avoided. Not only the quality of negativity in its structure, but the irreducibly negative operation of that theater as a whole, must be maintained and reaffirmed at every step. Exactly how this process works can be made clearer by a discussion of the question of *acting*.

The Paradox of the Actor

In the *Buch der Freunde*, Hofmannsthal — relying, as usual, on his memory rather than his library — misquotes Diderot's *Paradoxe sur le comédien* as follows: "Die meisten Menschen fühlen nicht, sie glauben zu fühlen; sie glauben nicht, sie glauben, daß sie glauben" (*RAIII* 236). Actually, Diderot distinguishes between most mediocre actors, who would simply reject the proposition that their art has nothing to do with genuine passion, and "quelques autres" of whom it could be said, "qu'ils croient sentir, comme on a dit du superstitieux, qu'il croit croire," actors, in other words, who are less certain about their genuine passion, but whose art still depends on their believing in its existence (Diderot 311). And precisely Hofmannsthal's misquoting ought to provide us here with an clear insight into his own thought on the question of acting and feeling.

It is evident that Hofmannsthal means to contrast the deludedness of "most people" with the relatively clear thinking of a small group; and since he associates his thinking with Diderot's *Paradoxe*, it seems fair to infer that that small group is meant to be constituted by those theatrical actors who are fully in command of their craft. But does the implied contrast then have the form: whereas most people only believe that they feel or believe, competent actors *actually* feel, *actually* believe? No one with even the most perfunctory knowledge of Diderot — and Hofmannsthal is by no means normally a perfunctory reader — could draw this conclusion. What Hofmannsthal means to suggest can only be: whereas most people believe that they feel or believe, competent actors understand clearly that they do *not* genuinely feel or believe (this being exactly Diderot's point), and restrict themselves accordingly to a mastery of the supposed outward signs of feeling or belief.

The consequences of this idea are considerable. For if "most people," plus the elite group with whom they are contrasted, add up to *all* people, then it follows that "genuine" feeling or belief simply does not operate in life. Or perhaps we might wish to say — with an eye to the "Vorspiel für ein Puppentheater" — that genuine feeling or belief, for all we know, may in some sense exist, but if so, then in a way that is entirely disconnected from any form of communicable meaning. The main implication, however, remains the same: that the theatrical actor, merely by competently executing his or her craft, by being precisely a "mere" actor, not a "natural" person, offers us a more accurate and complete representation of truth than could possibly characterize the supposedly communicated meaning of any poetic text. Thus, again, the importance of the theater of adaptation emerges, since any undermining of the category of meaning, in the theater, will tend to bring acting itself, with its cargo of truth, more clearly into focus. And in the special case of the *Großes Welttheater*, we can now form a more complete idea of why it is important that the acting of the inner play approaches the status of absolute or intransitive acting, acting regulated by a minimum of the distracting operation of "role."

Of course, the *Buch der Freunde* comes fairly late in Hofmannsthal's work (1921), and a single misquotation of Diderot does not seem like much on which to build a philosophical theory of acting. But on the other hand, the whole of our argument so far on the theater of adaptation favors that theory. And the very character of the theory makes it unreasonable to expect from Hofmannsthal a systematic exposition of it; such an exposition would necessarily presuppose the direct communicability of a belief about inner human existence, a belief according to which precisely that form of communicability is excluded. Again, the closest we can come to an adequate exposition is in the theater itself, especially in the performance of plays like the *Großes Welttheater*, or perhaps plays modeled on *La vida es sueño*, where the idea of treating one's own life as a dream suggests the possibility of living without the aid of convictions concerning one's "genuine" thoughts or feelings.

And yet, there are after all a number of other texts in which we can follow the development of Hofmannsthal's idea of acting. At the end of *Der Tor und der Tod* (1893), for example, Claudio reproaches himself for having lived his life like "ein schlechter Komödiant" (*GDI* 296); and the opposite of a "bad actor" is not a somehow genuine or complete or natural human being, but rather a *good* actor, who takes his craft (the "Klang der eignen Stimme" as it were) seriously enough to make it operate among other people in the service of what we are now in a position to call truth.[4] Or much later in Hofmannsthal's career, we recall the dramatic scene "Das Theater des Neuen," in which Homolka seeks to win over his Josefstädter colleagues for Brecht's *Baal*, by suggesting that the task of a truly "new" theater must be to rescue its time from enslavement to the concept of the "individual." ("Individualität ist eine der Arabesken, die wir abgestreift haben" [*DIII* 510]). For reasons that we have already noted (in discussing the difficulty of a systematic exposition of Hofmannsthal's theory of acting), the ideas here edge toward the ridiculous, the tone toward the satirical. But Waldau, who begins by finding himself entirely baffled by this type of thought, then saves the day when it occurs to him that precisely actors, by their profession, have *already* abandoned any belief in their natural individuality: "Denn wenn man schließlich das Schicksal hat, nur man selbst zu sein, indem man immer ein anderer wird . . ." (512). The idea that the natural or genuine individual does not exist, which is clearly an absurd idea when individuals discuss it seriously, becomes by contrast perfectly obvious and convincing when regarded as a description of the craft of acting. This "new" theater, then, for all its revolutionary pretensions, will in the end be merely a reaffirmation of what has always been the theater's philosophical mission, and the single true "meaning" of every play performed.

To complete the picture, we might turn finally to Hofmannsthal's short prose pieces on the famous actress Eleonora Duse. In 1892 he emphasizes Duse's ability to convey "the philosophy of her role" (*RAI* 476), which still implies acting as the transmission of poetic meaning. But in "Die Duse im Jahre 1903," we read:

> Mehr als jemals ging diesmal, während sie auf der Bühne stand und spielte, etwas Größeres vor als das Schicksal dieser Figuren [her roles], etwas Allgemeineres, etwas von so hoher Allgemeinheit, daß es dem tragischen Leben erhabener Musik sehr nahe verwandt war. . . . Es lebt in dieser Schauspielerin eine solche Seele, daß vor der Erhabenheit ihrer Gebärden jedes Stück, in welchem sie spielt, aus seinen Fugen geht und nur mehr sie da ist, ihre Natur, die unfähig ist, sich zu verbergen. (484–85)

Here the idea of absolute or intransitive acting is almost fully developed. We must not be confused by the terms "Seele" and "Natur." Hofmannsthal is not talking about the qualities of a particular person, but rather about a maximum of "Allgemeinheit," which in this context can only mean sheer acting as *itself* the vehicle of truth.

Moreover, once we have grasped this theory of acting and its fundamental relation to the theater of adaptation, we are able to account for Hofmannsthal's interest in the Oedipus material as a vehicle for that theater. Again, it is a question here of allegorical reflections, in the myth, of the essential but historically obscured theatrical situation. For the actor, like Oedipus, is from the outset saddled with a fate. He or she is doomed, in pursuing the theatrical craft, to pass beyond the limits of normal "individual" existence and to become something more "general," an icon, a symbol, a vessel of truth. And he or she, like Oedipus, fulfills this doom *precisely by striving to avoid it*, by striving repeatedly to be fully contained within the radical individuality of dramatic roles. ("Und sie [Duse] will Schauspielerin sein, und sie strebt sich zu verhüllen, und sie bietet die ganze dämonische Kraft ihres Leibes auf, in tausend Verwandlungen den Strahl ihres Wesens zu brechen" [485].) In *Ödipus und die Sphinx*, when Ödipus is first told of the heroic deed the Thebans require of him, he imagines himself ("Ihr guten Götter! . . . Baut ihr / dem Heimatlosen solche Taten auf" [*DII* 462]) as a kind of anonymous nomad who repeatedly receives the opportunity to define himself individually as the doer of a particular deed (as the actor of a particular role, in the allegory), and then always leaves it behind him for the next. And like the actor, he never manages actually to realize this vision of himself, for wherever he goes he is inevitably recognized for who he truly is — first unconsciously by Jokaste, then explicitly by the Sphinx — always inevitably recognized as the doomed vessel of truth.

Thus not only the Oedipus myth in general, but also Hofmannsthal's addition of *Ödipus und die Sphinx*, a story of how Oedipus becomes king of Thebes and marries Jokaste, makes sense in relation to the theater of adaptation. In response to Phönix's insistence that, after receiving at Delphi the prophecy of his parricide and incest, he should have pressed the original question of who his real parents are, Oedipus says: "Nicht zweimal redet / der Gott. Den er sich wählt, von dem wird er / begriffen" (398). The idea that he has been "chosen" by fate, in other words, for all its horror, still awakens in Oedipus a kind of pride that prevents him from asking the question that would have prevented his fate. His perverse pride in his vocation is the vehicle by which his vocation is realized, but in a sense he must necessarily strive to avoid. Or in the allegory: it is the actor's following of his vocation as, precisely, an actor — not a speculator, not an asker of questions, not a person who ever fails to focus on the particular — that proves the vehicle by which his vocation is realized, but on a level entirely different from the one on which he follows it.

Even Kreon, for Hofmannsthal, assumes allegorical significance here. It is Kreon whose use of theater terminology in the phrase, "sich

. . . mit Taten schminken" (429), establishes the connection between acting in the sense of doing deeds and acting in the sense of playing roles. But in using this phrase, Kreon marks himself as the man who wishes to *avoid* becoming an actor. He goes through the motions of maneuvering politically for the throne of Thebes, and his very name means "ruler." But when the time comes to take the final step that will secure him the kingship, he refuses. He wishes to *be* king, but somehow without ever *becoming* king ("und aus dem Schlaf / mich wecken kämen sie und legten mir / die Krone auf mein Bett" [432]), without ever passing through a moment of clear focus upon the goal, without ever "putting on the make-up" of a king. In this respect, Hofmannsthal takes his cue from the speech in *Oedipus the King* (Sophocles, lines 582–615; *DVI* 353) where Kreon states his natural preference for royal privileges without royal responsibilities.

Kreon, in Hofmannsthal, is thus the diametrical opposite to Oedipus, and the two figures between them allegorize the truth that there is no alternative in human existence to the condition of being an actor, that even the most determined resistance to this condition, the most consistent refusal to "put on make-up," is itself a form of acting, a deliberate shaping and focusing and particularizing of one's existence. Kreon in the end becomes king of Thebes after all, and king in exactly the sense he had wanted to avoid, faced with decisions that are too much for his vacillating temperament — should Oedipus be granted his wish for exile? (Sophocles, lines 1515–20; *DVI* 381–82) — and faced, if we look ahead to *Oedipus at Colonus*, with complete civic disaster. The lesson of the theater, *as* theater, remains what it had been in *Der Tor und der Tod*: that the substance of human life is not feeling or passion or conviction, but only *choice*, and that the only true choice is between being a good actor (Oedipus) and being a bad one (Kreon).

The Paradox of the Author

Several problems remain. Especially: (1) if the renewal of the theater that Hofmannsthal envisages is only a renewal of how the theater regards itself; and (2) if this renewal requires a reduction in the importance of poetic meaning in drama, so that the truth-bearing quality of absolute performance can come into focus; and (3) if Hofmannsthal therefore constructs a theater of adaptation and, to ensure that the character of this theater is properly understood (see condition 1), selects texts for it in which significant aspects of the theater itself are allegorized: then how are these allegories, these uses of text to influence spectators' view of their theater, at all *different* from precisely that literary "meaning" against which they are employed? Is there any actual hope for a renewal of the theater in Hofmannsthal's sense, or does the theater always automatically re-poeticize itself in the process of renewal? And does it really matter if there is no hope? What is the use of truth as we imagine it is conveyed by absolute performance? Why should we not be content with our belief in "individuality," in our genuine convictions and passions, however delusive this belief might be?

All these questions point toward *Der Turm*, but not in the sense that the play provides answers to them. On the contrary, the most striking thing about *Der Turm* — especially in the original long version published in *Neue deutsche Beiträge* (1923, 1925) — is that for all its enormous rhetorical weight and density, it is not an "answer," in any respect, to anything whatever, that it is constituted entirely by ambiguity, indecision, equivocation, inconclusiveness, rhetorical *emptiness*. Sigismund, the heir to the throne, is imprisoned as a child due to a prophecy that he will overthrow his father the king; summoned to court as a young man, in his confusion he is led to strike out at the king and thus fulfill the prophecy. In Act V, now that he has survived years of solitary philosophical training, his rebellion and defeat at court, the collapse of his father's regime, Julian's huge ambitions and tragedy, and his own capture by Olivier, we expect that the play will finally shape itself into some form of relatively coherent philosophical-political vision. Sigismund himself seems to expect this when his consciousness of having now learned "die Sprache der Welt" is balanced by a philosophical remark, to the Doctor who has been his companion for much of the action, that "nichts ist da oder nicht da: alles, indem es ist, war schon da" (*DIII* 360). But the gypsy woman is already present on stage when he says this; and Graf Adam soon appears with news of "die Grünen" (361), who turn out to be the troops of the Kinderkönig. Sigismund does his best, even in the scene with the gypsy, to maintain a practical, political-military focus; but he cannot. The real gypsy is replaced by her spectral double (365); the whole character of the stage thus changes from reality to symbolic vision; Sigismund now receives his death, which on this stage, however, is not even an unequivocally real death; and the play is then closed by the Kinderkönig, whose appearance simply begs any serious political (or philosophical) questions we might have wished to consider.

And yet, on the other hand, the play is anything but perfunctory. It moves, in fact, with a ceremonial deliberateness that apparently seemed excessive even to Hofmannsthal, when he produced a shorter version for the first book publication at the Bremer Presse. Brother Ignatius, at one point, has occasion to say:

> In Rom hab ich Theaterspielen sehen, in einem grossen Saale, aber schlecht. Was sie nicht anging agierten sie mit gespreizten Leibern und schleppten gebauschtes Zeug hinter sich drein, wie Schlangenschweife. (296)

And he could almost be talking about the play in which his own scene takes up much more time than is justified by its contribution to the central action. The "puffed-up cloth" that those Roman actors supposedly drag around might even suggest inordinately long speeches; for it is certainly true that all the major characters in *Der Turm* are given more than enough room to develop their positions and feelings in language. Julian, in fact, is not finally silenced even by death.

Why does this play *talk* so much, yet in the end not arrive at anything like a meaning? Or does this question contain its own answer? Here, perhaps, the theater of adaptation approaches its audience with an unprecedented directness, unmediated by the complications of allegory. The naked confrontation between ego and universe (we recall the *Puppentheater* Poet) is enacted over and over, not only by Sigismund, but by Basilius, Brother Ignatius, Julian, even Olivier; the stage does not represent a world (how can it be a world, with practically no women?), but is exclusively the locus of this confrontation. Poetic vision is not avoided or suppressed or attenuated, but in its very kernel, as the collision of ego and universe, is the only thing that actually happens in this play. And yet, this staging of pure poetic vision, even for Sigismund, is ultimately *empty.* "Gebet Zeugnis: ich war da. Wenngleich mich niemand gekannt hat" (381), says Sigismund — looking at the Doctor, thus including even him in the "niemand"! What communicative value will such "testimony" have, if its object is strictly unknown even to the witness, if there is "kein Platz in der Zeit" (381) for it? Sigismund's demeanor may be joyful, but when he dies on the words, "Hier bin ich, Julian!" (381), he still thus associates his death with Julian's descent into "Nichts!" (351).

The whole substance of the play is poetic vision, which, however, repeatedly proves ineffectual, non-communicable, and so in effect evaporates, leaving, in the theater, nothing but performance. Here is theater of adaptation reduced to absolute simplicity. *Der Turm* is not even really any longer an adaptation of *La vida es sueño*. It merely makes the *gesture* of being an adaptation; and in this case, the gesture is better than the reality, since the actual "original" is now too distant to be effective as a counterforce to its own undermining of the new text's meaning. In the same way, moreover, *Der Turm* merely makes a *gesture* at the theme of living one's life as if it were a dream, thus mobilizing the association of this idea with the actor's detachment, but without embarking on a necessarily obscure allegorical elaboration of it.

And yet, even without the specific complications of allegory, these ideas can still be regarded as aspects of the text's, or of the *author's* meaning, of what the author wishes to accomplish with his work. How do we get around this objection? How does Hofmannsthal? To the extent that this question can be answered, the answer is suggested by our discussion above of Hofmannsthal's response to the actress Eleonora Duse (1858–1924). Like the actress, every author begins by submerging himself entirely in each particular work; and like the actress, every author finds over time, in spite of himself, that this submergence becomes less and less complete, that he himself tends to become something "more," and "more general," than his works, in the very act of continuing to produce them. Hofmannsthal grows especially conscious of this process around the time of *Der Turm*.[5] In the sketch of a letter to an older man like himself, he says: "Unser eigentliches Geheimnis war unsere Haltung im Leben, die Perspektiven unserer Äußerungen — damit waren wir Vorläufer, Vorfühler — " (*SW31* 213). Not the utterances themselves, but the perspective from which they emerge, now becomes crucial. And in order for *Der Turm* to be effective in the manner I have suggested, this authorial perspective — in relation to which the play itself (the text, the structure of meaning) crumbles into non-essentialness — must be present and operative even for an audience in the theater. "Gebet Zeugnis: ich war da. Wenngleich mich niemand gekannt hat." These words are spoken not only *in* the play — where they do not signify much — but also, as it were, from *behind* it, by an author who thus insists on his separation from the knowable text, an author whose role is completed by simply "being there," not by saying anything specific.

But how can we be sure this actually happens? What evidence have we? Obviously we cannot be sure, there can be no conclusive evidence. We can understand that the theatrical situation required by *Der Turm* is more easily imaginable in the case of an older author with a long public career behind him, an author who is more likely to be pre known, pre-understood, pre-judged by tonight's audience, who is thus more likely to "be there" *for* that audience. But there is no place in the logic of textual or cultural criticism for anything like certainty in this matter. What we have described is the situation that *must* obtain if *Der Turm* is to have a culminating function in the theater of adaptation, but with nothing like a guarantee that it *does* obtain.

Hofmannsthal himself can be no surer of his ground here than we are, which is why he is willing (under Reinhardt's influence) to revise *Der Turm* and give it a fairly clear philosophical and political message after all. In the end, that is, Hofmannsthal turns his back on the theater of adaptation, and on his years of struggle with it. But in doing so, he also provides us — as it were inadvertently — with a justification of that theater, an answer to our final question concerning the *importance* of truth as it is conveyed by the possibility of absolute or intransitive performance.

The most significant change in the last version of *Der Turm* is the development of the figure of Olivier, who is permitted to give expression to what Hofmannsthal evidently considers the main political danger of the time. In the last scene, for instance, when the Doctor approaches him in a posture of supplication, pleading for Sigismund's life, Olivier responds: "Gebärdet Euch nicht. Die Pfaffen- und Komödiantensprache ist abgeschafft. Es ist ein nüchterner Tag über der Welt angebrochen" (*DIII* 467). In this new atmosphere of "sobriety," he implies, serious things will at last be taken seriously, people will be taken at their word and held to their word. What matters now is the "utterance" itself, not the "Haltung," the attitude, the theatrical pose behind it, the utterance as meaning, doctrine, ultimately dogma. Society will be constituted no longer by the fluid interaction of actorly types and moves, but by the clash of uncompromising positions or formulations, and ultimately therefore by the hegemony of one such position, one established order. "Denn ich und einige, wir haben uns aufgeopfert und nehmen dem Volk die Last des Regimentes ab, damit es nicht schwindlig werde" (468), says Olivier. The dizzying, disorderly quality of human existence (as represented, for example, in the uncenteredness of the theater of adaptation) will finally be brought under control; and control in this sense is by definition radically impersonal, hence a violation of the single actual form in which humanity is manifest.[6]

Or to put it differently, Hofmannsthal imagines a coming hegemony of the *nameless.* In his last speech, Olivier says:

> Jawohl! man sollte nach Recht vor uns liegen, für das, was wir auf uns genommen haben, aber wir verschmähen es, und auch mit unseren Namen soll kein Götzendienst getrieben werden, darum halten wir sie geheim. (*DIII* 468)

And it is against the threat of the nameless that the theater of adaptation, by way of its inevitable arrival at the idea of absolute or intransitive authorship, is erected. For the work or product of absolute authorship — if there is such a thing, which cannot be decided — can be, precisely, nothing but name, not even a particular name, but the quality of name as such, as an instance of language entirely dissociated from meaning, language as sheer performance ("Komödiantensprache" in the strictest conceivable sense), which does nothing but bear witness: "ich war da."

Notes

[1] On the importance of this text in general for Hofmannsthal's idea of the theater, see Karl Pestalozzi, "'Daß du nicht enden kannst, das macht dich groß . . .': Hofmannsthals Schwierigkeiten mit Dramenschlüssen," *Hofmannsthal-Forschungen*, Vol. 7, ed. W. Mauser (Freiburg i. Br.: n.p., 1983), 99.

[2] See Bennett, *Hugo von Hofmannsthal: The Theaters of Consciousness*, 75–79, for an interpretation of the poem "Die Beiden" in this sense.

[3] See Bennett, *Hugo von Hofmannsthal*, chapters 15–16, esp. 293–99, for a related argument: that the ethical aspect and the metaphysical aspect of the thinking of the *Großes Welttheater* are conducted in such a way as to produce oppositions by which anything that might qualify as the play's meaning is reduced to an absolute minimum.

[4] See the more complete argument in Bennett, *Hugo von Hofmannsthal*, 70–75.

[5] On Hofmannsthal's paralleling of himself and Goethe in this respect, see Bennett, *Hugo von Hofmannsthal*, 303–4.

[6] This point, concerning Hofmannsthal's sense of a pressing political danger, could be developed with the aid of the perceptions on Freud and mass psychology in Thomas A. Kovach, "*Acheronta movebo*: A New Light on the Figure of the Physician in Hofmannsthal's *Turm*," in Erika Nielsen (ed.), *Focus on Vienna 1900: Change and Continuity in Literature, Music, Art and Intellectual History* (Munich, 1982), 77–83.

Works Cited

Bennett, Benjamin. *Hugo von Hofmannsthal: The Theaters of Consciousness*. Cambridge: Cambridge UP, 1988.

Diderot, Denis. *Oeuvres Esthétiques*. Ed. Paul Vernière. Paris: Garnier Frères, 1968.

*Hugo von Hofmannsthal (standing, fourth from left) and Richard
Strauss (sitting, middle) with others involved in the premiere of*
Der Rosenkavalier, *January 26, 1911, at the Dresden Staatsoper.
Left of Hofmannsthal is Max Reinhardt, Director of the Kleines
Theater, Berlin; on right is Alfred Roller, set and costume designer.
Left of Strauss is Count Nicholas von Seebach, Director of the Staatsoper;
on right is Ernst von Schuch, conductor.
Courtesy Richard Strauss Institute.*

JOANNA BOTTENBERG

The Hofmannsthal-Strauss Collaboration

I N THE HISTORY of opera, a genuine collaboration between composer and librettist is a fairly recent phenomenon. The artistic dominance of librettists in the seventeenth and early eighteenth century diminished, and gradually composers became the more prominent creators of operas. Only after the mid-nineteenth century was a greater equality of librettist and composer achieved, through Wagner's writing of his own libretti, providing a model for later artists, and also through collaborations between respected writers (most often dramatists) and composers. Only rarely, however, has a composer significantly influenced an opera scenario (plot outline) and libretto, or a librettist influenced the musical form. One such collaboration was that of Hugo von Hofmannsthal and Richard Strauss. Their work together lasted from 1906 until Hofmannsthal's death in 1929, and produced six operas, one ballet, several smaller projects for theater, and an extensive correspondence that documents their collaboration. Strauss and Hofmannsthal seldom met, so they discussed their projects in letters. These were first edited and published in 1925 by the artists themselves, with the idea of giving both critics and audiences insight into the making of the operas, the problems that arose during the work process, the details of writing and composing, the ideas and effects they wanted to convey in the operas, and also the practical matters of staging.

What is opera? From the literary perspective, it is a play set to music; from the musical perspective, an illustrative dramatic composition. Yet an opera that corresponds to either of these descriptions is an exception. Generally considered as either music *or* drama by critics, opera is most accurately described as theater that joins words, music, and visual elements in a dramatic form. Words and music are sequential, temporally-bound, but the experience of opera in performance is often immediate, non-sequential. The temporal relationship of opera's components is often perceived only in retrospect.

The creation of an opera depends on the quality of communication between composer and librettist. The librettist addresses the composer in words, the composer responds in music. Words and music, joined in opera and in song, are in some ways disparate elements. In a successful collaboration, a balance is achieved in the art work between sensual, emotional, and intellectual components. Hugo von Hofmannsthal came to opera because his own artistic medium, words, seemed to him insufficient for a full expression of human experience. In an early poem, "Zukunftsmusik" (1891), he wrote: "Worte sind Formeln, sie können's nicht sagen," and in his notes from 1893 to 1894, "Das Drama ist die vornehmste Kunstform, weil darin am meisten verschwiegen wird" (*RAIII* 372). He remained ambivalent about language throughout his life, and felt that music can reveal dimensions of character and action that words cannot adequately convey. Hofmannsthal perceived musicality as a quality of his own poetry, and he came to Richard Strauss because he believed that Strauss's music would complement his dramatic texts. This perception also led him to ballet collaborations, in which he provided outlines and ideas for staging. Although this activity was important to him, he always worked on other projects while writing his libretti, and does not seem to have considered these to be of great significance in the context of his work as a whole.

The initiative toward a collaboration for the musical stage was taken by Hofmannsthal. In 1900 he offered Richard Strauss a ballet scenario, *Der Triumph der Zeit*, which was declined. Three years later, Strauss saw a performance of Hofmannsthal's play *Elektra*, and recognized in it a potential opera. Hofmannsthal had reinterpreted the Elektra myth in his adaptation of Sophocles, and Strauss's adaptation of the play was, in some respects, a new interpretation of Hofmannsthal. This is especially true of his treatment of Orest, whose minor role in the play is further reduced in the opera, and of Agamemnon. Although the murdered king does not appear in the play, he is evoked through Strauss's music. For Hofmannsthal, the tragedy of the Mycenaean dynasty is always secondary to the personal tragedy of Elektra, and serves the dramatic function of motivating her internal crises. But Strauss focused from the first notes of the opera on the family tragedy, with the "Agamemnon motif" that recurs as a leitmotiv throughout the opera. Hofmannsthal's retrospective comments suggest that he did not consider his *Elektra* successful, and that he probably found in music the potential salvation of a play he regarded as incomplete and unsuitable for the stage.

The play was designed as a psychological drama for a small stage (Max Reinhardt's Kleines Theater in Berlin), where the actors' gestures and expressions could easily be seen by the audience, and every word could be clearly heard. Strauss wrote his opera for a large opera house, with the largest orchestra he had ever used; but there are no ensemble scenes or choruses to balance the orchestra. Most of Strauss's text changes intensify emotional expression, but it is expression to be heard rather than seen, and it is sustained through the orchestra. His alterations shorten the first half of the play and lengthen the second half, thereby allowing for more lyrical passages. In the case of *Elektra*, the intentions of the composer diverged in some respects from those of the dramatist. Hofmannsthal's total compliance with Strauss's wishes in this case may indicate his eagerness to learn from the composer about libretto requirements. Elektra's last words in Hofmannsthal's play, retained in the opera, express her joy in revenge, and also the inadequacy of language to express her intense emotions: "Wer glücklich ist wie wir, dem ziemt nur eins: schweigen und tanzen!" (*DII* 234). At such a moment, words have no purpose.

Two weeks after the premiere of *Elektra* (January 25, 1909 in Dresden), Hofmannsthal wrote to Strauss that he had conceived a complete opera scenario. This sketch, which combined ideas of Hofmannsthal and his friend Harry Kessler, became the next opera, *Der Rosenkavalier*. In Hofmannsthal's foreword to the 1927 edition of the libretto, he recalls how he created a setting with characters representing the social strata of Maria Theresa's Vienna, and also comedy types transcending time and place. In a letter to Strauss two years after the premiere, Hofmannsthal explained his choice of this subject based on the form and style he wanted. After *Elektra*, he felt that they must return to the recitative-aria form, and for *Der Rosenkavalier* he wanted to create a libretto that would be conversational in style, but would also require set pieces. This choice was made partly because of Strauss's musical treatment of *Elektra*, a symphonic style in which the large orchestra sometimes overwhelms the voices, and thus obscures Hofmannsthal's text.

The preliminary scenario shows that Hofmannsthal conceived his comedy characters before the plot was developed, and that he first conceived them as types. Some of the characters, as well as certain plot elements, are taken from several plays of Molière, as well as from an eighteenth-century French novel, *Les Aventures du Chevalier Faublas*, by Louvet de Couvray. Strauss had different priorities for opera scenarios. An interesting, lively, well-developed plot line was his main concern, and this was what Hofmannsthal's scenario lacked. Strauss's suggestions to make the plot more dramatic, particularly in the second act of *Der Rosenkavalier*, were accepted and implemented by Hofmannsthal, who recognized that they would give dramatic unity to the opera. By the time he wrote the foreword to *Der Rosenkavalier*, he understood his own method of approaching a subject better, and had coined a term to explain how plot grows out of character relationships: "das Alloma-tische," meaning the reciprocal transformation of characters.

The libretto of *Der Rosenkavalier* exists in two different versions, which have the same plot but differences in the text of some scenes: the comedy version published in Hofmannsthal's works, and the libretto version published to accompany the opera. Perhaps Hofmannsthal felt that he must maintain contact with the spoken theater in his operatic work, for he considered the comedy version of *Der Rosenkavalier* as a potential play. He designed this libretto for recitative-aria form, for he wanted the voices, not the orchestra, to have primary musical impor-tance, and tried to guide Strauss toward composing music that would complement the verbal text and allow the words to be clearly under-stood. Strauss began composition before the libretto was completed, receiving the text one act at a time, and sometimes only one scene at a time. The score of the first two acts was already in print before the composer had even received the final version of Act III. Because of per-sonal factors, as well as differences in the work processes of the com-poser and librettist, this was the case with the subsequent operas as well (with the exception of *Arabella*), although both artists recognized the disadvantages of this working method.

After Strauss's positive response to the draft of the first act, Hof-mannsthal wrote on May 12, 1909 that he was trying to learn about comic opera's requirements, and that he hoped his libretto would bring out the most individual qualities of Strauss's music, the mixture of the characteristic, grotesque, and lyrical (*Bw* 60). Strauss was delighted, and requested more lines. In his enthusiasm, he composed the final love duet in Act III before he had even received Act II, and Hof-mannsthal had to provide lines for Strauss's simple, lovely melody. Oc-tavian and Sophie sing together:

> OCTAVIAN: Spür nur dich, spür nur dich allein
> und daß wir beieinander sein!
> Geht alls sonst wie ein Traum dahin
> vor meinem Sinn!
>
> SOPHIE: Ist ein Traum, kann nicht wirklich sein,
> daß wir zwei beieinander sein,
> Beieinand' für alle Zeit
> und Ewigkeit! (*DV* 104)

The form of the opera's finale was a topic of intense discussion in the correspondence. Strauss wrote on September 7, 1910 that he would guarantee an effective finale (*Bw* 101–2); Hofmannsthal accepted the judgment of the composer, who did indeed come through.

In terms of public success, and of the artists' working relationship, *Der Rosenkavalier* was the high point of the collaboration. Both men were responsible for the continuing success and the artistic qualities of this opera; but Strauss's changes to the original scenario not only enlivened the plot and intensified the action on stage, but also gave the drama a depth that was missing in Hofmannsthal's first version. All of the subsequent operas were measured in one way or another against this one, by critics and by the artists themselves.

Hofmannsthal's ideas for the next two operas were both developed shortly after the *Rosenkavalier* premiere. *Ariadne auf Naxos* was a genuinely new idea, an experimental work bringing together the three worlds that were Hofmannsthal's most important sources of subjects: the heroic world of Greek myth, the comic-satiric world of Molière, and the burlesque world of the *commedia dell'arte*. Although Hofmannsthal considered his idea for a fairy-tale opera (*Die Frau ohne Schatten*) more important, *Ariadne* occupied him first. It was planned as an interim work, a short opera within a play. Hofmannsthal wrote a play scenario, provisionally titled "Die kluge Gräfin," which could be a framework for *Ariadne*. This was not used, however, because he decided a new play would draw the audience's attention away from the opera. In the search for a suitable framework he turned to Molière, for several reasons. First, he wanted the dramatic frame set in that time; then, he had already adapted Molière for Max Reinhardt's theater, and he was strongly attracted by the works of Molière; finally, his Molière-influenced *Rosenkavalier* had been a great success.

The comic idea in Hofmannsthal's abandoned scenario was that two troupes of entertainers, one *commedia dell'arte* and the other *opera seria*, would perform on the same evening in the palace of a wealthy patron; this, he thought, would produce an amusing situation, involving comedy, irony, and an interesting stylistic mixture. He replaced his scenario with Molière's *Le bourgeois gentilhomme*, with the plan of condensing its five acts into two. As a further source of comedy, Hofmannsthal decided Monsieur Jourdain would command that the *commedia* and the *opera seria* be performed simultaneously. This performance would take place with Jourdain and his guests seated and chatting on stage, and would conclude the play (*Bw* 116). Hofmannsthal's main reason for choosing this play was Jourdain, for this complex comic figure could justify the mixture of *opera seria* and *opera buffa*, and also give the work the ironic dimension Hofmannsthal wanted. As a diversion within a play, the opera was necessarily short and accompanied by chamber orchestra. It was intended to occupy Strauss, giving Hofmannsthal time to work on the libretto of *Die Frau ohne Schatten*.

The subject of the *opera seria* is Ariadne's encounter with the young god Bacchus on the island of Naxos, where she has been abandoned by Theseus. She believes he is the messenger of death, for which she longs. Hofmannsthal concentrates on the themes of Ariadne's fidelity to Theseus and her transformation through Bacchus; and increasingly, as the opera develops, on the god's transformation through his encounter with Ariadne. The Ariadne-Bacchus relationship was not so central in Hofmannsthal's first conception; the focus was rather on the relationship of *opera seria*, *commedia dell'arte*, and Molière's play. His shift of emphasis meant that the three-way balance was upset, and neither the play nor the *commedia* could fulfill its purpose as originally planned. The ironic corrective to Ariadne's romantic pathos that should have been provided by the comic figures was largely lost.

Each opera of the Strauss-Hofmannsthal collaboration is in some ways experimental, but *Ariadne* is, as its author called it in a letter of December 13, 1912, "ein einmaliges Experiment" (*Bw* 206). There were numerous problems during the writing of this libretto and the composition of the opera. One problem area was in the different perceptions of the opera's characters by the librettist and the composer. They disagreed on the character of Zerbinetta, the female lead of the *commedia* troupe, and Ariadne's counterpart. Strauss found her much livelier and more interesting than Ariadne. He wanted her to have a greater musical role, and gave her four of the six set pieces he requested. By giving more music to the *commedia* characters, Strauss shifted the emphasis toward the *opera buffa*, which the *opera seria* frames, just as it is framed by Molière's play. But for Hofmannsthal, Ariadne's transformation remained "das Eigentliche," and Zerbinetta a mere "Zutat" (*Bw* 125).

Both artists recognized at the premiere that *Ariadne* was not viable in its existing form, and they perceived the coupling of this play with the opera as the main problem. Soon after the disappointing premiere and ensuing performances, they decided to drop the play. Hofmannsthal began work on a new *Vorspiel* that would enable the opera to be performed on its own; but the decision to revise, including writing the Prologue and rewriting parts of *Ariadne*, was made only in 1916. The setting of the Prologue is backstage before the performance, and the characters include not only the comedians, the prima donna and tenor, and several servants of the wealthy patron, but also a new character, the young Composer. His central role caused some friction between the artists, for Strauss didn't like him. Hofmannsthal had embodied in this figure the antitheses of the opera: the romantic ideal and the real world, and a naive belief in absolute fidelity (the Composer and

Ariadne) contrasted with a casual, almost cynical approach to love (Zerbinetta and the comedians). The high point of the Prologue is a brief flirtation between Zerbinetta and the Composer, the realist and the idealist. Zerbinetta tells him, "Ein Augenblick ist wenig, ein Blick ist viel" (197). Then, as she asks him to forget this moment of their meeting, he asks: "Vergißt sich in Äonen ein einziger Augenblick?" (198). Although the central argument of Hofmannsthal's libretto is prefigured in this meeting, he did not plan it as the lyrical climax Strauss made of it.

Ariadne auf Naxos is a unique case in this collaboration, and a rarity in operatic repertoire, in that it was re-created in a different form as a direct result of its poor reception. In preparing it for performance with the Prologue, Strauss decided to make cuts in Zerbinetta's part and the comedians' scenes, in order to balance the two parts of the opera. These cuts changed the emphasis of the original opera within a play, and also changed its end. The comedians and Jourdain disappeared, and the operatic illusion remained unbroken.

While writing the libretto of *Ariadne*, Hofmannsthal was already planning the opera that would become *Die Frau ohne Schatten*. As in *Ariadne*, the plot was built on two contrasting worlds, supernatural and human, embodied in two couples, the Emperor and Empress, and the dyer Barak and his wife. Hofmannsthal explained that the action would develop in eleven situations, alternating between the two worlds. There are, in fact, three levels in *Die Frau ohne Schatten*: 1. the supernatural world of the ruler Keikobad, his servants, and the unborn children; 2. the human world of the dyer Barak and his family; 3. the world of the human Emperor and half-human Empress (Keikobad's daughter) that is between them. Hofmannsthal gave the representatives of each level a characteristic diction, which he hoped would be supported by the music.

This is the first libretto in which he did not depend to some extent on the spoken theater. *Elektra* was a stage play adapted for opera; Molière's plays influenced *Der Rosenkavalier*, which Hofmannsthal wanted to be performable also as a play; *Ariadne auf Naxos* was, in its first version, a short chamber opera within a Molière play he adapted. Hofmannsthal needed to develop his characters from within, which is difficult within the limitations of the libretto form. To Strauss he expressed concern that music, which can superbly typify emotions, would conceal the characteristic qualities of language and gesture. He tried to guide the composer in bringing out the qualities of the characters through music, explaining each character in terms of typical or individual qualities, and of his or her dramatic role. He intended the Empress as the central figure, but she didn't really interest Strauss, who felt that

the human couple would elicit more sympathy. Although Hofmannsthal was aware of this, he insisted on their subordination in the
dramatic scheme to the rather passive Empress.

While working on this libretto, Hofmannsthal wrote his narrative version of *Die Frau ohne Schatten*, in which he developed symbolic levels
that open this subject to different interpretations. In the narrative, the
unborn children of the two couples appear, and to some extent guide
the course of action; the falcon and the fishes are stronger symbols; the
trials of the two couples are preordained; and the Empress here has fore-
knowledge of her own destiny. Parallels with Mozart's *Zauberflöte* are
obvious in the narrative, in which the preordained trials lead to a higher
consciousness, and thus make intelligible the rather confusing events that
precede them. A letter of December 19, 1913 to Strauss suggests that
Hofmannsthal wanted to explain the opera's meaning through the narrative version, possibly because he felt the libretto could not do justice to
this complex subject. In this letter, he calls the narrative the "Vorform
des Stoffes," although he wrote it later (*Bw* 253–54).

With its complexity of plot, character, style, diction, and symbols,
this opera presented problems for both librettist and composer. The
relative silence and passivity of the Empress made her hard for Strauss to
characterize musically, a problem he had already experienced with Ariadne. To some extent, Hofmannsthal shows her inner development in
Act II; but her transformation into a full human being is shown through
words and gestures too subtle for opera, which must rely on key words
and strong gestures to convey character development. In a long letter to
Strauss of July 25, 1914, Hofmannsthal tried to help the composer over
his difficulties with Act III, which was unclear to Strauss. This shows the
extent to which he relied on Strauss to give clarity and force to what he
himself had left vague. Toward the end of his explanation Hofmannsthal
wrote, in reference to the Empress, but also as a general principle: "Wie
denn überhaupt das Dichterische erst dann realisiert ist, wenn alles Äu-
ssere verinnerlicht und alles Innere veräusserlicht wird" (*Bw* 285). This
sentence is important for understanding Hofmannsthal's aesthetics, as
well as his strengths and weaknesses as dramatist and librettist. The Empress is inwardly transformed through her experiences in the human
world; however, her transformation is not verbally expressed except in
the final scene of Act II and the temple scene of Act III. Hofmannsthal
relied on the music; but the composer could not understand the Empress, and needed a stronger verbal characterization on which to base
his music. Hofmannsthal's characterization of the dyer's wife through
words and gestures is very strong, and her transformation is at least as
intense and total as that of the Empress. It is also dramatically more

credible, because it is better motivated and more understandable on the emotional level.

Certain flaws in *Die Frau ohne Schatten* became clear to the artists only after they had experienced it in performance, but they could not agree on whether the fault was in the scenario, the libretto, or the score. Strauss perceived it in the subject itself, which he considered too complex and cerebral for the opera stage. Hofmannsthal thought his own scene divisions might be to blame, and suggested changes in the staging (*Bw* 476). He also recognized that his own choice and treatment of this subject were to some extent responsible for the opera's heaviness and opacity; for the composer's music was largely determined by what he received from the librettist, and it became evident that this romantic opera with ethical dimensions was not really suitable for Strauss. Although they were disappointed, both artists continued to love this opera, which Strauss called their *Schmerzenskind*.

Between the 1919 premiere of *Die Frau ohne Schatten* and Hofmannsthal's conception in 1923 of the scenario that became *Die Ägyptische Helena*, the collaboration was dormant. Although each worked on other projects during these years, the artists continued their correspondence, with occasional discussion of potential projects together. By this time Hofmannsthal was well aware of the difference between his own tastes and his partner's in operatic subjects and in other aesthetic matters, and found most of the subjects Strauss proposed during this period unacceptable. These all tended toward operetta as form, political satire as content. After Hofmannsthal's repeated rejection of modern settings, Strauss proposed various settings in ancient Greece or Rome. In his letters Hofmannsthal seemed quite clear about what kinds of operatic subjects he did not want, but not about what he did want. However, he did consider some of the texts Strauss suggested as models. During this period Strauss composed his opera *Intermezzo*, with his own libretto based on an actual episode in his marriage.

The search for new subjects led the artists in different directions. Hofmannsthal offered Strauss several ideas for ballets and *divertissements*, but no opera scenario. In 1919, he wrote of three ideas for musical works, all completely different in style; he hoped to give Strauss a scenario for one of them by the following spring. He did not reveal their subjects, only that all three were in a light genre. Presumably one was "Danae," a scenario made into an opera by Strauss and Josef Gregor after Hofmannsthal's death, and another was "Lucidor," a source of the later opera *Arabella*. A letter of December 6, 1919 to his friend Rudolf Pannwitz (*HvH-RP* 459) suggests that the third subject was *Die Ägyptische Helena*.

Hofmannsthal and Strauss.
Silhouette by M. Bithorn, 1914.

Drawing of Hofmannsthal and Strauss
in a Viennese café, 1925.
Courtesy of Richard Strauss Institute.

In 1922 Strauss and Hofmannsthal collaborated on a ballet, *Die Ruinen von Athen*. But Hofmannsthal continued to search for operatic material, and at last was able to offer Strauss a suitable mythological subject, which would become *Die Ägyptische Helena*. Hofmannsthal wrote to his friend Carl Burckhardt on October 9, 1923 that this would be a beautiful pendant to *Ariadne*, its stylistic mixture bringing the heroic together with the fairy tale on the one hand, comedy on the other. Only after sketching the scenario for the first two acts did Hofmannsthal write about it to Strauss, who in a letter of September 8, 1923 responded enthusiastically, with requests for ballet interludes, choruses of elves and spirits: "Am liebsten einen zweiten 'Rosenkavalier' ohne dessen Fehler und Längen! Den *müssen Sie mir noch schreiben*, ich habe in diesem Stimmungsgebiet noch nicht mein Letztes gesagt. Etwas Feines, Lustiges, und Gemütvolles!" (*Bw* 492).

Hofmannsthal's conviction that myth is the truest mode of perception, together with Strauss's wish for a mythological subject, led him to reflect on the homeward journey of Helena and Menelaus after the fall of Troy. He saw the Trojan War as a parallel to the war that had just destroyed his own world, and in that sense it could be considered a modern setting. He was interested in the psychological situation of the reunited couple, and wanted to explore the dramatic possibilities that could lead to their reconciliation. In Euripides' version of the legend he found a motif that could be used both to facilitate and to impede this reconciliation. This was the "phantom Helena," sent to Troy by the goddess Hera in order to give the Greeks a motive for destroying the Trojans. The real Helena was spirited away to Egypt, where she remained for ten years under the protection of Poseidon, faithful to her husband, while the great heroes died for an illusion. This motif was used to introduce the story of the nymph Aithra's efforts to save Helena from being killed by her jealous husband.

For this libretto Hofmannsthal put together motifs from Stesichoros, Homer, and Euripides; he also invented some new characters. This eclectic mixture of motifs and characters complicates the plot and diminishes its dramatic qualities. The first act of a drama should provide the basis for a conflict that can be developed and then resolved in the subsequent acts; Act I of *Helena* lacks such a basis. The background and the indications of future conflict are provided not by the central characters, but by theatrical inventions, the seashell and the elves. Aithra's magic potion for suppressing memory is actually the element that brings about the dramatic conflict, but this is not yet made clear in Act I.

Hofmannsthal was uncertain how to develop the plot in Act II. The sheik, his son and slaves were introduced to provide some action but, as usual, Hofmannsthal tried to give them symbolic dimensions. The action is contrived and confusing, because of the heterogeneous plot elements. After Aithra's magical transport of the couple to a desert oasis, external conflict arrives with the desert sheik; internal conflict arises through the confusion of magic potions, and through Helena's decision to restore her husband's memory and put herself at his mercy. Dramatically the whole conception is problematic, but Strauss seems to have accepted it without question. The genesis of this opera followed a pattern similar to that of *Ariadne auf Naxos* and *Die Frau ohne Schatten*: Hofmannsthal designed a light fable with magical elements, based on fairy-tale or classical mythology, and as he developed it, became increasingly serious. The result of this process in *Die Frau ohne Schatten* was lyrical drama that, through Strauss's music, became romantic opera. But *Die Ägyptische Helena*, despite the original intentions of both artists, became a hybrid that was neither the operetta form nor the modernized mythology they had envisioned.

Hofmannsthal's ideas for his last libretto brought together two of his earlier projects: a short story published in 1910 with the title "Lucidor. Figuren zu einer ungeschriebenen Komödie," and a fragment for a Viennese folk comedy, "Der Fiaker als Graf" (1924). This fragment provided the setting for Act II of *Arabella*, with its elements of Viennese local color. "Lucidor" centers on the younger of two sisters, who is forced to masquerade as a boy, because this is less expensive for their father, a down-at-heel count addicted to gambling. In his scenario, Hofmannsthal made the older sister, Arabella, the central character rather than Lucidor (Zdenka in the opera), a change that made the story more suitable for music. The main plot involves the arrival of a wealthy Croatian count, Mandryka, who has fallen in love with Arabella's picture, and has come to Vienna to ask for her hand in marriage. The secondary plot involves a love triangle. Zdenka is in love with Matteo, a young soldier who worships the beautiful but remote Arabella. Arabella ignores him, but in order to make him happy and keep him near her, Zdenka writes messages of love to Matteo, signed with Arabella's name.

Strauss's reaction to this scenario was cautious and critical. In a letter of December 18, 1927 he compared it to *Der Rosenkavalier*, suggested additional romantic intrigue to liven the plot, and requested more serious emotional conflicts, to justify the involvement of music (*Bw* 605). Hofmannsthal assured him that Mandryka would provide action. However, Strauss had received the libretto of the first act without knowing how the plot would be further developed. Concerned with motivating the dramatic action, Strauss practically rewrote the scenario for the second and third acts. His purpose was to stimulate his librettist's imagination, and Hofmannsthal seemed enthusiastic about these new ideas for the plot. He accepted most of Strauss's suggestions, thus giving the composer a greater part in actually designing the plot than he had in any other collaborative work. These suggestions concerned the arousal of Mandryka's jealousy through a misunderstanding, when he overhears Zdenka offering Matteo the key to Arabella's room. Neither man knows that Zdenka will actually be waiting in the dark room, hoping Matteo will believe she is Arabella. This scene takes place at the ball, and the furious Mandryka publicly insults Arabella, who goes home mystified and hurt by this behavior. There, the misunderstandings are cleared up, and Mandryka must beg for Arabella's pardon. Matteo has found his true love in the girl he had taken for a boy, and the girls' father can return to his interrupted card game.

The scenario was debated and developed even as the libretto was being written. Strauss had a clear idea of the musical structure he needed for *Arabella*, and he tried to influence both the dramatic structure and the emotional content of the libretto so that it would be in accord with his musical plans. His greatest need here, as in the previous works, was conflict that is visible and audible onstage, and that also has a moral dimension to move the audience. In an expression of gratitude for Strauss's criticism and suggestions on August 5, 1928, Hofmannsthal also identified his own strength and weakness as a dramatist: "Hier haben Sie mir geholfen, ein wenig über meinen Schatten springen, der sich zu gern mit dem Zuständlichen der Figuren begnügt, statt ihr letztes in der Aktion zu suchen" (*Bw* 657). Strauss began composition of *Arabella* only after Hofmannsthal's death, so there was no discussion with his librettist during the composition of the music, and no reciprocal influence of the artists on the final form of either libretto or score. However, their letters during the writing of the libretto contain a number of significant statements on opera and on their collaboration. These give the *Arabella* correspondence particular value, as a distillation of the wisdom both artists had acquired through their long experience together.

Summary of the Collaboration[1]

With his choice of subjects for *Der Rosenkavalier*, *Ariadne auf Naxos*, and *Die Frau ohne Schatten*, Hofmannsthal consciously tried to influence Strauss's musical style and guide him in certain directions. Each of these subjects represents an attempt by Hofmannsthal to achieve a specific aesthetic ideal of his own, and to guide his partner toward the best musical realization of this ideal. After the problems with the creation of

Ariadne and *Die Frau ohne Schatten,* and their poor reception by the public and critics, he seems to have changed his attitude toward Strauss in this respect. While the poet became involved in other projects, but offered no new ideas for operas except "Danae," the composer wrote his own libretto for *Intermezzo.* Hofmannsthal was ambiguous in his reception of this opera. Although its subject repelled him, he recognized that in *Intermezzo* Strauss had made a significant stylistic breakthrough as a composer: the development of a *parlando* style that facilitated comprehension of the dialogue. In *Die Ägyptische Helena* and *Arabella,* therefore, Hofmannsthal tried to give Strauss subjects that would accord with this musical style, and also with the composer's own wishes.

Strauss chose a finished play (*Elektra*) as the first opera subject; he had relatively little influence on the development of the next three operas; and in the last two, he had some influence on the choice of form and genre, but not on the choice of subject. The correspondence tells us much about the librettist's preferences for subjects; the composer's preferences are demonstrated in his other nine operas. He composed three operas before his collaboration with Hofmannsthal, one during the collaboration, and five after Hofmannsthal's death. For all but one of these (*Die schweigsame Frau*), the choice of subject was either totally or primarily the composer's. Certain tendencies are apparent in Strauss's subject choices: toward satire, parody, and humorous confessional, and toward Greek myth with a modern slant. Although Hofmannsthal did not allow him an active role in choosing and shaping their opera subjects, Strauss did exert what influence he could. Hofmannsthal exercised his prerogative as a dramatist to distinguish what he perceived as beneficial or harmful in the composer's ideas.

Hofmannsthal's desire to work within certain forms and genres was a strong factor in determining his choice and design of opera subjects. Molière's comedies influenced the design of *Der Rosenkavalier* and *Ariadne auf Naxos;* Viennese operetta partly determined the subjects of both *Der Rosenkavalier* and *Arabella;* Jacques Offenbach's operetta influenced the design of *Die Ägyptische Helena;* and both *Der Rosenkavalier* and Johann Strauss's *Die Fledermaus* influenced the design of *Arabella.* Hofmannsthal's statements in the correspondence and elsewhere indicate that he usually conceived the form of an opera before the idea for its subject. He was proud of the fact that he and Strauss did not repeatedly use a successful operatic form (although Strauss might have been quite happy to do so), but that he experimented with forms that were either genuinely new, as in *Ariadne auf Naxos,* or at least new to them, as in *Die Frau ohne Schatten,* which actually belongs to the tradition of German Romantic opera.

Hofmannsthal reinterpreted Greek myths in *Elektra* and *Die Ägyptische Helena*, in the former under the influence of the new science of psychoanalysis and the new artistic movement of Expressionism, in the latter as a light, ironic treatment of a universal ethical issue. In *Der Rosenkavalier* he created a pseudo-historical world that related ironically both to a historical milieu and to a timeless comedy motif; in *Ariadne* the ironic interplay of theatrical forms moves on the one hand toward farce, on the other toward Baroque allegory; in *Die Frau ohne Schatten* the fairy-tale genre of German Romantic opera is used to present an ethical theme in symbolic form. Only in *Arabella* did the poet deliberately approach a form of his own plays: social comedy that depends on dialogue for its effect. Thus each work is really, as Hofmannsthal wrote to Strauss in a letter of September 18, 1919, a "Genre für sich" (*Bw* 451). Hofmannsthal thought he was acting for Strauss's own good in steering him away from subjects, genres, and musical tendencies he himself found distasteful. This was not always to the advantage of the collaboration, although Strauss did sometimes express gratitude for his librettist's guidance.

Artistic autonomy was very important to Hofmannsthal in his collaboration with Strauss. At least during the early stage, this meant that he worked within the literary and dramatic forms with which he had experience, and tried to preserve the autonomy of his text, or at least of its underlying conception, from music. *Der Rosenkavalier* has been performed without music several times, and Hofmannsthal certainly had this in mind, in case it failed as an opera. The first version of *Ariadne* was conceived as an integral part of his own Molière adaptation, more as a scene in a Hofmannsthal play than as a Strauss opera. *Die Frau ohne Schatten* was not conceived as a potential play, but it was preserved as a narrative, and in that form it was enriched with all the detail, subtlety and symbolism Hofmannsthal could not, for musical and dramatic reasons, put into the libretto. Up to this point, Hofmannsthal seems to have maintained literary connections to his libretti for two main reasons: to preserve his artistic autonomy, and to ensure the survival of the "Hofmannsthal" work if the "Strauss" work failed. These considerations became less important to him in later years. With *Arabella* he still maintained connections to literature, but here the creative process was reversed. Instead of putting his libretto material into a narrative or dramatic form in order to enrich it or to preserve it, he took two of his earlier texts, one narrative and one dramatic, both still essentially sketches, and preserved them by merging them into a libretto.

With *Elektra* Hofmannsthal was willing to oblige Strauss by fitting his own text to the composer's wishes; with *Der Rosenkavalier*, though he still deferred to Strauss in musical considerations, he consciously tried, through the form and style of his libretto, to influence the musical treatment; with *Ariadne* this became an effort to restrict the composer's musical choices. A balance was achieved in *Die Frau ohne Schatten* between Hofmannsthal's consideration of Strauss's wishes and musical style, and his attempts to influence and guide the composer. A "counter-curve" in the balance of artistic influence and autonomy can be found in the last two collaborations, with Strauss's influence most pronounced in the design of the *Arabella* scenario. Since he had not begun composition of this opera at the time of Hofmannsthal's death, and he was unwilling to alter what his partner had written, one can only speculate on how he would have further influenced this libretto, had Hofmannsthal lived longer.

Once he had established the formal and generic framework of a new opera subject, Hofmannsthal usually conceived the characters before the plot. He developed an idea through a configuration of characters, whom he first treated either as types, stock figures of the theater, or as allegorical figures. To the types belong the *Rosenkavalier* characters (with the exception of the Marschallin, who also was conceived initially as a type), the comedy figures of *Ariadne*; and at least the secondary characters of *Arabella*. To the allegorical figures belong Ariadne and Bacchus, the two couples of *Die Frau ohne Schatten*, and Helena and Menelaus. All of these latter personify different aspects of the problem of marriage and fidelity, one of Hofmannsthal's central themes.

Both Hofmannsthal and Strauss loved the theater and had a strong dramatic sense, but their talents and sensibilities were in some respects quite different. They searched for artistic means through which they might complement each other, but they were only partially successful in realizing their ideas together. In Hofmannsthal's conception of drama, the action develops out of characters in a situation, more than out of the revelation and development of character resulting from the action. This and certain other tendencies in Hofmannsthal's plot design were less favorable for his operas than for his plays, because of the retarding effects of music on the action. These include his concern with formal and stylistic elements, his stronger emphasis on character and atmosphere than on action, his initial conception of characters either as types or as allegorical figures, and his symbolic conceptualization of themes. Other tendencies were particularly favorable for opera, however: his conception of characters as contrapuntal necessities, his emphasis on the importance of *Gestalten* rather than *Reden*, and his conviction that music conveys some aspects of experience better than language.

The influence Strauss exercised on the development of Hofmannsthal's opera scenarios was almost always beneficial. When the subject was congenial to him, Strauss had an unerring sense for what was needed to generate drama, a sense Hofmannsthal acknowledged as superior to his own. The composer's influence was most pronounced in the changes he initiated in the scenario of Act II of *Der Rosenkavalier*, the role of Zerbinetta in *Ariadne auf Naxos* and of the Composer in the Prologue; and the entire *Arabella* scenario, especially the first two acts. Even in *Elektra*, though he could not really change the scenario, Strauss's text cuts and transpositions in adapting the play for opera reveal his sure dramatic sense.

Hofmannsthal wrote to Strauss on July 13, 1928 that the poet's real creation is the speech of the characters, and finding the right tone for each work, to bring it to life (*Bw* 638–39). In this collaboration, *character* is the area of closest artistic rapport, for Strauss had little interest in the broad themes and ethical issues underlying Hofmannsthal's operatic conceptions, and Hofmannsthal had little interest in the external action for which Strauss pleaded. In their correspondence they returned with each new project to the relation of character, thought, and action. Both artists worked toward the dramatic as the most important quality in their operas; but their correspondence and the opera texts indicate that they approached drama from different directions. Hofmannsthal tended to move from themes expressing ideas, to characters who embody these ideas, to the action that develops out of the characters and gives them dramatic purpose. Strauss started from a plot, proceeded to the characters who motivate and carry out the action, then to ideas (except in his last opera, *Capriccio*, which embodies ideas in characters, and cannot really be called a dramatic action). If this process is visualized as a crossing of two paths, the point of intersection is *character*. This is the dramatic component on which the artists came closest together and communicated best. Language expresses thought better than music can; music expresses action better than language can; character is the vehicle of both thought and action. Strauss highly valued the lyricism of Hofmannsthal's language, but not the undramatic self-containment that characterized at least some of his leading roles, most notably Ariadne, the Empress, and Arabella. The musico-literary synthesis in opera is a conjunction of two kinds of dramatic mimesis, representation and presentation. Representation portrays emotions, and thus tends to individualize them in characters. Presentation expresses emotions, thus moving toward their universalization. This conjunction was problematic in the Hofmannsthal-Strauss collaboration.

The creative tension in Strauss between the dramatic composer and the symphonic composer, and in Hofmannsthal between the dramatist, narrative poet, and lyric poet, produced tensions in their artistic relationship as well. Hofmannsthal's manner of placing characters in contrast was one of his greatest strengths. This is good for music, but not necessarily for drama; contrast alone is not sufficient to create the conflict drama requires. Tension between the artists sometimes impeded their work together, particularly when one tried to force the other into a decision or direction he considered wrong. When writing a libretto, Hofmannsthal did not always have time to refine and revise his work, for Strauss, who was eagerly waiting, composed sections of the libretti as he received them. The only exceptions to this procedure were the first and last operas of the collaboration. In the other four operas, both artists were somewhat disadvantaged. Strauss could only plan his score on the basis of the scenario, and Hofmannsthal could not revise his own text which had already been set to music, even if subsequent developments might require this. However, their close interaction generally benefited the operas, serving as a check and balance system.

Symbols in opera must be made sufficiently clear through the verbal text before they can be given musical form. In the libretti, some symbols were clearly specified by Hofmannsthal: the axe in *Elektra*, the shadow in *Die Frau ohne Schatten*, the sword in both this opera and in *Die Ägyptische Helena*, the potions in *Helena*, and the glass of water in *Arabella*. Strauss's treatment of such well-defined symbols was, in general, effective. He also created through music symbolic dimensions not present in the libretti. Some examples of symbols defined through musical means are: Agamemnon, who in Hofmannsthal's play was not the dominating presence Strauss made of him; the silver rose, which Strauss invested with a magical significance not explicit in the libretto; the Emperor's falcon, who became through music a powerful spirit-presence. Ambiguous symbols and allegory were difficult for Strauss to compose effectively, and Hofmannsthal often had to explain these to him. After *Der Rosenkavalier*, Hofmannsthal's symbolism became increasingly connected with a moral message, although both artists wanted to avoid this, and therefore less plastic, more difficult to express through music.

In a collaboration between a poet and a composer, different artistic media are joined and a balance between sensual and intellectual forms is attempted, with opera's essential third term, *emotion*, as mediating force between the physical and the spiritual elements. Like character, emotion is an axis of this collaboration; both artists confirmed its central importance in their work. But Hofmannsthal sometimes had difficulty expressing emotion directly and convincingly through words. The words of the Empress in Keikobad's realm, from Act III of *Die Frau ohne Schatten*, are one example of this. Strauss found the text for the opera's finale, sung by both couples, lacking in clarity and in the heightened emotion he needed here:

> Schatten zu werfen,
> beide erwählt,
> beide in prüfenden
> Flammen gestählt.
> Schwelle des Todes nah,
> gemordet, zu morden
> seligen Kindern
> Müttern geworden. (*DV* 378)

On the other hand, the chorus of the unborn children, which follows this song and ends the opera, beautifully expresses the meaning of this opera:

> Vater, dir drohet nichts
> siehe, es schwindet schon
> Mutter, das Ängstliche,
> das euch beirrte.
> Wäre denn je ein Fest,
> wären nicht insgeheim
> wir die Geladenen,
> wir auch die Wirte. (378)

The deep structure of Hofmannsthal's texts was not always understood by Strauss, but he always perceived the surface structure, the sound and syntax of the poetry, as beautiful. He wrote to his librettist several times that beautiful words could compensate him for lack of action; and in such cases, he quite consciously composed along the surface. Numerous examples could be cited; three mentioned by Strauss (*Betrachtungen und Erinnerungen* 170) are the Act III trio in *Der Rosenkavalier*, the duets in *Arabella*, and the final lines of *Die Ägyptische Helena*. One excerpt from these words that so inspired the composer is a part of the love duet between Arabella and Mandryka in Act II:

> ARABELLA: Der Richtige, wenns einen gibt für mich,
> der wird auf einmal da sein,
> und wird mich anschauen und ich ihn
> und keine Winkelzüge werden sein und keine Fragen,
> nein, alles hell und offen, wie ein lichter Fluß, auf dem die Sonne
> blitzt!

> MANDRYKA: So fließt die helle stille Donau mir beim Haus vorbei,
> und hat mir dich gebracht! Du Allerschönste!
> Und heute Abend noch, vor Schlafenszeit —
> wärst du ein Mädchen aus der Dörfer einem meinigen,

> du müßtest mir zum Brunnen gehen hinter deines Vaters Haus
> und klares Wasser schöpfen einen Becher voll
> und mir ihn reichen vor der Schwelle, daß ich dein Verlobter bin
> vor Gott
> und vor den Menschen, meine Allerschönste! (546–47)

Hofmannsthal saw expression as the proper goal of language in drama, and also essential to opera. He was a master of verbal nuance, both of sound and sense. A short example of such nuance is Zerbinetta's rondo, which Hofmannsthal himself praised as a jewel of song-writing. Within the strict limits of the rondo form, predetermined by Strauss, Hofmannsthal succeeds in expressing the central problem of *Ariadne auf Naxos*, the notion of *Treue*:

> Als ein Gott kam jeder gegangen,
> Und sein Schritt schon machte mich stumm,
> Küßte er mir Stirn und Wangen,
> War ich von dem Gott gefangen
> Und gewandelt um und um!
> Als ein Gott kam jeder gegangen,
> Jeder wandelte mich um,
> Küßte er mir Mund und Wangen,
> Hingegeben war ich stumm!
> Hingegeben war ich stumm!
> Hingegeben war ich stumm!
> Kam der neue Gott gegangen,
> Hingegeben war ich stumm! (207–8)

Early in the collaboration he realized that the sense had to be sacrificed to a considerable extent in opera, but that the sound — the sonority of the words, their rhythmic-metric scheme, their tone color — was important for the composer, and for the opera. Hofmannsthal's changing attitudes toward Strauss's alterations in the verbal texts of the operas reflect his developing self-awareness as librettist. He shortened or expanded his texts to suit Strauss's needs, and rarely insisted that a particular phrase or passage be retained. When he did so, it was almost always for the sake of dramatic clarity, not for the sake of his poetry, for he knew that the dramatic action in opera is essentially carried by music.

This collaboration was extraordinary not only in the number and diversity of its products, but also in the relationship of the two artists who, despite their differences in temperament and aesthetic sensibilities, were able to put their art before personal considerations, and to seek excellence together. On the occasion of Strauss's sixtieth birthday on June 4, 1924, Hofmannsthal expressed his gratitude for the composer's unfailing support, discernment, and creative response to his librettist's efforts: "Hiermit haben Sie mich gelohnt, soweit ein Künstler einen anderen lohnen kann" (*Bw* 517). In his letter to Hofmannsthal's wife on July 16, 1929, the day after the poet's sudden death, Strauss expressed his deep appreciation and affection for his friend and collaborator:

> Noch nie hat ein Musiker einen solchen Helfer und Förderer gefunden — Niemand wird ihn mir und der Musikwelt ersetzen! Die Nachwelt wird ihm das Denkmal setzen, das seiner würdig ist, das er in meinem Herzen immer besessen — unauslöschliche Dankbarkeit in treuestem Freundesherzen wird die Empfindung sein, die ich in Bewunderung ihm bis an mein Lebensende bewahren will. (*Bw* 698)

Notes

[1] For a more detailed discussion of the collaboration, see Joanna Bottenberg, *Shared Creation: Words and Music in the Hofmannsthal-Strauss Operas*, German Studies in Canada, vol. 6, ed. Manfred Kuxdorf (Frankfurt am Main: Peter Lang, 1996). The following comments are excerpted from pages 307–38 of this book.

Works Cited

Bottenberg, Joanna. *Shared Creation: Words and Music in the Hofmannsthal-Strauss Operas*. German Studies in Canada 6. Ed. Manfred Kuxdorf. Frankfurt am Main: Peter Lang, 1996.

Hofmannsthal, Hugo von. "Einleitung zum Vorabdruck." *Neue Freie Presse* 26 Mar. 1912.

———. *Hugo von Hofmannsthal-Carl Burckhardt: Briefwechsel*. Ed. Carl J. Burckhardt. Frankfurt am Main: S. Fischer, 1956.

———. *Hugo von Hofmannsthal-Harry Graf Kessler: Briefwechsel*. Ed. Hilde Burger. Frankfurt am Main: Insel, 1968.

———. *Hugo von Hofmannsthal-Rudolf Pannwitz: Briefwechsel 1907–1926*. Ed. Gerhard Schuster. Frankfurt am Main: S. Fischer, 1993. (Abbreviated as *HvH-RP*)

Strauss, Richard. *Betrachtungen und Erinnerungen*. 3rd ed. Ed. Willi Schuh. Zurich: Atlantis, 1981.

———. *Richard Strauss-Hugo von Hofmannsthal: Briefwechsel*, 4th ed. Ed. Willi Schuh. Zurich: Atlantis, 1970. [Abbreviated as *Bw*]

W. E. YATES

Hofmannsthal's Comedies

HOFMANNSTHAL WAS NOT one of those playwrights who come to comedy through practical experience of work in the theater; rather, it could almost be said that his absorption with the theater grew organically together with his conception of comedy. This was multifaceted and developed gradually, as his thematic material developed. He did not write easily; he left far more plans than completed comedies, and his comic masterpiece, *Der Schwierige* (1920, first publication in book form 1921), had a gestation period of over a decade. There is a considerable body of interpretative literature devoted to the comedies, the main critical cruxes having been most subtly summarized by Hans-Albrecht Koch. But there is no disagreement about the fact that his work in the comic mode culminates in two major plays, *Der Schwierige* and *Der Unbestechliche* (1956, no translation published), both of which were performed after the end of the First World War — the former directed by Kurt Stieler in the Residenztheater in Munich in November 1921, the latter by Rudolf Beer in the Raimundtheater in Vienna in March 1923. It is on these two comedies and the thematic threads developed in them that the present essay will chiefly concentrate.[1]

When Hofmannsthal was writing his early lyric dramas, the ideal form he envisaged was, so he told Marie Herzfeld in August 1892, a verse *proverbe* (used in Musset's sense, implying graceful delicacy of poetic sentiment) with a moral, "das Proverb in Versen mit einer Moral" (*Briefe 1890–1901* 62). In a brief outline that he wrote in 1921 for the critic Max Pirker on the subject of his dramatic work ("H. als Theaterdichter"), he traced the roots of his comedies back to the first of the short verse dramas, *Gestern* (1891, no translation published):

> Die Reihe der Lustspiele: "Gestern" als Embryo des poetisierten Gesellschaftslustspiels; "Der Abenteurer und die Sängerin," desgleichen auf höherem Niveau. Erster Versuch "Silvia im 'Stern'" (1907), unvollendet [. . .]. Sodann "Cristinas Heimreise" (1908–1909), "Rosenkavalier" (1910); "Der Schwierige" (1920). Dazwischen Pläne und Entwürfe zahlreich. [. . .] (*RA II* 131).

Der Abenteurer und die Sängerin (no translation published) — based on an episode from the memoirs of Casanova — was one of three short plays that he published together in 1899 under the title *Theater in Versen*. The collective title, introducing a specifically theatrical dimension, is clearly programmatic. One of the plays included, *Die Frau im Fenster* (translated as *Madonna Dianora*, 1916), which is partly in prose, had indeed provided Hofmannsthal with his first theatrical premiere, a matinee at Otto Brahm's Deutsches Theater in Berlin in May 1898; the following March the other two, *Die Hochzeit der Sobeide* (*The Marriage of Sobeide*, 1920) and *Der Abenteurer und die Sängerin*, were performed at the Deutsches Theater and simultaneously at the Burgtheater in Vienna. It is well known that by about 1900, dissatisfied with the predominantly lyrical idiom of his early work, Hofmannsthal resolved to devote himself to more socially oriented forms of writing. One reason for this was that he was committed to an element of social responsibility in art. This idea is most clearly developed in the lecture "Der Dichter und diese Zeit" which he delivered in various German cities in December 1906 and published the following year. The whole continuity of a culture essentially depends on those few who have creatively shaped its language; therefore the creative writer has a responsibility toward the generality of people, and specifically to exercise a kind of cultural "leadership" (*RAI* 55–67). This concern for the cultural responsibility of the artist intensified Hofmannsthal's interest in the theater as the most "social" of art forms: in it the human interaction of which drama is made is enacted before an audience functioning in effect as a microcosm of the whole community.

He always thought of his plays as belonging in the Burgtheater, the historic court theater, though in the event no fewer than nineteen of his plays were produced not there but at the Deutsches Theater in Berlin, under the direction of his long-time collaborator Max Reinhardt, the Austrian-born theater director who succeeded Brahm at the Berlin theater in 1905. The model of comedy that Hofmannsthal — like his contemporary Arthur Schnitzler — drew from the Burgtheater was a polished comedy of manners (*Konversationsstück*), whose classic representative was the nineteenth-century Viennese playwright Eduard von Bauernfeld. Bauernfeld had furnished the Burgtheater with a succession of comedies from the 1830s onwards; a few of them were, indeed, still performed there in the 1890s. His plays, characteristically recapturing the conversation of elegant society, were a natural model for aspiring dramatists at the end of the century. Hofmannsthal would make this very point about Schnitzler in 1922 in the first of his "Vienna Letters" in *The Dial,* explicitly pointing to the connection with the *Konversati-*

onsstück, "the drama of conversation as it was nurtured in the Burgtheater [. . .] in the years between 1860 and 1890," when the genre "was just at its height on this stage."[2] He himself wrote an appreciative essay on Bauernfeld in 1893 after the appearance of a selection of posthumous dramatic texts (*RAI* 185–89), and his debt can be seen throughout his oeuvre from the fragment *Silvia im "Stern"* (fragments published 1905 and 1909, first full edition 1959) onwards — at its strongest in *Der Schwierige*.

The Burgtheater also provided French models of high comedy, especially in the works of Molière. These were familiar territory to Hofmannsthal, who was a French specialist *manqué* (he had written a doctoral dissertation on the language of the poets of the *Pléiade* and subsequently a post doctoral thesis on Victor Hugo, with a view to becoming a recognized university lecturer — a plan he abandoned only in 1902). But in the summer of 1908, a year after the publication of "Der Dichter und diese Zeit," he paid a short visit to Paris, which included visits to the Comédie Française, and this confirmed his admiration of Molière's work; in a letter to Kessler of September 4 1908, he expressed his admiration for it as the supreme achievement in the comic genre — the equivalent to the supremacy of Shakespeare within the contrasting conventions of English theater (193). His reading of comic literature was international, ranging from Goldoni to the dialect comedy of the Viennese satirist Nestroy,[3] but Molière remained his classic model, and by January 1911 he was writing to his father not only of Molière's historic importance for the development of modern comedy but also of his own hope that he would contribute to establishing Molière fully on the German stage in new prose translations.[4] That was shortly before the premiere of *Der Rosenkavalier* (January 26, 1911; published 1911, libretto translated as *The Rose-Bearer*, 1912), which contains various motifs drawn from Molière, notably from *Monsieur de Pourceaugnac*, *Le Médecin malgré lui*, and *Le Bourgeois gentilhomme*. The year after that he again defined Molière's classic status as the dramatist in whom all the elements of comedy are united: "Molière vereinigt die Elemente des Komischen" (*RAIII* 512–13); and in the five years 1912 to 1916 he read his works intensively. One product was a free reworking of *Les Fâcheux* entitled *Die Lästigen* (1917); another was his translation of *Le Bourgeois gentilhomme*, which was first performed in Berlin (at the Deutsches Theater) in April 1918, the title part being played by the outstanding Viennese comic actor of the time, Max Pallenberg. Later, when he came to composing *Der Unbestechliche*, he would again draw inspiration from a French model, in this case Beaumarchais's *Le mariage de Figaro* — the figure of the unsubmissive servant Figaro providing the basis for Hofmannsthal's servant Theodor, another role created by Pallenberg.

In the period around 1907 to 1909, a number of factors came together significantly in Hofmannsthal's work: his conviction of the cultural responsibility of the artist to the wider community, a determination to meet the demands of practical theater, "die Erfüllung traditioneller theatralischer Forderung" (*RAII* 130), and his interest in French comedy and Burgtheater tradition as providing traditional models. He was now concerned not only to explore the moral growth of individual characters[5] but also to relate his material to the society it was rooted in, and comedy as well as the morality play (while revising *Cristinas Heimreise* [1910; translated as *Cristina's Journey Home*, 1916] he was also working on *Jedermann* [1911]) would serve him as vehicles for treating the concerns of his own age. Comedy — taking this to include his comic libretti, from *Der Rosenkavalier* to *Arabella* (1933) — was to prove the more satisfactory because of the subtlety it allowed in representing nuances of interaction between individuals in a recognizable social setting. In Hofmannsthal's adoption of traditional comedy as a preferred medium, then, his engagement with the theater was inseparably linked to his engagement with social reality. It is this latter feature that is uppermost in his much-quoted later formulation "das *erreichte Soziale: die Komödien*" (*RAIII* 611).

Traditionalist that he was, he readily took over the familiar scheme of comedy, an action featuring complications in a love intrigue and an orthodox happy ending bringing the union of at least one pair of lovers. The Casanova type who figures in numerous variants in Schnitzler's work and who continued to be adopted by other Viennese playwrights of Hofmannsthal's generation (for example, Raoul Auernheimer's *Casanova in Wien*, 1924) plays a central role in prewar works such as *Cristinas Heimreise* and also *Der Rosenkavalier*, where Baron Ochs is a grotesque caricature of the immoral philanderer. *Der Rosenkavalier* proved something of an aberration; Octavian's deception of Ochs in his disguise as "Mariandel" in Act I, the crude sexism Ochs displays toward Sophie in Act II, and the rough and tumble farce of the scene in the inn in Act III are all alien to the decorous tone Hofmannsthal would cultivate in his later prose comedies. He himself was well aware of the development in his work in comic form, tracing a line from *Die Abenteurer und die Sängerin* to *Der Schwierige*, on which he was working when he wrote to Pannwitz:

> [. . .] für die nächste Phase ist es die Comödie, in der ich mich geben u[nd] mich finden muss, in ihr kann ich meine Elemente zusammenfassen [. . .] Der "Abenteurer" u[nd] der "Rosencavalier" (eine leicht-

sinnige Improvisation) deuten in dieser Richtung, Cristinas Heimreise
ist der erste zum Teil misslungene Versuch [. . .] (*SW12* 476–77)

Cristinas Heimreise was a "failure" critically, a victim of the reviewers'
fixed image of Hofmannsthal as a supposedly decadent aesthete, but
also artistically.[6] In his best comic work Hofmannsthal was to achieve a
psychological and linguistic subtlety rooted in a social background
imagined in depth and in detail; this is still missing from the stylized
characterization centering on the contrast between the seducer Flo-
rindo and the good-hearted ship's captain Tomaso, with whom Cristina
is finally united. After a Berlin production in 1926 he was content to
accept Leopold von Andrian's description of the work as an "uneigent-
liches Theaterstück" (*SW11* 835–36). As Bennett observes, Tomaso
represents the first step in Hofmannsthal's development of a new type
of adventurer, capable of finding his way to the stability of marriage;
but the development would come to fruition only in *Der Schwierige*
(Bennett 101). Hence the considerable formal problems Hofmannsthal
encountered in this transitional stage in shaping his material to a satisfactory dénouement; this is especially clear in the various stages of his
treatment of the *Cristinas Heimreise* material, which underwent a series
of revisions and reworkings.[7] The difficulty is perhaps not wholly solved
even in his later work: *Der Schwierige*, after all, ends with the lovers,
Hans Karl Bühl and Helene Altenwyl, having disappeared from view,
Der Unbestechliche with a sudden repentance on the part of the erring
husband that has not convinced all commentators as being convincingly
motivated. But in these plays Hofmannsthal presents more many-sided
characters; here he tackles issues related to the moral development of
the individual within a more complex social setting, and is therefore
able to bring the lovers together in marriage by way of a more complex
process. The moralist in him was concerned precisely to stress the fun
damental seriousness of the idea of marriage in his mature comedies:
"Es ist alles was ich davon denke in meinen Lustspielen gesagt, oft in
einer mit Willen versteckten und beinahe leichtfertigen Weise" (*Hof-
mannsthal-Burckhardt* 226, letter of September 10, 1926). But he was
congenitally inclined to schematize his own work, nudging his readers
into readings that he formulated long after the work concerned was
composed. While planning *Der Unbestechliche* he referred to it not as a
moralizing work but using such generic terms as "Gesellschaftslustspiel" and "Gesellschaftscomödie" (*SW13* 133, 149) — suggesting
links with the traditional comedy of manners but also implying a conscious thematic thrust, comedy about social relations, social values,
even about society itself. That is, the terms do not just describe the
tone of the comedy but point to its import as well. In a similar double

sense he would also use the terms "Gesellschaftscomödie" and "Gesell-schaftslustspiel" about *Der Schwierige*: the former, apparently drawn from a conversation with Reinhardt, comes in one of his earliest notes about the play, made in December 1909, and again in September and October 1917, during his work on the first act, in letters to Auern-heimer, Pannwitz, and Andrian;[8] "Gesellschaftslustspiel" on November 2, 1919, in a letter to Schnitzler. In that case the term reflects his awareness that the play depicts a specific — vanishing — society, that of the Austrian aristocracy (*SW12* 490); that is, the traditional form is consciously chosen to reflect his traditionalist conception of the old or-der under threat after the war.

But in treating current social, cultural and even political concerns, his aim in both plays was to do so with a deceptive lightness of touch. A much-quoted aphorism sums up his artistic intentions: "Die Tiefe muß man verstecken. Wo? An der Oberfläche" (*RAIII* 268). To give artistic form to profundity, you have to conceal it — and best of all, on the surface; that is, what seems superficial may hide ideas and feelings of depth. Nor was this mere theory: one of the most significant obser-vations in Hofmannsthal's letters from the time when he was compos-ing *Der Schwierige* is one in a letter to Pannwitz written on November 26, 1919: "An dem Lustspiel bessere ich beständig, es noch leichter, oberflächlicher zu machen" (*SW12* 491).

Significantly the aphorism about surface lightness as a means of "con-cealing" profundity appeared in 1922, the very year in which he wrote *Der Unbestechliche*, in the volume entitled *Buch der Freunde* (1922, 1929). Another aphoristic note, drawn from the Romantic poet Novalis, that he quoted in a short 1921 essay entitled "Die Ironie der Dinge," runs: "Nach einem unglücklichen Krieg müssen Komödien geschrieben werden" (*RAII* 138). Comedy, he explains, presents a world in disarray, a world in which the individual character is confronted with a complex of topsy-turvy values; that is just what war does also, as the confusion of post-1918 Europe has illustrated. The result is a network of irony, which can be expressed artistically only in irony; hence the development of "Romantic irony" in reaction to the French Revolution and the upheav-als of the Napoleonic period:

> [. . .] Die wirkliche Komödie setzt ihre Individuen in ein tausend-fach verhäkeltes Verhältnis zur Welt, sie setzt alles in ein Verhältnis zu allem und damit alles in ein Verhältnis der Ironie. Ganz so verfährt der Krieg, der über uns alle gekommen ist, und dem wir bis heute nicht entkommen sind, ja vielleicht noch zwanzig Jahre nicht entkommen werden. [. . .]

Mit alldem befinden wir uns ganz und gar im Element der Komödie — oder vielmehr in einem Element so allseitiger Ironie, wie keine
Komödie der Welt es aufweist, es sei denn die Komödie des Aristo-
phanes; und auch diese ist während eines für die Vaterstadt des Dichters höchst unglücklichen, ihr Schicksal besiegelnden Krieges
entstanden. [. . .]

Für alle diese Dinge waren die Dichter empfindlich, die vor hun-
dert Jahren da waren, und ganz natürlich, sie hatten die französische
Umwälzung und die napoleonische Zeit durchleben müssen, sowie
wir diese jetzigen Krisen durchzuleben haben. Darum machten sie aus
der Ironie ein Grundelement ihrer Lebens- und Kunstgesinnung und
nannten sie die "romantische Ironie." [*RAII* 138, 140–41]

Comedy works by achieving an effect of distance, which allows the dis-
passionate effect of ironic objectivity; the artistic imagination is drawn to
comedy as the supreme medium in which to capture that distance and to
treat cultural and political issues of immense urgency with the "lightness"
that alone brings them into manageable scale. Hofmannsthal's starting
point, it is clear, is still not just political events, but the responsibility of
the artistic temperament in relation to such events. This is reflected in
both the major comedies, which reflect in ironic mode his imaginative
engagement with an age hostile to the values he most cherished.

In the war he had come to see the whole world order as disintegrating; he became ever more convinced that the Catholic Austria to
which he belonged had a cultural mission as a repository of traditional
values that were under threat throughout Europe, first from the Bolshevik revolution in Russia and, after the war, from the disintegration
of the multi-national Habsburg Empire. He remained committed to
the idea of a cosmopolitan "conservative revolution." This was a term
that was in currency in the early 1920s and was adopted by Hofmannsthal in the sense of a cultural restoration, a preservation of humane internationalist standards[9] — a process which is summed up at
the end of the address that he gave at the University of Munich in
1927 under the title "Das Schrifttum als geistiger Raum der Nation."
This cultural concern, which underlay his involvement in the Salzburg
Festival, informs much of the dramatic writing of his last years. The
mature comedies *Der Schwierige* (first planned in 1909 but not completed until 1920/21) and *Der Unbestechliche* both reflect a coming
together of this engagement with political and cultural circumstances
and his continued fascination with the artistic imagination.

The two central characters, the "difficult" Viennese aristocrat Hans
Karl Bühl and the "incorruptible" Bohemian servant Theodor, are not
obvious representatives of the artistic imagination: neither of them is a

creative artist, and both are firmly embedded in a social setting where concern seems on the surface to center on traditional comic issues, master-servant relationships and relations between the sexes. But returning from the front at the age of nearly forty with a new sense of the meaning of human life, Hans Karl has the genuine artist's perception that life is shaped by language: "Durchs Reden kommt ja alles auf der Welt zustande" (*DIV* 403). The artistic element in his temperament is also suggested by a delicate sensitivity to nuance that he shares with Helene Altenwyl. (At one point Hofmannsthal seriously considered calling the play not *Der Schwierige* but *Die Schwierigen* [*SW12* 229–30]). Hans Karl's difficulties in committing himself to a social engagement or to making a speech in a parliamentary debate are an equivalent to the traditional difficulty of artist-figures, from Goethe's Tasso to the characters of Hofmannsthal's own lyric dramas, in accommodating themselves to social responsibility.

But in Hans Karl's case the problem is specifically linked to his sensitivity to language. However simply he believes that he sees things, he cannot translate this clarity of understanding in correspondingly clear expression. Thus he is incapable of explaining to his elder sister Crescence why he is unwilling to attend the soirée at the Altenwyls' home; later he is equally incapable of putting into words why he is withdrawing his premature farewell from Helene and apologizing to her: "Ich drück' mich elend aus, aber meine Gedanken darüber sind mir ganz klar" (*DIV* 427).

The liveliness of his imaginative sensibility is manifest in the dialogue with Helene in Act II that is widely recognized as a key passage in the play,[10] in which he explains his admiring appreciation of the silent mime of the circus clown Furlani. At the soirée which Crescence has persuaded him to attend in order to plead for Helene's hand on behalf of her son Stani, he tells Helene of his admiration for Furlani's act, which consists in creating confusion on all sides, but always with style and elegance — something of the feeling we have about Hans Karl himself:

> Er outriert nie, er karikiert auch nie. Er spielt seine Rolle: er ist der, der alle begreifen, der allen helfen möchte und dabei alles in die größte Konfusion bringt. [. . .] Und dabei behält er eine Elegance, eine Diskretion, man merkt, daß er sich selbst und alles, was auf der Welt ist, respektiert, er bringt alles durcheinander, wie Kraut und Rüben; wo er hingeht, geht alles drunter und drüber, und dabei möchte man rufen: "Er hat ja recht!" (378)

He has told Crescence explicitly that he derives more pleasure from Furlani's mime than from the cleverest conversation: "Mich unterhält er viel mehr als die gescheiteste Konversation von Gott weiß wem" (373). His mistrust of language, reflected in his characteristic reticence, is based on the inexpressible quality of significant experience: precisely in a life in which "everything comes about as a result of speech," what ultimately matters is "inexpressible": "[. . .] in einem Leben, wo doch schließlich alles auf die letzte unaussprechliche Nuance ankommt" (403). The shortcomings of language as a medium of communication are given a purely comic illustration in Hans Karl's telephone conversation with Adolf Hechingen (367), in which a series of trivial physical mishearings stand for deeper failures of communication. At the deeper level, Hans Karl's insights are clearly related to those of the fictional Lord Chandos, who seeks a means of self-expression other than conceptual language, "eine Sprache, von deren Worten mir auch nicht eines bekannt ist" (*Erz* 472), and Furlani's silent mime is a comic correlative of what, reflecting on *Ein Brief* (1902), Hofmannsthal termed "der Anstand des Schweigens" (*RAIII* 601). Hofmannsthal himself linked the two works specifically in respect of their treatment of language, defining "die Rede als soziales Element, als *das* soziale Element" and pointing in this context to threads running throughout his work, "zu dem Lord Chandos des 'Briefes' und zu dem 'Schwierigen'" (*RAIII* 615); in a carefully formulated letter of February 14, 1921, to his fellow-dramatist Anton Wildgans (who had just been appointed director of the Burgtheater), he again relates his comedy in respect of the linguistic problem to *Ein Brief* (*SW12* 504).

Moreover, Hans Karl suffers the perennial fate of the creative artist: those around him impose on his utterances their own cut-and-dried interpretation, reducing them to what they believe to be their real gist, even if this means contradicting what he is actually saying. In the first act, Crescence tells him outright: "Wenn du sagst, im allgemeinen, so meinst du was Spezielles" (338). Then the maid Agathe, dismissing his explanation of a letter — apparently about the sanctity of marriage — that he wrote to her mistress Antoinette from the field hospital, insists: "Auf die Worte kommt's nicht an. Aber den Sinn haben wir gut herausbekommen" (347). And his nephew Stani rejects out of hand the idea that Antoinette's husband Hechingen should take literally Hans Karl's protestations of friendship: "Pardon, Onkel Kari, bei dir darf man nichts wörtlich nehmen" (358). In these circumstances it is not just attendance at a soirée that is bound, as he puts it to Crescence, to be "ein unentwirrbarer Knäuel von Mißverständnissen" (337).

In treating the shortcomings of language as a vehicle of expression, *Der Schwierige* reverts to one of Hofmannsthal's recurrent themes. If "Ein Brief," once assumed to be a confessional or autobiographical document, is now recognized as being a fictional exploration, in a specific Renaissance setting, of the fundamental problem of language for the literary artist, so too the contrast Hans Karl makes in his conversation with Helene between the inadequacy of his expression and the internal clarity of his thoughts in effect restates the artist's perennial struggle to translate a perception or vision or idea into words — a multi-layered process of the imagination that makes the would-be intellectuals in the play such as the self-important academic Brücke or the gushing Countess Edine look ridiculously pretentious.

The servant Theodor in *Der Unbestechliche*, who speaks a comically stiff German, a mixture of Slav idiom and awkward formality, is on the surface a still more unlikely representative of the artistic imagination. The plot is that of a light-hearted moral comedy, based on the familiar theme of infidelity. Before his marriage Count Jaromir has lived what Theodor calls a "ein Junggesellenleben [. . .] von einer beispiellosen Frivolität und eiskalten Selbstsucht" (*DIV* 469). Married but not reformed, he is now actively planning adultery under the nose of his wife and family, inviting to the estate in Lower Austria where the play is set two old flames, Melanie Galattis and Marie am Rain. This constitutes an offence not just against moral and social laws — "Das spricht ja Hohn allen göttlichen und menschlichen Gesetzlichkeiten" (470) — but also against the standards which the servant Theodor represents, and is thus in Theodor's eyes a personal slight: "das ganze Leben, das er geführt hat, war eine fortgesetzte Beleidigung meiner Person" (468). The first four acts conform to a traditional pattern of comedy, with the servant outwitting his master. Jaromir's responsibilities are symbolized in his young son, also called Jaromir, who first articulates the news that Theodor is fed up with what he calls "das Ganze": "Das Ganze paßt ihm nicht" (464–65). Scenes featuring the child are strategically placed at the beginning of Acts II and III and the end of Act IV, so that in effect they frame the episodes with Melanie and Marie.[11] The final act then brings Jaromir's moral awakening in response to a direct appeal from Anna, his loving wife.

The action is set in 1912, not long before the outbreak of the First World War (just as *Le mariage de Figaro* takes place shortly before the French Revolution); whereas the society of *Der Schwierige*, complete with an Upper House of parliament that did not in fact meet after 1919, seems to project a continuation of the old order in the post-war world, the society portrayed in *Der Unbestechliche* is on the brink of disintegration, the fragility of its authority implicit in the threat to moral order represented by Jaromir's philandering intentions.

The title *Der Unbestechliche* has obvious revolutionary overtones, suggesting specifically an echo of the French Revolution, when the "incorruptible" Robespierre, who was known for his rigid rectitude, ushered in the Reign of Terror. As his preparatory notes (*SW13* 224) show, Hofmannsthal was well aware of the historical overtones, but also of the differences.[12] Theodor may rail against the privilege his master enjoys, most eloquently in his long tirade to the maid Hermine at the end of Act IV (510), but far from being disruptive, his activity leads to a restoration of domestic order. The Robespierre echo in the title points ironically to a revolutionary quality in his take-over of power within the household, but his is a revolution designed not to upset the order but to restore it — an equivalent on the level of formal social comedy to the idea of "conservative revolution." Written at the height of Hofmannsthal's involvement with the Salzburg Festival, *Der Unbestechliche* reflects the cultural traditionalism informing his preoccupation with the cultural plight of post-war Europe. He had been acutely conscious of the dangers inherent in the disintegration of the Austro-Hungarian monarchy while the war was still in progress, expressing his fears most gloomily in July 1917 in a letter to Eberhard von Bodenhausen in which he analyses "die eigentliche Agonie des tausendjährigen heiligen römischen Reiches deutscher Nation" and foresees the "cataclysmic" effects that would follow from the demise of what he calls "die einzige Institution, die auf Höheres als auf Macht u[nd] Bestand und Selbstbehauptung gestellt war" (*Briefe der Freundschaft* 235–36). Events would confirm his worst fears: ten years after the end of the war he wrote to a politician friend, Josef Redlich, that the break-up of the monarchy was not just a political disaster: it had so uprooted the stable order of things that, as he put it, his very "existence" as an imaginative writer was called into question by the collapse: "[. . .] weil mein eigenes dichterisches Dasein in diesem Zusammensturz fragwürdig geworden ist" (*Hofmannsthal-Redlich* 116). The artist, then, is existentially endangered by the modern world; the artist, too, in keeping with Hofmannsthal's long-held view of the artist's responsibility for "leadership," is the proper revolutionary — now in the sense of the "conservative revolution."

Jaromir in *Der Unbestechliche* is, as it happens, a writer, and was so conceived in Hofmannsthal's very first notes when he was planning the play in August 1920 (*SW13* 149–50). He has, we quickly learn, a shallow literary reputation: that is, he is not a true artist, but a sham — a modern sham. His published work consists of no more than indiscretions; specifically, he has made his affair with Marie am Rain the subject of a sensationalist *roman à clef*, which Theodor derides as "ein[en] sogenannten Schlüsselroman ohne einen literarischen Wert" (469). In Act II, Theodor scares Melanie Galattis by talking of diary notes on which Jaromir's next novel will be based, notes that are fluttering through

Jaromir's open window as he speaks. Hermine then hides them among Melanie's writing-things, and when in Act IV Melanie reads them they only confirm that Jaromir is planning to base his next novel on his affair with her. Her departure with the notes for the novel in her case brings together the two linked strands of the action, Jaromir's immorality and his writing; his reform in the final act is signaled not just by his discovering his true love for his wife, but also by his giving up any thought of completing the novel. First he is frantic to find the manuscript, and says it is indispensable to him (517); but after his conversion he forbids Anna to go on looking for it and condemns it as "ein abscheuliches Überbleibsel aus meiner zu langen Junggesellenzeit" (520).

Theodor's role in this reflects his function as a counterweight. Again it is the four-year-old child who provides the interpretative key, in that he believes Theodor is a magician. This motif comes up first at the end of the sixth scene of Act I (463), then at the beginning of the ninth scene (465), and again at the very end of Act IV, when Theodor is speaking to the child: "Wie sagt der Zauberer zu dem Kinde?" (512). In Hofmannsthal's work, from his early poems onwards, "magic" is repeatedly used as a metaphor for *art*. [13] Anna may loyally see Jaromir as a "Phantasiemensch" (462), a man of imagination, but the one who succeeds in stimulating the imagination of the child is Theodor; it is he who, like the artist, has "magical" powers. In routing the pseudo-novelist Jaromir, he brings about a "conservative revolution" in the household he serves; the restoration of moral order on the domestic front stands suggestively for the restoration of a lost political and social order.

Hofmannsthal scholars have to be watchfully skeptical toward his determination to impose an interpretative shape on his own development, whether in the abstractions about human development in his self-analytical notes *Ad me ipsum*, written from 1916 onwards (published posthumously in 1931), or in his association of his writing with a South German and Austrian "Baroque" heritage. To see *Der Schwierige* and *Der Unbestechliche* in those terms, concentrating principally on the moral development of Hans Karl and Jaromir, runs the risk of reducing them to a lifeless formula and understates the extent to which both plays engage in the wider problems of their time. In the case of *Der Schwierige*, the whole structure of the society depicted had been revolutionized between the conception of the play and its completion. Despite the dates mentioned in the text, there is no strong case for arguing that in the finished work the action is set during the war. [14] Hofmannsthal himself told Karl Zeiss in the summer of 1918 that it is based on the assumption that the war is over (*SW12* 484). Although this statement predates the completion of the text, the lack both of uniforms and of any allusion to action still in progress confirms that he was striving to evoke *not* a wartime mood but rather the survival in the post-war period of a society that by then no longer existed. In short, the depiction of aristocratic society is consciously unrealistic, indeed idealized, and this did not escape contemporary reviewers. Felix Salten, for example, reviewing Reinhardt's 1924 production at the Theater in der Josefstadt, was one who noted that there was no reflection at all of the social revolution to come.[15] To the extent that an idealized society is made to stand for certain qualities amid the changes threatened in the post-war world, the process is overtly mythopoeic.

In that framework, the rivalry between Hans Karl and Neuhoff for the hand of Helene, and indeed for the affections of Antoinette, takes on a wider significance. The construction of *Der Schwierige* — flirtation focused on Antoinette, proposals of marriage on Helene — systematically contrasts Hans Karl with his nephew Stani and the Prussian Neuhoff. Hans Karl has had an affair with Antoinette, Stani is currently having an affair with her, Neuhoff attempts to start an affair with her; Stani decides to marry Helene, Neuhoff in his would-be masterful way proposes marriage to her, Hans Karl actually becomes engaged to her. The strand of the plot leading to the disappointment of the naively unsubtle Stani enacts a defeat of the up-and-coming younger generation by the older generation — a defeat paralleled by the dismissal of the scheming new servant Vinzenz who has planned to take over the authority in Hans Karl's household of the trusted older servant Lukas.

What Neuhoff self-importantly perceives as his "duel" with Hans Karl over Helene — "Es war ein Zweikampf zwischen mir und ihm, ein Zweikampf um Sie!" (402) — amounts to a re-run, on the personal level, of a national rivalry, a political contrast projected on the comic action. His traditionalist manners have beaten off the claims of the younger generation as represented by Stani within his own family and by the emblematically named Neuhoff: the "duel" ends with Hans Karl winning the day, as first Helene and then Antoinette summarily rebuff Neuhoff's advances. That this is not mere chance is prefigured in the key passage in which Hans Karl defines Furlani's act:

> Aber das, was der Furlani macht, ist noch um eine ganze Stufe höher, als was alle andern tun. Alle andern lassen sich von einer Absicht leiten und schauen nicht rechts und nicht links, ja, sie atmen kaum, bis sie ihre Absicht erreicht haben: darin besteht eben ihr Trick. Er aber tut scheinbar nichts mit Absicht — er geht immer nur auf die Absicht der andern ein. (379)

Furlani is "seemingly" not set on a specific goal, but it is an act: in fact he achieves his aim with the unruffled elegance and discretion that

Hans Karl admires in him. So too Hans Karl's victory over Neuhoff is carried off with an unobtrusive elegance, an apparently effortless artistry, that deceives the eye — not least Neuhoff's eye. Translated into the terms of political rivalry between Austria and Germany, it is course fanciful wishful thinking, part of the time-warp in which the play is set: a victory of supposedly traditional Austrian characteristics of discretion and subtlety over supposedly North German characteristics of brash pushiness which the post-war world would never see.

Both Hans Karl and Jaromir belong to the familiar type of the elegant philanderer. In conformity with universal comic tradition, the action of both plays turns on flirtation and marriage; but as in all the best comedies, in each case the action has a representative or symbolical force. What occurs on the surface serves to suggest wider issues. Hofmannsthal uses the union of lovers, the traditional ending of comedy, to impose a moral framework, a reaffirmation of moral order.

There are indeed commentators who interpret this as the main thrust of the plays, seeing Hans Karl's central concern in his extolling of marriage to Antoinette (394–95) and taking literally the comically heavy-handed self-perception of Theodor (another emblematically named character) as the agent of a higher power.[16] But while the moral dimension is more subtly suggested than in *Cristinas Heimreise*, where the heroine simply realizes "Gut ist die Ehe" (*DIV* 209), the motif is still on the surface, and in both plays the ending moves our attention away from the marriage theme (Hans Karl's and Helene's absence, Theodor's pursuit of Hermine). Much more far-reaching are the resonances in terms of political and cultural history.

The mythopoeic implications are not spelled out on the surface; but the defensive concern, with threatened values associated with a nostalgically presented Austrian aristocracy, clearly contributed to the mixed reception that both plays have encountered. This is especially obvious in the case of *Der Unbestechliche*, in that Beer's original production failed in Berlin precisely because it was felt to be rooted in a specifically Viennese tradition of high comedy, and because it dealt with the Austrian landed aristocracy in a vanished prewar era (Rühle 438–41) — a setting with little appeal in the ultra-modern theater of 1920s Berlin. If *Der Schwierige*, by contrast, has been elevated to classic status, it is because its treatment of the theme of language has distracted attention from its political overtones. In fact, that it centers on a figure who is characterized as discreetly reticent, and who, far from being a comic butt (as the central figures of the Molière comedies admired by Hofmannsthal are), is, like his mirror-image Furlani, essentially right where all around him are blunderingly insensitive, makes for problems in production. That this would be the case was something that Hofmannsthal foresaw while he was still writing the play. He read material from his draft of the first two acts to Max Reinhardt and Reinhardt's assistant Arthur Kahane in November 1917 and reported their reaction to his wife: "Sie meinen, lachen wird man wenig (sie haben beide fast gar nicht gelacht) aber darauf kommt es nicht an" (*SW12* 482). In fact, both plays have continued to prove themselves over the last forty years or so in highly successful productions in Vienna: *Der Unbestechliche* in a touring Volkstheater production by Hans Rüdgers starring Harry Fuss as Theodor and Franz Morak as Jaromir (1970) and in a much-praised 1983 Burgtheater production directed by Rudolf Steinboeck and starring Josef Meinrad as Theodor; *Der Schwierige* in a number of productions that have brought out the comic potential of individual roles: Crescence (Adrienne Gessner) and Edine (Lilly Stepanek) in a 1959 Burgtheater production by Ernst Lothar; Hans Karl (Peter Weck) in a 1974 Theater in der Josefstadt production by Ernst Haeussermann; Helene (Julia Stemberger) in a 1991 Burgtheater production by Jürgen Flimm; Antoinette (Petra Morzé) in a 2000 Theater in der Josefstadt production by Otto Schenk. None of the productions have made all the characters equally comic; we are, after all, in a world not of knock-about farce but of high comedy. Hofmannsthal's great art lies in combining breadth of significance with characterization of rare depth, richness, and subtlety. The roll call of distinguished directors and actors who have risen to their challenge is itself a tribute to their many-sidedness and vitality.

Notes

[1] It draws on arguments advanced in previous essays by the present writer, notably: Introduction to edition of *Der Schwierige* (Cambridge: Cambridge UP, 1966), 1–35; "*Der Schwierige*: The Comedy of Discretion," *Modern Austrian Literature* 10, 1 (1977): 1–17; "Hofmannsthal and Austrian Comic Tradition," *Colloquia Germanica* 15 (1982): 73–83; "Hofmannsthal and the Renaissance; or: Once More unto 'Ein Brief,'" *Publications of the English Goethe Society* 61 (1992): 99–118; *Schnitzler, Hofmannsthal, and the Austrian Theater* (New Haven and London: Yale UP, 1992), 185–99; "Hidden Depths in Hofmannsthal's *Der Unbestechliche*," *Modern Language Review* 90 (1995): 388–98.

[2] Hofmannsthal, *Aufzeichnungen* 269. The letter was first published in English: *The Dial* (New York), 73, 2 (August 1922): 206–15 (quotation from p. 207).

[3] See especially Bauer and most recently Thomasberger, the latter drawing on hitherto unpublished material: 73–74 and 77–78.

[4] Letter first published in Fiedler, *Max Reinhardt und Molière*, 9–10. On Hofmannsthal's Molière translations see Fiedler, *Hugo von Hofmannsthals Molière-Bearbeitungen*.

[5] Most comprehensively expounded by Rösch in relation to the comic libretti as well as the principal prose comedies. See also Mauser for a concise discussion of *Der Schwierige* in relation to the recurrent themes of Hofmannsthal's comedies.

[6] The reception of the play is concisely and instructively summarized by Joyce, 4–9.

[7] These are fully documented in *SW11* 21–359; see also especially Pestalozzi (passim).

[8] *SW12* 221, 477–9. Particularly revealing is the letter of September 5, 1917, to Auernheimer: "eine kleine dreiactige Gesellschaftscomödie, mit einem 'Charakter,' dem 'Schwierigen' als Mittelpunkt, eine Conversationscomödie, weiter nichts" (477).

[9] On the idea of "conservative revolution" see especially Wuthenow (passim).

[10] For further (differently argued) discussions of the passage, see, for example, Gray 311–13 and McKenzie 46–48.

[11] The fullest discussion of the role of the child is to be found in Lindken, the fullest scene-by-scene analysis of the play in Altenhofer.

[12] See McKenzie 55.

[13] E.g. "Ein Traum von großer Magie," "Zum Gedächtnis des Schauspielers Mitterwurzer."

[14] For a calculation of these see Frühwald; the counter-argument — that there is not a strong case for arguing that in the finished work the action is set during the war — is convincingly put by Stern.

[15] *Neue Freie Presse*, 18 April 1924. The text of this review is not reproduced in Joyce but is reprinted in Rühle 529–33.

[16] For a carefully argued statement of this reading of *Der Schwierige*, see McKenzie 48–52; for the most thorough reading of metaphysical symbolism in *Der Unbestechliche* see Polheim.

Works Cited

Altenhofer, Norbert. *Hofmannsthal's Lustspiel "Der Unbestechliche."* Homburg v. d. H.: Gehlen, 1967.

Bauer, Roger. "Hofmannsthals Diener und lustige Personen." *Hofmannsthal-Forschungen* 8 (1985): 7–16.

Bennett, Benjamin. *Hugo von Hofmannsthal: The Theaters of Consciousness.* Cambridge: Cambridge UP, 1988.

Fiedler, Leonhard M. *Max Reinhardt und Molière.* Salzburg: Otto Müller, 1972.

———. *Hugo von Hofmannsthals Molière-Bearbeitungen: Die Erneuerung der comédie-ballet auf Max Reinhardts Bühnen.* Darmstadt: Agora, 1974.

Frühwald, Wolfgang. "Die sprechende Zahl. Datensymbolismus in Hugo von Hofmannsthals Lustspiel 'Der Schwierige.'" *Jahrbuch der Deutschen Schillergesellschaft* 22 (1978): 572–88.

Gray, Ronald, *The German Tradition in Literature.* Cambridge: Cambridge UP, 1965: 301–26.

Hofmannsthal, Hugo von. *Briefe 1890–1901,* Berlin: S. Fischer, 1935.

Hofmannsthal, Hugo von — Eberhard von Bodenhausen. *Briefe der Freundschaft.* Ed. Dora von Bodenhausen. Berlin: Diederichs, 1953.

Hofmannsthal, Hugo von — Carl J. Burckhardt. *Briefwechsel.* Ed. Carl J. Burckhardt. Frankfurt am Main: S. Fischer, 1956.

Hofmannsthal, Hugo von — Harry Graf Kessler. *Briefwechsel* 1898–1929. Ed. Hilde Burger. Frankfurt am Main: Insel, 1968.

Hofmannsthal, Hugo von — Josef Redlich. *Briefwechsel.* Ed. Helga Fussgänger. Frankfurt am Main: S. Fischer, 1971.

Joyce, Douglas A. *Hugo von Hofmannsthal's Der Schwierige: A Fifty-Year Theater History.* Columbia, SC: Camden House, 1993.

Koch, Hans-Albrecht. *Hugo von Hofmannsthal.* Darmstadt: Wissenschaftliche Buchgesellschaft, 1989.

Lindken, Hans-Ulrich. "Die Rolle des Kindes in Hofmannsthals Lustspiel 'Der Unbestechliche.'" *Österreich in Geschichte und Literatur* 15 (1971): 32–44.

Mauser, Wolfram. *Hugo von Hofmannsthal: Konfliktbewältigung und Werkstruktur. Eine psychosoziologische Interpretation.* Munich: Fink, 1977.

McKenzie, John R. P. *Social Comedy in Austria and Germany 1890–1933.* Bern: Lang, 1992: 35–60.

Pestalozzi, Karl. "Hofmannsthals Schwierigkeiten mit Dramenschlüssen am Beispiel von *Cristinas Heimreise*" [1983]. Karl Pestalozzi, Martin Stern. *Basler Hofmannsthal-Beiträge*. Würzburg: Königshausen & Neumann, 1991. 139–53.

Polheim, Karl Konrad. "Sinn und Symbol in Hofmannsthals Lustspiel *Der Unbestechliche*." *Sinn und Symbol: Festschrift für Joseph P. Strelka zum 60. Geburtstag*. Ed. Karl Konrad Polheim. Bern: Lang, 1987. 249–64.

Rösch, Ewald. *Komödien Hofmannsthals: Die Entfaltung ihrer Sinnstruktur aus dem Thema der Daseinsstufen*. Marburg: Elwert, 1963.

Rühle, Günther. *Theater für die Republik 1917–1933 im Spiegel der Kritik*. Frankfurt am Main: S. Fischer, 1967.

Stern, Martin. "Wann entstand und spielt 'Der Schwierige'?" *Jahrbuch der Deutschen Schillergesellschaft* 23 (1979): 350–65.

Thomasberger, Andreas. "Nestroy: ein Lehrer Hofmannsthals?" *Nestroyana* 21 (2001): 72–79.

Wuthenow, Ralph-Rainer. "Hugo von Hofmannsthal und die konservative Revolution." *Goethe-Jahrbuch* (Tokyo) 3 (1961): 8–26.

A performance of Jedermann *on the steps of the Salzburg Cathedral, 1920. Courtesy of Max Reinhardt Archives, State University of New York at Binghamton.*

JUDITH BENISTON

Hofmannsthal and the Salzburg Festival

IN THE AFTERMATH of the First World War, the work of cultural critic Rudolf Pannwitz was to influence markedly Hofmannsthal's ideas for reconstruction, fostering his conservatism and encouraging him in the belief that Austria was the legitimate heir to the German cultural tradition. For three years following the publication of Pannwitz's *Die Krisis der europäischen Kultur* (1917), he conducted an intense but increasingly acrimonious correspondence with Pannwitz himself. One of several sources of disagreement was Pannwitz's outspoken criticism of the planned Salzburg Festival. On November 4, 1919 Pannwitz warned Hofmannsthal that his collaborators Richard Strauss and Max Reinhardt were merely exploiting his prestige and would toss him aside as soon as they found a writer who was, as Pannwitz put it, "kinomäsziger" (*Briefwechsel* 416). In the same letter he predicted, with his usual disdain for orthographic convention, that "diese Salzburger sache kann nach meinem tiefsten instinkte auch nicht ein schatten von dem werden was Sie davon erwarten oder verlangen" (417). For him, Reinhardt's production of *Jedermann*, which inaugurated the Festival in August 1920, was indeed a profanation of Hofmannsthal's work.

Hofmannsthal broke off relations with Pannwitz in November 1920, but made a point, in a postscript to his very last letter, of defending the Salzburg production:

> Die Jedermann Aufführung in Salzburg schien mir im vorhinein, etwas was so leicht Profanierung werden könnte, dass ich mich fürchtete, und zaudernd den letzten Tag vor der Aufführung erschien. Dann war es das Unahnbarste, Wirklichste Beglückendste was ich im Zusammenhang mit Menschen, mit Publicum, wie Sie's nennen wollten, je hätte erleben oder zu erleben auch nur hätte ahnen können: durch die tausendfach gebrochene, in tausend wirklichen einfachen Menschen sich brechende directeste stofflich-simpelste und zugleich religiöseste Wirkung auf eine ganze *Bevölkerung*, von der kaum der Hundertste die Namen Hofmannsthal oder Reinhardt auch nur gekannt hätte. Das Publicum der aus Wien u. Berlin zugereisten Fi-

nanzleute verschwand darüber, war nicht da, so wenig als die Later-
nenpfähle auf dem Domplatz. Es war die Einzige ganz grosse Ermuti-
gung auf diesem Gebiet die ich je erlebt habe. (555–56)

Like the vast majority of critical responses to this event, Hofmannsthal's
commentary stressed both its riskiness and its remarkable success. For
him, the revelation was not so much the play, on which he had written
at length when it was first performed in 1911, as the audience. Juxta-
posing images of wholeness and fragmentation, he saw the simplicity of
the play's message to have been matched by that of the spectators who
were spiritually receptive to it. As this group expanded in his mind's eye
to become "eine ganze *Bevölkerung*," the lampposts around the cathedral square disappeared, and with them the metropolitan element of the
audience — which Hofmannsthal unequivocally identified with modern
capitalist society. Recalling the same production five years later, he
wrote, "es herrschte hier durchaus das siebzehnte Jahrhundert [. . .], in
welchem aber der noch frischere, kräftigere Geist früherer Jahrhunderte
einbehalten war" and attributed the effect to "ein Einschlag von ländlichen oder landstädtischen Elementen" (*DIII* 172) in the audience.
Writing about the premiere of *Das Salzburger große Welttheater* in
1922, he again stressed the disparate nature of the festival audience —
foreign visitors and the new moneyed elite alongside "sehr viele einfache
Menschen aus dem Volk, Bauern und Bäuerinnen, die Kleinbürger unserer kleinen ländlichen Alpenstädte, Priester und Klosterfrauen" (*RAII*
290) — but claimed that the combination of text, setting (the Kolle-
gienkirche) and production had transformed them, this time without
exclusion, into a homogenous and naively receptive *Volk*.

    While in *Der Rosenkavalier* the Marschallin merely stops her clocks
at dead of night, it appears that for Hofmannsthal the Salzburg Festival
was a very public means of turning them back, of re-establishing contact with the south-German Baroque tradition and with a premodern
notion of cultural community. It is via Hofmannsthal's preoccupation
with the motif of time — a thread which runs throughout his oeuvre —
that I propose to approach both his contribution to the cultural profile
of the Salzburg Festival and his two festival plays, *Jedermann* and *Das
Salzburger große Welttheater*. Since the Festival's early institutional
history has been traced in detail by Steinberg, as well as by Fuhrich and
Prossnitz, I will keep my comments on that aspect relatively brief. The
primary focus will be on the nature of Hofmannsthal's traditionalism
and on the ways in which human attitudes toward time underpin the
moral and spiritual message of his two festival plays.

Festival Ideology

The Salzburg Festival drew on and combined two aspects of the town's cultural identity: the Mozart legacy, which Hofmannsthal declared to be "über und unter den Zeiten" (*RAII* 259), and the Catholic Baroque heritage. Max Reinhardt's very visual style of theatre, which Hofmannsthal viewed as a continuation of Baroque traditions (252), was increasingly out of place in Berlin; he had long felt drawn to Salzburg, had by 1916 made known his desire to stage open-air productions there and in the following year proposed to the directorate of Vienna's Imperial court theaters that a festival theater be built outside the town center at Hellbrunn, in the grounds of the former Archbishop's palace. At around the same time, local plans to enhance the town's prestige by building a Mozart-Festspielhaus began to gain momentum as Friedrich Gehmacher, a local merchant, won the support of Heinrich Damisch, the music critic of Vienna's *Deutsch-österreichische Tageszeitung*, and together they launched the Salzburger Festspielhaus-Gemeinde on August 1, 1917. Although correspondence reveals that Damisch and Gehmacher were (like Pannwitz) wary of Reinhardt (Holl 158, 171–73), the two impulses came together a year later when he agreed to join the Artistic Advisory Committee along with composer Richard Strauss and conductor Franz Schalk. Hofmannsthal's involvement with the Festival officially began five months later, when he and the stage designer Alfred Roller were co-opted onto the same committee, and continued until his death in 1929.

Steinberg's assertion that Hofmannsthal was "the principal spiritual and institutional founder of the Salzburg Festival" (Steinberg xi) nevertheless requires some qualification. Most obviously, he provided, in *Jedermann* and *Das Salzburger große Welttheater*, the two works that formed the core of the spoken (that is, non-operatic) repertoire in the interwar period, with the former continuing as the centerpiece of the postwar Festival. However, Reinhardt, whose directorial skill was undoubtedly a major reason for their success, exerted far greater influence over the spoken repertoire as a whole, which was long dominated by his taste for religious morality plays and theatrical spectacle. Hofmannsthal gamely involved himself in international fundraising (Steinberg 65–69), but Strauss and Reinhardt were far better known abroad. Hofmannsthal did, however, distinguish himself as a publicist; from 1919 onwards he produced some eight essays promoting the Festival, including the anonymously circulated pamphlet "Die Salzburger Festspiele" (1919), and was the only figure closely associated with it to present the event and its repertoire in the context of a comprehensive cultural vision.

There are a number of reasons why, in the early years of the First Republic, Salzburg should have become the focus for Hofmannsthal's cultural endeavors. Most obviously, it was a town to which he had a longstanding personal attachment. On August 21, 1906 he wrote to Eberhard von Bodenhausen: "ein Tag in dem entzückend schönen Salzburg, — so sehr die Landschaft meiner Jugend, meiner Träume, vielfach der Hintergrund meiner Poesie, ist das Schönste Liebste was ich denken kann" (*Briefe der Freundschaft* 86). Ideologically, Salzburg had particular appeal for Hofmannsthal because the idea of establishing a festival there could be justified on the basis of the theories of cultural geography that had been put forward by Austrian-born academic Josef Nadler. His *Literaturgeschichte der deutschen Stämme und Landschaften*, three volumes of which had appeared by 1918, was a great solace and inspiration to Hofmannsthal, who discovered it during the war and became an enthusiastic propagandist after he had read Nadler's account of the Austrian Baroque in 1918 (Volke 39–40). His thesis, which Hofmannsthal rehearses at some length in "Festspiele in Salzburg" (1921), is that the variety of literary and cultural development within the German-speaking area should be attributed to differences in regional geography and ethnic character: the Austrian and south-German peoples — or rather "Stämme," to use Nadler's preferred term — are distinguished by an inborn theatrical talent and enthusiasm for theater. Fostered by the amphitheatral shape of many Alpine valleys, this talent first manifested itself in the proliferation of religious folk drama, and reached its high point in the Baroque era. The argument and terminology of this essay, and indeed of Hofmannsthal's Salzburg propaganda as a whole, owe a considerable debt to Nadler. In "Festspiele in Salzburg" he even gives Nadler a footnote as he cites verbatim the claim that, since the mid-seventeenth century, Salzburg had been the undisputed cultural center for the whole region between Munich, Vienna, and Innsbruck. Viewed through this lens, the Festival idea became "der eigentliche Kunstgedanke des bayrisch-österreichischen Stammes" (*RAII* 255) and Salzburg the only place to hold it.

Drawing on Nadler's work, Hofmannsthal had little difficulty after the collapse of the Empire in transferring to Salzburg that Austrian patriotism which had emerged in his wartime essays. For example, the touchingly optimistic thesis, set out in "Die österreichische Idee" (1917), that the postwar future of Austria-Hungary would be guaranteed by its ancient provenance, its geographical centrality within Europe, and its cosmopolitanism, appears in barely modified form in "Die Salzburger Festspiele," the catechism-like publicity pamphlet that was Hofmannsthal's most authoritative statement on the Festival. In it he cites an unbroken theatrical tradition going back five hundred years as legitimation, and asserts that Salzburg is at the heart of Europe: "Es liegt halbwegs zwischen der Schweiz und den slawischen Ländern, halbwegs zwischen dem nördlichen Deutschland und dem lombardischen Italien; es liegt in der Mitte zwischen Süd und Nord, zwischen Berg und Ebene." For him the town mediates not only geographically but also temporally and culturally: "es liegt als Bauwerk zwischen dem Städtischen und dem Ländlichen, dem Uralten und dem Neuzeitlichen, dem barocken Fürstlichen und dem lieblich ewig Bäuerlichen" (*RAII* 261). The idea of Salzburg as a cultural watershed was not new — in 1900 Hermann Bahr had called it "Die Hauptstadt von Europa" (Bahr 122–29) — but in 1919 the emphasis on reconciliation between peoples recalled both the Europeanism of the *Goethezeit*, to which Hofmannsthal drew attention, and that cosmopolitanism which, under the *Vielvölkerreich*, had been a supremely Austrian value. Bearing out Steinberg's contention that "Hofmannsthal was a grand synthesizer" (Steinberg 76), this was combined with his Nadlerian rhetoric to produce a *rooted* cosmopolitanism[1] that sought simultaneously to preserve a European cultural heritage and to showcase a supposedly autochthonic folk tradition.

Hofmannsthal had long been concerned with the relationship between tradition and individual talent, and Nadler's work fascinated him because it provided him with a theoretical approach to precisely that issue, allowing him to see himself as a late representative of the Austrian Baroque tradition. As he told the readers of the American journal *The Dial*, the artist was no longer a lone genius but "Ausdruck einer in weite Vergangenheit zurückführenden Pluralität" (*RAII* 289), and all the more so in Austria where in the early 1920s so many "Vergangenheiten" were helping to constitute the new form of the state and its cultural profile. Looking back on Nadler's impact a few years later, Hofmannsthal concluded:

> Er [Nadler] hat die geistigen Leistungen auf ein letztes sie Bewirkendes zurückgeführt, das die Individuen überdauert und während sie historisch werden gegenwärtig bleibt wie das Dasein unserer Berge und Flüsse; man nenne das Mythologie — so ist es die faszinierendste und ermutigendste, die man sich denken kann. (*RAIII* 149)

By associating a myth of cultural continuity with the Alpine landscape, Hofmannsthal was able to bridge the gap between Empire and Republic, convincing himself that the rationale behind the Festival and, with it, the roots of his creativity were independent of political upheavals.

That neither Nadler's work nor much of what Hofmannsthal made of it stands up to detailed scholarly analysis has been exhaustively demonstrated.[2] With the benefit of hindsight, the association is also unfortunate insofar as the combination of ethnicity and regionalism, on which Hofmannsthal founded his ostensibly suprapolitical concept of Austro-Bavarian identity, not only encouraged Nadler to bring the fourth edition of his history — published under the revised title *Literaturgeschichte des deutschen Volkes: Dichtung und Schrifttum der deutschen Stämme und Landschaften* (1938–1941) — into line with the Nazi ideology of *Blut und Boden*, but also gave the Festival, in the eyes of some, an ominous socio-political subtext.

It is no coincidence that, in turning toward Salzburg, Hofmannsthal also turned away from Vienna. A pragmatic reason for this was Reinhardt's failure, following the directorial crises of 1917/18, to gain a foothold at the Burgtheater, which considerably reduced Hofmannsthal's own chances of establishing his work there. Regrettably, one must also suspect an element of cultural antisemitism on Hofmannsthal's part. This is most explicit when, in a letter of September 2, 1917 to Rudolf Pannwitz, Hofmannsthal warns him against "ein gewisses intellectuelles Wiener Judenmilieu, das für mich das Schlimmste vom Schlimmen ist." He goes on to characterize it in terms of "äffisch betastende Neugierde, geldwechslerische verfluchte Unrast — keine Substanz, keine Ehrfurcht, keine Frommigkeit — zu nichts Distanz, zu nichts Glaube — alles betastend, beleckend, alles auflösend, alles zerschwätzend" (*Briefwechsel* 55–56). As Jens Rieckmann has demonstrated, Hofmannsthal had since the 1890s come to associate Viennese Modernism with a stereotypical view of the Jewish intellect as critical, reflexive, and prone to dilettantism (Rieckmann 476–78). His hostility mounted as he personally grew away from that milieu, effectively seeking a second assimilation, not into the liberal bourgeoisie, as his paternal grandfather had done, but into a "baroque" cultural nexus that combined aristocratic and *völkisch* elements.

For Hofmannsthal, the antithesis of this relentless modernity fuelled by capitalism lay in an idealized image of the Alpine peasant world and its cultural traditions. In his collection of aphorisms entitled *Buch der Freunde* (1921) he wrote: "Der Gegenwart entflieht, wer unter die Bauern geht. Der Bauer und die Gegenwart liegen in einem gesunden ewigen Streit, und über der Natur und den Sternen schwebt eine unverwelkliche Zeit, die nichts von der schalen Gegenwart weiß" (*RAIII* 273–74). This "other" time frame, which found a potent symbol in the mountains and lakes of the Salzkammergut, can be glimpsed both in Hofmannsthal's idea of a festival calendar that would harmonize with the Church's year and the pattern of the seasons rather than the commercial theater schedule (*RAII* 258), and in the repeated invitation to festivalgoers to regard themselves not as a novelty-seeking "Publikum" but as part of a pre-modern *Volk*: "Das Volk rechnet mit Jahrhunderten. Für den Kern des Volkes ist das Große immer neu" (259). Hofmannsthal's ideal was that this notional audience would come to regard the Festival "wie ein Selbstverständliches" (267), as part of a living tradition rather than as the product of a conscious traditionalism that it more correctly was.

It should be made clear at this point that there were significant discrepancies between Hofmannsthal's original intentions for the Salzburg Festival and the form in which it was ultimately realized, not least because his approach in his publicity essays was fundamentally mythopoeic, constructing what he regarded as an attractive cultural narrative in the hope that it would appeal to others. Although in the interwar period some festivalgoers did make a point of dressing up in folk costume, the more fanciful of Hofmannsthal's claims about audience composition were contradicted at the time by reviews noting that the high ticket prices excluded most of the local population. Furthermore, as W. E. Yates has emphasized, Salzburg in the early 1920s was less a great cultural center than a small provincial town, struggling like the rest of the Republic against severe economic hardship; although the governor of the province of Salzburg, Franz Rehrl, regarded the Festival as a boon to the region, sectors of the local population opposed it on religious, antisemitic, cultural, xenophobic, and practical grounds (Yates 206–8).

One area in which Hofmannsthal was prophetic was in his ideal of rooted cosmopolitanism. As Herbert Ihering commented in 1931, the Salzburg Festival was characterized by "Mozart plus Fremdenverkehr. Bayreuth plus internationale Saison," all the more paradoxical because, in Ihering's view at least, the star attraction for this international audience was what Austria and Salzburg alone could offer, the unique experience of *Jedermann* in the cathedral square (Ihering 73). Notwithstanding this, the repertoire, in which opera and spoken drama remained essentially separate, never achieved that degree of *völkisch* coherence originally envisaged by Hofmannsthal, although in the 1920s his own work was supplemented by two other modern folk dramas, Max Mell's *Das Apostelspiel* in 1925 and Richard Billinger's *Das Perchtenspiel*, brought to Salzburg by the Innsbruck-based Exl-Bühne three years later. In 1933, four years after Hofmannsthal's death, Reinhardt also mounted a memorable production of Goethe's *Faust*, the work that Hofmannsthal had placed at the heart of his *völkisch* agenda, describing it as "das Schauspiel aller Schauspiele, zusammengesetzt aus den theatralischen Elementen vieler Jahrhunderte, und reich genug an Sinnfälligem, Buntem und Bewegtem, um das naivste Publikum ebenso zu fesseln wie den Höchst-gebildeten" (*RAII* 259). Hofmannsthal's *Jedermann* and *Das Salzbur-ger große Welttheater*, both of which were influenced by Goethe's *Faust* (Beniston 149–53, 227–29), have in common with it that they too draw on centuries of theatrical tradition, with the explicit objective of ad-dressing a challenging modern problematic within that framework. As Walter Weiss has argued, the result is complex and Janus-faced, a "zwei-deutige Synthese von Rückbindung und Innovationsanspruch" (113) which becomes particularly uneasy when cultural conservatism tips over into political prescription.

Jedermann

By the time *Jedermann* opened the Salzburg Festival in August 1920, the play had been in print for some nine years and had, until the out-break of war in 1914, been widely staged throughout the German-speaking world. In the context of Hofmannsthal's oeuvre it is com-monly viewed alongside his prewar adaptations of Greek drama and of Thomas Otway's *Venice Preserv'd*, as an exercise in learning to handle large-scale dramatic forms and an attempt at cultural appropriation. From the outset the play was also closely associated with the name of Max Reinhardt: premiered at Zirkus Busch in Berlin on December 1, 1911, it began life as one of his experimental arena productions, along-side Hofmannsthal's adaptation of *Oedipus Rex* and Karl Vollmoeller's wordless mystery play *Das Mirakel*, which was premiered three weeks after *Jedermann* and followed it to Salzburg in 1925. Thematically, *Je-dermann* witnesses to a growing concern with ethical issues, and in particular with the pernicious social and psychological effects of mod-ern materialism, that was to remain with Hofmannsthal well into the 1920s. These contexts are all relatively familiar and well documented; what has so far not been appreciated, and will be explored here, is the central importance for Hofmannsthal's morality play of the theme of time, as a vehicle to articulate both human failings and perspectives be-yond them. This gives *Jedermann* a surprising affinity with *Der Rosen-kavalier*, which was written immediately before the final version of the morality play and premiered in January of the same year.[3]

The genesis of Hofmannsthal's *Jedermann* can be traced back to 1903 when his friend Clemens von Franckenstein wrote to him de-scribing a production of the English *Everyman* play mounted in Lon-don by the Elizabethan Stage Society. Although impressed by the late-fifteenth-century text and by his friend's account of its theatrical effec-tiveness, Hofmannsthal's initial response was to plan a modernized prose version, four scenes of which were completed before he shelved it in favor of other projects in 1906. When he returned to the material four years later, at the behest of Reinhardt (who had seen the London production in 1901), what he produced was far closer to the spirit of the medieval morality play — an archaizing verse drama, part adaptation, part pastiche, which nevertheless reflected some of his most pressing concerns about twentieth-century society.

Hofmannsthal's comments about the relationship between his text and its sources need to be treated with circumspection: initially dubbing himself "der Restaurator, sehr bescheidne und ängstliche Restaurator" (*SW9* 261), he appended a list of sources to the first five editions of the play. However, following its success at the box-office, he became less self-effacing, replacing this with a less precise account of the play's origins. Although in 1918 he even asserted "entscheidende schöpferische Elemente" (276), his postscript to Pannwitz quoted at the start of this essay demonstrates that, when he glimpsed the possibility of assimilating his work into the indigenous folk culture, he cheerfully reverted to anonymity.

In truth Hofmannsthal's *Jedermann* interweaves a number of sources. The English *Everyman* play furnished the title and the central event — God sending his emissary, Death, to call an allegorical Everyman to account for his life — but arguably more important as a source of inspiration was Hans Sachs's *Ein comedi von dem reichen sterbenden menschen, der Hecastus genannt* (1549). Whereas in the English morality play the title figure is summoned by Death as soon as he steps on stage and is genuinely universal, in Sachs he is not only defined as wealthy but also shown in the enjoyment of that wealth. Hofmannsthal followed this model, devoting the first half of his play to what he called "Jedermanns Tageslauf," a depiction of the selfish, ungodly, superficially pleasurable but ultimately unsatisfying existence which Jedermann's money has allowed him to build. The figure of Mammon and the banquet scene, constituting respectively the moral and theatrical high points of Hofmannsthal's play, also have a basis in Sachs, as do the allegories Werke and Glaube, which were preferred to the larger complement of allegories in the English text.

The opening of Hofmannsthal's play, taken directly from his English model, announces that the issue of time — in the form of human mortality — is fundamental to its message:

> Darin euch wird gewiesen werden,
> Wie unsere Tag und Werk auf Erden
> Vergänglich sind und hinfällig gar. (*DIII* 11)

With the exception of the banquet scene, the whole play is characterized by urgency and impatience: God dispatches Death to summon
Jedermann "mit dieser Stund und heutigem Tag" (12); Jedermann becomes irritated as his schedule is held up by a series of uncomfortable
encounters; Death grants him a mere hour to prepare himself for his final journey; and, as he achieves redemption, his mother hastens to
mass, summoned by bells that signal not a division of human time but
the onset of eternity.

The first few scenes of *Jedermann* have in common with the lyrical
drama *Gestern* that they oblige the central figure to reflect on and defend
his lifestyle and the attitude to time on which it is founded. Meeting an
impoverished former neighbor, Jedermann and "Gesell" (his toadying
companion) try to avoid confrontation by claiming to be in a hurry, "Ja,
wie gesprochen, wir müssen eilen, / Dürfen uns gar nit länger ver-
weilen" (14). Lack of time for others is symptomatic of a deficient social
conscience, as the pair proceed to propound a self-satisfied capitalist
philosophy that recalls the merchant Dreißiger and his clerk Pfeiffer in
Gerhart Hauptmann's naturalistic play *Die Weber* (1893). Although Jedermann will later order servants to bring chests of money out of his
house, he tells the neighbor that he cannot simply share his wealth, since
it is not at his disposal; in order to be productive it must go out and
work on his behalf, ironically wrestling "Mit Tod und Teufel" (16).

The subsequent encounter with a debtor and his destitute family
contrasts the remoteness of the institutionalized relationship between
debtor and creditor with the immediacy of human suffering and charity.
While the neighbor refused to accept the change in his circumstances
which time had wrought (no other explanation is offered, and one is
reminded of the English idiom "to fall on hard times"), the Debtor
warns Jedermann that his hard-heartedness will result in "zeitlich und
ewig Schmach." Jedermann responds by pointing out that unpaid debts
are the product of an unrealistic attitude toward time:

> Wer hieß dich Geld auf Zinsen nehmen?
> Nun hast du den gerechten Lohn.
> Mein Geld weiß nit von dir noch mir
> Und kennt kein Ansehen der Person.
> Verstrichne Zeit, verfallner Tag,
> Gegen die bring deine Klag. (18)

With this riposte Jedermann unwittingly demonstrates the senselessness
of his own refusal to believe in a day of reckoning and of his attempt to
take his wealth with him to the grave. Despite his bravado, Jedermann
is rattled by allusions to his mortality in this scene and abandons his

plan to view the garden he is buying for his mistress, both because he is no longer in the mood and because the light is failing: "Auch wird es duster [*sic*] schon und grau" (22). That repeated references to the quality of light are made in the course of the play reinforces the emphasis on transience.

The effectiveness of *Jedermann* is also enhanced by the fact that, especially in German, the vocabulary of divine reckoning — *Schulden, Rechenbuch, Erlösung* — is also that of worldy calculation, and both are habitually subject to temporal conditions. Ultimately Jedermann avoids a final reckoning because Christ has, by His death on the Cross, "Jedermannes Schuldigkeit / Vorausbezahlt in Ewigkeit" (69). That the link between the themes of time and materialism was from the outset fundamental to Hofmannsthal's conception for the play is suggested in a note written in 1904: "Jedermann suchte das Unendliche im Endlichen, durch Häufung des Endlichen" (*SW9* 137). The accumulation of material wealth can be seen as an attempt to compensate for the inability to hold onto time; what the character fails to realize is that the eternal and timeless can be grasped by humankind only in symbolic form.

Jedermann's third encounter, that with his pious elderly mother, is once again overshadowed by anxiety about time. The son's first words on catching sight of her are: "Drück mich nit gern vor ihr beiseit, / Hab aber wahrlich nit viel Zeit"(*DIII* 24), and he repeatedly tries to cut short the conversation by feigning concern about her being outside at dusk. Although his mother's first speech is a complaint that her son's worldly affairs leave him little time for her, the main focus of the scene is not Jedermann's lack of filial piety but his spiritual health. While his mother is comfortable with the idea that her days on earth are numbered, Jedermann repeatedly dismisses the thought, telling her that the time for taking stock of his life, for repentance and reform, lies some way in the future: "Bin jung im Herzen und wohl gesund / Und will mich freuen meine Stund" (26). Jedermann's reluctance to marry, to establish and maintain socially and spiritually validated bonds, is symptomatic of his unwillingness to accept time as constitutive of the human condition. It is, however, clear in the subsequent dialogue with his mistress, Buhlschaft, that he is conscious of aging and fearful of becoming an "ältlich, unbequemer Mann" (29). Now approaching forty, he resembles the Marschallin in *Der Rosenkavalier* insofar as he cultivates a love relationship with a younger partner as a temporary escape from the tyranny of time. Symbolic of this is the pleasure garden which he plans to buy for his mistress, as a secular "Angebind" (22) and a token of thanks for the respite from mid-life crisis which she provides. In imagining this garden, which he illogically envisages as "einen ungequälten Ort" (23), shady at all hours of the day, Jedermann is at his most ostrich-like, but also his most lyrical.

It is in a spirit of defiance, as a glorious celebration of worldly pleasure as victory over time, that the banquet scene is conceived. Its fragility is, however, nowhere clearer than when a guest proposes the song "In süßen Freuden geht die Zeit" (36) and is immediately rebuked by his neighbor for suggesting "ein geistlich Lied," presumably one that would castigate the vanity of such indulgence. The original speaker protests that the song in question is in fact a *Tagelied*, waking a pair of lovers after a night of illicit passion; but the preceding exchange has already shown up the illusory nature of that escape from time and responsibility. Notwithstanding this, it is striking that, while every other human figure who professes loyalty to Jedermann is shown to let him down, Buhlschaft is treated rather more kindly. Although fearful of the snake beneath flowers that is death, for the duration of the banquet she is loving and solicitous toward her increasingly melancholy companion. In response to his contention that the assembled company are so parasitic that he could buy and sell them and think no more of it than of a broken fingernail, she asks, "Geht die Red gleicherweis auf mich?" (33) The question is answered only with a look. Rather than testing her profession of love, "Dein bin ich heut und ewiglich" (33), by asking Buhlschaft to accompany him, Jedermann anticipates her response in a speech phrased entirely in the conditional:

> Wenn ich dann spräch: Bleibst du bei mir?
> Willst dort bei mir sein so wie hier?
> Willst mich geleiten nach der Stätte
> Und teilen mein eiskaltes Bette?
> Fielest ohnmächtig mir zu Füßen,
> So hätte ich meine Frag zu büßen!
> [. . .] Wenn ich müßt sehen mit eigenen Augen,
> Wie deine süßen Schwür nit taugen
> Und wie du lösest deine Händ
> Aus meinen Händen gar am End
> Und deinen Mund von meinem Mund
> Abtrennest in der letzten Stund.
> Oh weh. (33–34)

Hofmannsthal spares both Jedermann and the audience the pain of this parting, as Buhlschaft leaves the stage anonymously, presumably at the direction "*Es flüchten viele*" (41).

Insofar as *Jedermann* is centrally concerned with human attitudes toward time and their implications for moral and spiritual life, Hofmannsthal's claim in the essay "Das alte Spiel von Jedermann" (1911) that the core of its message is "menschlich absolut, keiner bestimmten Zeit angehörig, nicht einmal mit dem christlichen Dogma unlöslich verbunden" (*DIII* 90) is valid. Although Heinz Rölleke has argued, in a reading of the play that breaks off at the point when Death appears, that Hofmannsthal was far less interested in Jedermann's redemption than in his earthly failings (Rölleke 106), it is striking that the preoccupation with time continues. Once he has glimpsed in the frail figure of Werke the lasting joy and comfort that he might have derived from embracing greater social responsibility, the main cause of Jedermann's anguish is that he cannot turn back the clocks:

> So wollt ich ganz zernichtet sein,
> Wie an dem ganzen Wesen mein
> Nit eine Fiber jetzt nit schreit
> Vor tiefer Reu und wildem Leid!
> Zurück! und kann nit! Noch einmal!
> Und kommt nit wieder! Graus und Qual!
> Hie wird kein zweites Mal gelebt! (61)

Regret at the opportunities missed is far stronger than fear of what might lie before him. Only briefly does Jedermann consider the prospect of being "verloren für alle Zeit" (61) and, having rediscovered his faith in a realm that is not trapped in time, he tells Glaube of his joy and relief in terms which again present the overcoming of mortality as a matter of turning back the clocks: "Oh, deine Worte sind gelind, / Mir ist, als wär ich neugeboren" (64).

It is at this point in the text that productions of Hofmannsthal's *Jedermann* have traditionally inserted a recitation of the Lord's Prayer, forcefully reminding the spectator of the conventional Christian understanding of that realm beyond time. As Nehring has demonstrated, the nature of Hofmannsthal's personal religious belief is notoriously elusive (Nehring 79–82). By referring to *Jedermann* as a "dieses allen Zeiten gehörige und allgemein gültige Märchen" (*DIII* 89) and inviting comparisons between his role and that of the Brothers Grimm (Rölleke 95–98), Hofmannsthal tried to locate it in a folk tradition rather than a religious one. However, once the play was transferred from a secular to a sacred setting, from circus arena to cathedral square, it was inevitably perceived more narrowly as a Catholic festival play, a perception that was encouraged by details of staging. As Raoul Auernheimer noted in his review of the Salzburg premiere, the facade of the cathedral was not a distant backdrop but a functional part of the scenery: whereas in Berlin and in the published text a repentant Jedermann is led off stage by a monk, presumably to make his confession and/or receive the sacraments (what exactly he does is not specified), in Salzburg he made his exit into the cathedral and was met at the door by a fully robed Catholic priest. Auernheimer also observed that at the end of the play Glaube symbolically returned to the Church (11). This intermingling of institutional reality and theatrical illusion inevitably offers a narrower definition of the realm beyond time to which Jedermann finds access: it is represented by the symbols and monuments of Baroque Catholicism and by Salzburg's ancient mountain landscape.

Das Salzburger große Welttheater

Das Salzburger große Welttheater, which replaced *Jedermann* in the Festival repertoire in 1922 and 1925, and was the only work which Hofmannsthal wrote specifically for Salzburg, has a number of similarities to *Jedermann*. Once again worldliness goes hand in hand with a defective human attitude to time, which in the later text jeopardizes both the salvation of the individual and the survival of an ancient social order. The *Welttheater* metaphor is glimpsed in *Jedermann*: in an exchange which Hofmannsthal took directly from his English source, Death explains the difference between props and property: "Nichts da, war alls dir nur geliehen. / Bist du dahin, erbts einen andern, / Und über eine Weil schlägt dem seine Stund / Und er muß alles hier lassen und wandern" (*DIII* 42). In *Das Salzburger große Welttheater* this becomes the explicit organizing principle of the whole play, and Death, rather than merely being on his way, is constantly visible on stage. The idea "daß die Welt ein Schaugerüst aufbaut, worauf die Menschen in ihren von Gott ihnen zugeteilten Rollen das Spiel des Lebens aufführen" (107) is taken from Calderón's Corpus Christi play *El gran teatro del mundo* (1655), together with the play's title and the six figures — King, Rich Man, Farmer, Beggar, Beauty, and Wisdom — who represent human society.

If *Jedermann* lost some of its universality at Salzburg, the model for Hofmannsthal's *Welttheater* could not have had a more impeccable Catholic pedigree. Since the 1890s precisely this *auto sacramental*, with its defense of the hierarchical *Gottesstaat*, had been an axiomatic text for Austria's conservative Catholics.[4] Hofmannsthal employs several tactics in an attempt to liberate his play from association with this tradition (which included productions in Vienna in 1897 and 1923). His preface stresses that the *theatrum mundi* topos is not exclusively Catholic property but belongs to a treasure trove of myths and allegories created in the middle ages and freely available to subsequent generations. One can also note a repeated avoidance of institutionalized vocabulary in Hofmannsthal's interpretations of his *Welttheater*, and he made concerted efforts to market it as an indigenous folk drama rather than a narrowly Catholic one, signaling this not only with the inclusion of "Salzburg" in the title but also by the fact that the cast for the premiere included Josef Meth, director of the Bauerntheater in nearby Bad Reichenhall, as the Farmer, and local dialect poet Otto Pflanzl as the Hanswurst-like figure of Vorwitz.

Hofmannsthal made most free with his Spanish model, which he knew primarily in Joseph von Eichendorff's translation, in the early part of *Das Salzburger große Welttheater*, replacing the sonorous, measured verse of the Baroque archetype with a lively prose introduction to the *theatrum mundi* topos which, unlike its model, does not assume detailed prior knowledge of its poetic and theological implications. In place of the harmonious and respectful interaction of creator and created, Hofmannsthal introduces comedy, dissent, and foreboding. Using insect metaphors reminiscent of Mephistopheles in the prologue to Goethe's *Faust*, an irreverent Frau Welt responds with incredulity to the suggestion that the play of human life would be an appropriate subject for "ein Fest und Schauspiel" (110) to entertain its divine creator. This limited understanding bears out the comment, made by Glaube in *Jedermann*, that the world is "gefangen in der Zeit / Und bleibt in solchen Schranken stocken" (70). It is also true of her entourage: Vorwitz, a dim-witted comic figure whose meddlesome curiosity and worldly, trivializing commentary provides a counterpoint to that of Wisdom, and the Widersacher, an adversarial pedant who opposes the divine order with a secular concept of rights that is strongly colored by the Enlightenment.

A note of foreboding emerges as an Angel warns Frau Welt of the need to put on a good show: "Hat der Herr dich nicht einmal schon ersäuft, und als du am letzten warst, einen neuen Weltstand über dich aufgehen lassen!" (111–12) Anticipating the Beggar's revolutionary demand, the reference to a new world order makes clear that, despite the impression of permanence created by mountains and lakes, the world is subject to time and therefore also to change. The point is driven home as one of the prophets and sibyls, whose every word "glänzt durch die Zeiten" (109), summons up a Büchneresque image of the world as a wild horse, rushing headlong into the darkness with the devil on its back.

Dissent surfaces as the unborn soul commanded to play the Beggar initially refuses on the grounds that the role consists only of suffering and humiliation, and finds little comfort in its finite nature. The Beggar's desire for "eine Rolle, in der Freiheit ist" (120) is explored by the

Widersacher in terms which recall the ideals of the French Revolution: alongside freedom he demands "natürliche Gleichheit des Schicksals" (119) and an end to the fraternal enmity that is born of inequality. In invoking the ideals of 1789 (the Widersacher signals his historicity with the phrase "in unserer erleuchteten Zeit" [119], Hofmannsthal takes up a theme from lectures he had given in Scandinavia in 1916. There he had expressed the hope that the Great War would herald "einen neuen geläuterten Freiheitsbegriff" (*RAII* 33), one that was predicated on a harmonious relationship between the individual and the higher law and did not require anything so legalistic as a social contract. It is an acceptance of these principles, and a redefinition of liberty, equality and fraternity, that is effected by the Beggar's transformation (Beniston 243–44).

Amongst the six figures of Hofmannsthal's play within the play, it is striking that the King and Beauty, who appear first, speak almost entirely in the present tense. This suggests that that they live unreflectively in the present: while an unchanging landscape and ancient dynastic tradition give the King a sense of permanence, Beauty believes herself to be the embodiment of a timeless ideal, an illusion to which the King gives fervent lyrical expression:

> Helenas Werke sind nicht einst gewesen,
> Sie werfen ab Jahrtausendlast,
> Sind wieder, sind von heut, sind ewig da!
> Was jemals herrlich war, ist wieder nah. (*DIII* 124)

While King and Beauty both revel in centrality, Wisdom, for Hofmannsthal an allegory drawing together "alles dessen [. . .], was wir an Hohem, Unselbstischem, Gott-Gleichem in uns tragen, sei es nun aus religiöser oder aus profaner Tradition" (*RAII* 288), defines herself by retreating to the periphery and exchanging the "Wirbel, der inmitten dieser Welt" for "Ewigkeit" (*DIII* 125). In so doing she introduces a conflation of spatial and temporal metaphors later echoed by the Beggar and makes clear that any notion of "worldly wisdom" is out of the question.

The Rich Man and Farmer, who enter together, have in common a less solipsistic, more interactive relationship with their surroundings and, in reflecting on past achievements and future aspirations, noticeably deploy a wider range of tenses. Congratulating the King on the modernity of his outlook, the Rich Man pays only lip service to the traditional order, proclaiming that "Der Gott der neuen Zeiten heißt Verkehr, / Ihm sei dein Reich zum Tempel umgebaut" (126). As an industrialist scarring the earth in his quest for wealth, he combines the worldly ambition of Faust with the ruthlessness of Mephistopheles.

Less repentant and more aggressive than Jedermann, he alone is ultimately excluded from the play's "goldne Gnadenkette" (163). The
Farmer, whom Hofmannsthal described in his third "Wiener Brief" as
"Bauer — der bei uns den gesicherten konservativen kleinen Besitz bedeutet" (*RAII* 288), exploits the land in a more traditional fashion but
is no less reprehensible and materialistic in his claim to exclusive owner-
ship. As such, he is far removed from the idealized image of the Alpine
peasant which litters Hofmannsthal's essayistic work. The Farmer's final
speeches foreground his evasiveness in humorous fashion as he repeatedly attempts to brush Death aside, saying that he has no time and, like
Jedermann, ends by admitting that he had hoped for a few more years:
"Du laßt an ja ka Zeit, / Jetzt tuats mi g'reun, daß mi so wenig
g'reut!" (*DIII* 159).

As Hofmannsthal repeatedly asserted, it was in the role of the Beggar that his major innovation lay. For the Beggar of *Das Salzburger
große Welttheater* is a misnomer; he does not beg; he is a representative
of the disinherited and disaffected proletariat that had demanded its
rights in the Revolutions of 1917 and 1919. In the Salzburg premiere,
Alexander Moissi gave his performance "etwas Russisches, und das Ge-
spenst des Bolschewismus stand sehr deutlich hinter seinen außeror-
dentlichen, sparsamen und unvergeßlichen Gebärden" (*RAII* 293).
With the entry of the Beggar one has for the first time in Hofmannsthal's play a glimpse of modern individualism: in contrast to the
static allegories which surround him, the Beggar has been shaped by
past experiences, he has developed over time, becoming embittered and
marginalized following the loss of his wife and children. In this sense he
is certainly more sinned against than sinning, and is rightly furious
when Wisdom (and seemingly also Hofmannsthal) confuses social and
metaphysical evil, suggesting that the premature deaths of his loved
ones were somehow metaphysically necessary rather than being the result of poverty and civil unrest. However, in his dialogues with the
other figures the Beggar reveals himself to be hardly less materialistic
than they are, threatening the social order largely out of jealousy at
what they have and he does not. His list of grievances even includes
their supposed mastery over time: "[Ihr] habt die Zeit und noch den
Zeitvertreib, / Ihr habt den Tag und habt als zweiten Tag die Nacht /
Mit Fackeln, Kerzen, Glanz und Pracht" (*DIII* 132). In other words,
he would like to have the luxury of succumbing to the same illusions as
the other worldly figures. Although the Beggar rejects the explicit
prompting of the Widersacher, this appears to be how Hofmannsthal
reads the secular concept of rights which he represents.

The crisis of the Beggar's revolt, which Hofmannsthal described as "die Drohung des Chaos an die geordnete Welt" (*RAII* 287), is resolved not by dramatic means but thanks to a miraculous Pauline conversion, a moment out of time, of which he says, "Mir hat die Sternenuhr die große Zeit geschlagen" (*DIII* 148). Thereafter, rather than attempting to live his life differently within society, the Beggar withdraws into the forest, now accepting a marginality which he, like Wisdom, expresses in temporal terms:

> Was schiert mich, was ihr habt? Ich bin so voller Freuden
> Und will in Wald, daß ich umblitzt von Ewigkeit
> Mich beieinander halt, an keinen Hauch der Zeit
> Die innre Himmelsfülle zu vergeuden! (147)

In renouncing human time, the Beggar renounces not only human company but also his sense of differentiated identity:

> Was weiß ich, wer ihr seid — was weiß ich, wer ich bin?
> Als wie von Ewigkeit
> Ist mir der Wald bereit,
> Da ich ein schuldlos Kind
> Auf moosigem Stein gelegen. (147)

Whereas it is only in the moments before his death that Jedermann exchanges time for eternity and comes to view the future in terms of a memory of prelapsarian innocence, the Beggar in Hofmannsthal's *Welttheater* supposedly lives out the rest of his life in this fashion. In this difference lies the truth of Hofmannsthal's comment that his solution to the problem of proletarian discontent is poetic and spiritual rather than practical (*RAII* 288). Herein also lies a major reason why *Das Salzburger große Welttheater*, despite being a poetic *tour de force*, did not find wide acceptance in the manner of *Jedermann* and only twice replaced it in the Festival repertoire (in 1922 and 1925). Whereas one can envisage, not least in terms of his attitude to time, how Jedermann and the society of which he is only too representative could live in a more responsible fashion, the stoicism which appears to be expected of the Beggar makes far less sense in that modern socio-political context to which Moissi's performance alluded. Expressed another way, there is no trace in Hofmannsthal's *Welttheater* of anything resembling that fragile but precious synthesis of "Zeit und Ewigkeit" glimpsed by the lovers in his Vienna operas (Vilain 118) and suggested in the figure of Jedermann's mother.

Despite the emphasis in the introductory section of *Das Salzburger große Welttheater* on the mechanics of the *theatrum mundi* topos, the inner action appears to exemplify the sentiments voiced by the Marschallin in the first act of *Der Rosenkavalier*:

> Die Zeit, die ist ein sonderbares Ding.
> Wenn man so hinlebt, ist sie rein gar nichts.
> Aber dann auf einmal,
> da spürt man nichts als sie:
> sie ist um uns herum, sie ist auch in uns drinnen.
> In den Gesichtern rieselt sie, im Spiegel da rieselt sie,
> in meinen Schläfen fließt sie.
> Und zwischen mir und dir da fließt sie wieder. (*DV* 42)

Time, aging, and mortality make themselves felt just as suddenly and palpably in *Das Salzburger große Welttheater*. The sequence begins with Frau Welt's song. Its title, "Flieg hin, Zeit, du bist meine Magd" (150), which recalls the delusion of Jedermann with respect to Mammon, is ironic, insofar as its message is as applicable to her in the (very) long term as to the other worldly allegories — and she knows it, ending "Flieg hin, Zeit! die Zeit ist noch weit!" Following this, Beauty looks in the mirror and, seeing the face of an old woman, laments that her former self has been violated and destroyed. Raising the alarm achieves little, however, as time is now all around the figures of the inner action in the form of a rushing wind; the beat of Death's drum magnifies the racing heartbeat, and all are reduced to puppet-like impotence as they circle around each other in a dreamlike pantomimic *Totentanz*. That in Reinhardt's Salzburg production this sequence was widely regarded as the theatrical high point of the play has led Cynthia Walk to suggest that the socio-political message which Hofmannsthal hoped to convey via the transformation of the Beggar was overshadowed by the less controversial idea of *media in vita in morte sumus* (Walk 106–14). As I have demonstrated, the two issues cannot be divorced.

Although there can be no doubt in *Das Salzburger große Welttheater* that Hofmannsthal is critical of King, Rich Man, Farmer, and Beauty, and ensures that they receive their just deserts, he ultimately upholds the principle of order which they collectively embody; individual players in the world's theater may have been found wanting, but Frau Welt is dismissed with the words, "Tritt weg, Welt, denn deinen Auftrag hast du erfüllt, und dein Meister ist mit dir zufrieden" (*DIII* 162). If the Beggar evokes the spectre of Bolshevism, so this vindication of the *status quo*, which Karl Kraus famously condemned as "das große Welttheater der zum Himmel stinkenden Kontraste" (4), constitutes an unmistakably conservative response to that challenge. As Walter Weiss has demonstrated (113–14), it has a disturbing similarity to the corporatist model of the state proposed by right-wing social theorist Othmar Spann in *Der wahre Staat* (1921), and one can hardly dismiss as coincidence the fact that *Das Salzburger große Welttheater* was the work chosen to represent the Austrian *Ständestaat* at the 1937 World Exhibition in Paris.

That Hofmannsthal exploited the sacral dimension of text and setting in order to invite the festival audience to celebrate with him the overcoming of the Communist threat, and in so doing appeared to make common cause with the forces of reaction, has rightly been regarded as a matter of regret by many commentators. Within Hofmannsthal scholarship, unease with regard to the political and cultural conservatism of his later work, of which *Das Salzburger große Welttheater* is arguably the most awkward example, has exacerbated that tendency toward compartmentalization which is inevitable given the breadth of his oeuvre; it has also meant that many thematic and stylistic continuities — such as the preoccupation with time, highlighted in this essay — remain to be explored.

Notes

[1] Unless referring to the German *Kulturnation*, I prefer "rooted cosmopolitanism" to Steinberg's concept of "nationalist cosmopolitanism" (Steinberg 84–115), since Hofmannsthal rarely used the term "Nation" without qualification when referring to either Weimar Germany or the Austrian First Republic.

[2] On Hofmannsthal's distortions of Austrian cultural history see Yates, *Schnitzler, Hofmannsthal, and the Austrian Theatre* 206–7; and Yates, "Hofmannsthal and the Austrian Comic Tradition" 73–83.

[3] On *Der Rosenkavalier* see Vilain, "'Stop all the Clocks': Time and Times in the 'Vienna Operas' of Hofmannsthal and Strauss."

[4] For a discussion of the text against this background, see Beniston, *"Welttheater": Hofmannsthal, Richard von Kralik, and the Revival of Catholic Drama in Austria, 1890–1934*.

Works Cited

Auernheimer, Raoul. "Der Salzburger "'Jedermann.'" *Neue Freie Presse, Vienna* 27 August 1920, reproduced in *Resonanz: 50 Jahre Kritik der Salzburger Festspiele*. Ed. Max Kaindl-Hönig. Salzburg: Salzburger Nachrichten Verlagsgesellschaft, 1971. 9–13.

Bahr, Hermann. "Die Hauptstadt von Europa: eine Phantasie in Salzburg." *Das Hermann-Bahr-Buch*. Berlin: Fischer, 1913. 122–29.

Beniston, Judith. "*Welttheater*": *Hofmannsthal, Richard von Kralik, and the Revival of Catholic Drama in Austria, 1890–1934.* London: Modern Humanities Research Association, 1998.

Fuhrich, Edda, and Gisela Prossnitz. *Die Salzburger Festspiele: Ihre Geschichte in Daten, Zeitzeugnissen und Bildern, I: 1920–1945.* Salzburg and Vienna: Residenz-Verlag, 1990.

Hofmannsthal, Hugo von — Eberhard von Bodenhausen. *Briefe der Freundschaft.* Berlin: Diederichs, 1953.

Hofmannsthal, Hugo von — Rudolf Pannwitz. *Briefwechsel 1907–1926.* Ed. Gerhard Schuster. Frankfurt am Main: Fischer, 1993.

Holl, Oskar. "Dokumente zur Entstehung der Salzburger Festspiele. Unveröffentlichtes aus der Korrespondenz der Gründer." *Maske und Kothurn* 13 (1967). 148–79.

Ihering, Herbert. "Salzburger Internationale." *Börsen Courier, Berlin,* 13 August 1931, reproduced in *Resonanz: 50 Jahre Kritik der Salzburger Festspiele.* Ed. Max Kaindl-Hönig. Salzburg: Salzburger Nachrichten Verlagsgesellschaft, 1971. 72–73.

Kraus, Karl. "Vom großen Welttheaterschwindel." *Die Fackel,* 601–7 (1922). 1–7.

Nadler, Josef. *Literaturgeschichte der deutschen Stämme und Landschaften.* 4 vols. Regensburg: J. Habbel, [1]1912–1928. *Literaturgeschichte des deutschen Volkes: Dichtung und Schrifttum der deutschen Stämme und Landschaften.* Berlin: Propyläen-Verlag, [4]1938–1941.

Nehring, Wolfgang. "Religiosität und Religion im Werk Hugo von Hofmannsthals." *Numinoses und Heiliges in der österreichischen Literatur.* Ed. Karlheinz F. Auckenthaler. Bern: Lang, 1995. 77–98.

Reinhardt, Max. "Denkschrift zur Errichtung eines Festspielhauses in Hellbrunn." *Max Reinhardt, Schriften: Briefe, Reden, Aufsätze, Interviews, Gespräche, Auszüge aus Regiebüchern.* Ed. Hugo Fetting. Berlin: Henschelverlag Kunst und Gesellschaft, 1974. 176–82.

Rieckmann, Jens. "Zwischen Bewußtsein und Verdrängung: Hofmannsthals jüdisches Erbe." *Deutsche Vierteljahrsschrift* 67 (1993). 466–83.

Rölleke, Heinz. "Hugo von Hofmannsthal: Jedermann." *Interpretationen: Dramen des 20. Jahrhunderts.* 2 vols. Stuttgart: Reclam, 1996. I, 93–108.

Steinberg, Michael P. *The Meaning of the Salzburg Festival: Austria as Theater and Ideology, 1890–1938.* Ithaca and London: Cornell University Press, 1990.

Vilain, Robert. "'Stop all the Clocks': Time and Times in the 'Vienna Operas' of Hofmannsthal and Strauss." *The Austrian Comic Tradition: Studies in Honour of W. E. Yates.* Ed. John R. P. McKenzie and Lesley Sharpe. Austrian Studies 9. Edinburgh: Edinburgh University Press, 1998. 185–201.

Volke, Werner. "Hugo von Hofmannsthal und Josef Nadler in Briefen." *Jahrbuch der Deutschen Schillergesellschaft* 18 (1974). 37–88.

Walk, Cynthia. *Hofmannsthals "Großes Welttheater": Drama und Theater.* Heidelberg: Carl Winter Universitätsverlag, 1980.

Weiss, Walter. "Salzburger Mythos? Hofmannsthals und Reinhardts Welttheater." *Zeitgeschichte* 2 (1975). 109–19.

Yates, W. E. "Hofmannsthal and the Austrian Comic Tradition." *Colloquia Germanica* 15 (1982). 73–83.

———. *Schnitzler, Hofmannsthal, and the Austrian Theatre.* New Haven and London: Yale University Press, 1992.

KATHERINE ARENS

Hofmannsthal's Essays: Conservation as Revolution

SCHOLARLY STEREOTYPE WOULD have it that Hugo von Hofmannsthal, like his Hans Karl Bühl in *Der Schwierige* (1921), was in many ways lost after the First World War. Yet such generalizations ignore the constancy of his cultural preferences as expressed from the earliest of his essays on. Well before the turn of the century, Hofmannsthal argued that cultural change was inevitable and necessary, but that it should never be engaged in a precipitous manner, since change must be based on the European heritage as lived and experienced by all. No wonder, then, that Hofmannsthal sought out cultural innovators like Max Reinhardt, the Ballets Russes, and other figures of *avant-garde* culture after the First World War. Like these artists, Hofmannsthal sought a revolution from within rather than a wholesale clean-sweep of older forms.

Throughout his career, Hofmannsthal's essays document his interest in finding in that common European culture a space for pluralistic discussion that could transcend class and national boundaries. He sought in that space not a cultural nationalism that would soon become fascism, but rather a cure for Europe's historical disruption. In his account, that space would, first and foremost, be occupied by *eine mittlere Sprache*, a language "in the middle" that could mediate among all parts of society, as a reference point for discussions of the new society's common needs. This common cultural space would also be faithful to the historical experience of the group, enabling the building of a bridge between past and future, one much like that Hofmannsthal attempted in his work with Reinhardt in staging *Jedermann* for the Salzburg Festival in 1922. He did not sense the danger in the vision of the *Volk* that others were gathering around him, yet he did consistently use his essayistic voice to argue for modernization.

Particularly the late essays "Der Schrifttum als geistiger Raum der Nation" and "Wert und Ehre deutscher Sprache" (both 1927) stem from an Austria that experienced the First World War and then, as a ruined country, rethought its cultural legacy as part of Europe. In these works, Hofmannsthal is by no means simply looking backward (as critics like Michael Steinberg argue), but rather continuing a long-term project begun at the start of his career: the renovation of western traditions for a new generation. Resisting not modernization, but modernism (with its insistence on a birth *ex nihilo* and on stylistic experimentation), these essays document Hofmannsthal's hopes for a cosmopolitan art that was not elitist or nationalist — an art that mediates rather than excludes because it grows from the historical experience of the group, not just from an elite.

This point can be argued most effectively with reference to Hofmannsthal's essays, taking them as the genre he used for cultural advocacy, but not necessarily as literary products in their own right. That point, however, has been obscured because of many of the pieces collected as "essays" originally served very different purposes: some were speeches to specific audiences or to commemorate deaths, anniversaries, or official functions; many were reviews of books, artists, and theater (mainly, actors); a few offer overt political commentary (mostly from the First World War); and others were taken from forewords and other publicity on books, especially when, in his late career, Hofmannsthal began to use editing and publishing as a way to advocate for his own vision of what the literary heritage needs to be. The "essays" were, in addition, originally scattered widely across journals and newspapers, and thus do not reflect Hofmannsthal's engagement with a particular audience. The scholar's difficulties in dealing with these texts are exacerbated further by the current edition status. The ten-volume Fischer paperback edition breaks the essays down into three volumes (8: 1891–1913; 9: 1914–1924; and 10: 1925–1929), with the third volume also containing "Aufzeichnungen"; an added fourth volume includes some famous "essays" of a different sort under the title of "Erfundene Gespräche," including the "Brief des Lord Chandos." Those "Erfundene Gespräche" are included in Vol. 31 of the new *Sämtliche Werke*, although the three or four volumes that will be dedicated to the essays have not yet appeared.[1] Some of the "essays" in each of these volumes, moreover, are actually drafts that may not have been intended for publication. As a final complication, the paperback edition has the texts divided into thematic groups (theater reviews or art reviews are distinguished from book reviews and author appreciations, for example).

Yet this appearance of diversity is in many ways deceiving. In general, Hofmannsthal's themes remain consistent throughout his essayistic work. First and foremost, he is a constant advocate for the classics of

German-language literature, of the past and present, and especially for distinguishing an Austrian canon from a German one. Thus, he will advocate for authors of the Viennese Volkstheater (a form he will draw on himself in *Ariadne auf Naxos* and *Rosenkavalier*), including Eduard von Bauernfeld and Raimund. At the same time, he supports the roots of all German-language literature, especially as represented in German Classicism and Romanticism. These essays are almost all notices of book editions or anniversary commemorations, used to highlight artistic excellence rather than arguing their cases in detail.

More crucial to an assessment of Hofmannsthal's program may be his many essays on canonical European literature, especially those associated today with the roots of Modernism — figures from Decadence and Naturalism (D'Annunzio and Pater through Wilde and Ibsen) to Balzac, Shakespeare, and Marlowe. These essays make the case for a common body of *European* literature, for work that reflects Europe's commonly held values. He is careful not to exclude authors or to narrow his canon to the point where his audience's favorites might be excluded; thus aside from traditional canonical literature, he will even include some contemporary German-language literature, to highlight it as part of this European heritage (even figures as recent as Hans Carossa).

A third, small set of essays refers to the theater and art icons preferred by the Modernist generation. From the performing arts, he includes the actress Eleonora Duse, the dancer Nijinsky, and particularly Mozart. Among painters he will highlight, notably, Van Eyck and Franz Stuck. These essays, however, seem to be incidental efforts, until his interests move toward his own revival of theater forms in plans for the Salzburg Festival, after the First World War.

On the few occasions when Hofmannsthal approaches the politics of the day, he usually does so from the humanistic point of view (such as when he decries the brutality of the First World War). Despite his preference for elite culture, however, Hofmannsthal is not overtly elitist, or ethnic-nationalist in inspiration. For instance, when he offers the "Ankündigung A. E. I. O. V. Bücher aus Österreich" (*RAII* 428), he uses the essay to make the case for a single Austria, composed of many ethnic groups; his proposed book series will include a volume of Slovenian folksongs (albeit in German translation), as well as political speeches from Austrian history.

Thus, in these various forms, the cultural relations between Austria and Germany, and those between Austria and Europe, remain at the forefront of Hofmannsthal's essays. This evidence has, however, rarely been collected as a serious index to Hofmannsthal's career. Let us now turn to some of these essays, in order to see how very consistent Hofmannsthal's arguments for Europe remain. The goal will be to set Hofmannsthal into an interwar context as a voice that tried to foster modernization, yet that fell decisively outside of the experimental modernism associated with writers like Joyce and Woolf. His appeal to a revitalized history rather than to experiments has been questioned by subsequent history, but this appeal had an integrity in its time.

Nationalism and Cosmopolitanism

From early in his career, Hofmannsthal conceived of cultures in terms of what today we would call *Geistesgeschichte*, in the theory that a culture was geographically and historically rooted in its own environment.

Hofmannsthal's 1893 discussion of the publication of one of Vienna's *Volkstheaterdichter*, Eduard von Bauernfeld, is indicative of his sense of history. The essay is typical for his early phase, comparatively florid in evoking *Anno dazumal* and cultural treasures. "Eduard von Bauernfelds dramatischer Nachlass" underscores how women and servants of his own day were different from those of the Biedermeier (*RAI* 187). In consequence, he believes that it is a mistake to play period works in contemporary clothes, a decision obscuring the earlier era's distinctiveness and difference (*RAI* 188). Artists, too, must be recognized as belonging to a specific era: "Die Dichter verarbeiten meist ihr Leben lang die Erlebnisse einer gewissen Epoche ihrer Entwicklung, wo ihr Fühlen intensiv war und dagegen das meiste Spätere als eine matte Wiederholung erscheint" (*RAI* 186).

The vehicle for that historical preservation of culture is language: "so weht aus der Sprache ein Hauch der Heimat, der jenseits aller Worte ist. In ihr bewegen sich wie dunkle verfließende Schatten so viele Gesichter, soviel Landschaft ist in ihr, soviel Jugend, soviel Unsägliches" ("Französische Redensarten" [1897] *RAI* 237). Language is alive, possessing the power of influencing how the world sees itself (*RAI* 238); it is also the vehicle through which a worldview is revealed to and imposed on a group (his term is *Prägung*) ("Der Dichter und diese Zeit" [1906] *RAI* 58). For this reason, the great books of Europe, from Balzac through Oscar Wilde, are crucial, since bad writing will help a culture's spirit to deteriorate. Instead, the poet acts as the eyes and ears of the age, passing on what can affect souls, as the person who records the culture's experience and *Bildung* in language (*RAI* 77).

Hofmannsthal characterizes his age as being in descent from the start of the modern era, a culture that originated in the decades between 1790 and 1820, "in denen ohne Handelsgeist, Spekulationsgeist, politischen Geist 'sich der Deutsche mit allem Fleiß zum Genossen einer höheren Epoche der Kultur bildet'" ("Vom dichterischen Dasein" [1907] *RAI* 84). How far this era got ahead of itself is exemplified by Mozart: "Österreich ist zuerst Geist geworden in seiner Musik und in dieser Form hat es die Welt erobert" ("Österreich im Spiegel seiner Dichtung" [1916] *RAII* 13). His successors were Grillparzer, Raimund, Nestroy, and Rosegger — representatives of a great intellectual tradition that was *Austrian* and not *German* or *Prussian*, resting on several hundred years of history and shared cultural experience that the Germany of Hofmannsthal's own era did not possess.

The Germany of the First World War was, for Hofmannsthal, in many ways a falsification. Its culture had, for example, pushed to eliminate foreign words from its German (just as, in the United States, sauerkraut became liberty cabbage). In consequence, its norm for the German language is a version of the language that has no historical roots, and is actually North German in its historical inspiration. Colloquial Austrian German, in contrast, was grounded in historical truths in many shadings. It was, he claims, the most mixed (*gemengteste*) and culturally rich language of the world, including a language of the military and one for diplomacy: "Aber wir haben und hatten auch neben der bürgerlichen eine aristokratische Sprache und neben der Sprache der Innern Stadt eine Vorstadtsprache; und diese wieder ist nicht gleich der Sprache der Ortschaften rings um Wien, ganz zu schweigen vom flachen Lande" ("Unsere Fremdwörter" [1914] *RAII* 363). All these variants of Austrian are aspects of real language that must be accommodated in literature and in education as part of the living heritage of the German-speaking nation. But the era of the First World War has not met this challenge, since the political entity that has emerged as Germany does not understand, or even notice, Austria: "Es darf, auch in dem heutigen sehr ernsten Zusammenhang, ausgesprochen werden, daß Österreich unter den Ländern der Erde eines der von Deutschen ungekanntesten oder schlechtest gekannten ist" ("Wir Österreicher und Deutschland" [1915] *RAII* 390).

Hofmannsthal thus draws careful distinctions between political entities and cultural ones — the Austria that, in the days of Franz Joseph, had no official name nonetheless had a culture that had been broken apart by the Treaty of Versailles. His Austria is a cultural entity specifically marked as especially European as the continent's defense against the Turk. Hofmannsthal admits that there is a relationship between Germany and Austria, "Stammesverwandtschaft mit dem einen der großen Volkselemente Österreichs" ("Wir Österreicher und Deutschland" [1915] *RAII* 391). But *Reichsdeutsche* (he uses the word) do not understand the historical entity which is Austria, "kein schlechthin Bestehendes, sondern eine ungelöste Aufgabe" (*RAII* 393–94), subject to a "pure spiritual imperialism" and representing a challenge to Germany-in-Europe:

> Denn Österreich bedarf ohne Unterlaß des Einströmens deutschen Geistes: Deutschland ist ihm Europa. . . . Was wir Österreicher von Deutschland beständig verlangen müssen, ist das Reinste seiner geisten Kraft. Ein Reinstes aber kann von Staat zu Staat, wie von Individuum zu Individuum, nur unter einer hohen Spannung gegeben werden. Wo uns Deutschland ein Minderes gibt, als sein Höchstes und Reinstes, wird es uns zu Gift. Das Höchste deutschen Lebens, unter einer hohen Spannung gegeben und genommen, ist auch für unsere Slawen, ob sie es in verworrenen und getrübten Zeiten Wort haben oder nicht, Leben des Lebens. Und dies an sie zu geben sind wir ihnen schuldig. ("Wir Österreicher und Deutschland" [1915] *RAII* 394)

This paradox recurs throughout Hofmannsthal's essays: Germany (especially cherished figures like Goethe) is the course of German-language culture: "Wir empfingen von den Deutschen wieder und wieder einströmendes Volksgut" ("Wir Österreicher und Deutschland" [1915] *RAII* 394). Yet Austria has taken the best of that German Europe and made it into something else that the Germany of postwar Europe has not been able to appreciate.

While Hofmannsthal's use of terminology like *Volksgut* is disturbing in retrospect, he leaves no doubt that he was speaking of European history rather than genetics (or eugenics). His Europe is not a political nation, but rather a cultural heritage that can turn the *masses* back into the *people*:

> Die Mission Österreichs, an die ich glaube und für die ein ungeheueres Blutopfer in diesen Monaten von unsern Völkern vereint mit dem ungarischen Volk gebracht wird, ist eine europäische: wie könnten wir es ertragen, jenes Europa, von dem wir unsere tausendjährige Mission empfangen haben und das sie uns beständig erneuern muß, woanders wir nicht erstarren und absterben sollen, als ein im geistigen und sittlichen Sinne nicht mehr existierendes zu denken? Österreich bedarf mehr als alle andern eines Europa — es ist ja doch selber ein Europa im Kleinen. ("Krieg und Kultur" [1915] *RAII* 417)

Hofmannsthal's European Austria came to its cultural maturity around 1800 and is endangered a century later by its two dominant trends: "Provinzialismus" and "Übertriebenen Partikularismus" ("Österreich im Spiegel seiner Dichtung" [1916] *RAII* 21). Therefore, the German *Wesen* that Austria inherited is different from the German Reich in its political incarnation of the First World War era ("Österreich im Spiegel seiner Dichtung" [1916] *RAII* 23).

Hofmannsthal's Austrian culture thus correlates with real, lived experience, not simply with a political entity: "Kultur ist uns kein Totes und Abgeschlossenes, sondern ein Lebendiges, das Ineinandergreifen der Lebenskreise und Lebenskräfte, des Politischen und des Militärischen, die Verbindung des Materiellen mit dem Sittlichen" ("Österreich im Spiegel seiner Dichtung" [1916] *RAII* 24). The future of that Austria-as-culture, however, requires not just Germany, or an isolationist world, but a commitment to Europe: "ohne einen Hauch von geistigem Univeralismus kann ein zukünftiges Österreich weder gewollt noch geglaubt werden" ("Österreich im Spiegel seiner Dichtung" [1916] *RAII* 25). This Austria results from the legacy of the *Heiliges Römisches Reich* and the Catholic Church, with Austria as a *Grenzkolonie* ("Die österreichische Idee" [1917] *RAII* 455, 456).

The author's approach to Austrian culture and its future in Europe remains consistent: Europe needs the German inheritance as Austria uses it, not as represented in Prussia. This is not *Deutschtümelei* of the traditional sort, because he carefully estranges Austria from Germany and approximates it to the future of Europe. His Austria is still necessary to define the form Europe's future will assume:

> Dies Europa, das sich neu formen will, bedarf eines Österreich: eines Gebildes von ungekünstelter Elastizität, aber eines Gebildes, eines wahren Organismus, durchströmt von der inneren Religion zu sich selbst, ohne welche keine Bindungen lebender Gewalten möglich sind; es bedarf seiner, um den polymorphen Osten zu fassen. ("Die österreichische Idee" [1917] *RAII* 457)

Hofmannsthal's Austria is an example of European assimilation, a bulwark against the East, and a moral authority because of its history. It is an organic whole, as he will underscore in a set of notes on "Preusse und Österreicher" [1917]. He clearly explains which of the two potential German nations has historical authority: "Preussen: Geschaffen, ein künstlicher Bau, von Natur armes Land, . . . Disziplinierbarste Masse, grenzlose Autorität . . . Österreich: Gewachsen, geschichtliches Gewebe, von Natur reiches Land . . ." (*RAII* 459). History has determined that Austria's culture has created a superior type of citizen through its culture, with a healthier cognitive style (Austrians will, for example, decline dialectics [*RAII* 460]). Even the art of the two German nations differs, with Berlin's theater focusing on the "pathological and bizarre," or on decorativeness, while Austria's theater, in the tradition of Mozart's opera, develops "aus der aristokratischen und zugleich volkstümlichen Kultur des alten Österreich" ("Proposition" [1917] *RAII* 231, echoed in "Das Reinhardtsche Theater" [1918]).

In the postwar era, Hofmannsthal takes up the widespread postwar trope (promulgated most visibly by Hermann Bahr) that the Baroque is Austria's natural inheritance, part of the south's heritage, with its emphasis on pageantry: "Das Festspielgedanke ist der eigentliche Kunstgedanke des bayrisch-österreichischen Stammes" ("Deutsche Festspiele zu Salzburg" [1919] *RAII* 255). Because two German states share this legacy, the *Festspiel* belongs on the border, to unite various strands of culture, wedding Mozart to Goethe and Schiller: "So tritt Weimar zu Salzburg: Die Mainlinie wird betont und zugleich aufgehoben. Süddeutsche Stammeseigentümlichkeit tritt scharf hervor und zugleich tritt das Zusammenhaltende vor die Seele" ("Deutsche Festspiele zu Salzburg" [1919] *RAII* 255). Poets like Ferdinand Raimund embody this inheritance of the *Theatrum mundi*, as "ein Individuum und . . . auch zugleich eine Welt. Die Grenzen zwischen ihm und allem andern, was zu dieser Welt gehört, sind ganz fließend. Er gehört einer Gemeinschaft an: Wien, und er teilt mit dieser Gemeinschaft alles, was er hat" ("Ferdinand Raimund" [1920] *RAII* 118). Thus Raimund's link to the community enabled him to stage the language and culture he shared with the people.

In Hofmannsthal's estimation, however, the World War threatened this cultural legacy and showed where it needed modernization. Austria's and Germany's opponents had a political language that could be practical, a language that his own country did not have ("Adam Müllers Zwölf Reden über die Beredsamkeit" [1920] *RAII* 123). The two countries, like Belgium and France, remain distinct, despite their many commonalties:

> Der Zusammenhang Österreichs mit der Gesamtheit des Deutschtums, andererseits die Freiheit und teilweise Fremdheit, mit der Österreich dem im neuen Reich vereinigten Deutschtum gegenüber steht, ist weit mehr als bloßer Sprachzusammenhang. Er ruht darauf, daß Österreich ein Teil des alten Reichs, sowohl des Heiligen Römischen Reiches als dann des Deutschen Bundes war, und dies bis vor sechsig Jahren, während etwa die Schweiz sich schon vor mehr als vierhundert Jahren faktisch und formal vom alten deutschen Reich abgelöst hat. ("Bemerkungen" [1921] *RAII* 473)

Passages like this argue the actual priority of Austria over Germany, despite the latter's current political dominance. The optimal Austria that Hofmannsthal seeks is universal, blended, and humane in a way that the German Empire is not. In part, that is due to Austria's internationalism, based on its Catholic heritage and on the heritage of the seventeenth century, which Hofmannsthal thinks is broader than that of the eighteenth. This Austrian situation is a more universal situation that must be added to the current state of the "Prussian German Empire" of the day: "daß das gegenwärtige Deutsche Reich nicht das ganze Gesicht des deutschen Wesens in Europa zeige, daß dieses Gesicht nicht ohne die in Österreich erhaltenen Züge eines älteren und höheren Deutschtums erkannt werden könne" ("Bemerkungen" [1921] *RAII* 476). Hofmannsthal's Austrians are thus again presented as better representatives of German culture than the Germans are, since the Germans have moved further away from its direct political inheritance. Thus this is *Deutschtümelei*, yet not tied to the political entity born out of the German Reich in any of its current forms.

Hofmannsthal will not change his idea about the configuration that Europe took on after the First World War. The German language, as represented in a set of live dialects in the community, remains the anchor for the community and for the group's future. He is interested in what he calls "real power," not prestige. That power, however, is not found in a political nation or in its ability to make propaganda ("neuen Begriffen das Pathos zu geben") to save a dying way of life, no matter what kinds of story it can tell of itself:

> Denn die Welt um uns, die wir die Wirklichkeit zu nennen gewohnt sind, ist ein Kampf (und ein Ausgleich) von Mächten, die Fiktionen sind; ihnen aber eine neue Fiktion zu gesellen oder überzuordnen, ist die Befugnis der geistigen Potenz. Eine Gruppe, die es unternimmt, einer absterbenden Wirklichkeit neue Wirklichkeit aufzudrängen, muß zumindest sich selbst als eine Elite empfinden, um dann, wenn ihr Werk nicht vergeblich war, von der nächst heraufkommenden Epoche als eine solche empfunden zu werden. (*"Europäische Revue*: Eine Monatsschrift" [1926] *RAIII* 79)

The situation in Hofmannsthal's day is that German culture has a language, but no self-consciousness — which his Austria may well have.

This vision of Austria as a European culture sheds unusual light on perhaps the two greatest of Hofmannsthal's late essays, ones that, however, were not originally journalistic. The first is a speech: "Das Schrifttum als geistiger Raum der Nation: Rede, gehalten im Auditorium Maximum der Universität München am 10. January 1927" (1926) (*RAIII* 24–41); the second is the introduction to a collection of maxims about the German language: "Wert und Ehre deutscher Sprache" (1927) (*RAIII* 128–33). "Das Schrifttum" is, notably, dedicated to Karl Vossler, noted philologist and rector of the university. Both again tie the question of the German language into then-current debates about nationalism.

Hofmannsthal's vocabulary seems off-putting today, but it does not diverge significantly from his earlier explications. First and foremost, he seeks a community as the heart of a nation (which, he notes, America does not have):

> Nicht durch unser Wohnen auf dem Heimatboden, nicht durch unsere leibliche Berührung in Handel und Wandel, sondern durch ein geistiges Anhängen vor allem sind wir zur Gemeinschaft verbunden. . . . In einer Sprache finden wir uns zueinander, die völlig etwas anderes ist als das bloße natürliche Verständigungsmittel; denn in ihr redet Vergangenes zu uns, Kräfte wirken auf uns ein und werden unmittelbar gewaltig, denen die politischen Einrichtungen weder Raum zu geben, noch Schranken zu setzen mächtig sind, ein eigentümlicher Zusammenhang wirksam zwischen den Geschlechtern, wir ahnen dahinter ein Etwas waltend, das wir den Geist der Nation zu nennen uns getrauen. ("Das Schrifttum," *RAIII* 24)

That understanding is mediated in writing, as a *Schrifttum,* a body of writing of all sorts, including anecdotes, political speeches, and newspaper articles. In this, Hofmannsthal is decisively combating the emergence of a self-declared elite in literature, and wants to consider again a body of writing that remains part of the community. He wishes to avoid divisions in class enforced through such writing ("der unglückliche Riß in unserem Volk zwischen Gebildeten und Ungebildeten" [*RAIII* 24]).

Thus the effective writing that reflects the core of the nation is not simply elite (although voices like Goethe did speak to those groups). In countries with a better-developed sense of public discourse, like France, Hofmannsthal finds a better-developed popular literature, and a language that can mediate among (and hence bond) all sectors of society: "Die Blüte dieser Tendenz ist die Sprachnorm, welche die Nation zusammenhält und innerhalb ihrer dem Spiel widerstreitender Tendenzen — der aristokratischen wie der nivellierenden, der revolutionären wie der konservative — Raum gewahrt" (*RAIII* 25). When these "tendencies" continue to pay attention to each other and remain in productive rivalry, then there is a nation. Thus "writing," *Schrifttum, écriture,* defines the real space of the nation, the space between audience and writer, binding all into a whole that is not *zerrissen* (fractured).

Hofmannsthal is clearly utopian in his hopes (or rather, a strict Kantian, in the sense of "Was ist Aufklärung?"). But what is more crucial here is his warning that an elite culture cannot be elitist — that the self-declared upper classes cannot isolate themselves from the public face of the nation, which he describes very much in the way that Benedict Anderson would later call an *imagined community.*

> Die Nation, durch ein unzerreißbares Gewebe des Sprachlich-Geistigen zusammengehalten, wird Glaubensgemeinschaft, in der das Ganze des natürlichen und kultürlichen Lebens einbeschlossen ist; ein Nationsstaat dieser Art erscheint als das innere Universum ... Der Raumbegriff, der aus diesem geistigen Ganzen emaniert, ist identisch mit dem Geisterraum, den die Nation in ihrem eigenen Bewußtsein und in dem der Welt einnimmt. (*RAIII* 27)

This "inner universe" defines the power, role, rights, and duties within a nation defined as a community. Yet Hofmannsthal refuses to equate that nation with the Germany of his era, which does not have the necessary preconditions (cultural traditions) to become an imagined community. His accusation that Germany has the "disease of abstraction" echoes both Marx's *Theses on Feuerbach* and Benjamin's *Theses on the Philosophy of History*. His era's Germany has the *idea* of a community or nation, rather than the reality, since there is nothing natural, traditional, about it.

Significantly, he also begins to reverse the image of the poet-genius that has been cherished by the *Bildungsbürgertum* in the wake of German Classicism. In this vision, the poet cannot create or lead the nation, but must rather embody and articulate what the nation already is on the basis of its history and experience. The nation, not the poet, is the agent of national formation or change:

> Um die Sprache ringt [der Dichter] zuzeiten wirklich — aber nicht mitzuwirken an der Schöpfung der Sprachnorm, in der die Nation zur wahren Einheit sich bindet, sondern als die magische Gewalt, die sie ist, will er sich sie dienstbar machen, seine geistige Leidenschaft ist so groß, in den höchsten Momenten wird er wirklich ein leidenschaftlich Erschautes bis in den Rhythmus seines Leibes in sich nachzittern fühlen und dann wahrhaft Dichter sein. (*RAIII* 33)

This poet is in the service of the nation as almost a channeller, one responsible for making extant currents of language visible and significant. That poet does not, however, create the language, but rather take it into himself, lending form to its ineffability.

Hofmannsthal's final assessment of his Europe's *imagined community* grows out of his concept of history. Like his younger contemporaries Ernst Cassirer, Max Horkheimer, and Theodor W. Adorno, he decides that the Enlightenment is not yet complete. Yet the Austro-German nation he seeks originated earlier, in the Renaissance and Reformation, which actually started the social and political processes that were to bring Europe out of the middle ages and into an era of freedom and new humanity: "Der Prozeß, von dem ich rede, ist nichts anderes als eine konservative Revolution von einem Umfange, wie die europäische Geschichte ihn nicht kennt. Ihr Ziel ist Form, eine neue deutsche Wirklichkeit, an der die ganze Nation teilnehmen könne" (*RAIII* 41).

This quotation is often adduced as Hofmannsthal's acceptance of a proto-Nazi nationalism. But he means to point not to the extant German nation, but rather to a historically-grounded community aware of its heritage and working toward a common future — toward a "conservative revolution" that will change Europe, but not by sweeping it away. Instead, he wants to preserve the "German reality" in which *all parts* of the nation can participate. This is, in the context of Hofmannsthal's essay work, a late Enlightenment Europe fulfilling the potential of the Renaissance and Reformation, not the strand of Modernist Europe that tries to overcome its past rather than to ennoble or sublate it in a new synthesis of spirit and life.

This is, I believe, a period-correct reading of Hofmannsthal's project, one that bespeaks his possible naiveté about the ability of a group to resist co-optation by a self-declared elite like the Nazis. Yet it is echoed in his other great cultural history essay of the era, "Wert und Ehre deutscher Sprache" (1927). There again he begins with the need for the German language to function as a mediator, to join the community into a commonality that is missing in today's politics, so that "das in jedem Wort Mitverstandene" will join each hearer into a commonality:

> . . . das gesellige Element, worin sich beide, der Redende und der Angeredete, zusammen wissen; von dem Einzelnen, der ihm gegenübersteht, nicht zu sehr dessen Sich-Unterscheiden, nicht der individuelle Anspruch, der ja leicht zu Ablehnung herausfordert, sondern die Verflochtenheit, gemäß der ein jeder zu den Gruppierungen innerhalb der Gesamtheit, den Einrichtungen, den Unternehmungen in gewissen typischen Verhältnissen steht. Nicht so sehr das, was er für sich ist, soll in seiner Sprache sich ausprägen, als das, was er vorstellt. In seinem Sprechen repräsentiert sich die Gesamtheit. Es herrscht in einer solchen Umgangsrede zwischen den Worten ein Etwas, daß sie untereinander gleichsam Familie bilden, wobei sie alle gleichmäßig verzichten, ihr Tiefstes auszusagen. (*RAIII* 128–29)

In his diagnosis, the community of German-speakers in his world has only a language of utility, a series of individual languages without a center. But in a recourse to history, that nation may be rediscovered:

> Die Sprache ist ein großes Totenreich, unauslotbar tief; darum empfangen wir aus ihr das höchste Leben. Es ist unser zeitloses Schicksal in ihr, und die Übergewalt der Volksgemeinschaft über alles Einzelne.
> Unmittelbar schreiten wir durch sie in das Volk hinein, das fühlen wir. (*RAIII* 132)

The works that contain that "highest life" will be those he will later try to include in the Salzburg Festival: *Faust*, his own *Ariadne*, mystery plays like his own *Jedermann*, and the Johann Strauss, Jr. operetta *Die Fledermaus.*

That Salzburg Festival would later help to label Hofmannsthal as a conservative instead of a conservator, as I argue here. He, however, saw the Festival as a way to reinvoke the center of the traditional German-language culture he sought to set against Prussian Germany, "den süd-deutschen (bayrisch-österreichischen) Theatergeist" ("Das Salzburger Programm" *RAIII* 178). He is, on the one hand, asserting the necessity of a national theater in the sense familiar since Schiller, yet with a distinct social goal rather than simply an educational one: to unite social politics, urban and rural groups. This is, explicitly, not the modernist theater of cities like Berlin that portray only the crass and evil, not the rest of the nation ("Das Publikum der Salzburger Festspiele" *RAIII* 184–85).

Critics, however, have tended to read these recommendations in the context of his late enthusiasm for Josef Nadler's *Literaturgeschichte*, the work of a scholar who later became a centerpiece of Fascist culture. Hofmannsthal never wrote an extended essay on Nadler, but we have his 1924 to 1928 notes for an essay for the *Deutsche Vierteljahrsschrift für Literaturwissenschaft und Geistesgeschichte* (*RAIII* 639–40). They are fragmentary, but they again help to contextualize Hofmannsthal's ongoing engagement with a conservative revolution.

On the one hand, he approves completely of the overall approach of the book, which eschews artificial aesthetic categorizations like "Realist" or "Neo-Romantic," but rather: "Der Inhalt ist — eine Ergänzung von Gervinus — der Prozeß der Staatswerdung — und das Sicheingliedern des Geistigen" (*RAIII* 149). This assesses Nadler fairly as a *Geistesgeschichtler* in the tradition of Gervinus and Dilthey, interested in what Hofmannsthal calls "unzerstörbare Lebensbegriffe" and "fortwirkende Vergangenheit" that are part and parcel of a nation's mind and experience (*RAIII* 147). This mind and experience, he continues, take many forms in a nation's voice, from political tract to art, and so it is Nadler's achievement to have rewritten the history of writing as the history of affiliations ("die Filiationen"), and thus to have contributed to a future uniting of the nations: "Das Buch läßt nichts verlorengehen, es zeigt das Geistesleben der Nation als kontinuierlichen Prozeß der Selbst-Bewußtwerdung" (*RAIII* 148).

Yet Hofmannsthal does not approve of Nadler without restriction, as a longer note, "Zur Theorie oder These Nadlers," confirms. The text is too deterministic: "Bedenklich Determinismus — alles Höhere

des Menschen aus seinem Niedersten entwickeln — eine Art Freudia-
nismus — dem Bedenklichen der Zeit verwandt —" (*RAIII* 150).
Hofmannsthal will not accept the restricted place given to the individual in any ethnic-nationalist overreading of historical process, nor
Nadler's confusion of forcefulness with art — as he would not have accepted Nadler's later engagement in the Nazi mass culture that cut
Germany off from Europe.

Hofmannsthal's essayistic voice is thus not dulled in his later works.
He remains convinced about art, but not necessarily about artists as
leaders; he is a conservator, but not one who denies the need for
change and progress.

Europe and the Ethics of Historical Aesthetics

The question of Hofmannsthal's adherence to Europe and its history is
not only a political one, however. Europe has an artistic heritage as well
as a history. Just as he considers the nation a cultural unit throughout
his career, Hofmannsthal's criteria for aesthetic excellence remain re-
markably consistent. In all cases, Hofmannsthal is careful not to fly in
the face of public taste and interest, even as he tries to evaluate art and
aesthetics sympathetically. He remains firm in his resolve to make art
cater to the heart of the nations whose identities he seeks.

His approach to literature is already established in one of his earliest
reviews, on "Algernon Charles Swinburne," an essay written in 1892
and published in 1893. Swinburne attracts Hofmannsthal's attention as
a very popular poet who had been passed over for poet laureate, "weil
er nichts Heiligeres zu tun weiß, als auf dem reichen blauen Meer mit
wachen Augen die unsterbliche Furche zu suchen, aus der die Göttin
stieg" (*RAI* 148). This image from the close of the essay evokes the
world of Aestheticism in terms that his contemporaries would recognize. Yet as Hofmannsthal hints, that "rich blue sea" that houses an unseen goddess is beautiful, but not necessarily either useful or part of
life, just as these artists are not: "Die Luft ihres Lebens ist die Atmosphä-
re eines künstlich verdunkelten Zimmers, dessen weiche Dämmerung
von den verbebenden Schwingungen Chopinscher Musik und den Re-
flexen patinierter Bronzen, alter Samte und nachgedunkelter Bilder erfüllt ist" (*RAI* 144). Poets like Swinburne serve at best an abstract
beauty, "der moralfremden, zweckfremden, lebenfremden," that vio-
lates morality and "healthy common sense" (*RAI* 143).

This is much the same criticism leveled against Gabriele
D'Annunzio in several essays (1893, 1894, 1895). In the first, Hofmannsthal accuses D'Annunzio of being overly decorative:

Man hat manchmal die Empfindung, als hätten uns unsere Väter, die Zeitgenossen des jüngeren Offenbach, und unsere Großväter, die Zeitgenossen Leopardis, und alle die unzähligen Generationen vor ihnen, als hätten sie uns, den Spätgeborenen, nur zwei Dinge hinterlassen: hübsche Möbel und überfeine Nerven. Die Poesie dieser Möbel erscheint uns als das Vergangene, das Spiel dieser Nerven als das Gegenwärtige. (*RAI* 174)

These artists may be in some ways the "consciousness" (*Bewußtsein*) of the generation, but they are not positive: they are "Vampire, lebendige Leichen" (*RAI* 175, 174). Artists like D'Annunzio who evoke moods and emotions rather than a well-rounded reality represent the "Triumph der Möbelpoesie" (*RAI* 183). They are altogether *wirklichkeitsfremd*, escapist, as he reiterates in 1894, calling them static (*starr*) and artificial in their worldviews. They lack the ability to reveal (*Offenbarung*) (201). Such emotive and beautiful artificiality may appeal to France, Italy, and "other barbaric countries." The essay's closing line is decidedly two-edged: "Es gibt da und dort einige junge Menschen, die sich zu freuen verstehen, daß solch ein Künstler am Leben ist" (*RAI* 202). Only "a few of the young" will appreciate that art — a statement which can be read as designating that youth as special, or the art as appealing only to certain over-sensitive juveniles.

As Hofmannsthal picks this point up in 1895, he offers even more devastating criticism. D'Annunzio is a strong poet, able to conjure up pasts as vivid backdrops, but not as life or reality: "Das Dasein war ihm ein ungeheurer Mechanismus. Die Schicksale der Menschen und der Dinge stürzten bei ihm nebeneinander hin durch das Leere" (*RAI* 207). As he summarizes in his 1894 "Walter Pater" essay, such aestheticized art is idealized: "Das ist Ästhetismus, in England ein großes, berühmtes Wort, im allgemeinen ein übernährtes und überwachsenes Element unserer Kultur und gefährlich wie Opium" (*RAI* 196). The aesthetes reach beauty, but never *Dasein*, reality. Pater, D'Annunzio, and Swinburne all evoke beauty and show it to us, but they remain outside of society, staring at the blue sea for a goddess who will never emerge, no matter how much they pine for her.

Hofmannsthal's 1896 essay on "Gedichte von Stefan George" takes this point to its limit: George uses his historicist talent in the present to evoke the requisite nymphs and Greek temples. Hofmannsthal cites Pater — "there is style in it" (*RAI* 214) — to describe George's poetry as undeniably beautiful but essentially useless. By using the hyperaesthete Pater to "compliment" George, Hofmannsthal consigns the poet to the same juvenile world that D'Annunzio occupies:

> Die angeborene Königlichkeit eines sich selbst besitzenden Gemütes
> ist der Gegenstand der drei Bücher. Nichts ist der Zeit fremder, nichts
> ist den wenigen wertvoller. Die Zeit wird sich begnügen, aus den
> schlanken tyrannischen Gebärden, aus den mit schmalen Lippen spar-
> sam gesetzten Worten, aus dieser leichtschreitenden hochköpfigen
> Menschlichkeit und der im unsicheren Licht der frühen Mor-
> genstunden gesehenen Welt einen seltsamen Reiz zu ziehen. Einige
> wenige aber meinen, nun mehr um den Wert des Daseins zu wissen als
> vorher. (*RAI* 221)

The beauty of George's poetry is "alien to the age," and "valuable to
the few," while purporting (falsely) to reveal existence. George cannot
do what greater artists like Victor Hugo were able to, in Hofmannsthal's estimation. In *Studie über die Entwickelung des Dichters
Victor Hugo* (1901), he notes that Hugo achieves the epitome of art
that the aesthetes miss: "Poesie ist Weltgefühl; es wird in den Werken
eines poetischen Genies immer ein Bild der Welt sein" (*RAI* 275).

For Hofmannsthal, then, art centers its optic on people, and not
furniture or stage sets. The aesthete could not be further removed from
art's purpose of bearing witness to the truth, as his 1905 "Sebastian
Melmoth" essay on Oscar Wilde notes, heartbreakingly. Wilde's person
and his fate were intertwined from the first, like Oedipus, seeing but
blind to the inevitable:

> Der Ästhet war tragisch. Der Geck war tragisch. . . . Man sagt: "Er
> war ein Ästhet, und dann kamen unglückselige Verwicklungen über
> ihn, ein Netz von unglückseligen Verwicklungen."
>
> Man sollte nicht mit den Worten alles zudecken. Ein Ästhet! Da-
> mit ist gar nichts gesagt. Walter Pater war ein Ästhet, ein Mensch der
> vom Genießen und Nachschaffen der Schönheit lebte, und der war
> dem Leben gegenüber voll Scheu und Zurückhaltung, voll Zucht. Ein
> Ästhet ist naturgemäß durch und durch voll Zucht. Oscar Wilde aber
> war voll Unzucht, voll tragischer Unzucht. Sein Ästhetismus war et-
> was wie ein Krampf. Die Edelsteine, in denen er vorgab mit Lust zu
> wühlen, waren wie gebrochene Augen, die erstarrt waren, weil sie den
> Anblick des Lebens nicht ertragen hatten. . . . Unablässig forderte er
> das Leben heraus. Er insultierte die Wirklichkeit. (*RAI* 342–43).

Those last lines are the crux of the matter: the purported aesthete's frozen eyes could not bear the view of life . . . he insulted reality. Wilde,
too, was in his velvet room — until he went out of it, believing he was
above history.

Hofmannsthal thus returns to familiar ground: art must be part of a
community and of its present, as well as at one with its historical traditions. Significantly, he does not restrict these desiderata to verbal art,
but will also extend them to stage performers. Thus he will prefer Eleo-

nora Duse over Sarah Bernhardt, since the former evokes reality on the stage while the latter is histrionic. He approaches in this way two dancers who are taken today as founders of modern dance: Ruth St. Denis, and Isadora Duncan. In 1906, St. Denis is "Die unvergleichliche Tänzerin" (*RAI* 666), whose art is tied to both his present and to the Orient (she had taken her troupe to Calcutta, Japan, and other destinations in the Orient to perform and imbibe local performance customs).

There is much that is stylized about her performance, especially in costumes and staging, but, in Hofmannsthal's estimation, she becomes "den Tanz an sich" when when she performs a solo that starts inside a stage temple, lit from above, rising from a kneeling prayer position. Her work compares to Rodin's in embodying not poses, but a "rhythmischer Fluss" (*RAI* 499). Hofmannsthal even attributes to her the power of "Urworte orphisch," leaving Rilke unnamed but present as a benchmark for artists who can make the past live for the present. Still, her performance is not part of Europe, because it is sensuous and exotic, but it is also much more:

> So also tanzt sie. Es ist die berauschendste Verkettung von Gebärden, deren nicht eine an die Pose auch nur streift. Es sind unaufhörliche Emanationen absoluter sinnlicher Schönheit, deren nicht eine Konvention ist, zumindest nicht europäische Konvention, sondern allenfalls die Konvention höchsten, strengsten, hieratischen, uralten Stiles. . . . [Ihr Tanz] geht an die Grenzen der Wollust und er ist keusch. Er ist ganz den Sinnen hingegeben, und er deutet auf Höheres. (*RAI* 499–500)

St. Denis reinvokes the truth of past eras, but never in a museal or historicist mode because she unites past and present, the imminent and the transcendent, beauty of the body and the mind. Hers is a creation of absolute beauty, absolute presence, but also absolute engagement with the here and now — she does not hide in velvet rooms, but is elemental and indefinable: "Das ein völlig Fremdes vor uns darstellt, ohne die Prätension des Ethnographischen, des Interessanten, einfach nur um seiner Schönheit willen" (*RAI* 497). This is the kind of revelation he misses in George's work.

St. Denis' competitor, Isadora Duncan, does not measure up, because Duncan was an ethnographer looking at the past from the outside, too sentimental and historicist for Hofmannsthal. As he summarizes:

> Die ungeheure Unmittelbarkeit dessen, was sie [St. Denis] tut, diese strenge, fast abweisende Unmittelbarkeit, dies Kommentarlose, der grandiose Ernst ohne Pedanterie, alles dies schafft um sie herum den leeren Raum, den das Außerordentliche immer um sich hat [. . .]. Die Duncan, so charmant sie ist, wirkt neben ihr unendlich sentimental. Es

war das Geheimnis der Duncan, daß sie wußte, was Tanzkunst ist. Dieses da ist eine geborene große Tänzerin. Das Tanzen der Duncan, an diesen inkalkulablen Gebärden gemessen, war ein Zeigen, fast ein Demonstrieren. Diese tanzt. Die Duncan hatte etwas von einem sehr gewinnenden und leidenschaftlich dem Schönen hingegebenen Professor der Archäolgie. Diese ist die lydische Tänzerin, aus dem Relief herabgestiegen. (*RAI* 501)

That "relief" necessarily evokes the unnamed Rilke; but his use of the term "sentimental" is key. He is using it as Schiller had, to refer to art in which the mind is too divorced from the experience for the result to seem natural. Calling Duncan a professor of archeology devoted to beauty echoes on his earlier assessment of Swinburne's "furniture poetry" — beautiful, but lacking life.

These assessments also echo in Hofmannsthal's most famous piece of short prose, his 1902 "Ein Brief," an "Invented Conversation,"[2] which can also be read as a critique of aestheticism. The letter closes with an interesting duplicity, stating that it is his last: "diese[r] voraussichtlich letzt[e] Brief[. . .], den ich an Francis Bacon schreibe." Yet this letter may not necessarily be "the last letter" that Chandos ever would write, as critics prefer to read this passage, but perhaps better noted as "the last letter that he would write *to Bacon*."

When Chandos seeks refuge in the country, he is not only echoing the history of the family of which he is a fictional member (the Elizabethan Baron Chandos was known for the lavish hospitality of his estate, Sudeley House), but also taking a position vis-à-vis Francis Bacon's cultural politics (cf. Schultz in Works Cited). Born 1561, Bacon's career began as a barrister and queen's/king's counsel; after Elizabeth's 1603 death, Bacon continued in the service of James I in various capacities, including Lord Chancellor. In 1621, having fallen out of official favor, Bacon was imprisoned, which helped turn him toward philosophy. He died in 1626, because of bronchitis contracted in an experiment in preserving food with snow (memorialized in Bertolt Brecht's short story "Das Experiment" [written 1938–39]).

Bacon's most famous work in philosophy is the *Novum Organum* (1620), a treatise on the methodology of acquiring knowledge from nature. His famous Book II demonstrates the limits on the deductive method of science and recommends the inductive method instead, based on observed facts. As part of that discussion, Bacon enumerates the ways in which language can cause human error (as "idols," popular stereotypes). Most Hofmannsthal scholars believe that his Chandos has rejected Bacon the rationalist and fled from language at the onset of a linguistic crisis,[3] yet they ignore the historical Bacon's critique of language. Hofmannsthal's Chandos seems to believe that, by leaving society, he can enter a lost prelapsarian state, becoming one with nature. Moving out of culture in this way, he is left in a profound state of speechlessness, attempting to commune with mute nature in a language that is nothing like any of those in the real world (*Erz* 472). Hofmannsthal's Chandos thus has not only taken language's inadequacies to heart, but he has also turned overly subjective, inward directed, individualistic; in so doing, he is also rejecting Bacon's science, which relies on the objectivity of observation within a community.

By comparison with his evaluations of Swinburne and Duncan, this result might be conscious humor on Hofmannsthal's part — his Chandos is an egocentric self-performer, withdrawn from Europe's traditions, a kind of Elizabethan Oscar Wilde doomed to isolation. Thus the "Lord Chandos Letter" may be a very different invented conversation than critics have realized, the story of an objectionable aesthete who indulges his own sensibilities and holds to an outdated belief in experiencing nature rather than observing it, looking backward instead of embracing Bacon's modern Europe.

Toward a Revolutionary Conservatism

This reading of "Ein Brief" would pull it very much in line not only with Hofmannsthal's other essays, but with other strands of interwar thought that disappeared with the Second World War.

First and foremost, Hofmannsthal defines a nation as a psychological and anthropological community, much as Dilthey or Jakob Burckhardt (*Die Kultur der Renaissance in Italien*) did. This is strictly opposed to the economic model of class stratification from Marxist historiography, as well as to the Hegelian idea that the state is the fundamental unit of human existence, the basis for all historical sensibility. Hofmannsthal is instead steering a middle course that seems more Kantian in inspiration — relying on social conflicts and discourse to improve the whole. Hofmannsthal was thus engaged in a work of historical conservation that specifically decried the elitism of the *Bildungsbürgertum*, while nonetheless supporting the value of *Bildung* itself.

Perhaps more importantly, Hofmannsthal takes as the origin of the modern era the Renaissance rather than the Enlightenment, a move shared by Ernst Cassirer but specifically decried by the Frankfurt School, especially by Habermas's *Strukturwandel der Öffentlichkeit*. He is, therefore, drawing a line between the modern era and more radical forms of Modernism. Hofmannsthal refuses to see the Enlightenment as a closed-off and completed nationalistic era against which artists of the present had to react (as the Frankfurt School would have it, positing it as a dialectic). The modern Europe starting with the Enlightenment is, instead, an unfulfilled project that has lost its historical staging ground in an era when Prussian Germany was attempting to co-opt the cultural legitimacy that more properly belongs to Europe as a whole (or even to the lost Austria). Hofmannsthal definitely overestimates the power of public culture, but he is not arguing for any sort of German restoration — the nation he seeks still needs to be formed and called into life, acknowledging its art. Moreover, that nation is a willed affiliation of individuals that shares experience, not an ethnic community, as the Nazis would have it. Naively, Hofmannsthal assumes (as do many others of his era) that even Slavs can become German, when that "German" means a specific form of European culture deriving from Renaissance-humanist values.

As we have seen, these themes recur throughout Hofmannsthal's essays. His aesthetic sensibility remains highly tuned — he will never dispute the value of great books, or what we term canonical literature. Yet the Hofmannsthal in these essays has decisively distanced himself from aestheticism, even as he espouses aesthetics. In his eyes, the poet dare not claim leadership, because that would mean isolation; instead, the artist is the one who engages and gives form to the historical experience of his group — not the creator of its future. From this perspective, the essays remain largely untapped keys to Hofmannsthal's adaptations of European dramatic forms — to his vain hopes for recreating a common European culture that would not fall prey to the leveling and elitist assumptions of cosmopolitanism, but which would valorize the national voice of a German culture that had not yet existed in its full form.

Notes

[1] Bernd Schoeller, with Rudolf Hirsch (Vols. 8 and 9) and Ingeborg Beyer-Ahlert (Vol. 10), have done a commendable job of documenting and annotating the essays; the *Sämtliche Werke* will have variants and will have the advantage of a chronological arrangement, rather than one by topics, as Schoeller et al. have done. When they appear, they should be the editions of record.

[2] A more completely argued version of this section can be found in Chapter 4 of Katherine Arens, *Empire in Decline*. There, the similarity of his work to that of Fritz Mauthner, who had long claimed the kind of work in language philosophy that Hofmannsthal used here. Regardless of the truth of the matter, Mauthner, not Hofmannsthal, was first identified with "linguistic skepti-

cism" to a broad public. At one point, Mauthner tried to get Hofmannsthal to acknowledge that the first volume of Mauthner's own *Beiträge zu einer Kritik der Sprache* (1901) influenced the 1902 "Lord Chandos Letter," a suggestion which Hofmannsthal more or less politely denied (see Stern 22). In the *Erfundene Gespräche und Briefe (SW31)*, the editor Ellen Ritter agrees that "[e]in Vergleich zwischen beiden läßt kaum einen Zweifel daran, daß die Erzählung Mauthners ["Phantasie," from *Aus dem Märchenbuch der Wahrheit*] Hofmannsthals Fragment unmittelbar beinflußte. Ebenso wird es sich auch mit dem Chandos-Brief und Mauthners *Sprachkritik* verhalten haben . . ." (281). Gerhard Fuchs, in contrast, is doubtful about Mauthner influencing Hofmannsthal (2). H. Stefan Schultz's "Hofmannsthal and Bacon: The Sources of the Chandos Letter" is still definitive.

[3] Jacques Le Rider also offers a reading of the *Brief* that does not lead to speechlessness, but he points to an identification of Bacon with Stefan George (p. 125). Michèle Pauget believes, in contrast, that Bacon and Chandos are *Doppelgänger* in the essay (105).

Works Cited

Arens, Katherine. *Empire in Decline: Fritz Mauthner's Critique of Wilhelminian Germany*. Frankfurt am Main: Peter Lang, 2001.

———. "Linguistic Skepticism: Towards a Productive Definition." *Monatshefte*, 74, No. 2 (Summer 1982): 145–55.

Brecht, Bertolt. "Das Experiment." *Prosa 3: Sammlungen und Dialoge. Werke*, Bd. 18. Frankfurt am Main: Suhrkamp Verlag; Berlin: Aufbau Verlag, 1995: 362–72.

Fuchs, Gerhard. "Fritz Mauthners Sprachkritik: Aspekte ihrer literarischen Rezeption in der österreichischen Gegenwartsliteratur." *Modern Austrian Literature*, 23, Nr. 2 (1990): 1–21.

Hofmannsthal, Hugo von. "Ein Brief." In *Erfundene Gespräche und Briefe (Sämtliche Werde XXXI)*, ed. Ellen Ritter. Frankfurt am Main: S. Fischer, 1991: 45–55.

———. *Gesammelte Werke: Reden und Aufsätze I, 1891–1913*. Ed. Bernd Schoeller. Frankfurt am Main: S. Fischer, 1979.

———. *Gesammelte Werke: Reden und Aufsätze II, 1914–1924*. Ed. Bernd Schoeller. Frankfurt am Main: S. Fischer, 1979.

———. *Gesammelte Werke: Reden und Aufsätze III, 1925–1929*. Ed. Bernd Schoeller and Ingeborg Beyer-Ahlert. Frankfurt am Main: S. Fischer, 1979.

Kühn, Joachim. *Gescheiterte Sprachkritik: Fritz Mauthners Leben und Werk.* Berlin: De Gruyter, 1975.

Le Rider, Jacques. *Hugo von Hofmannsthal: Historismus und Moderne in der Literatur der Jahrhundertwende.* Trans. Leopold Federmair. Wien: Böhlau, 1997 [French original, 1995].

Pauget, Michèle. "Der Brief des Lord Chandos in seinem Verhältnis zum mythischen Denken: Seine Aktualität im französischen Sprachraum." In: Sigurd Paul Scheichl and Gerald Stieg, eds. *Österreichische Literatur des 20. Jahrhunderts: Französische und österreichische Beiträge.* Innsbrucker Beiträge zur Kulturwissenschaft, Germanistische Reihe Band 21. Innsbruck: Institut für Germanistik der Universität Innsbruck, 1986: 99–114.

Schultz, H. Stéfan. "Hofmannsthal and Bacon: The Sources of the Chandos Letter." *Comparative Literature*, 13, Nr. 1 (Winter 1961): 1–15.

Steinberg, Michael P. *The Meaning of the Salzburg Festival: Austria as Theater and Ideology, 1890–1938.* Ithaca, NY: Cornell UP, 1990.

Stern, Martin, ed. and intro. "Der Briefwechsel Hofmannsthal-Fritz Mauthner." *Hofmannsthalblätter*, Heft 19/20 (1978): 21–38.

The Legacy

NINA BERMAN

Hugo von Hofmannsthal's Political Vision[*]

I S IT USEFUL, or even possible, to separate an artist's work from his or her essayistic writings or even private activities? This question continues to provoke critics, who engage in discussions of the relation between the form and content of aesthetic representations, or of the perceived contradictions between aesthetic works and politically problematic nonfictional writings. Similar concerns stimulate debates over the contradictions between the writings of intellectuals and their public or private actions. Analyses of the work of Richard Wagner or Martin Heidegger are two of the most prominent examples of this dilemma, and critics have taken diametrically opposed positions regarding the ways in which to approach these cases. Regarding Heidegger, for example, Richard Rorty has argued that one has to be able to distinguish between Heidegger's achievements as a philosopher and his political actions. Others, however, believe that the contested political views can be detected in the philosophy or artwork itself. Bernard Williams suggests, for instance, that the views expressed by Wagner in his political writings emerge clearly in his artwork, such as the *Ring-cycle*, where "a higher, transcendental, politics, of a peculiarly threatening kind" is celebrated.[1]

In similar but perhaps less dramatic ways, Hugo von Hofmannsthal is often debated as a writer whose literary texts are distinguished by their high aesthetic merit, but whose political views have been challenged as problematic.[2] In an essay on Hofmannsthal's war-time essayistic writings, Franz K. Stanzel identifies the questionable aspects of the writer's political views. After all, in essays such as "Die Bejahung Österreichs" (1914), "Krieg und Kultur" (1915), "Österreichische Bibliothek. Eine Ankündigung" (1915), and "Die Österreichische Idee" (1917), Hofmannsthal had not only greeted the war as a rejuvenating and redeeming event, but had also glorified Austrianism in the highest terms. After presenting a detailed analysis denouncing Hofmannsthal's political views, Stanzel ends his essay with the following sentences: "Our findings cannot diminish the stature of H. as poet, dramatist, literary essayist and critic. They require, however, a fresh evaluation of the public role adopted by Hofmannsthal as political essayist during the Great War" (178).

In this concluding statement, Stanzel implies a split between the content of Hofmannsthal's political essays and that of his literary writings. It is unlikely that Stanzel meant to refer exclusively to the technical skills of the writer, leaving aside the issue of the content of his fictional writings. His statement thus suggests a polarity between the message of the war-time essays and that of the literary writings. But can the split between the political essays and the fictional work be maintained?

In the following I argue for a two-fold approach. Hofmannsthal articulates his conservative and paternalistic political vision, which is quite distinct from the German nationalism of the Wilhelmine or National Socialist era, throughout his career, before and beyond the wartime period. It will be shown that this political vision is expressed not only in his essays and letters, but in his literary work as well. However, distinct aesthetic features of the literary texts allow room for varying interpretations, and leave questions regarding the specific political message of these texts unanswered or open. By focusing on the writer's early prose texts we will see how Hofmannsthal articulates his fears of a new democratic political order, of changes in gender relations and of threats to German political superiority within the Habsburg Monarchy. Hofmannsthal's aesthetically eminent early prose texts are seen here as documents that elucidate a specific historical moment, namely the period before the First World War, a period distinguished by rapid and large-scale transformations which generated enthusiasm and anxiety alike. In times of change such as this, elements of the emerging order inevitably are imbued for some with a sense of ambivalence; they conflict with the traditional order and bear the signs of illegitimacy.[3] Hofmannsthal's texts speak to the issues resulting from the fundamental changes early twentieth-century society underwent, and formulate themes, such as problematic femininity, which reappear throughout the writer's career.

The short narratives, "Das Märchen der 672. Nacht" (1895), "Soldatengeschichte (1896), "Reitergeschichte" (1899), and "Erlebnis des Marschalls von Bassompierre" (1900) shall exemplify that Hofmannsthal writes as a member of a specific class, as a man, and as a citizen of the Habsburg monarchy who is visibly disconcerted by the challenges to his social status.[4] Hofmannsthal's views need to be understood in the context of debates over the fate of the Habsburg Empire; his enthusiasm for the constitutional monarchy refers to the specifically Austrian model, which was multinational and multicultural (although here, as elsewhere, multiculturalism did not imply equal and harmonious relationships between the different ethnic groups).[5] Nevertheless, the specific stance which Hofmannsthal adopts in his writings becomes most evident when contrasted to that of other contemporary texts that articulate their concern with societal changes in a different manner. Key plays written by representatives of Naturalism and Expressionism, for example, take a more sympathetic approach to the lower classes, which appear in Hofmannsthal's texts as threatening to the social order. While Hofmannsthal laments the demise of the aristocratic world, members of the women's or the working-class movements are pursuing their goals of political participation and full citizenship rights for all adult members of the society. The utopian spirit contained in these movements is nowhere to be found in Hofmannsthal's writings. My analysis will show that, in contrast to other literary figures of the era, such as Heinrich Mann, Karl Kraus, or Gerhard Hauptmann, who were critical of the aristocratic order, Hofmannsthal clearly identified with the aristocratic paradigm.

It is imperative to keep these alternative points of view in mind when considering Hofmannsthal's work. In my analysis, I take his text literally: rather than interpreting his narratives as expressions of an ontological crisis, I suggest that his working class and his female characters are really about the working class and social conflict.[6] In what follows, I explore the ways in which the narratives convey the anxieties surrounding class and gender transformations under way during Hofmannsthal's era. Finally, I consider the question of the texts' political message in light of the narrators invented by Hofmannsthal and in light of his essayistic activities.

The Challenge From Below

To one degree or another, modern social orders are always under revision, but the scope and pace of changes occurring in Europe around 1900 were unprecedented. The struggle for democracy was undoubtedly one of the most fundamental transformations under way. Hofmannsthal's early narratives articulate concerns regarding these changes in relations between members of different social classes. In three of the selected stories, the central characters are members of the middle or upper class, and reveal sensibilities that distinguish them from those of the lower classes, who are presented in stark contrast. In "Reitergeschichte," the upper-class character is not at the center of the story line, but is nevertheless portrayed in opposition to the problematic lower middle class character. In all of these cases, the danger that leads to the downfall of the central protagonists emanates from environments of poverty and low social status which are given an especially repulsive nature through their association with ugliness and disease. The common theme of these stories is the contested status of the aristocratic and bourgeois order, and the threat of transgression or even dissolution of the social order. It is precisely the aristocracy and the wealthy bourgeoisie whose privileges were challenged around 1900 in Austria (and other parts of the German-speaking world and Europe), and whose fate is explored in Hofmannsthal's early narratives.

The social status of the son of a merchant in "Märchen" is most precarious. Devoid of a name of his own, his life-style is made possible by the legacy and wealth of his parents, who died at a moment not specified in the story. His demeanor, and the ambiance of the world in which he lives, seem almost that of an aristocrat; work is never mentioned, implying complete financial independence. Bored with social life, he retreats into a *Dingwelt* [order of things] of aesthetic objects which he prefers to social relations with the outside world. In his house and in his garden he is surrounded by this symbolic world of beautiful artifacts. The young man, however, does not experience this world as lifeless and empty, he takes pleasure and comfort in its beauty:

> Allmählich wurde er sehend dafür, wie alle Formen und Farben der Welt in seinen Geräten lebten. Er erkannte in den Ornamenten, die sich verschlingen, ein verzaubertes Bild der verschlungenen Wunder der Welt. (*Erz* 45)

Hofmannsthal's "Märchen" is cast in terms familiar from other Aestheticist art, such as Joris-Karl Huysmans's *À rebours* (1884; *Against Nature*, 1959) or Oscar Wilde's *The Picture of Dorian Gray* (1890/91). The protagonist's symbolic *Dingwelt* facilitates a relationship to the world which he cannot experience outside of the aesthetic realm. The beautiful artifacts function as a substitute for the *Lebenswelt*, for an authentic experience of life, and their beauty elevates the *Dingwelt* to a realm endowed with meaning and truth. The artifacts symbolize an antimodern stance in that they provide a connection to an era of courtly glamor during which the status of both the aristocracy and the bourgeoisie was uncontested, an era whose defining power structure was under siege at the time of the writing of Hofmannsthal's short narrative.

While many critics have seen Hofmannsthal's "Märchen" as a rejection of aestheticism, Theodor W. Adorno interprets aestheticism not as an avoidance, but as a critique of the social realm.[7] Adorno argues that an obsession with the *Dingwelt* is not solely an affirmation of the beautiful, but stems from a fear based on experiences in society. The aesthete attempts to save himself by renouncing his social identity and by substituting it with fetishized objects (234). The asocial nature of this *Dingwelt*, which in spite of its beauty reminds him of the futility of life, is further apparent in the social seclusion of the young man. Although he does occasionally enter the public sphere, he does not interact directly with human beings, rather takes notice of them with a surveying gaze. The distance expressed in the attitude of the onlooker transforms human beings encountered in the public sphere into objects of observation; his need for distance also shows how frightening the public sphere is to him. In Adorno's interpretation, the responsibility for the aesthete's flight is thus assigned to society itself, and not seen in the presumed character weakness of the protagonist.

The only social contacts the young man maintains are relationships to his servants; an old female housekeeper, an old man, and two young women, one approximately fifteen years old, the other two or three years her senior, share the young man's solitary life. He is incapable, though, of interacting with them in an intimate and trusting way. The merchant's son perceives his servants with ambivalence. As the narrator comments, their presence adds an element of anxiety to the protagonist's aesthetic world: "Er fühlte sie leben, stärker, eindringlicher, als er sich selber leben fühlte" (*Erz* 49). Danger emanates from these servants, and throughout the text, the merchant's son dreads his servants because they force him "in einer unfruchtbaren und so ermüdenden Weise an sich selbst zu denken" (*Erz* 50). He experiences them as dangerous, because their vitality reminds him of his own inertia. This atmosphere of fear and danger arising from the presence of members of the lower classes escalates when the merchant's son forsakes the security of his aesthetic *Dingwelt*: his death occurs in the social sphere of the metropolis, where he is rendered vulnerable, unprotected by the walls of his beautiful prison of choice.[8]

The story of the Marshall of Bassompierre is similarly explicit in its association of lower class individuals with a threat to the social order and especially the well-being of the political elites.[9] In this narrative, which is the only of the four stories told from the perspective of a first-person narrator, the influential Marshall is seduced into an erotic adventure by a beautiful shop-keeper who offers herself to the Marshall, seemingly out of pure admiration for his power and social standing. In arranging the meeting with the woman, one of the Marshall's servants admonishes him to take special precautions to protect himself from the plague which is said to have not only affected "niedrigen und schmutzigen" people but also "ein Doktor und ein Domherr" (*Erz* 133). He advises the Marshall to bring his own mattress, linen, and blankets to the place of the rendezvous. The Marshall meets the woman, spends a passionate night with her, and is so enchanted with his lover that he demands to see her again. The woman, on the other hand, exudes an air of mysteriousness; she seems to carry a secret and at some point bursts out in tears, asserting that she never belonged to any one but her husband and the Marshall. In an emotional scene, she insists that she does not want to meet him in the same place and suggests the house of her aunt. At that point, the observant reader will be reminded of the potential threat of the plague, from which the Marshal would not be able to protect himself by bringing his own linen to this new meeting place.

Nevertheless, the Marshall is full of passion for the mysterious beauty and can barely await the night of the second encounter. His impatience leads him to the woman's house the very next day, to at least catch a glimpse of her. However, the house is dark apart from one room which seems empty at first. When the Marshall's servant investigates the place once more, he sees a man in the illuminated room, who he assumes to be the woman's husband. The Marshall walks up to the window and sees a tall and handsome man, who, upon closer investigation, reminds him of a prisoner he once guarded for the king. The night of the planned encounter, the Marshall arrives at the house of the aunt, but instead of a passionate lover, he is greeted by a stark picture of two naked bodies, laid out in a room where people are engaged in the usual procedures that follow the death of plague victims. Based on their physical characteristics, the corpses are presumably those of the mysterious woman and her husband.

The couple's mystery is not explicitly resolved in Hofmannsthal's story, but the reader is led to assume that the woman gave her diseased body to the Marshall to avenge her husband's mistreatment as a prisoner of the king.[10] While much here has to remain speculative and we do not know anything about the social background of the man, he potentially symbolizes a threat to the aristocratic order. If indeed this man is identical with the prisoner of the king who was under Bassompierre's supervision, and thus was most likely not an ordinary criminal, then he could have presented some sort of challenge to the political order. The woman, rendered as a simple working-class character, is the vehicle to this challenge of the existing order's power.

Associating poverty as well as femininity with disease and death are classic strategies to stigmatize women and working-class people. Bram Dijkstra and Elisabeth Bronfen have shown how the association of death and disease with femininity appears an especially powerful tool of social control of women.[11] At the same time, these representational conventions reflect the anxieties experienced by men or socially advantaged groups when faced with challenges to their power. Even when used metaphorically, these images express general anxieties of disintegration. The reader can only speculate about the specific nature of the struggle hinted at in this story; much as in the narrative about the young son of a merchant, many questions remain unresolved in the story of Marshall Bassompierre, and the reader is left to do some guesswork as to the causes for the conflicts. However, the air of anxiety is overwhelming and the challenge to aristocratic and bourgeois male power beyond question.

The social background of the dragoon Schwendar in "Soldatenge-schichte" is not explicitly stated; however, from the descriptions of Schwendar's sensibilities and from those the protagonist gives of his fellow soldiers, the reader is encouraged to deduce that his emotional and intellectual education is more sophisticated than that of any of the people who surround him. The discrepancy between Schwendar and the rest of the company is voiced in the opening paragraph: "[E]s war ein halblautes dumpfes Gespräch, wie es niedere Menschen führen, wenn sie sich beengt und unfrei fühlen." Among these lower-class indi-viduals, Schwendar sits as a "todte[r] Punkt," "ein [. . .] traurige[r] Mensch" (*Erz* 67). While the others demonstrate healthy appetites, he is slower, his entire disposition distinguished by fragility and fearfulness. He is clearly different from the robust people around him.

When Schwendar watches over his sleeping comrades, he describes them with references to their social background, physicality, and habits. The first soldier, Corporal Taborsky, a shoemaker in his civilian life, is rendered with relative sympathy as a good and simple person. The sec-ond man, the dragoon Cypris, also has likable features, however, the appealing aspects are reduced to his face, which is described with words that relate the man to an animal, by describing his nose with the term "Nüstern" which evokes the nose of a horse (77). The other soldiers are defined to an even greater extent through their physicality which is rendered as abominable and implicitly suggests a corrupted character. "Der starke Nekolar" is "riesengroß," the strongest man in the com-pany (77). His hair is compared to that of an otter, and the way his body is thrown over the bed is likened to that of a man who attempts to fight a great oddly colored animal with his youthful gigantic body. The last person is outright "hässlich" and "gemein," and the narrator repeats the word "hässlich" twice in the same sentence, in addition to calling him "feig" and "unverschämt" (77).

The view of this most despicable character inspires Schwendar to think of his friend Thoma, who is incarcerated for the theft of Schwen-dar's old silver watch, a valuable heirloom dear to the protagonist. This memory in turn reminds the young man of the death of his mother, which he recalls as a betrayal and personal assault against himself. Abandoned by those he loved and robbed of the comfort and security of friendship and family, his redemptive moment comes when a light from outside falls through the window and promises hope beyond the ugliness and repulsiveness of his existence among the primitive soldiers.

Again, Hofmannsthal sketches a young hero who has lost his connection to the parent generation, and whose social status is endangered for various reasons. In these descriptions, Schwendar has to defend his identity against an onslaught of base, socially, intellectually, and emotionally inferior human beings. Even an ethnic component is brought into the narrative, as the names of the fellow soldiers are exclusively Slavic, an aspect which I will return to in the conclusion.

In "Reitergeschichte," Hofmannsthal also takes the reader into the world of soldiers.[12] The story focuses on questioning the brute force that is practiced by the soldiers.[13] The central character, First Sergeant Anton Lerch, brings to the fore key aspects of problematic violence. His demise begins when he is first confronted with an enticing vision of comfort and power, but his actual downfall is foreshadowed when he encounters images of ugliness and poverty. After his troop declares victory over the city of Milan, the squadron enters the defeated city. Lerch feels the rush of victory and imagines a life "von Behaglichkeit und angenehmer Gewalttätigkeit ohne Dienstverhältnis" (*Erz*, 124–25). He dreams of a social status based on the power of a victor who can afford to arbitrarily defy the civilian order and whose status affords him the leeway of discretionary behavior.

However, these dreams of wealth and power are challenged when, later in the day, Lerch comes upon a small and deeply impoverished village. Deathlike and silent, dirty and ugly, the village is almost completely void of people, apart from a few repulsive and filthy characters. The state of the village is reflected in the baseness of the animals that Lerch watches: two bleeding, biting rats and ugly, dirty, decrepit dogs mirror the repugnant state of the village and its inhabitants. When the dogs begin to attack Lerch's horse, the young man attempts but fails to shoot one of the animals and then leaves hastily. But soon he is confronted with the next repulsive scene: a cow, on its way to the slaughterhouse, blocks his way.

Depressed and disoriented, Lerch escapes from the village, only to be faced with a vision of himself riding on his horse, an apocalyptic rider, an omen of his own death. Soon afterwards he finds himself in the middle of the next battle, his comrades surrounding him. The battle is won, and victorious once more, Lerch rides through the sunset which colors everything in red, so that he seems to be riding through a landscape of blood. Blood appears to be everywhere, on trees, sabers, on the soldiers, and even on the bugle of the squadron's bugler. The intoxicating effect of repeated victorious fighting gradually overcomes the soldiers, who are increasingly excited and seem in a trance, blood-thirsty, battle-thirsty.

This emotional high is suddenly interrupted by Captain Baron Rofrano, who orders the soldiers to give up the horses they won in battle. Upon this order, Lerch fights an internal battle between the etiquette demanded on account of his rank, acquired during years of compliance with the military order, and the emerging desire for comfort and power. Defying the order to give up the horse, he is killed by the Captain.

In what ways are class issues articulated in this story? The punishment Lerch ultimately receives is the result of his transgressive dreams: Lerch envisions a life beyond his legitimate status and for this, he is killed.[14] The danger that emanates from the ugliness and poverty of the village is the mirror image to the visions of comfort, sexuality, and power Lerch is captured by earlier in Milan. Lerch's fantasies are interpreted as dangerous through the juxtaposition with the ugliness of the village.[15] The Captain emerges as a figure who reestablishes the order which has been threatened by the transgressive dreams of the intoxicated First Sergeant, who contests the limits of his inferior rank. Although the reader might empathize with Lerch's dreams in the first part of the story, the turn to bloodthirsty and defiant behavior makes an identification with Lerch quite problematic. In fact, here lies Hofmannsthal's skill as a writer: because the reader is initially willing to follow Lerch's dreams of power and comfort, the shock at the end can work very well as a lesson and a warning for the reader. While the Captain is not an entirely sympathetic character in the narrative, his behavior is justified by the danger imminent in Lerch's rebellion. The action of Captain Baron Rofrano, who seizes the moment that requires discipline to be restored and an end to be put to the desire to kill and conquer, is legitimized through the problematic image of Anton Lerch. The sole aristocratic character of the story thus becomes the guarantor of the social order.[16]

In all four narratives, Hofmannsthal articulates concerns about the stability of the social and political order. Members of the lower-classes emerge as threatening to social peace, either because they challenge the continuity or well-being of the protagonists ("Märchen," "Soldatengeschichte," "Marschall") or because their transgression has to be aborted by an upper-class member to ensure the persistence of the existing social hierarchy ("Reitergeschichte"). Interestingly, however, in each of the stories, Hofmannsthal's narrator adopts a different stance toward the events narrated; I will come back to this question of the narrative perspective at the end of my analysis.

The Challenge From Within

Just as members of the lower-classes emerge as carriers of danger and disorder, women in Hofmannsthal's early prose texts also threaten the protagonist's stability. These demonized figures are not to be understood simply as a reaction to the women's movements emerging during the second half of the nineteenth century. While the demonization of women can be identified as a strategy to gain social control over women, the prevalent figure of the *femme fatale* and the general discourse on problematic femininity in the *fin de siècle* must be seen as the symptom of a wider social crisis. Gerd Stein, for example, demonstrated that this demonization occurred at a historical moment when women were entering the public sphere and demanding political and social emancipation (Stein 11–20). However, at the same time, the deadliness of the *femme fatale,* one of the most prominent types of the demonized woman, mirrors those apocalyptic fears which were connected to political and social transformations of modernization. Like the images of working-class individuals, images of threatening women speak to the multiple insecurities experienced by large segments of European society at the turn of the century, and especially by bourgeois and aristocratic men.[17]

The *femme fatale* is, as Carola Hilmes has shown, a specific type of demonized woman (Hilmes 10). She is beautiful, sexual, seductive, power-driven, passionate, childless, independent, self-confident, cold-hearted, destructive — and deadly, for the man and/or herself. The exceptionality of the *femme fatale* was often emphasized by exotic otherness (Allen 3). While most of these attributes were present in earlier models of problematic femininity, the uniqueness of the *fin-de-siècle femme fatale* lies primarily in the unprecedented numbers of its cultural representation around 1900, as part of a larger debate on problematic femininity. Sigmund Freud's belief in a natural "deficiency of the female" — which led to the theoretical construct of a castration complex in the woman — and Otto Weininger's definition of "woman as the sexual being par excellence" illustrate some of the ways in which turn-of-the-century patriarchal culture connected sexuality and femininity (Hilmes 42).

Hofmannsthal created several versions of the *femme fatale* in his writings, such as the witch in "Der Kaiser und die Hexe" (1897). In one way or another, all the female figures in "Märchen" are representative as well in that they are connected to decay, danger, the uncanny, original sin, and death. Only the old female servant does not fall into the category of *femme fatale.* Nevertheless, on account of her age, the young man still associates her with death and with his dead mother. The other female figures in the narrative are all quite young: a girl of about four years, a young woman approximately fifteen years old, and another who is two to three years her senior. Nonetheless, the protagonist experiences them all as dangerous and mysterious, and encounters with these prototypical demonized females foreshadow the young man's death. Although the narrator claims that women cannot meet the needs of the merchant's son and that he does not desire them, their destabilizing influence on him is crucial. Confrontations with both of the young servants, recollections of their image while astray in the city, and a frightening scene with a little girl in a greenhouse create the destabilization that ultimately leads to the protagonist's destruction. Hofmannsthal's characters deeply resonate with the contemporary association of woman and danger; however, in several scenes, the use of mirror images also suggests the connection between the female characters and Hofmannsthal's protagonist. Rather than suggesting a fear of actual women, these images of women become vehicles to express the identity crisis and the anxieties of a destabilized male ego facing a world of disintegrating traditional orders.

In "Soldatengeschichte" the reader is again led to associate women with death. The first woman mentioned in the narrative is the dim-witted aunt of the protagonist Schwendar, who killed herself in a gruesome manner shortly after his birth by drowning herself. The image of this aunt is evoked when Schwendar glances into a barrel filled with water, which brings about memories of the traumatic event. He recollects how as a boy he often stared into the very barrel in which his aunt drowned herself, and how in staring into the dark water, his own face appeared out of the water's depth. As a mirror-image of the protagonist, this female character brings to the fore Schwendar's death-wish, his depression, his obsession with death. The second female character recalled by the protagonist is his mother. More specifically, he recalls the death of his mother when he experiences a sensation similar to that which the loss of his mother had evoked in him. He feels abandoned, and expresses his hatred for the mother who left him alone "in dieser Hölle" (*Erz* 73). The memory of the abandonment enrages him, and Schwendar sets out on a rampage with his sword against trees and bushes, and even a small rabbit falls victim to his outburst.

The memories of the two female figures and the lack of any mention of his father suggest that the protagonist's destabilized self-image is connected to the missing parents and family members. Just as the young son of a merchant in "Märchen" is introduced as one without parents and family, Schwendar lacks the access to the comfort and stability that can be derived from family. While the male figure is entirely absent, the female figures are connected with despair (the aunt) and abandonment (mother). The death of the mother, however, also fore-shadows the redemption the protagonist experiences at the end of the story: Schwendar's view of heavenly light mirrors the mother's vision of the Virgin Mary just before she dies. And just as the mother seemed to have drawn internal peace from this vision, Schwendar is healed and reconciled with existence through the experience of a transcendent sign. While the image of the mother thus ultimately leads to redemption (in an almost Faustian manner), the absence of the father points to the disturbance of the social order, where tradition and continuity are no longer guaranteed. In addition, the heavenly solution suggested at the end removes Schwendar from the worldly environment; redemption comes from an order that lies outside of the social.

In "Soldatengeschichte," the female characters thus mirror and explain the protagonist's depression, but they also foreshadow his salvation. In "Reitergeschichte," the destructive aspect of femininity comes to the fore again. As mentioned before, Lerch rides through Milan after its defeat, and he sees a woman he seems to have known from before in a window of a recently built bright yellow house. The vision of this enticing *femme fatale* is the starting point for Lerch's demise. Seeing the woman, whose name is Vuic, inspires him to imagine a life of comfort and uncontested power and instills in him a desire to claim the woman. Emboldened by the victory over the city, Lerch allows himself transgressive and violent thoughts, and he imagines a life of prestigious social status. As the story continues, Lerch's desire for material wealth and sudden rewards ultimately brings about his death, when he refuses to let go of the horse he won in battle and is shot for this transgression by Captain Rofrano. Again, the image of a woman foreshadows death and stands for illicit desire, which in this case is the transgression of social boundaries and the aspirations of the lower-class First Sergeant to augment his social standing and power.

In a most explicit way, the shopkeeper in "Marschall" is associated with disease and death. The association of the young woman with the plague, her seemingly childless state, her death and that of her husband, and the fact that the first-person narrator could have infected himself with the disease, makes this female character clearly a representation of the *femme fatale*. The Marshall is lured into his potential death through this image of an enticing woman; apart from the illicit affair, however, she brings to the fore the conflict between the two men, the Marshall and her husband. Again, the woman emerges as a vehicle with which to address issues concerning the social order. Like the longing for Vuic in "Reitergeschichte," the desire for the shop-keeper initiates the protagonist's plunge into what could have become his downfall. In both cases, however, the demise, potential or actual, is ultimately not a result of illicit sexual desire, but due to the conflicts that are related to the contested social order.

Hofmannsthal's Narrators

The four narratives highlight issues central to the political and social order of German-speaking countries around 1900. If we were to focus on the position of the narrator in each of the four texts, what might we deduce regarding the political vision of the author? Each narrative offers a different answer.

In "Märchen," the ambivalence of the narrator makes it impossible to decide the interpretation of alliances put forth, that is, whether identification should be with the protagonist (and society is held responsible for his demise) or whether criticism of the protagonist is expressed (and his asocial nature brings about his death). Throughout the text, a tension arises between the information given by the narrator (where he seems to report the inner monologue of the young man) and the judgments the narrator passes on the young man. Hofmannsthal invented a narrator who is unreliable in an almost Kafkaesque manner, luring the reader into perpetual attempts to solve the puzzle of the young man's biography. In "Soldatengeschichte," the sympathies of the narrator are more clearly in favor of Schwendar, whose salvation at the end of the story redeems his darker characteristics. The positive view of his redemption elevates Schwendar's earlier perceptions of his fellow comrades, and the narrative thus condones and confirms these views. In "Marschall," the narrator leaves the reader hanging once more; because of the sparse information about the woman's husband, that is, Bassompierre's former prisoner, the reader cannot decide whether the revenge taken was legitimate or not. Interestingly, the reader is encouraged to experience the story through the eyes of the first-person narrator, which suggests at least the possibility of identification. However, this first-person narrator turns out to be a questionable character, his pursuit of the woman is illicit from the beginning, and as the narrative unravels, shady aspects of the Marshall's political life are revealed. Thus, the reader's sympathies might ultimately be with the woman and her husband, but again, the position taken is not entirely clear.

"Reitergeschichte" is similarly complex in the way the narrative perspective entails a commentary on the protagonist's actions. While the reader experiences the events through the eyes of Anton Lerch, rendered by an omniscient third-person narrator, the killing of Lerch at the hands of Captain Baron Rofrano presents a dilemma. The reader is initially lured into joining in with Lerch's youthful enthusiasm, only to gradually see this euphoria turn bloodier and greedier. Thus the killing of Lerch emerges as a necessary step to protect the social order, and while the reader might be surprised by the drastic action of Rofrano, it follows as a logical response to the transgressive behavior of the First Sergeant. However, this action collides with the reader's initial sympathy for Lerch.

When it comes to evaluating the political purport conveyed through the figure of the narrator in these early prose texts, we are faced with narrators that display differing positions. If the narrators are seen as tools that enable the writer to express political points of view, the commentary Hofmannsthal makes about the political and social order through these figures is far from coherent. The one aspect, however, that emerges consistently is the fact that the social and political order is contested, that lower-class and female characters pose a threat to the existing order and often generate situations that result in crisis. The ambivalence of the narrator in "Märchen" and "Marschall" and even the more clearly defined attitude in "Reitergeschichte" and "Soldaten-geschichte" opens up a space for the reader to draw his or her conclusions. With his meticulous observations of the social and political crisis around 1900, Hofmannsthal has created invaluable documents illuminating the internal conflict of Austrian *fin-de-siècle* society. A reader might not agree with the stance Hofmannsthal's narrators are taking, but the descriptions put forth by Hofmannsthal allow the reader to come up with a range of interpretations.

Conclusion in Light of Hofmannsthal's Political Essays

Hofmannsthal's early prose expresses the anxieties experienced by upper-class Austrian men (and to some extent, women) whose power was contested and embattled at the time. A close reading of Hofmannsthal's early prose texts shows that the sense of crisis voiced here is not that of an ontological crisis about the meaning of life in the modern world. His protagonists do not experience a Heideggerian homelessness.[18] Rather, they are endangered by the actions of lower-class people who throughout these texts are represented without the appeal of the "Volk" as we know it from texts by writers of Romanticism or Naturalism. The lower-class people in Hofmannsthal's texts are not depicted compassionately; rather the protagonists experience them as threatening, violent, dirty, and primitive.[19] In all instances under discussion here, the lower-class characters contribute to bringing about the death of the (not always sympathetic) protagonists or alternatively, have to be killed (Anton Lerch) to protect the existing order. The narratives converge in that they express the state of crisis (merchant's son, Marshall) and formulate a need for leadership (Rofrano) and vision (Schwendar).

Images of women in these early prose texts bring to the fore the fragility of the protagonists. I have interpreted these female figures in a two-fold manner: on the one hand, they are indicative of an attempt at social control of women who were in the historical context striving for a redefined social role, for the right to vote, full citizenship, and an expanded presence in the workplace. But the many mirror images that are present tie the protagonists to these images of femininity, and thus also comment on the destabilized self-image of the men in Hofmannsthal's narratives. The precarious status Hofmannsthal identified for his social class is reflected in these images of dying or diseased women.

In addition to employing tropes of class and gender, Hofmannsthal also tied the dangers his protagonists experience to non-German or non-Austrian territories. The locale of "Märchen" is the Orient, long associated with danger to the national Austrian body. In "Soldatengeschichte," the problematic male characters all bear Slavic names (Taborsky, Cypris, Nekolar, Karasek), with the exception of his former friend Thoma. The dragoon Moses Last is not described in repulsive ways, but encourages speculation in that his first name suggests a Jewish background, but his family name "Last" marks this implied Jewishness as a predicament.[20] "Reitergeschichte" is set in Italy, and the aristocrat who restores order at the end of the story is identified as a member of the Italian aristocracy (Baron Rofrano), much in line with the German-Italian legacy of the Holy Roman Empire Hofmannsthal invokes in positive ways. The enticing female character, however, is identified as Slavic; her name is Vuic and the narrator connects this ethnic background with a certain cunningness ("[Vuic] lächelte ihn in einer halb geschmeichelten slawischen Weise an" [*Erz* 124]). The multicultural aspect of the Habsburg Empire appears to be — at best — deeply conflicted.[21]

The elements I have identified in these early prose texts — anxieties about a changing social order, fear of lower-class members and women, assertion of the aristocratic order, assertion of the preeminence of a German-based Habsburg order — still leave many blanks to be filled in. The author's message is simply not clear, mostly on account of the ambivalent narrator, and the texts leave spaces for the reader to decide what conclusions to derive from the portrayal of the society. I suggest then that his writings, rather than containing a clear political vision, first and foremost document the crisis of the Austrian (male) upper-class around 1900.

While the fictional texts contain room for interpretation, Hofmannsthal's essayistic work leaves little doubt about his political views. For one, Hofmannsthal was consistently elitist and suspicious of "the people." As Walter Dimter has shown, the young Hofmannsthal was critical of the Austrian working-class movement, and did not hesitate to voice his disdain for the "Pöbel" (Dimter 89–91). Later, in "Das Schrifttum als geistiger Raum der Nation" (1926; *RAIII* 24–31), Hofmannsthal privileges a vision of the nation as consisting of "searching" individuals over the idea of a mob-based nationalism. While Hofmannsthal's notion of a "konservative Revolution" (41) is aimed at condemning the revolutionary visions of extremists on the left and the right alike, his understanding of politics is based on an aristocratic and liberal bourgeois ideal of independent individuals. The essay also highlights the different dimensions of Hofmannsthal's political vision. While he first develops an idea of the nation that is not connected to soil, but ultimately expressed in a spiritual and intellectual commonality, that is, a specific world view, the essay ends with a transference of this idealist understanding of nationality into the realm of the political. Ultimately, the intellectual-spiritual connection (which he endows with a religious responsibility) translates into political action. He envisions an overcoming of all division between individuals and their synthesis in the political body of the nation (40). This highly mystified idea of politics, which stigmatizes division within the nation, clearly opened the way for a nationalist politics that aimed at downplaying issues of social status and ideological orientation in favor of an almost religious understanding of the nation.

While Hofmannsthal seems to reject the idea of a nation based on blood and soil, he clearly privileges the German-language cultures over other European cultures. In "Deutsche Erzähler" (1912), he proclaims the superiority of the German over the French (*RAI* 430). In "Boycott fremder Sprachen?" (1914), his advocacy for language learning does not conceal the ultimate goal behind this activity, namely to achieve hegemony (*RAII* 352). Within the hierarchy of nations, Austria emerges as the better Germany, just like the Habsburg Empire is the blueprint for his notion of a multicultural Europe ("Preusse und Österreicher: Ein Schema" [1917; 459–61]). Much as he argues that a true nation is not based on blood and soil, he sees Europe as an "idea" that transcends geographical boundaries ("Die Idee Europa" [1917; 43–54]).

But while Hofmannsthal evokes the idea of a multicultural Austria or Europe, he clearly insists on German cultural leadership within these entities. In "Grillparzers politisches Vermächtnis" (1915; 405–10), "Geist der Karpathen" (1915; 411–16) and "Österreichische Bibliothek" (1916; 432–39) he voices his appreciation for Slavic and other peoples of the Habsburg Empire. But the stance he takes is still paternalistic. Given the negative characteristics associated with the Slavic figures of the stories I just discussed, his valuation of Slavic and other cultures is questionable. Ultimately, colonization and cultural-political domination is never questioned, whether in Eastern Europe or later in Morocco.[22]

Michael P. Steinberg has described the tension contained in this contradiction between Hofmannsthal's cosmopolitanism and his German-culture nationalism as "nationalist cosmopolitanism" (84–115). As the evidence from his essays shows, Hofmannsthal's political vision is consistently elitist (with a strong preference for aristocratic orders),[23] paternalistic, based on a privileging of Christian (mostly Catholic) traditions and an idea of Europe under German-culture leadership.[24] In contrast to Hofmannsthal's essayistic output, his early prose texts seem to be more complex and insightful. The skillfully crafted literary texts portray the crisis of the time with its many contradictions and valences. The openness and ambivalence of the literary texts is often reduced to definitive statements in Hofmannsthal's non-fictional writings. We are left with a tension between the skills and visions of a writer and those of an essayist, who seems to be the profane mirror image of the artist.

Notes

* I would like to thank Karen Brettell who helped me to update my bibliography on Hofmannsthal. I am also grateful to Rebecca Lorins for her thoughtful editorial comments.

1 Bernard Williams, "Wagner and Politics," *The New York Review of Books*, 2 Nov. 2000: 43. For an earlier discussion of Wagner's political views, see Marc A. Weiner, *Richard Wagner and the Anti-Semitic Imagination* (Lincoln: U of Nebraska P, 1995), 1 passim.

2 For a detailed analysis, see, for example, Heinz Lunzer, *Hofmannsthals politische Tätigkeit in den Jahren 1914 bis 1917* (Frankfurt am Main: Lang, 1981).

3 "Alles Neuartige, das als Anomalie auftritt, gerät damit ins Zwielicht einer unaufhebbaren *Ambivalenz*. Von der alter Ordnung aus betrachtet erscheint dasselbe als Verstoß, was auf eine künftige Ordnung hin betrachtet ein Vorstoß ins Neuland sein mag." Bernhard Waldenfels, *In den Netzen der Lebenswelt* (Frankfurt am Main: Suhrkamp, 1985), 142.

4 For detailed information regarding the textual history of the individual narratives, see the commentary included in *SW28 (Erzählungen 1*, ed. Ellen Rit-

ter; 201–14, 217–21, 222–24) and *SW29* (*Erzählungen* 2, ed. Ellen Ritter; 298–303).

⁵ For a discussion of writers critical of the Wilhelmine system, see Peter Sprengel, *Literature im Kaiserreich: Studien zur Moderne* (Berlin: Erich Schmidt, 1993). Joseph P. Strelka's *Zwischen Wirklichkeit und Traum: Das Wesen des Österreichischen in der Literatur* (Tübingen: Francke, 1994) sheds light on the differences between the Austrian and the Prussian model. A discussion of Hofmannsthal can be found pp 210–24.

⁶ Here I differ from analysts such as Joachim Pfeiffer, who disregards the social and political context of the period in favor of philosophical considerations about the ontological situation of a generally defined humanity. See *Tod und Erzählen: Wege der literarischen Moderne um 1900* (Tübingen: Niemeyer, 1997). Rudolf Hirsch takes a similar approach in, "Reitergeschichte und andere Erzählungen," *Beiträge zum Verständnis Hugo von Hofmannsthals* (Frankfurt am Main: S. Fischer, 1995), 20–25. The article was originally published in 1975.

⁷ See my review of the critical discussion of Hofmannsthal's aestheticism in *Orientalismus, Kolonialismus und Moderne: Zum Bild des Orients in der deutschsprachigen Kultur um 1900* (Stuttgart: Metzler, 1997), 179–81.

⁸ See my detailed discussion of "Märchen" in *Orientalismus, Kolonialismus und Moderne* 165–259.

⁹ On the genesis of this narrative, see Henry Remak, "Novellistische Struktur: Der Marschall von Bassompierre und die schöne Krämerin (Bassompierre, Goethe, Hofmannsthal)," *Essai und kritischer Forschungsbericht* (Bern: Frankfurt am Main, 1983).

¹⁰ The night which the Marshall spends with the woman is rendered in an atmosphere of mystery and danger ("kalter Lufthauch," "fahle widerwärtige Dämmerung," "farbloser, wesenloser Wust," "Hart- und Dunkelwerden ihres Gesichts" [135–36]). The woman also insists that she never belonged to anyone other than her husband and the Marshall, but the motive for her pursuit of the Marshall remains unnamed. Her tears and generally mysterious behavior, the fact that her husband is handsome, and the fact that she lures the Marshall to the house of her aunt (where he finds her dead with her husband) all indicate that this encounter is not romantic at the core.

¹¹ Elisabeth Bronfen, *Over Her Dead Body: Death, Femininity, and the Aesthetic* (Routledge: New York, 1992); Bram Dijkstra, *Idols of Perversity: Fantasies of Feminine Evil in Fin-de-Siècle Culture* (New York: Oxford UP, 1986).

¹² Both "Reitergeschichte" und "Soldatengeschichte" draw on Hofmannsthal's experience of service in the army from October 1894 to September 1895, during which he was haunted by bouts of depression.

[13] A discussion of the political aspects of the narrative can be found in Volker O. Durr, "Der Tod des Wachtmeisters Anton Lerch und die Revolution von 1848: Zu Hofmannsthals *Reitergeschichte*," *The German Quarterly* 45 (1972): 33–46. Gerhard Träbing gives an overview of the critical discussion in "Hofmannsthals *Reitergeschichte*: Interpretationen und Observationen 1949–1976," *Sprache im technischen Zeitalter* 21 (1981): 221–36.

[14] See also Marilyn Scott who discusses Lerch's story with a focus on the nexus of gender and military order. "Order and Masculinity in Hugo von Hofmannsthal's "Reitergeschichte," *Geschichte der österreichischen Literatur*, vol. 2, ed. Donald G. Daviau and Herbert Arlt (St. Ingbert: Röhrig Universitätsverlag, 1996), 500–517.

[15] Here as well as in the other prose texts under discussion, the material, physical and social worlds emerge as instrumental in bringing about the downfall of the hero. This contradicts theses put forth by Georg Braungart who has argued that the crisis of language and meaning experienced around 1900 was often countered by a new appreciation of physicality and sensuality. Hofmannsthal's early prose texts do not exemplify these tendencies. Georg Braungart, *Leibhafter Sinn: Der andere Diskurs der Moderne* (Tübingen: Niemeyer, 1995). See the passage on Hofmannsthal's "Ein Brief," 219–30.

[16] If we were to see the Captain in a more negative light, empathy would grow for Lerch, which in turn would condone the kind of violence he increasingly engages in. Based on the textual evidence, in particular the portrayal of Lerch, it seems unlikely to me that Hofmannsthal wanted to render a positive image of illicit behavior.

[17] For a discussion of this topic in the Viennese context, see Sander Gilman, "Male Stereotypes of Female Sexuality in Fin-de-siècle Vienna," *Difference and Pathology: Stereotypes of Sexuality, Race, and Madness* (Ithaca: Cornell UP, 1985), 39–58.

[18] Nancy Hartsock approaches this issue from a different angle: "Why is it, exactly at the moment when so many of us who have been silenced begin to demand the right to name ourselves, to act as subjects rather than objects of history, that just then the concept of subjecthood becomes 'problematic'?" "Rethinking Modernism: Minority vs. Majority Theories," *The Nature and Context of Minority Discourse*, eds. Abdul R. JanMohamed and David Lloyd (New York: Oxford UP, 1990), 26.

[19] The same holds true for lower-class characters in Thomas Mann's early narratives, such as *Der Tod in Venedig*.

[20] Regarding Hofmannsthal's ambivalent relationship to his Jewish heritage, see, for example, Jens Rieckmann, "Zwischen Bewußtsein und Verdrängung: Hofmannsthals jüdisches Erbe," *Deutsche Vierteljahresschrift für Literaturwissenschaft und Geistesgeschichte* 67.3 (1993): 466–83.

[21] Here I disagree with Jacques Le Rider who finds Hofmannsthal's multicultural Habsburg appealing. "Hugo von Hofmannsthal and the Austrian Idea of Central Europe," trans. Rosemary Morris, *The Habsburg Legacy: National Identity in Historical Perspective*, eds. Ritchie Robertson and Edward Timms (Edinburgh: Edinburgh UP, 1994), 121–35. On the feudal aspects of the Habsburg Empire and the economic exploitation and political oppression of southern and eastern regions, see Oscar Jászi, *The Dissolution of the Habsburg Monarchy* (Chicago: U of Chicago P, 1929); David F. Good, *The Economic Rise of the Habsburg Empire, 1750–1914* (Berkeley: U of California P, 1984); Iván T. Berend and György Ránki, *The European Periphery and Industrialization 1770–1914*, trans. Éva Pálmai (Cambridge: Cambridge UP, 1982).

[22] On ideas of colonization in Slavic territory, see "Unsere Militärverwaltung in Polen" [Our Military Rule in Poland, 1915], *GW Reden und Aufsätze II*, 421–28, and "Die Österreichische Idee." I have elaborated on the writings based on Hofmannsthal's trip to Morocco in "K.u.K. Colonialism: Hofmannsthal in North Africa," *New German Critique* 75 (Fall 1998): 3–27.

[23] Hofmannsthal's predilection for aristocrats is well-documented in letters and other sources. Several of Hofmannsthal's closest friends were members of the aristocracy, such as Leopold Andrian Reichsfreiherr von Andrian-Werburg.

[24] Hofmannsthal's longing for pre-reformation, Catholic times, is expressed in "Wert und Ehre deutscher Sprache," *RAIII* 128–33.

Works Cited

Adorno, Theodor W. "George und Hofmannsthal: Zum Briefwechsel: 1891–1906." *Gesammelte Schriften 10: I. Kulturkritik und Gesellschaft I. Prismen, Ohne Leitbild*. Ed. Rolf Tiedemann. Frankfurt am Main: Suhrkamp, 1977. 195–237.

Allen, Virginia M. *The Femme Fatale: Erotic Icon*. New York: The Whitston Publishing Company, 1983.

Dimter, Walter. "Von der Idee Österreich zur Idee Europa: Hugo von Hofmannsthals kulturkritische Anstrengungen." *Nationaler Gegensatz und Zusammenleben der Völker: Österreich-Ungarn im Spiegel der deutschsprachigen Literatur; ein Modell für Europa?* Ed. Peter Mast. Bonn: Kulturstiftung der deutschen Vertriebenen, 1994. 87–103.

Hilmes, Carola. *Die Femme fatale: Ein Weiblichkeitstypus in der nachromantischen Literatur*. Stuttgart: Metzler, 1990.

Rorty, Richard. "On Heidegger's Nazism." *Philosophy and Social Hope*. London: Penguin, 1999. 190–97. (Essay originally published in 1990.)

Stanzel, Franz K. "The Poet in His Time: Hofmannsthal and the Great War." *Literature, Culture and Ethnicity: Studies on Medieval, Renaissance and Modern Literatures. A Festschrift for Janez Stanonik*. Ed. Mirko Jurak. Ljubljana: Ucne delavnice, 1992. 171–79.

Stein, Gerd. *Femme fatale — Vamp — Blaustrumpf: Sexualität und Herrschaft*. Ed. Gerd Stein. Frankfurt am Main: Fischer, 1985.

Steinberg, Michael P. *The Meaning of the Salzburg Festival: Austria as Theater and Ideology, 1890–1938*. Ithaca: Cornell UP, 1990.

DOUGLAS A. JOYCE

Hofmannsthal Reception in the Twentieth Century

HOFMANNSTHAL RECEPTION, embracing as it does the ever-changing course of Hofmannsthal criticism, is the account of a young, exceptional talent, a *Wunderkind*, who by virtue of precocity and circumstances achieved early recognition and fame.[1] With early recognition came acceptance, admiration, even adulation, but also misperception, miscomprehension, and misrepresentation. Early interest centered on the phenomenon of Hofmannsthal/Loris, the fascination of the teenage prodigy, later the mature artist and family man of Rodaun. Hofmannsthal's talent captured the imagination and attracted other talents, and as he had an open, approachable manner, his talent opened doors to that of others, not all of which were compatible with his own. The young Hofmannsthal had many friends and admirers, but from the beginning Hofmannsthal was a controversial figure, and response to his writings and his personality was polarized. Hofmannsthal was familiar from an early age with critical hostility and an adverse press.

As Hofmannsthal's productivity developed, critics failed to comprehend the protean nature of his talent and the stages of his artistic development: the literary aestheticism and moral consciousness of the early poetry and verse dramas; his explorations in Greek and Jacobean tragedy; his commitment to comedy, libretti, and festival theater; and not least, a steady flow of essays and correspondences dating from his years as a teenager. Each was a stage in his growth as an artist; each gave fuel to his detractors and played into a discordant reception. In his lifetime Hofmannsthal was largely known for his early works.[2] Rehabilitation came later — much later — through scholarly research, theater performances and practices, as well as political, social, and philosophical change.

Aesthete, unworldly ("weltfremd"), decadent, Viennese *fin-de-siècle* — these were the epithets attached to the young Hofmannsthal; they formed the central focus of Hofmannsthal's early reception. From epithets to clichés to stereotype there developed the myth of Loris:

charming purveyor of beauty and melancholy, eternally youthful, word genius with a star-bright future, but acceptable only to a limited circle, and in reality not meeting the needs and expectations of the time. Three writers in particular — Hermann Bahr (1863–1934), Stefan George (1868–1933), and Rudolf Borchardt (1877–1945) — were instrumental in establishing Hofmannsthal's early reputation and reception. Hofmannsthal's association with these figures goes a long way toward explaining the stereotype.

It was as much the prodigal exuberance of youthful creativity as exceptional circumstances that brought the young Hofmannsthal to public attention. In 1890 the first of Hofmannsthal's published poems appeared. Hofmannsthal was then sixteen and still two years from matriculation in the Akademisches Gymnasium. In the fall of the same year, Hofmannsthal was introduced to the circle of young literary talents who gathered at the famed gathering spot for artists, the Café Griensteidl. The following year appeared more poems, the one-act "dramatic study" *Gestern*, and no fewer than six essays or book reviews on works by contemporary authors such as Bahr, Paul Bourget (1852–1935), Henri-Frédéric Amiel (1821–1881), and Maurice Barrès (1862–1923). These writers represented the new psycho-literary tendencies in France, which rejected the ideology and aesthetic of Naturalism (Zola) and emphasized the turn to the "inner life," the cult of the individual, the dilemma of conscience, the precariousness of personal relationships, and the search for renewed affiliations between the individual and society.

The Hermann Bahr review, published in the *Moderne Rundschau* (April 1891), dealt with Bahr's play "Die Mutter" (*RAI* 100). With this essay the seventeen-year-old Hofmannsthal — ironically — sparked his own reception. The review, written in a fresh, energetic prose, spoke sympathetically of Bahr's restless energies, placed the play within the context of contemporary styles, and stated unambiguously the writer's dissatisfaction with Bahr's attempt to create a colloquial tone. It was written with brilliant perceptions and open-mindedness, critical but without censure, and with courteous distance. The review was signed: Loris.[3]

Hermann Bahr, already an established author and known particularly for his essay collections *Zur Kritik der Moderne* (1890) and *Die Überwindung des Naturalismus* (1891), recorded his reaction to the young Hofmannsthal in as many as three articles (1892–1893) devoted to the subject of Loris. In the first of these articles ("Loris," January 1892) — an article that may claim to have inaugurated Hofmannsthal reception — Bahr included an account of his meeting with the young man. Bahr reported that he read Hofmannsthal's review upon returning to Vienna from St. Petersburg, that he was elated with the discovery of a new poetic voice, and was eager to meet Loris. The tone of Bahr's article was ecstatic — Bahr was wonderstruck. He was deeply affected by the freshness and authority of Loris's style, the depth of his perception, and his light, unforced, and slightly ironic charm. Indeed, Bahr claimed that in Loris's review he had been tousled and pulled to pieces ("zerzaust und zerrupft") with so much grace that he experienced it more as a caress. Bahr professed he had made up his mind that Loris was a Frenchman, or someone who had spent a considerable time in France, well-educated and well-traveled, probably between 40 and 50 years of age. He was not prepared for the energetic young man who, on April 27, 1891, strode across the room at the Café Griensteidl and introduced himself: "Ich bin nämlich Loris" — an ordinary Viennese man, not yet 20 years old! (Hofmannsthal was in fact 17.)

Despite Hofmannsthal's limited productivity, Bahr's enthusiasm was unbounded. Hofmannsthal/Loris represented something original and innovative. He praised *Gestern*, Hofmannsthal's maiden play published later that same year (1891), as the terminal work of Naturalism and as the initial work of a future art which would supplant Naturalism. At the same time, Bahr recognized the enigmatic nature of this new talent. First, Loris's art lacked feeling and passion; he seemed to look on life as from a distant star, hence the sense of moderation, grace and dignity, but also coldness, *sécheresse* (Bahr's word), and the ironic haughtiness of his verses. Second, Bahr wrote candidly of the elements of aesthetic sensibility and over-refinement in Hofmannsthal's personality. Loris embodied youthfulness — "So möchte man seine fröhliche Gesundheit rühmen, die sonst heute der gepeinigten Jugend fehlt" ("Das junge Osterreich" in Bahr/Wunberg 150) — but the youthfulness had a double side: Loris had none of the "Räuber" (Storm and Stress) about him, for the youth began as a man, by nature mature and self-disciplined. Further, Bahr associated Loris with the impassioned apostles of beauty, like the English Pre-Raphaelites and the French Symbolists, who escaped from the raw wilderness of daily life into glowing dreams of the past. Bahr concluded that Loris was both epigone and modern, lyrical and critical, sick and healthy, perverted and pure, Symbolist and Naturalist all at the same time — an inexhaustible riddle.

What is most important is that Bahr established a connection between Hofmannsthal and Goethe. Modern literature, for all its progress, Bahr claimed, lacked a commitment to moral questions. It lacked the quality Bahr called "das Wilhelm-Meisterliche," the pains and doubts concerning the meaning of existence, the sense of promoting moral education. The secular, the transitory divided the age from the eternal. In Bahr's view, Loris was the sole figure among the young writers who was concerned with moral problems. Loris sought certainties for the course of life, for the relation of man to the world, for the significance of things. His aims were reawakening and edification. Loris had the quality of "das Wilhelm-Meisterliche."[4]

Reading Bahr's articles today, we see that Bahr made astute observations about the talented young Hofmannsthal, and articulated some of the conflicting qualities that later became so much a part of Hofmannsthal reception. The question arises: How much did Bahr's "discovery" and promotion of Hofmannsthal/Loris contribute to the perception of Hofmannsthal as aesthete, unworldly ("weltfremd"), decadent, *fin-de-siècle?* The answer lies largely in the ideologically driven culture of the time, the expectations and criteria which contemporaries imposed on their understanding of the young Hofmannsthal. Bahr perceived the complexity of Hofmannsthal's talent, the incompatible elements that made up that talent. However, the critics (those who read Bahr) failed to discern Bahr's finely drawn distinctions: they read Bahr — and saw Hofmannsthal — in terms of either/or, and overlooked completely Bahr's claim for Hofmannsthal's interest in moral questions. This accounts for the praise and adulation which friends and readers sympathetic to Aestheticism (witness the George circle) gave to Hofmannsthal in the last decade of the century and the early years of the next. At the same time, those who subscribed to the Realist and Naturalist aesthetic reacted resolutely against Aestheticism, both the French and English varieties. Many contemporaries (essayists, press critics, and literary historians) in search of the poet of the new age considered Hofmannsthal's poetry — and his language — suspect and failed to recognize that the talented young voice spoke with remarkable insight. The stereotype that emerged rested as much on incomprehension, incapacity, and envy, as on contending cultural factions.

Another writer to court the young Hofmannsthal was Stefan George. Hofmannsthal was seventeen years of age and Stefan George was twenty-three when they met in the Café Griensteidl in December 1891, the same year in which Bahr met Loris. George pressed — and pressed passionately — for Hofmannsthal's friendship, but what followed was a fifteen-year (1891–1906) tortuous and tension-ridden relationship, recorded in the Hofmannsthal-George correspondence. The conflict lay in fundamental differences in personal qualities and artistic-cultural aims (Volke 28–35).

The importance of Hofmannsthal's association with Stefan George and his circle should not be underestimated. In George, Hofmannsthal met an immensely talented, refined poet, a kindred spirit who confirmed Hofmannsthal in his calling,[5] and who, in the *Blätter für die Kunst*, gave Hofmannsthal his first regular forum (between 1891 and 1903).[6] In addition, George published the first collection of Hofmannsthal's poems.[7] For his part Hofmannsthal was one of the first to present George to the public in the essay "Gedichte von Stefan George" of 1896.[8] And again in 1904, Hofmannsthal's essay "Das Gespräch über Gedichte"[9] made George's poetry central to a discussion of modern poetry. While Hofmannsthal was collaborating on the *Blätter für die Kunst* he was accepted by the George circle. After the break between them in 1906, Friedrich Gundolf became the chief spokesman for the "circle's" hostility to Hofmannsthal.

Hofmannsthal's name was early associated with George's, fostering the misperception that Hofmannsthal and George were alike in their views on life and art, and encouraging a clichéd view of the relationship.[10] By 1897 phrases such as "schwärmerische Jüngerschaft," "Blasiertheit," "weltfremd," "unentschiedener halber Charakter" and "Produkt einer durchsättigten Kultur," were already appearing in Vienna and Berlin journals.[11]

The association with Rudolf Borchardt, coming a few years later, reinforced the connection with George's name and circle, and tied Hofmannsthal's reputation more closely to his early work. Rudolf Borchardt, student of theology, classical philology, and archaeology, as well as aspiring poet, made the initial approach to Hofmannsthal in May 1901. A cordial friendship developed between the two men which, despite some uneven moments, lasted up to Hofmannsthal's death in July 1929 (Volke 81–82). Borchardt's public lecture, "Rede über Hofmannsthal," in Göttingen in 1902 (Wunberg 86–113) was directed not specifically to the subject of Hofmannsthal but to the nature of the "modern age" ("die Moderne") and Hofmannsthal's place in the future of German literature. Borchardt named Hofmannsthal and George as representatives of the new generation. Borchardt treated both writers as parallel, but different, neither writer more eminent than the other. The parallelism was ambivalent — Borchardt described Hofmannsthal's lyrical corpus as "der höchste rein dichterische Ausdruck des Zeitalters neben den besten Werken Stefan Georges" — leading to a facile and false identification of the two poets. Hofmannsthal remonstrated over the incompleteness, the work-in-progress character of Borchardt's presentation — Borchardt himself entitled it "Torso" when it was published in 1907 — and Friedrich Gundolf took up the challenge of Borchardt's misrepresentation of Stefan George in an essay "Das Bild Georges" of 1910.

Later, in 1924, Borchardt's "Eranos" letter merely aggravated the earlier misunderstanding. The letter, published as part of a *Festschrift* for Hofmannsthal's fiftieth birthday, set out to give a picture of a changing European culture and to establish Hofmannsthal as the mature spokesman of the historical and spiritual world of the Habsburgs. Hofmannsthal protested the letter, not for its general content, but for Borchardt's wrong emphasis. Hofmannsthal claimed that Borchardt, for all his learning, had played into the hands of his detractors by placing the emphasis on his early work: " . . . es ist das mot d'ordre der böswilligen und sonst fatalen Litteraten geworden, mich auf mein Jugendoeuvre festzulegen" (*HvH-Borchardt Bw* 185–86). This was, in fact, the case: Borchardt, writing in 1924, had not cited any work of Hofmannsthal's after the "Balzac" essay of 1908!

Rudolf Borchardt, who has been described as "one of the decisive factors in the history of Hofmannsthal reception,"[12] bears much responsibility for the establishment of the "Loris myth." Borchardt's comparison between Hofmannsthal and George reinforced the impression that Hofmannsthal was a dedicated follower of George's artistic ideology, and nurtured the pejorative image which came to dominate discussion of Hofmannsthal's person and reputation.

What was Hofmannsthal's response to his own reception, specifically to the clichés and stereotypes which early developed around his name? At the beginning, Hofmannsthal's attitude to reception was ambivalent, and wavered between indifference and staunch commitment. On one hand, in a letter to his father in May 1896 (Hofmannsthal was then twenty-two) he wrote: "Mich interessiert das Äußere, das Durchdringen der Generation schon fast gar nicht mehr. Auch über das sogenannte Verstehen und sogenannte Nichtverstehen von seiten des Publikums bin ich ganz beruhigt" (*Briefe 1890–1901* 192). On the other hand, in an address "Poesie und Leben," published in the same month in *Die Zeit* (Vienna), he declared: "Ich halte Wirkung für die Seele der Kunst . . . Wenn sie nicht wirkte, wüßte ich nicht, wozu sie da wäre" (*RAI* 18). Hofmannsthal early learned the experience of unfavorable reception and a bad press. Writing to Clemens Freiherr zu Franckenstein in December of that year, Hofmannsthal observed: "Die Gedichte ['Lebenslied' and 'Gute Stunde'] in der *Rundschau* haben in Wien einen unglaublichen Lärm hervorgerufen durch ihre völlige Unverständlichkeit" (*Briefe 1890–1901* 208). And on March 23, 1899 he reported to Arthur Schnitzler on the Berlin premieres of *Die Hochzeit der Sobeide* and *Der Abenteurer und die Sängerin*: "Hier sind meine armen Stücke von einer beispiellos bösen Presse erschlagen worden und mußten nach dem dritten Mal abgesetzt werden" (*HvH-Schnitzler Bw* 120).

Hofmannsthal valued a favorable criticism and an honest opinion. On April 1, 1897 Hofmannsthal wrote to Ria Schmujlow-Classen, thanking her for a favorable article in the *Sächsische Arbeiter-Zeitung* of the previous December (*Briefe 1890–1901* 209–10), and in a letter to his father of October 1897 he commented on a forthright opinion he had received from Gustav Schwarzkopf, adding: "Es ist mir recht wichtig, weil ich ja nicht die Bewunderung der gewissen modernen Clique haben will, sondern einen möglichen Eindruck auf das Publikum" (*Briefe 1890–1901* 235). As an emerging professional author, Hofmannsthal was concerned with reviews and readership; he was also aware of the effect of a work on a particular public — and the need to reach a wider public. Clearly he was conscious of his own reception, but by all accounts not yet fully aware of the implications of the stereotype ("Ästhet," etc.), and at twenty-three years he had much to learn about dealing with an unfavorable press. Above all, Hofmannsthal had to come to terms with the sharp differences between the theatrical climate in Vienna and that in Berlin where, despite consistently lukewarm reception, he had the support of Otto Brahm and Max Reinhardt.[13]

Hofmannsthal's transition from lyric poetry to drama, first by way of Greek and Jacobean tragedy, then by way of comedy and libretto, is a development now familiar to scholars and public alike. At the time, however, this transition was not viewed with much understanding, let alone tolerance; Hofmannsthal encountered critics who had neither the interest nor the talent to comprehend his new theatrical course. The critics of the *Elektra* premiere (play) on October 30, 1903, under Max Reinhardt's direction in the Kleines Theater in Berlin, failed to see the play as a recreation of a mythic situation with contemporary implications. They faulted Hofmannsthal's interest in hysteria and Freud for misleading him dramatically, "die Verirrung eines Talents,"[14] styling him little more than an artistic practitioner of psychoanalysis.[15] *Das gerettete Venedig* (1905), which had its premiere January 21, 1905 in Otto Brahm's Lessing Theater, fared no better. Hofmannsthal was coupled with the would-be poets ("Wie-Poeten"), aesthetes, and "Formkünstler" who surrendered essentials in favor of effect and atmospheric decoration. Hofmannsthal, like the Romantics (so it was claimed), showed a fondness for the perverse and the sadistic.[16]

1910 saw the premiere of *Cristinas Heimreise*, Hofmannsthal's first comedy for the spoken stage; this year was critical for Hofmannsthal, who by then was committed to comedy and aspiring to productive activity — and a wider audience — in the German-speaking theater (*Briefe 1907–1909* 305, 324, 352, 367, 396–97). A large body of critical opinion, polarized and hostile, already existed when *Cristinas Heimreise* had its Berlin premiere at the Deutsches Theater on February 11, 1910 under the direction of Max Reinhardt. In the reception of Hofmannsthal's comedy, the majority of reviews followed accepted opinion: they drew heavily on the implications of the Loris myth, typed Hofmannsthal as "Ästhet," "wirklichkeitsentrückter Poet," "Wortkünstler" and "Undramatiker," and confirmed in the theatrical sphere a view of Hofmannsthal which already existed in the broader literary sphere.[17] Many critics, believing they perceived genuine weaknesses in the play, revealed attitudes which went beyond the earlier stereotype, namely, deep suspicion of Hofmannsthal's artistic medium — Hofmannsthal's language (Hofmannsthal as "Wortkünstler") — serious doubts about Hofmannsthal's capacity as a playwright, and a personal animosity or an attack *ad hominem*. There were few positive reviews.[18]

The image that the drama critics established in the reviews of *Cristinas Heimreise* was repeated in another form by the music critics in the reception of *Der Rosenkavalier*. The work was reportedly a success when it was first performed in Dresden on January 26, 1911 under the direction of Max Reinhardt. It was also produced in Munich and Cologne prior to its Berlin premiere on November 14, 1911 under the direction of Generalintendant Graf Georg von Hülsen-Haeseler. In contrast to *Cristinas Heimreise* of the previous year, Hofmannsthal was on this occasion librettist, sharing scrutiny with Richard Strauss and judged by *music* critics. If the drama critics saw in Hofmannsthal the "Ästhet," "wirklichkeitsentrückter Poet," "Wortkünstler," and "Undramatiker," and injected into their assessment a vindictive note of personal animus, the music critics, for their part, intensified the oppositional tone of the reaction by creating a distinction between librettist and composer which viewed Hofmannsthal not simply as overshadowed by Strauss's talent, but as exercising a wayward influence on the composer. The hostile critics who understood the work least praised Strauss and exonerated him from all defects in the work — the weaknesses of the work were held to be Hofmannsthal's responsibility.

Reflecting on these productions a few years later in a letter to Rudolf Pannwitz (January 16, 1918), Hofmannsthal described his precarious position by drawing a parallel between himself and Grillparzer: Grillparzer's literary reception had been "vergällt durch beständige Unlust des Publikums und Bosheit der Kritik," his own position he characterized by "die unbeschreibliche Anfeindung nach *Cristina* und *Rosencavalier* [*sic*] ohne *eine* Gegenstimme" (180). The attitude of "unbeschreibliche Anfeindung" was an inexorable reality, and for a poet who had consciously committed himself to the theater, "der Unverstand und Bosheit der Kritiker" was a heavy handicap already in 1910.

In his response to the critical reaction to the Berlin premiere of *Der Rosenkavalier* — the critics' suggestion of a qualitative difference between composer and librettist — Hofmannsthal interpreted the reaction, vindictive as it was, less as a threat to the collaboration between himself and Strauss than as a need to proselytize the press. Hofmannsthal's immediate concern in a letter to Strauss of December 18, 1911 "inmitten dieser Einöde wimmelnder Mittelmäßigkeit" (*RS-HvH Bw* 155) was for the first performance of their new work *Ariadne auf Naxos*. The first version of *Ariadne* was produced on October 25, 1912 in Stuttgart under the direction of Reinhardt. The ten months leading up to this premiere — the record is in the Strauss-Hofmannsthal correspondence — were months of intense activity, during which Hofmannsthal undertook to ease, as he put it in a letter of February 7, 1912, "[seine] schwierige und nicht dornenlose Position als Dichter-Librettist (über den ausschließlich *Musik*-Kritiker referieren)" (*RS-HvH Bw* 167). Hofmannsthal, with Strauss's encouragement and active support, undertook to proselytize press and public before the premiere of *Ariadne auf Naxos* in Stuttgart — thus the approach to several editors, publishers, and critics in that year. And to circumvent misconceptions and false interpretations, especially concerning the relation of the Ariadne theme to Molière, no fewer than five separate articles under Hofmannsthal's name appeared in the year 1912 in German and French publications. "Die schlimme Presse, die hetzt und faule Nachrichten in die Welt setzt," as Strauss called it in a letter of December 1912 (*RS-HvH Bw* 208), was a force both composer and librettist were obliged to recognize and contend with.

The effects of proselytizing were reflected in some measure in the reviews of the Berlin premiere of *Ariadne auf Naxos* (Neubearbeitung) which took place on November 1, 1916. However, despite some better informed, albeit reserved criticism, the older attitudes to Hofmannsthal persisted. The process of typecasting Hofmannsthal first as "Ästhet," "wirklichkeitsentrückter Poet," "Wortkünstler," "Undramatiker," and then as exemplar of "literarische Blutleere," which began in 1910 and 1911, was to receive official sanction by the scholarly world, in 1918 with Karl Justus Obenauer's study, "Hugo von Hofmannsthal. Eine Studie über den ästhetischen Menschen," and in 1920 with Walter A. Berendsohn's *Der Impressionismus Hofmannsthals als Zeiterscheinung* (Wunberg 257–82, 283–88). The struggle was not only with the daily press, but with the scholarly press as well.

Slight improvements through proselytizing could be seen in the reception of the next major work, *Die Frau ohne Schatten*. The reviews of the Vienna premiere (October 10, 1919. Conductor: Franz Schalk), written largely by uncomprehending and disapproving critics, reflected familiar elements. Hofmannsthal was labelled "Kunstdichter," "Ästhet," "Sprachartist." The competent, soundly argued reviews were a minority.[19] The reviews of the Berlin premiere (April 18, 1920. Director: Max von Schilling) were better reasoned, more knowledgeable, and reflected the welcome circumstance that Hofmannsthal and Strauss had at last made some progress in stimulating an informed response among the critics. Despite some hard-won advances, however, the event itself was again considered a Strauss achievement, even among the best informed critics. For the music critics, Hofmannsthal was still an imponderable, a gray eminence veiling Strauss's splendor.

When Hofmannsthal turned to the theater and to comedy in 1910 and 1911, he found himself the unwitting beneficiary of his own earlier reputation and the embodiment of a legend — the myth of Loris. This image, already fixed by 1910, represented the writer Hofmannsthal as journalists — and scholars — remembered him, or wished to remember him. The "aestheticism" of Loris, admired in the 1890s, was "frozen" in the 1910s in a stereotype which was soon fixed not only aesthetically, but politically and culturally. The strategy of insinuation and persuasion — the process of proselytizing — which Hofmannsthal and Strauss had been forced to adopt after 1911 had resulted at least in a mitigation of the harsh and insensitive criticism — "unbeschreibliche Anfeindung" — toward Hofmannsthal the librettist. However, due to radical changes in the sociopolitical and theatrical climate of the early 1920s, the stereotype came to represent all that was considered unprogressive and reactionary, oriented to the past and out of touch with contemporary reality. With this handicap Hofmannsthal proceeded into the last decade of his life. There were still important works to come: *Der Schwierige* (1921), *Das Große Salzburger Welttheater* (1922), *Der Unbestechliche* (1923), *Die ägyptische Helena* (1928), *Der Turm* (1924, 1927), and *Arabella* (posth. 1933).

Mortality imposes its own critical dimension: it signals reflection, reassessment, and an awareness of totality. Hofmannsthal's sudden death on July 15, 1929, was followed by a tide of tributes and reminiscences which swelled the years 1929 to 1931. In these years also began an important development, that is, interest in Hofmannsthal and his works as subject of serious academic attention. Studies appeared which constituted a clear shift away from the critical focus of earlier Hofmannsthal reception. One such study was Ernst Robert Curtius's study "Hofmannsthals deutsche Sendung" of 1929, Curtius' follow-up to Hofmannsthal's "Das Schrifttum als geistiger Raum der Nation" of 1926, in which Curtius contested the cliché of aestheticism, or Hofmannsthal as "*nur* Ästhet." In 1930 two important items from the Hofmannsthal *Nachlass* were published. The first of these was Max

Mell's *Loris. Die Prosa des jungen Hugo von Hofmannsthal*; the second, Walther Brecht's publication of Hofmannsthal's *Ad me ipsum* fragment, a document which would have far-reaching and, some would say, questionable consequences for Hofmannsthal research. In the same year (1930) appeared works by Friedrich Gundolf and Max Kommerell. Gundolf, no longer part of the George circle, returned to his earlier positive attitude to Hofmannsthal in a study entitled "Loris"; and Kommerell's inaugural lecture in Frankfurt am Main was notable for its systematic and critically affirmative assertion of the totality of Hofmannsthal's work, giving as much weight to Hofmannsthal's later as to his early work. (Kommerell, like Hofmannsthal, had freed himself from the dominance of George's personality.) In 1935, Richard Alewyn, who was destined to have a large influence on future Hofmannsthal research, published the first of his pioneering essays. At the same time the beginning of academic interest in Hofmannsthal was confirmed by Weber's recording of five dissertations for that year.[20] (Six dissertations are recorded for 1935 to 1939, including one Italian dissertation.) And before the end of the decade (1938), Karl J. Naef published his important study on Hofmannsthal's concept of "Praeexistenz." These were the emerging positive voices of the 1930s.

Active interest in Hofmannsthal declined during the Second World War, reaching a low point in 1942. (Weber records nine items for that year.)[21] Nevertheless the 1940s were distinguished for the initial work of such scholars as Emil Staiger, Hilde Cohn, Walter Naumann, Helmut Fiechtner, Grete and Heinrich Schaeder, and Andrew Jaszi. Scholarly investigation and interpretation initiated new aspects of reception, a reception based on objective historical findings and accumulated knowledge, leading to a better informed public (including critics) with broader critical expectations.

Between 1945 and 1959 there took place a radical transformation of critical perspectives leading to a clear turnabout in attitude to Hofmannsthal; this was due largely to postwar material and politico-technological developments and to new stimuli in Hofmannsthal research. The mood of the years following the Second World War was charged with political tension, economic stress, and psychological insecurity. Questions of the nuclear-technological age — nuclear deterrent or nuclear annihilation — loomed large in the thinking of the times. It was a somber, desperate atmosphere, filled with paradoxes, and always in the background the unseen and incomprehensible face of a new technocratic world. As a result the generation of readers, theatergoers, and critics that emerged in the decade after 1945 acquired new historical and cultural experience, and a basis for a fresh approach to Hofmannsthal.

The year 1945 marked a particular event in Hofmannsthal scholarship. This was the appearance of the first volume (*Erzählungen*) of the *Gesammelte Werke in Einzelausgaben* (15 vols.), edited by Herbert Steiner, an important interim edition, the last volume (*Aufzeichnungen*) of which appeared in 1959. This became the standard edition for researchers up into the 1970s. A second notable development of the postwar years was the indisputable fact that during the twenty-five-year period following Hofmannsthal's death in 1929 Hofmannsthal's name and works became part of the literary canon, an accepted part of the national cultural heritage. With active scholarship and a better informed public it was but a short step to the "Hofmannsthal Renaissance," which characterized the 1950s and the celebrations of the Commemoration Year 1954.[22] The vigorous flowering of research in the 1950s and 1960s made a persuasive and lasting impact on the understanding of Hofmannsthal's works, his artistic sensibility, and his development as an artist. The committed researchers whose investigations began in the 1950s and continued into the next two decades — Walter Jens, William Rey, Fritz Martini, Paul Requadt, Werner Kraft, Gerhard Baumann, Martin Stern, Wolfram Mauser, Richard Exner — stimulated new approaches to Hofmannsthal and shaped decisively Hofmannsthal reception in the second half of the century.

Hand in hand with political-cultural changes and developments in Hofmannsthal research went a more open and aesthetically broader critical vision. Postwar cultural developments encouraged a wider, more internationally oriented theatrical activity. This was due largely to the *Nachholbedarf*, the desperate need to make up for time lost during the years of Nazi rule, and the plethora of literary-dramatic forms that flooded the postwar literary scene. Radical political and technological developments, active Hofmannsthal research, and the broader international literary climate after 1945 created the conditions for new critical positions — and new aspects of reception.

A brief comment is called for on Hermann Broch's groundbreaking study *Hofmannsthal und seine Zeit* of 1951. This work was commissioned by the Bollingen Foundation as an introduction to a collection of Hofmannsthal's prose pieces; it evolved as Broch worked on it into an intellectual history of the years 1860 to 1920. Broch's special contribution was the perspective he created of Hofmannsthal viewed against the culture and art styles of the nineteenth century, a knowledge of which, Broch believed, was essential to an understanding of Hofmannsthal. Broch was cognizant of the deep divisions in Hofmannsthal's nature, to which he applied the word "schizophrenia" or split mind, and clarified Hofmannsthal's artistic and psychological responses to a culture already in the throes of decline. (In Hofmannsthal, Broch recognized parallels with his own situation.) Relating ethics and aesthetics, his study followed Hofmannsthal's progress as he became "the most eloquent spokesman for the rejection of aestheticism" (Steinberg 4). In addition, Broch placed Hofmannsthal in the broader context of European writers, declaring Hofmannsthal's kinship with Marcel Proust and James Joyce. (He might have added W. B. Yeats and T. S. Eliot.) Broch contrasted Hofmannsthal and Joyce brilliantly as visual and auditory artists. Broch established an artistic-psychological basis for understanding Hofmannsthal, and wrote with shrewd and sympathetic perception — one poet examined through another poet's penetrating insight. In Wunberg's words (32), Broch summed up everything that had been achieved up to that time, and made up for what had been overlooked.

The radical turnabout in attitude to Hofmannsthal — the popularity of his name in the 1950s — is evidenced in the reaction to performances of *Der Schwierige*, Hofmannsthal's comic masterpiece of his mature years. Long struggling against the critical misportrayal as a glorification of an effete and declining Viennese aristocracy, *Der Schwierige* was seen, between 1945 and 1959, in a context of contemporary developments. Actress Maria Fein in a dramatic reading of the play in Berlin in September 1953 — the reading was repeated in Zurich and Paris[23] — first stated the critical theme: the precariousness of the age, with its bewildering and alarming paradoxes, and the imperiled nature of human relationships — "the great problem of partnership ('Gefährtschaft') in its highest sense." In the productions that followed, especially the productions of the Commemoration Year ("Gedenkjahr") 1954, Hofmannsthal's comedy was seen as an important complement to the age, an artistic and ethical restorative to an age radically displaced socially and politically and desperately in search of moral and psychological stability.

In the meantime Hofmannsthal gained friends in high places. No less a person than West Germany's President Theodor Heuss, speaking at the Bad Hersfeld Festival in July 1954 — the occasion was performances of Hofmannsthal's *Jedermann*, *Das Salzburger Große Welttheater*, and *König Ödipus* — declared his support for a revised view of Hofmannsthal. Heuss[24] acknowledged Hofmannsthal's position as "Sprecher eines actuellen *Vergangenen*," who represented "die geistige Sublimierung des alten Österreich, ja des Österreich-Ungarn"; but in opposition to a one-sided and dated attitude to Hofmannsthal, Heuss stressed "das Erzieherische" and "die Ermunterung zur Selbstbildung" in Hofmannsthal's work, as well as the intention in Hofmannsthal's theatrical works (operas, comedies, and serious dramas), "mit den Bedrohnissen einer ent-gotteten Welt der Angst, der Bosheit, des plumpen und mörderischen Machtwillens innerlich fertig zu werden." In emphasizing "das geistig Produktive" in Hofmannsthal's *oeuvre* over the political ("Hofmannsthal war kein Politiker") Heuss confirmed — and re-affirmed — an essential relation between Hofmannsthal's work and the time.

Two developments of the 1960s and 1970s were important for the course of Hofmannsthal reception in the remaining decades of the century: the emergence of a new critical approach and methodology known as "Rezeptionsästhetik," sometimes referred to as "Rezeptions-geschichte" or "Wirkungsgeschichte," and the founding of the Hugo von Hofmannsthal-Gesellschaft. The aesthetics of reception, the new critical methodology formulated by Hans Robert Jauss, Karl Robert Mandelkow, and others[25] represented at the time a shift in critical-historical focus as well as a reinvigoration of German literary-historical criticism. The new position was based on the premise that the historical life of literature should be liberated from the static conventions of liter-ary history, that the renewal of literary history required the abandon-ment of the fixed attitudes of historical objectivity, and that the traditional aesthetic of productivity and presentation should be founded on an aesthetic of reception and effect (Jauss 26).

The aesthetics of reception focuses on the response which a work of art receives from a particular sociopolitical environment, and on the criteria of judgment which a particular group in that environment ap-plies. This is viewing literary activity through, as it were, the prism of social-political-cultural values. What is important is not only the critical horizon of a particular group, that is, the interaction between work and public, but also the interaction between author, critic, and public. Fur-thermore, the aesthetics of reception examines how aesthetic responses are shaped by sociopolitical attitudes, and how aesthetic responses are transformed over time and through changing sociopolitical environ-ments — Paul Stöcklein speaks of "Literary sociology" (1968) — or the interdependency of aesthetic values and sociopolitical attitudes. In short, this is a claim for the priority of receptionist norms over classical critical norms derived from Goethean philology.

The new methodology adapted easily to Hofmannsthal studies. Alongside the time-honored textual and interpretative studies on Hof-mannsthal, reception studies have appeared since the 1960s and 1970s which have shed light on Hofmannsthal's relationship to critics and public (Exner 114–34). A seminal study in Hofmannsthal reception was Gotthard Wunberg's *Hofmannsthal im Urteil seiner Kritiker: Dokumente für die Wirkungsgeschichte Hugo von Hofmannsthals in Deutschland*

(1972). Reception studies of individual works have followed: *Frau ohne Schatten* (Konrad, 1988), *Uraufführungen Hugo von Hofmannsthals in Berlin* (Sösemann, 1989), *Der Schwierige* (Joyce, 1993), and *Andreas* (Mayer, 1998–1999).

In the summer of 1967 the Deutsches Seminar of the Johann Wolfgang Goethe University in Frankfurt issued a circular letter to around 800 individuals interested in Hofmannsthal in Europe and around the world: Was there interest in forming an international Hofmannsthal organization? The letter received some 200 affirmative replies. Subsequently, and following legal preliminaries, the Hugo von Hofmannsthal-Gesellschaft was officially founded on February 1, 1968. Martin Stern (Basel) was the Society's first President. Succeeding presidents have been Klemens Köttelwesch (1980–1988), Werner Volke (1989–1995), Marcus Bierich (1995–2000).

The Society has attracted a large membership from all parts of the world, people interested in the life and writings of Hofmannsthal. (The Society's March 2000 membership catalogue listed 340 individual members — and 150 institutions — from 14 European countries, from the United States and Canada, from Brazil, Japan, Australia, and Israel.) Among its world-wide membership the Society has stimulated scholarly activity through conferences, workshops, and members' meetings held at regular intervals, and has developed the sense of scholarly community. The Society issued two publications: *Hofmannsthal-Blätter* (1968–1992), including research essays, bibliography, reports from the executive, and *Hofmannsthal-Forschungen* (1971–1986), with information on conferences, papers, and research projects.

The central objective of the Society's foundation, however, was the preparation and publication of a new critical edition of Hofmannsthal's works. This objective was achieved in 1975 with the appearance of the first volume. The project was facilitated in large part by the consolidation of several important Hofmannsthal collections at the Freies Deutsches Hochstift in Frankfurt.

In 1979, the fiftieth anniversary of Hofmannsthal's death, the editors of *Literatur und Kritik*, a journal devoted to Austrian writing, dedicated the June issue (No. 135) to Hugo von Hofmannsthal. Included in this issue were the replies to a questionnaire which the editors had directed to 30 Austrian writers: "What does Hofmannsthal mean to me?" ("Was bedeutet mir Hofmannsthal? Eine Rundfrage") The purpose of the survey was to determine what kind of presence Hofmannsthal — in large measure representative of his time — exerted in the current literary scene in Austria. The editors noted that 11 of the 30 writers did not reply, either out of overwork, or indifference, or lack of knowledge of Hofmannsthal's works. Based on the nineteen opinions received, the editors concluded that Hofmannsthal was still as controversial a writer as ever, one whose "classicality" ("Klassizität") was still denied on the basis of old and obsolete prejudices.

One third of the respondents were negative and reflected continuing older attitudes: resentment of Hofmannsthal's upper-class background and "classical" training; mistrust of Hofmannsthal's — assumed — artistic egotism; and the perception of Hofmannsthal's art as decadent, aloof, and lacking in human feeling. Prominent was the perceived failure of Hofmannsthal's social-political objectives — a claim supported by references to Hermann Broch's description of Hofmannsthal as "der Mann, der überall auf verlorenen Pfosten steht."[26] In addition, there were two strongly formulated antisemitic replies, ill-informed and vitriolic in tone.

The affirmative replies (12 in all) presented a more redeeming picture. The central focus was the affectionate recollection of Hofmannsthal's early works over the later works. Hofmannsthal's poetry was warmly remembered, and works such as *Andreas, Die Frau ohne Schatten, Der Schwierige*, and *Der Turm* were greatly admired; but for most of the respondents the works of Loris, up to the Lord Chandos letter, represented Hofmannsthal's real message — "Mein Hofmannsthal heißt Loris." The Lord Chandos letter received special consideration, as much for its analysis and prophetic warnings as for its painfully realized predictions, that is, the profusion of language forms faced by the generation of the 1960s. As one writer expressed it, the Lord Chandos letter signalled the decline of language from "Golden Age" to "Silver Age" to "Iron Age" to "Paper Age," with the dawning realization that numbers and signs might replace language altogether.

The same respondents acknowledged the cultural-educative aspects of Hofmannsthal's work. Hofmannsthal was seen as the mature writer who conquered aestheticism through ethics, who stood fast while Austria declined, and who, despite the lack of general recognition, has the potential to exert an influence fifty years after his death. Hofmannsthal showed a present generation (that is, 1960s and 1970s) that a writer need not be ordinary and make a big noise in order to be a true poet, and the "poet of Rodaun" provided a balance in the face of the Austrian masochism of Bernhard, Handke, etc. Most importantly, Hofmannsthal demonstrated the possibilities that lay within the reach of every individual, the feeling of belonging to a "sensitive, eclectic century" (that is, the nineteenth century), and the cosmopolitan awareness of being at home in England, France, and Italy, the conviction that one was a child of Greater Europe.

What was lacking in two thirds of the replies was a deep conviction of Hofmannsthal's place as an influential national writer whose achievements were relevant to present-day realities. If Hofmannsthal could be counted a spiritual force or mentor to the age (consider the 1950s), then he served at best a small, limited community. As the century moved into its last decades (1980 to 2000), it was clear that for this group of Austrian writers, and probably for other writers and members of the public, Hofmannsthal and his work had the status of a controversial classic.

However, Hofmannsthal's name enjoyed some currency as a national psycho-political icon. This was demonstrated at the time of the state visit of the Federal President Richard von Weizsäcker to Austria in March 1986. A week before the visit, *Die Presse* (Vienna) ran the account of an interview with the Federal President in Bonn, the headline above the article reading: "Sein Lieblingsautor ist Hofmannsthal." Weizsäcker informed his interviewer that for many years he held no one in greater admiration than Hofmannsthal, his visit to Austria would therefore be pervaded by recollections of Hofmannsthal.

A week later, the day of the Federal President's arrival in Vienna, *Die Presse* published an article — "Die Kraft der Erinnerung" — outlining what it was hoped the state visit would achieve, allowing for the current tense situation in Central Europe. The article concluded optimistically with the well-known lines — "Ich spreche von einem Prozess [. . .] eine konservative Revolution" — from Hofmannsthal's speech in Munich in 1927: "Das Schrifttum als geistiger Raum der Nation." The writer added: "What have we learned from the frightful lesson of the last decades? There is still no end to the problems." The "Hofmannsthal connection" was not mentioned in any of the subsequent reports in *Die Presse* of the Federal President's visit to Austria.

The scholarly world had another approach. In 1993, the *Hofmannsthal-Blätter* and the *Hofmannsthal-Forschungen* were succeeded by the *Hofmannsthal-Jahrbuch zur Europäischen Moderne*. Like its predecessors, the *Hofmannsthal-Jahrbuch* undertook to provide source and documentary materials, as well as a forum for scholarly discussion. However, in recognition of the larger international cultural scene, the editors of the *Hofmannsthal-Jahrbuch*, showing great foresight, broadened the editorial policy. Starting from the premise that Hofmannsthal and his works were related in a special way to the genesis and development of the modern age, the editors sought to focus on themes associated with the name of Hofmannsthal, and to treat Hofmannsthal's works in relation to the so-called classicism of the modern age ("die sogenannte klassische Moderne"), its origins and continuity. The editors expected that the articles appearing in the *Jahrbuch* would reflect the broad spectrum of what defined Hofmannsthal's role in his own time, that is, an acknowledgement of tradition and a blueprint for the future. The policy recognized the international level of investigation the editors believed Hofmannsthal research had reached, proceeding into the new century. The *Hofmannsthal-Jahrbücher* together with the new critical edition would be instruments for shaping future reception.

In line with the new technologies — media culture and mass communications — the Hofmannsthal Society recently (1999) opened its own internet website, *Hugo von Hofmannsthal Online*, with links for information on Biography and Bibliography, Critical Edition and Society Activities, Projects and Publications, and Forum. In December 2000, the Society announced by way of its website the appearance of a new and relevant study, *Hugo von Hofmannsthal und die Medien der Moderne*, a dissertation (Graz) by Heinz Hiebler. There is no doubt: the Hofmannsthal "industry" is alive and flourishing!

Hofmannsthal has left a valuable legacy of works, insights, and attitudes which are relevant today. Hofmannsthal is an example of a poet who developed in his art through difficult transitions: the transition from aesthetics to ethics, from poetry to drama, from the language of mythical thinking to the language of conceptualization, and from Austrian national state to a republican state. Each transition was made with much self-searching and spiritual reorientation. Each experience was resolved in a new and maturer level of creativity.

Hofmannsthal left a body of writing — poetry, drama, libretti, prose, and correspondence — which is impressive in its compass, variety, formal aspects, even in its incompleteness. His poetry is an expression of his commitment to beauty of language and formal perfection. His prose style — rhythmic, lucid, and flexible — is second to none in the German language. In his dramatic works, he created memorable figures for the spoken stage — Jedermann, Cristina, Hans Karl, Theodor, Sigismund — and in his opera texts he created figures — Elektra, the Marschallin, Oktavian, Baron Ochs, Zerbinetta, the Dyer's Wife, Barak, Arabella — which are recognized internationally.[27]

Imagination played an important role in Hofmannsthal's thought, both in the creation of a literary work and in its reception by the public. To this end he created works — lyrical, dramatic, and narrative — which speak directly to the imagination, requiring the reader's and spectator's imaginative response. For Hofmannsthal, understanding by reflection alone did not unlock the essential nature of an artistic image. He created figures that have within them the capacity for interpretative expansion. The energy of imagination, its development in reader and spectator, is integral to his views on reception.

Hofmannsthal led the way in recognizing and working with the instabilities of language (the Lord Chandos complex), and in healing, if not eradicating, the split between language and meaning. He foresaw the dangers of language deteriorating into ciphers and numbers.

Most importantly, in the tradition of Goethean and classical liberalism, Hofmannsthal has left a view of life which emphasizes the value of the individual, his totality, his possibilities. This is important in a world of broken values, material objectives, and intellectual cynicism. Hofmannsthal saw the individual as a part of a cosmopolitan, supranational culture. Hofmannsthal's political ideal — the ideal of an Imperial Austria under Habsburg rulership, which he fervently represented and fostered — collapsed, but his humanist-cultural thought remains.

Hofmannsthal's legacy, which also defines his modernity,[28] is based on a quality his writings share with those of only the greatest writers: the quality of inexhaustibility, of creative reinterpretation.

Notes

[1] This account of Hofmannsthal reception owes much in format and substance to Gotthart Wunberg's seminal study and invaluable source book on Hofmannsthal reception: Preface, 13–34.

[2] "[. . .] die Rezeptionsgeschichte Hugo von Hofmannsthals, ist das nahezu klassische Beispiel eines einmal fixierten und fortan ausschliesslich an seiner Erfüllung gemessenen Erwartungshorizontes; darin nur noch Byron vergleichbar oder Mozart, mit dem er die fama vom Wunderkind gemeinsam hatte. Selten ist ein Dichter so früh auf eine bestimmte Seite und Möglichkeit seiner Produktion, und damit zugleich auf ihre Grenzen festgelegt worden; selten allerdings war dazu auch so viel berechtigte und frühe Veranlassung. Überschwengliches Lob, Belehrung und Besserwisserei, Verachtung, Tadel und Verzückung haben ihn von Anfang an begleitet" (Wunberg, 15).

[3] Other pseudonyms used by Hofmannsthal were: Loris Melikow, Theophil Morren, and Archibald O'Hagan.

[4] "re: Hugo. Seine Dominante ist das Wilhelmmeistlerliche. Ruhiger Empfang der Dinge ist nicht seine Sache; er ist immer bekümmert, sie sich zu deuten. Alles soll geordnet, verbunden werden. Diese bunten, hastenden Verse fragen immer das Leben um seinen Sinn" (Hermann Bahr, *Tagebücher, Skizzenbücher, Notizhefte*. Vol. 2: 1890–1900 (1996), 78).

[5] Hofmannsthal affirmed his experience in a letter to Walther Brecht, dated February 20, 1929: "Man fühlte sich als Verbundene . . . die Bestätigung dessen, was in mir lag, die Bekräftigung, daß ich kein ganz vereinzelter Sonderling war" (*Bw George-HvH* 235).

[6] The majority of Hofmannsthal's major poems, as well as *Der Tod des Tizian*.

[7] *Ausgewählte Gedichte*. Berlin: Verlag der Blätter für die Kunst, 1902. Reprinted 1904.

[8] In *Die Zeit*, ed. Hermann Bahr (Vienna, March 1896).

[9] First published in *Die Neue Rundschau* (Berlin, February 1904).

[10] See Hermann Ubell, "Die Blätter für die Kunst," *Die Zeit*, 20 May 1899 (Wunberg 62–66).

[11] See Franz Servaes, "Jung-Wien. Berliner Eindrücke," 1897 (Wunberg 47–48); Gustav Gugitz, "Das literarische Jung-Wien," 1897 (Wunberg 49); Alfred Neumann, "Loris," 1897 (Wunberg 49–52).

[12] Wunberg, 487: "einer der entscheidenden Faktoren in der Rezeptionsgeschichte Hugo von Hofmannsthals." The full implications of Borchardt's effect on Hofmannsthal reception have yet to be investigated.

[13] Hofmannsthal's preference for the Berlin theatrical atmosphere over that in Vienna, Berlin being in his view the more vibrant center, is reflected in letters to his father, ca. March 1909 (*Briefe 1907–1909* 313 and 356).

[14] Paul Goldmann, *Aus dem polemischen Irrgarten*, Frankfurt 1905 (Wunberg 113–117).

[15] Maximilian Harden, *Die Zukunft*, August 27, 1904 (Wunberg 82–86).

[16] Heinrich Hart, *Der Tag*, January 25, 1905 (Wunberg 123–126).

[17] Similar sentiments and similar vocabulary — "Feinschmecker," "Museumsdirektor der Kultur," and "zarter und geschmeidiger Neuromantiker" — were to be found in Samuel Lublinski's study, *Der Ausgang der Moderne: Ein Buch der Opposition*, of 1909; Friedrich Gundolf's comparative comments on George and Hofmannsthal in *Das Bild Georges* of 1910, proclaimed Hofmannsthal as "Proteus der bildung, geschickt sich in alles zu verwandeln, ohne irgend etwas unentrinnbar zu sein." See Wunberg 209–228, 228–235.

[18] A review in the *Berliner Börsen Kurier* (February 12, 1910) described the tumult in the theatre caused by contending factions and the departure after the first act of one of the Hohenzollern princesses and her husband. See Joyce 5.

[19] Reviews of the Vienna premiere are discussed in Claudia Konrad's excellent study: *"Die Frau ohne Schatten" von Hugo von Hofmannsthal und Richard Strauss* (Hamburg: Karl Dieter Wagner, 1988), 166–79.

[20] Helmut A. Fiechtner, *Hofmannsthal und die Romanitas* (Vienna); Walter Perl, *Das lyrische Jugendwerk Hugo von Hofmannsthals* (Zurich); Paul Werner

Müller, *Hofmannsthal's Lustspieldichtung* (Basel); Emma Hannöver, *Weltanschauung und Stil: Eine stilpsychologische Untersuchung zu Hugo von Hofmannsthals Wesen und Werk* (Bonn); and Wilhelm Trappmann, *Das Ich-Du-Problem in seiner Existenzbedeutung im dramatischen Jugendwerk Hugo von Hofmannsthals* (Erlangen).

[21] Two points are to be noted about the statistics of the war years. First, of the 93 items listed by Horst Weber for the years 1939–1945, 38 items (more than one third!) appeared under British and American authorship, including 3 American dissertations — no German dissertations were recorded for the same period; second, this figure of 38 was larger by 12 than the number of items appearing under British and American authorship between the years 1929 and 1938! It is therefore evident, that, despite the clearly documented decline in interest after the early 1930s, Hofmannsthal maintained a dedicated and growing following, and that during the war years he even gained adherents, particularly in the Anglo-Saxon world.

[22] A brief statistic relating to the publication of various correspondences sheds light on the expanding understanding of the Hofmannsthal phenomenon. Of the 85 correspondence items listed by Horst Weber (*Hugo von Hofmannsthal: Bibliographie des Schrifttums, 1892–1963* [1966]) between 1904 and 1964, 44 items (50%) appeared between 1932 and 1954 (the Commemoration Year), including: *Briefe, 1890–1901, Briefe, 1900–1909,* and the correspondences with Wildgans, Beer-Hofmann, George, Strauss, Bodenhausen, and Borchardt. This fact strikingly points up the liveliness of scholarly activity.

[23] Also in Zurich (January 18, 1954) and Paris (date uncertain).

[24] *Hugo von Hofmannsthal: Eine Rede gehalten bei der Eröffnung der Festspiele der Stadt Bad Hersfeld am 3. Juli 1954.* Tübingen: Rainer Wunderlich Verlag Hermann Leins, 1954. Reprinted in *Würdigungen, Reden, Aufsätze und Briefe 1949–1955.* Ed. Hans Bott. Tübingen, 1955.

[25] Paul Stöcklein, Wolfgang Iser, Gunter Grimm, Peter Uwe Hohendahl.

[26] The source of the Broch statement has not been established.

[27] Review listings for the years 1981–1998, available in the *Hofmannsthal-Blätter* and *Hofmannsthal-Jahrbuch,* show that the musical works *Elektra, Der Rosenkavalier, Ariadne auf Naxos,* and *Die Frau ohne Schatten* are performed with regularity (*Arabella* less regularly); as for the works for the spoken stage, *Jedermann* is performed annually (at Salzburg), *Der Schwierige* frequently (*Cristinas Heimreise* and *Das Grosse Salzburger Welttheater* less frequently).

[28] Hofmannsthal's modernity, his spiritual relatedness to the contemporary world, has been argued for many years — by the Japanese scholar Takahoro Kikuchi on the basis of humanist idealism (1965), by F. M. Kuna on Hofmannsthal's association with T. S. Eliot (1966), and on grounds of comprehensiveness by Martin E. Schmid (1981).

Works Cited

Bahr, Hermann. "Loris." *Freie Bühne für den Entwicklungskampf der Zeit.* Berlin, January 1892.

———. "Das junge Österreich." *Deutsche Zeitung,* Vienna, 1893. All three items available in Hermann Bahr. *Zur Überwindung des Naturalismus: Theoretische Schriften 1887–1904.* Ausgewählt, eingeleitet und erläutert von Gotthard Wunberg. (*Sprache und Literatur* 46) Stuttgart: W. Kohlhammer, 1968.

———. "Symbolisten." *Die Nation. Wochenschrift für Politik, Volkswirtschaft und Literatur.* Ed. Theodor Barth. Berlin, June 18, 1892.

———. *Tagebücher, Skizzenbücher, Notizhefte. 1895–1905.* 4 vols. Ed. Moritz Czáky. Vienna, Cologne, Weimar: Böhlau, 1994–2000.

Borchardt, Rudolf. "Eranos-Brief." *Gesammelte Werke in Einzelbänden.* Prosa I, 90–130. Ed. Maria Luise Borchardt. Stuttgart: Ernst Klett, 1957.

Briefwechsel zwischen George und Hofmannsthal. Ed. von Robert Boehringer. 2. ergänzte Auflage. Munich and Düsseldorf: Helmut Küppen (formerly Georg Bondi), 1938. (Abbreviated as *Bw George-HvH.*)

Durzak, Manfred, ed. *Hermann Broch: Der Dichter und seine Zeit.* Stuttgart, Berlin, Cologne, Mainz: W. Kohlhammer, 1968.

Exner, Richard. "Forschungsgeschichte als Wirkungsgeschichte. Skizzierung einiger grundsätzlicher Probleme zur Rezeption Hugo von Hofmannsthals." In *Hofmannsthal-Forschungen I. Referate der zweiten Tagung der Hugo von Hofmannsthal-Gesellschaft* (Vienna, June 10–13, 1971), 114–34.

Heuss, Theodor. *Hugo von Hofmannsthal: Eine Rede gehalten bei der Eröffnung der Festspiele der Stadt Bad Hersfeld am 3. Juli 1954.* Tübingen: Rainer Wunderlich Verlag Hermann Leins, 1954. Reprinted in Theodor Heuss, *Würdigungen, Reden, Aufsätze und Briefe 1949–1955,* ed. Hans Bott. Tübingen, 1955.

Hugo von Hofmannsthal. Briefe, 1890–1901. Berlin: Fischer Verlag, 1935.

Hugo von Hofmannsthal. Briefe, 1900–1909. Vienna: Berman-Fischer Verlag, 1937.

Hugo von Hofmannsthal-Arthur Schnitzler. Briefwechsel. Ed. Therese Nickl und Heinrich Schnitzler. Frankfurt am Main: S. Fischer, 1964. (*HvH-Schnitzler Bw*)

Hugo von Hofmannsthal-Rudolf Borchardt. Briefwechsel. Ed. Marie Luise Borchardt and Herbert Steiner. Frankfurt am Main: S. Fischer, 1954. (*HvH-Borchardt Bw*)

Hugo von Hofmannsthal-Rudolf Pannwitz. Briefwechsel, 1907–1926. Ed. von Gerhard Schuster. With an essay by Erwin Jaeckle. Frankfurt am Main: S. Fischer, 1993.

Jaron, Norbert et al., eds. *Berlin-Theater der Jahrhundertwende: Bühnengeschichte der Reichsstadt im Spiegel der Kritik (1889–1914).* Tübingen: Max Niemeyer, 1986.

Jauss, Hans Robert. *Literaturgeschichte als Provokation der Literaturwissenschaft.* Konstanzer Universitätsreden 3. Konstanz, 1967. In *Literaturgeschichte als Provokation.* Frankfurt am Main: Suhrkamp, 1970, 144–207.

Joyce, Douglas. *Hugo von Hofmannsthal's "Der Schwierige": A Fifty-Year Theater History.* Columbia, SC: Camden House, 1993.

Kikuchi, Takehiro. "Der Dichter Hugo von Hofmannsthal und sein Lebenswerk in der geistigen Situation unserer Zeit." In *Universitas* 20 (1965), 499–506.

König, Ewald. "Sein Lieblingsautor ist Hofmannsthal. Wie der deutsche Bundespräsident über Österreich denkt." *Die Presse* (Vienna), March 12, 1986.

Konrad, Claudia. *"Die Frau ohne Schatten" von Hugo von Hofmannsthal und Richard Strauss: Studien zur Genese, zum Textbuch und zur Rezeptionsgeschichte.* Hamburger Beiträge zur Musikwissenschaft 37. Hamburg: Verlag der Musikalienhandlung Karl Dieter Wagner, 1988.

Kuna, F. M. "Wie modern ist Hugo von Hofmannsthal?" *Literatur und Kritik* 9–10 (1966): 77–78.

Mandelkow, Karl Robert. "Probleme der Wirkungsgeschichte." *Jahrbuch für Internationale Germanistik* Jahrgang II, Heft 1 (1970): 71–84.

Mayer, Mathias, ed. "Hofmannsthals *Andreas.* Nachträge, Nachfragen und Nachwirkungen. Teil I: Texte aus dem Umkreis des Andreas-Romans." In *Hofmannsthal-Jahrbuch* 6 (1998), 129–37.

———. "Hofmannsthals *Andreas.* Nachträge, Nachfragen und Nachwirkungen. Teil II: Hofmannsthals *Andreas* im Spiegel früher Kritik (1930–1954)." In *Hofmannsthal-Jahrbuch* 7 (1999), 101–97.

Rühle, Günther. *Theater für die Republik 1917–1933: Im Spiegel der Kritik.* Frankfurt am Main: S. Fischer Verlag, 1967. 331–37.

Schmid, Martin E. "Hofmannsthals Modernität. Tagung der Hofmannsthal-Gesellschaft in Marbach." *Neue Zürcher Zeitung*, August 28, 1981, 40.

Schulmeister, Otto. "Die Kraft der Erinnerung." *Die Presse* (Vienna), March 19, 1986.

Sösemann, Bernd, ed. *"Im Geschwätz der elenden Zeitungsschreiber." Kritiken zu den Uraufführungen Hugo von Hofmannsthals in Berlin.* Herausgegeben und mit Erläuterungen versehen von Bernd Sösemann unter Mitarbeit von Holger Kreitling. Berlin: Nicolaiische Verlagsbuchhandlung, 1989.

———. "Verrisse, Hymnen, Spötteleien. Das Spektrum publizistischer Kritik nach den Uraufführungen Hofmannsthals in Berlin." *Hugo von Hofmannsthal: Freundschaften und Begegnungen mit deutschen Zeitgenossen.* Ed. Ursula Renner and G. Bärbel Schmid. Würzburg: Königshausen & Neumann, 1991. 191–213.

Steinberg, Michael P., trans. *Hermann Broch: Hugo von Hofmannsthal and His Time. The European Imagination, 1860–1920.* Translated, edited, and with an introduction by Michael P. Steinberg. Chicago and London: University of Chicago Press, 1984.

Stöcklein, Paul. "Literatursoziologie. Gesichtspunkte zur augenblicklichen Diskussion." In *Literatur und Geistesgeschichte: Festgabe für Heinz Otto Burger.* Berlin: E. Schmidt, 1968. 406–21.

Strauss, Richard-Hugo von Hofmannsthal. Briefwechsel. Commissioned by Franz and Alice Strauss. Ed. Willi Schuh. Zürich, Freiburg i. Br.: Atlantis, 1978. (Abbreviated as *RS-HvH Bw*)

Volke, Werner. *Hugo von Hofmannsthal in Selbstzeugnissen und Bilddokumenten.* Rowohlts Monographien. Reinbek bei Hamburg: Rowohlt, 1967.

"Was bedeutet mir Hugo von Hofmannsthal? Eine Rundfrage. Österreichische Autoren antworten." *Literatur und Kritik* June 1979 (135): 276–301.

Weber, Horst. *Hugo von Hofmannsthal: Bibliographie des Schrifttums 1892–1963.* Berlin: Walter de Gruyter, 1966.

Wunberg, Gotthard. *Hofmannsthal im Urteil seiner Kritiker: Dokumente für die Wirkungsgeschichte Hugo von Hofmannsthals in Deutschland. (Wirkung der Literatur: Deutsche Autoren im Urteil ihrer Kritiker.* Band 4.) Ed. and introduced by Gotthart Wunberg. Frankfurt am Main: Athenäum Verlag, 1972.

———. "Öffentlichkeit und Esoterik. Zur Wirkungsgeschichte Hugo von Hofmannsthals." *Dichter und Leser: Festschrift für Hans Teesing.* Groningen: Wolters-Noordhoff, 1972. 47–75. (Expanded version of "Einleitung" to previous volume.)

Notes on Contributors

THOMAS A. KOVACH (editor) is Associate Professor in and Head of the Department of German Studies at the University of Arizona, Tucson. He is author of *Hofmannsthal and Symbolism: Art and Life in the Work of a Modern Poet* (1985) and of numerous articles on Hofmannsthal, Rilke, and other topics in German and Austrian literature, Judaic Studies, and intellectual history since 1750. He is co-translator of Franz Rosenzweig, *Ninety-Two Poems and Hymns of Yehuda Halevi* (2000).

KATHERINE ARENS is Professor of Germanic Studies and Comparative Literature at the University of Texas, Austin. She is author of *Empire in Decline: Fritz Mauthner's Critique of Wilhelminian Germany* (2001), *Austria and Other Margins: Reading Culture* (1996), and numerous articles on topics in Austrian and German intellectual history since 1750.

JUDITH BENISTON is Lecturer in German, University College London. She is author of *"Welttheater": Hofmannsthal, Richard von Kralik, and the Revival of Catholic Drama in Austria, 1890–1934* (1998) and co-editor of the journal *Austrian Studies*, to be relaunched in 2003.

BENJAMIN BENNETT is Kenan Professor of German at the University of Virginia, Charlottesville. He is author of several books on German literature and on European drama, including *Hugo von Hofmannsthal: The Theaters of Consciousness* (1988), *Beyond Theory: Eighteenth-Century German Literature and the Poetics of Irony* (1993), and *Goethe as Woman* (2001).

NINA BERMAN is Associate Professor in the Department of Germanic Languages and Literatures at The Ohio State University, Columbus. She is author of *Orientalismus, Kolonialismus und Moderne: Zum Bild des Orients in der deutschsprachigen Literatur um 1900*, and articles on minority literature, multiculturalism, colonialism, Hugo von Hofmannsthal, Karl May, Bodo Kirchhoff, and Albert Schweitzer.

JOANNA BOTTENBERG is Lecturer in German and Humanities at Concordia University, Montreal, Quebec. She is author of *Shared Creation: Words and Music in the Hofmannsthal-Strauss Operas* (1996), and essays on Hofmannsthal and Strauss, Wagner and Nietzsche, Otto Dix, Fritz Grasshoff, and Hannah Arendt.

Douglas A. Joyce is Professor Emeritus in the Department of Germanic Languages and Literatures at Trinity College, University of Toronto. He is Co-Founder and Associate Editor of *Seminar: A Journal of Germanic Studies*, and author of various essays and studies on German and Austrian literature, including *Hugo von Hofmannsthal's* Der Schwierige*: A Fifty-Year Theater History* (Camden House, 1993).

Ellen Ritter is author of a number of articles on various aspects of Hofmannsthal's work. She is editor of volumes XVIII (*Dramen 16*, 1987), XIX (*Dramen 17*, 1994), XXVIII (*Erzählungen 1*, 1975), XXIX (*Erzählungen 2*, 1978), and XXXI (*Erfundene Gespräche und Briefe*, 1991) of the *Kritische Ausgabe* of Hofmannsthal's works. She is also editor of the Fischer paperback edition of Hofmannsthal's three most celebrated stories, *Das Märchen der 672. Nacht. Reitergeschichte. Erlebnis des Marschalls von Bassompierre* (1998).

Hinrich C. Seeba is Professor of German at the University of California at Berkeley. He is co-editor of the Kleist edition in the Deutscher Klassiker Verlag (1987 and 1991) and Festschriften for Heinz Politzer (*Austriaca*, 1975) and Richard Brinkmann (*Literaturwissenschaft und Geistesgeschichte*, 1981), and author of books on Hofmannsthal (*Kritik des ästhetischen Menschen*, 1970) and Lessing (*Die Liebe zur Sache*, 1973), and of numerous articles on German literary and intellectual history and cultural studies from the eighteenth century to the present.

Andreas Thomasberger is Adjunct Professor of German Literature at the Johann Wolfgang Goethe Universität, Frankfurt am Main. He is author of books on Hölderlin (*Von der Poesie der Sprache*, 1982) and Hofmannsthal (*Verwandlungen in Hofmannsthals Lyrik*, 1994), and numerous essays on literature and culture from the seventeenth to the twentieth centuries, as well as editorial theory and practice. He is editor of *Franz Hessel, Lyrik und Dramatik* (1999) and Hofmannsthal, *Lyrische Dramen, Jedermann, and Elektra* (Reclam 2000–2001). He is also co-editor of two volumes in the Hofmannsthal *Kritische Ausgabe* devoted to the lyric poetry and dramas (*SW 1* 1984, *SW 2* 1988) and of Richard Beer-Hofmann, *Gesamtausgabe in sechs Bänden* (1993–1998).

W. Edgar Yates is Emeritus Professor of German, University of Exeter, United Kingdom. He is author of *Schnitzler, Hofmannsthal, and the Austrian Theatre* (1992), *Theatre in Vienna: A Critical History, 1776–1995* (1996), *Nestroy and the Critics* (1994), and of numerous articles on Austrian and German literature and cultural history. He has been a *Korrespondierendes Mitglied* of the Österreichische Akademie der Wissenschaften (phil.-hist. Klasse) since 1995.

Index

Adorno, Theodor W., 6–7, 11–12, 21, 41, 43, 191, 208–9, 224
Aestheticism (historical movement), 4, 6–7, 11–12, 28–30, 68–69, 74, 83, 194, 230
aestheticism (*Weltanschauung* or lifestyle), 4, 15, 38, 48, 198, 200, 208, 222, 227, 236, 239, 242
Akademisches Gymnasium, 2, 228
Alewyn, Richard, 6–7, 21, 42, 237
Alexander II (Russian Tsar), 37
Allen, Virginia, 224
Allomatische, das, 75
Altenberg, Peter, 31, 33, 37
Altenhofer, Norbert, 154–55
Amiel, Henri-Frédéric, 228
Andrews, Julie, 36
Andrian, Leopold von, 10, 20, 31, 61, 82, 143–44, 224
Andrian, Leopold von, works by: *Der Garten der Erkenntnis,* 82
antisemitism, 9, 12, 33, 36–39, 43, 164–65, 242
Arabian Nights, 69
Arens, Katherine, 18, 200–201, 251
Arnim, Achim von, works by: *Kronenwächter,* 73; (with Clemens Brentano) *Knaben Wunderhorn, Des,* 57
Artaud, Antonin, 99
Auernheimer, Raoul, 79, 142, 144, 154, 171–72, 178
Auernheimer, Raoul, works by: *Casanova in Wien,* 142

Bacon, Francis, 76, 85–89, 92, 94, 198–99, 201–2
Bahr, Hermann, 2–3, 30–31, 34, 38–39, 228–30, 245–46, 248
Bahr, Hermann, works by: "Moderne, Die," 31; *Mutter,*

Die, 31, 228; *Überwindung des Naturalismus, Die,* 228; *Zur Kritik der Moderne,* 228
Ballets Russes, 181
Balzac, Honoré de, xvi, 183–84, 232
Baroque, 1, 10, 28, 131, 150, 160–62, 164, 172–73, 188
Barrès, Maurice, 228
Barzun, Jacques, 42
Baudelaire, Charles, 7, 29–30
Bauer, Roger, 42, 154–55
Bauernfeld, Eduard von, 140–41, 183–84
Baumann, Gerhard, 238
Beaumarchais, Pierre Augustin Caron De, works by: *Mariage de Figaro, Le,* 141, 148
Beer, Rudolf, 139, 152
Beer-Hofmann, Richard, 2, 9, 20, 33, 38, 43, 247, 252
Beller, Steven, 37, 43
Belvedere, xviii (photo), 1
Beniston, Judith, 18, 166, 174, 178–79
Benjamin, Walter, 191
Benjamin, Walter, works by: *Thesis on the Philosophy of History,* 191
Benn, Gottfried, 12
Bennett, Benjamin, 18, 94, 115, 143, 155, 251
Berend, Iván T., 224
Berendsohn, Walter A., 235
Berger, Alfred von, 3
Bering, Dietz, 43
Berlin, 29, 31, 35–36, 38, 40, 118, 140–41, 143, 152, 155, 159, 161, 166, 187, 193, 231–36, 239, 241, 246, 249–50
Berman, Nina, 18, 251
Bernhard, Thomas, 242

Bernhardt, Sarah, 197
Beyer-Ahlert, Ingeborg, xiii, 19, 200–201
Biedermeier, 28, 184
Bierich, Marcus, 241
Blätter für die Kunst, 3, 6, 55, 231, 246
Bodenhausen, Eduard von, 34, 61, 155, 162, 179, 247
Bolshevik Revolution, 145, 175
Borchardt, Rudolf, 228, 231–32, 246–48
Bottenberg, Joanna, 18, 137–38, 251
Bourget, Paul, 228
Bowra, C. M., 7, 11, 21
Brahm, Otto, 29, 140, 233
Braungart, Georg, 223
Brecht, Bertolt, 18
Brecht, Bertolt, works by: *Baal,* 108; "Experiment, Das," 198, 201
Brecht, Walther, 75–76, 84 237, 246
Bremer Presse, 111
Brentano, Clemens, works by: (with Achim von Arnim) *Des Knaben Wunderhorn,* 57
Brentano, Franz, 3
Brettell, Karen, 221
Briese-Neumann, Gisa, 42
Broch, Hermann, 242, 247, 249
Broch, Hermann, works by: *Hofmannsthal und seine Zeit,* 2, 8–10, 21, 26, 32, 34, 43, 238–39, 250
Bronfen, Elisabeth, 210, 222
Burckhardt, Carl, 127, 137, 143, 155
Burckhardt, Jakob, works by: *Die Kultur der Renaissance in Italien,* 199
Burgtheater (Vienna), 140–42, 147, 153, 164
Burton, Robert, works by: *Anatomy of Melancholy,* 53

Byron, George Gordon (Lord), 29, 245

Calderón de la Barca, Pedro, works by: *El gran teatro del mundo,* 103–4, 172; *La vida es sueño,* 100–101
Canetti, Elias, 41
Carossa, Hans, 183
Casanova, Giacomo, 140, 142
Cassirer, Ernst, 191, 199
Celan, Paul, 41, 43
Celan, Paul, works by: "Todesfuge," 41
Chekhov, Anton, 28
Classicism, 25, 28, 90, 183, 191
Claudel, Paul, 7, 42
Coellen, Ludwig, 42
Cohn, Dorrit, 35
Cohn, Hilde, 237
Coleridge, Samuel Taylor, works by: "Inscription for a Time-Piece," 58
Comédie Française, 141
commedia dell'arte, 102, 121–22
Crassus, Marcus, 87, 92
Curtius, Ernst Robert, 236

D'Annunzio, Gabriele, xv, 28–29, 33, 183, 194–95
Decadence, 27–30, 39, 42, 44, 183
Derrida, Jacques, 94
Deutsches Theater (Berlin), 140–41, 234
Diderot, Denis, 106–7
Diderot, Denis, works by: *Paradoxe sur le comédien,* 106
Dijkstra, Bram, 210
Dilthey, Wilhelm, 26, 193, 199
Dimter, Walter, 220
Dresden, 119, 234
Dreyfus, Alfred, 37
Duncan, Isadora, 197–99
Durr, Volker O., 222
Durzak, Manfred, 248

Duse, Eleanora, xv, 108–9, 113, 183, 196–97

Eichendorff, Joseph von, 49, 52, 173
Eichner, Hans, 35
Eliot, T. S., 7, 11–12, 18, 21, 239, 247
Enlightenment, 173, 191–92, 199–200
Epigonentum, 27
Euripides, 127
Exner, Richard, 62, 238, 240, 248
Expressionism, 31, 131, 207
Eyck, Jan van, 183
Eyes Wide Shut, 36

Fackel, Die, 40, 179
Fascism, 11, 35, 181
Fein, Maria, 239
Felstiner, John, 43
Femme fatale, 7, 214–16, 224
Fiechtner, Helmut, 31, 34, 43, 237, 246
Fiedler, Leonhard, 154
fin de siècle, 13, 25, 26, 28–29, 32, 36, 39, 42, 214
First World War, 10, 139–40, 148, 160, 181–83, 185–87, 189, 206
Fischer, Jens Malte, 42
Flimm, Jürgen, 153
Franckenstein, Clemens Freiherr von, 166
Franckenstein, Georg von, 70
Frankfurt am Main, 19–20, 237
Frankfurt School, 11, 199–200
Franz I (Austrian emperor), 33
Franz Joseph I (Austrian emperor), 185
Freie Bühne für modernes Leben, 66
Freies Deutsches Hochstift (Frankfurt), 20, 241
French Revolution, 25, 144, 148, 174

Freud, Sigmund, 33, 35, 89, 115, 214, 233
Friedrich, Hugo, 8
Frühwald, Wolfgang, 154
Fuchsschlössl, 4
Fuhrich, Edda, 160
Fuss, Harry, 153

Gautier, Théophile, 30
George, Stefan, xv, 3, 6–7, 20, 28, 49, 55–56, 88, 195–97, 201, 224, 228, 230–32, 237, 246–47
George, Stefan, works by: "An Phaon," 56; *Die Bücher der Hirten und Preisgedichte, der Sagen und Sänge und der hängenden Gärten,* 56, 63
Gervinus, Georg Gottfried, 193
Gessner, Adrienne, 153
Gibbon, Edward, 30
Gibbon, Edward, works by: *History of the Decline and Fall of the Roman Empire,* 30
Gilman, Richard, 42
Gilman, Sander, 8, 10, 21, 43, 223
Goethe, Johann Wolfgang von, 1, 52, 59, 73, 75, 82, 90, 115, 146, 153, 165–66, 173, 186, 188, 190, 222, 229
Goethe, Johann Wolfgang von, works by: *Faust,* 165–66, 173–74, 193; *Wilhelm Meisters Lehrjahre,* 73; *Wilhelm Meisters Wanderjahre,* 82
Goldmann, Paul, 246
Goldoni, Carlo, 141
Gomperz, Theodor, 3
Good, David F., 224
Gray, Ronald, 154
Griechische Anthologie, 70
Griensteidl, Café, 2, 21, 228–30
Grillparzer, Franz, 27, 36, 65, 185, 234
Grillparzer, Franz, works by: *Arme Spielmann, Der,* 65; *König Ottokars Glück und Ende,* 27

Grimm, Gunter, 247
Grimm, Jakob and Wilhelm, 171
Gundolf, Friedrich, 231, 237
Gundolf, Friedrich, works by: *Das Bild Georges,* 231, 246

Haas, Willy, 10
Habermas, Jürgen, 199
Haeussermann, Ernst, 153
Hamann, Brigitte, 36, 42
Hamann, Richard, 42
Handke, Peter, 242
Hannöver, Emma, 246
Harden, Maximilian, 246
Hart, Heinrich, 246
Hartsock, Nancy, 223
Hauptmann, Gerhard, 207
Hauptmann, Gerhard, works by: *Weber, Die,* 168
Hebbel, Friedrich, 79
Hegel, Georg Wilhelm Friedrich, 199
Heidegger, Martin, 12, 205, 218, 224
Heine, Heinrich, 38–39, 44
Heller, Peter, 35
Henry VIII (English king), 90
Hermand, Jost, 38, 42–43
Herzfeld, Marie, 139
Herzl, Thedor, 37, 39
Herzl, Thedor, works by: *Judenstaat, Der,* 37
Heuss, Theodor, 239–40, 248
Hiebler, Heinz, 244
Hilmes, Carola, 214, 224
Hirsch, Rudolf, xiii, 19, 63, 80, 84, 200, 222
Hitler, Adolf, 11, 32, 36, 38
Hofmann, Isaak Löw, 1, 9, 33
Hofmannsthal, Anna Maria Josefa, 1
Hofmannsthal, Augustin Emil von, 1
Hofmannsthal, Christiane von, 5
Hofmannsthal, Franz von, 5

Hofmannsthal, Gertrud (Gerty) von (née Schlesinger), 40
Hofmannsthal, Hugo August Peter von, 1–2
Hofmannsthal, Hugo von, works by:
Abenteurer und die Sängerin, Der, 76, 79, 139–40, 142, 232
Ad me ipsum, xvii, 34, 53, 75–77, 87, 92, 150, 237
"Adam Müllers Zwölf Reden über die Beredsamkeit," 188
"Age of Innocence," 65, 78 83–84
Ägyptische Helena, Die, xvii, 4, 125, 127–28, 130–32, 134–35, 236
"Algernon Charles Swinburne," xv, 6, 29, 194
"Alte Spiel von Jedermann, Das," xvi, 171
"Amgiad und Assad," 69, 78
Andreas, xvii, 15, 65, 70, 71, 73, 241–42, 249
"Ankündigung A. E. I. O. V. Bücher aus Österreich," 183
Arabella, xvii, 4, 70, 79, 120, 125, 128–35, 142, 236, 244, 247
Ariadne auf Naxos, xvi, 4, 121, 123–24, 128, 130, 133, 136, 183, 235, 247
"Augenblicke in Griechenland," 79
"Ballade des äußeren Lebens," xv, 2, 13, 57, 60
"Ballade von einem kranken Kinde," 57
"Balzac," xvi, 183, 232
"Beiden, Die," xv, 4, 17, 61, 115
"Bejahung Österreichs, Die," 5, 205
Bemerkungen, 188–89

"Bergwerk zu Falun, Das," xvi, 79

"Betrachtungen, die geschnittenen Steine und die redenden Masken, Die," 57

"Bild spricht," 58

"Boycott fremder Sprachen?" 220

"Brief an Lili," 59

"Brief des letzten Contarin," 79

"Brief, Ein" (Letter of Lord Chandos), xvi, 4, 16–18, 40, 62, 76–77, 79, 82, 85, 89, 147, 153, 182, 198–99, 201, 223

"Briefe des Zurückgekehrten, Die," xvi, 73, 79

Buch der Freunde, xvii, 66, 73, 106–7, 144, 164

"Bühne als Traumbild, Die," xvi

Cristinas Heimreise, 139, 142–43, 152, 233–34, 247

"Danae," 125, 130

"Dein Antlitz . . .," 55–56

"Deutsche Erzähler," 220

"Deutsche Festspiele zu Salzburg," xvii, 188

"Dichter und diese Zeit, Der," xvi, 140–41, 184

Dominic Heintls Letzte Nacht, 71

"Dorf im Gebirge, Das," 78

"Duse im Jahre 1903, Die," 108

"Eduard von Bauernfelds dramatischer Nachlass," 184

"Ehe des Herrn von Ferschengelder mit Fräulein della Spina, Die," 73

"Einige Worte als Vorrede zu St.-J. Perse 'Anabasis,'" xvii

Elektra, xvi, 4, 18, 62, 97, 102, 118–19, 123, 130–31, 133–34, 233, 244, 247

"Englischer Stil," 59

"Erinnerung schöner Tage," 78–79

"Erlebnis," xvi, 2, 50, 57–58

"Erlebnis des Marschalls von Bassompierre," xvi, 15, 65, 72, 75–76, 78, 82, 206

"Europäische Revue: Eine Monatsschrift," 189

"Francis Vielé-Griffins Gedichte," xv

"Französische Redensarten," 184

"Frau im Fenster, Die," 52–53, 61, 140

Frau ohne Schatten, Die (opera text), xvii, 4, 7, 20, 75, 79, 104, 121, 123–25, 128–34, 235, 241–42, 246–47, 249

Frau ohne Schatten, Die (prose), xvii, 7, 15–16, 20, 65, 69, 74–80, 82, 84, 124

"Für Eberhard von Bodenhausen," 34, 61, 149, 162

"Gabriele D'Annunzio" (1893), xv, 33, 194

"Gabriele D'Annunzio" (1894), xv, 194

"Gedankenspuk," 57

"Gedichte," 56

Gedichte und kleinen Dramen, Die, 51

"Gedichte von Stefan George," xv, 56, 195, 231

"Geiger vom Traunsee, Der," 65

"Geist der Karpathen," 220–21

Gerettete Venedig, Das, xvi, 97, 102, 233

"Geschichte der beiden Liebespaare," 70, 78

"Geschichte des Cadet Offiziersstellvertreters," 69

"Geschichte eines österreichischen Officiers," 69

"Gesellschaft," 55, 61

Hofmannsthal, Hugo von,
  works by (continued):
    "Gespräch über Gedichte,
      Das," xvi, 70, 88, 231
    Gestern, 32, 57, 61, 139, 168,
      228–29
    "Glück am Weg, Das," 51, 78
    "Glückliches Haus," 60
    "Goldene Apfel, Der," 51, 69,
      78
    "Grillparzers politisches
      Vermächtnis," 220
    "Großmutter und Enkel," 61
    "Hebbels Eiland," 79
    "Herzog von Reichstadt, Der,"
      79
    "Hier lieg ich," 52
    Hochzeit der Sobeide, Die, 140,
      232
    "Ich ging hernieder . . .," 52
    "Ich lösch das Licht," 52
    "Idee Europa, Die," 220
    "Idylle," xv, 3, 57–58
    "In ein Exemplar von Gestern,"
      57
    "Inschrift," 51
    "Jedermann," xvi, 18, 26, 97,
      105–6, 142, 159–61, 165–
      73, 175–77, 181, 193, 239,
      244, 247
    "Junge Frau und die Nixe im
      Baum, Die," 78
    "Jüngling und die Spinne,
      Der," 52–53
    Jupiter und Semele, 77
    Kaiser und die Hexe, Der, xv, 4,
      59, 79, 214
    "Kaiser von China spricht,
      Der," xv
    Kleine Welttheater, Das, xv, 4,
      15, 57, 61
    "Kluge Gräfin, Die," 121
    "Knabe, Ein," 53
    "Knabengeschichte," 66, 78
    König Ödipus, 97, 239
    "Krieg und Kultur," 186, 205

    Lästigen, Die, 141
    "Leben," 50
    "Lebenslied," 60, 62, 232
    "Leise tratest . . .," 52
    "Lucidor," 65, 69–71, 78–79,
      82, 125, 128
    "Manche freilich . . .," xv, 2,
      54–56
    "Märchen der 672. Nacht,
      Das," xv, 3, 15, 65–66, 69,
      74, 78, 82–83, 206, 252
    "Märchen von der
      verschleierten Frau," 78–79
    "Mein Garten," 50
    "Mit Handschuhen für Leopold
      Andrian," 61
    "Neue Roman von d'Annunzio,
      Der," xv, 194–95
    "Novelle," 78
    Ödipus und die Sphinx, xvi, 97,
      109
    "Österreich im Spiegel seiner
      Dichtung," 185–87
    "Österreichische Bibliothek:
      Eine Ankündigung," 205,
      221
    "Österreichische Idee, Die," 5,
      162, 187, 205, 224
    "Paar im Berg, Das," 78
    "Philipp II. und Don Juan
      d'Austria," 79
    "Philosophie des
      Metaphorischen," xv
    "Poesie und Leben," xv, 6, 88,
      232
    "Preusse und Österreicher: Ein
      Schema," 187, 220
    "Prinzessin auf dem
      verzauberten Berg," 78
    "Prolog zu Der Tor und der
      Tod," 57
    "Proposition," 188
    "Publikum der Salzburger
      Festspiele, Das," xvii, 193
    "Reinhardtsche Theater, Das,"
      188

"Reise im nördlichen Afrika,"
  xvii, 79
"Reiselied," xvi, 57
Reitergeschichte, 65, 67–9, 78,
  82–83, 206, 212–13, 216–
  19, 222–23, 252
Rosenkavalier, Der, xvi, 4, 10,
  17–18, 26, 70, 119–21, 123,
  127–35, 141–42, 160, 166,
  169, 177–78, 183, 234–35,
  247
Ruinen von Athen, Die, 127
"Die Salzburger Festspiele,"
  xvii, 161–62
*Salzburger große Welttheater,
  Das*, xvii, 4, 10, 12, 16, 97,
  103–5, 107, 115, 160–61,
  166, 172–80, 236, 239, 247
"Salzburger Programm, Das,"
  193
"Schrifttum als geistiger Raum
  der Nation, Das," xvii, 11,
  145, 164, 181, 189–91,
  220, 236, 243
Schwierige, Der, xvii, 5, 17, 34,
  139, 141–48, 150–56, 236,
  239, 241–42, 247, 249, 252
"Sebastian Melmoth," xvi, 16,
  71, 196
"Shakespeares Könige und
  große Herren," 62
"Siebenbrüder," 78
"Siehst du die Stadt," 49, 61
Silvia im "Stern," 139, 141
"Soldatengeschichte," 66, 69,
  78, 206, 211, 213, 215–19,
  222
"Spiel vor der Menge, Das,"
  xvi, 97, 106
*Studie über die Entwickelung des
  Dichters Victor Hugo*, xvi,
  141, 196
"Südfranzösische Eindrücke,"
  xv
"Terzinen," xv, 2, 50, 55, 57,
  86

"Theater des Neuen, Das," 108
Tod des Tizian, Der, xv, 3, 14,
  26, 49, 61, 246
Tor und der Tod, Der, xv, 3, 6,
  14–15, 26, 30, 42, 48, 52,
  57, 60, 62, 71, 107
"Traum von großer Magie,
  Ein," xv, 2, 52, 154
Triumph der Zeit, Der, 118
Turm, Der, xvii, 5, 16, 21, 97,
  101, 111–15, 236, 242
"Über moderne englische
  Malerei," xv, 6, 70
Unbestechliche, Der, xvii, 5, 17,
  139, 141, 143–45, 148–50,
  152–56, 236
"Unsere Fremdwörter," 185
"Unsere Militärverwaltung in
  Polen," 224
"Unvergleichliche Tänzerin,
  Die," 198
"Venezianische Erlebnis des
  Herrn von S., Das," 73
"Verse für ein durch Wasser
  getriebenes Puppenspiel," 61
"Verse zum Gedächtnis des
  Schauspielers Josef Kainz,"
  xvi
"Verwandten, Die," 78
"Vom dichterischen Dasein,"
  185
"Vor Tag," xvi, 50, 58, 86
"Vorfrühling," xv, 2, 7, 53, 57
"Vorspiel für ein
  Puppentheater," 99, 102,
  106, 107
"Vox et praeterea nihil," 53
"Walter Pater," xv, 6, 29, 183,
  195
"Was die Braut geträumt hat,"
  61
"Wege und die Bewegungen,
  Die," 78
Weiße Fächer, Der, 4, 11, 47, 61
"Weltgeheimnis," xv, 2, 51, 55,
  57, 60

Hofmannsthal, Hugo von,
  works by (continued):
  "Wert und Ehre deutscher
    Sprache," 181, 189, 192, 224
  "Wir Österreicher und
    Deutschland," 185–86
  "Wo ich nahe, wo ich
    lande . . .," 51
  "Wolken," 49
  "Wort, Das," 57
  "Zukunftsmusik," 118
  "Zum Gedächtnis des
    Schauspielers Mitterwurzer,"
    154
  "Zum Programm der
    Salzburger Festspiele," xvii
Hofmannsthal, Raimund von, 5
Hohendahl, Peter-Uwe, 247
Holl, Oskar, 161, 179
Homer, 127
Horkheimer, Max, 191
Hugo, Victor, xvi, 3, 141, 196
Hugo von Hofmannsthal-
  Gesellschaft, 20, 240–41, 244,
  248–49
Huysmans, Joris-Karl, 28–29, 208
Huysmans, Joris-Karl, works by:
  À Rebours, 29, 208

Ibsen, Henrik, xv, 29, 31, 183
Ibsen, Henrik, works by: Ghosts,
  29; Pretenders, 29, 31
Ihering, Herbert, 165, 179
Immermann, Karl, 27
Immermann, Karl, works by:
  Epigonen, Die, 27
Impressionism (movement), 30,
  42, 235
Irving, John, 36
Irving, John, works by: World
  According to Garp, The, 36
Iser, Wolfgang, 247

Jacobsen, Jens Peter, 65–66
Jahrbuch des freien deutschen
  Hochstifts, 76

Janik, Allan, 43
Janz, Rolf-Peter, 42
Jaron, Norbert, 249
Jaszi, Andrew, 237
Jászi, Oscar, 224
Jauss, Hans Robert, 25, 44, 240,
  249
Jens, Walter, 238
Jewishness, 1–2, 4, 9–11, 21, 33,
  35–41, 43, 164, 219, 223
Joachim, Jacques, 30
Jodl, Friedrich, 3
Joyce, Douglas, 18, 154–55, 241,
  246, 249, 252
Joyce, James, 184, 239
Junges Deutschland, 38, 43
Junges Wien, 2, 3, 9–11, 29–31,
  34, 38, 44, 227–29, 246

Kafka, Eduard Michael, 30
Kafka, Franz, 40, 217
Kahane, Arthur, 153
Kant, Immanuel, 190, 199
Kant, Immanuel, works by:
  "Was ist Aufklärung?" 190
Kessler, Harry, 119, 137, 141, 155
Kikuchi, Takehoro, 247, 249
Kleines Theater (Max Reinhardt's
  Berlin theater), 118, 233
Klimt, Gustav, 34
Knackfuß, Hermann, 55, 63
Kobel, Erwin, 86, 93, 95
Koch, Franz, 37–38, 44
Koch, Hans-Albrecht, 20, 139, 155
Koch, Uta, 20
Koenig, Ewald, 249
Kommerell, Max, 237
Konrad, Claudia, 241, 246, 249
Konservative Revolution, 11, 136,
  191, 220, 243
Köttelwesch, Clemens, 19–20, 241
Kovach, Thomas A., 20–21, 62,
  88, 95, 115, 251
Kraft, Werner, 238
Kraus, Karl, 33–37, 39–40, 44,
  177, 179, 207

Kraus, Karl, works by: *Demolirte Literatur, Die,* 39; "Krone für Zion, Eine," 37; "Heine und die Folgen," 39
Kubrick, Stanley, 36
Kuna, F. M., 247, 249

Laermann, Klaus, 42
Lenau, Nicolaus, 48, 65
Le Rider, Jacques, 8, 21, 89, 95, 201–2, 223
Lindken, Hans-Ulrich, 154–55
Literatur und Kritik, 241, 249–50
Lombroso, Cesare, 39
Lombroso, Cesare, works by: *Genio et Folia,* 39
London, 29, 167
Loos, Adolf, 32, 345, 39
Lorenz, Dagmar, 42
Lorins, Rebecca, 221
Loris, 2, 29, 38, 227–30, 232, 234, 236–37, 242, 246, 248
Lothar, Ernst, 153
Lothar, Rudolf (real name: Rudolf Spitzer), 38
Lothar, Rudolf, works by: *Kritische Studien zur Psychologie der Literatur,* 38
Louvet de Couvray, Jean Baptiste, 119
Louvet de Couvray, Jean Baptiste, works by: *Aventures des Chevalier Faublas, Les,* 119
Lublinski, Samuel, 246
Lueger, Karl, 9, 33, 36
Lunzer, Heinz, 221

MacDonald, Dwight, 12, 21
Mach, Ernst, 3, 32, 37, 44, 89, 93
Mach, Ernst, works by: *Beiträge zur Analyse der Empfindungen,* 32, 89
Maeterlinck, Maurice, 28
Mahler, Gustav, 33–34
Mallarmé, Stéphane, 7, 29, 49
Mandelkow, Karl Robert, 240, 249

Mann, Heinrich, 207
Mann, Thomas, 27, 223
Mann, Thomas, works by: *Buddenbrooks: Verfall einer Familie,* 27; *Der Tod in Venedig,* 223
Maria Theresia, Empress of Austria, 4, 119
Marlowe, Christopher, 183
Martini, Fritz, 238
Marx, Karl, 191, 199
Marx, Karl, works by: *Theses on Feuerbach,* 191
Mauser, Wolfram, 115, 154, 156, 238
Mauthner, Franz H., 35
Mauthner, Fritz, 40, 200–202, 251
Mauthner, Fritz, works by: *Beiträge zur Kritik der Sprache,* 40
Mayer, Mathias, 19–21, 241, 249
McKenzie, John R. P., 154–55, 179
Meinrad, Josef, 153
Mell, Max, 165, 237
Menzel, Wolfgang, 38–39
Metternich, Franz, 28
Meyerbeer, Giacomo, 10
Michelangelo Buonarotti, 55, 63
Moderne Dichtung, 30–31
Moderne Rundschau, 31, 228
Modernism (movement), 8–9, 16, 21–36, 85, 95, 164, 183, 223
Molière (real name: Jean Baptiste Poquelin), 119, 121–23, 130–31, 141, 152, 154–55, 235
Molière, works by: *Bourgeois gentilhomme, Le,* 121, 141; *Fâcheux, Les,* 141; *Médecin malgré lui, Le,* 141; *Monsieur de Pourceaugnac,* 141
Morak, Franz, 153
Morton, Michael, 88–91, 94–95
Morzé, Petra, 153
Mozart, Leopold, 2

Mozart, Wolfgang Amadeus, 2, 124, 161, 165, 183, 185, 187–88, 245
Mozart, Wolfgang Amadeus, works by: *Zauberflöte, Die,* 124
Müller, Paul Werner, 246
Munich, 11, 139, 145, 162, 234, 243
Musil, Robert, 34
Musil, Robert, works by: *Mann ohne Eigenschaften, Der,* 34
Musset, Alfred de, 139

Nadler, Josef, 10, 162–64, 179–80, 193–94
Nadler, Josef, works by: *Literaturgeschichte der deutschen Stämme und Landschaften,* 162, 164, 179, 193
Naef, Karl J., 237
National Socialism (Nazism), 11, 21, 36, 164, 192, 194, 200, 206, 224, 238
Naturalism (movement), 65, 183, 207, 218, 228–30, 248
Naumann, Walter, 237
Nehring, Wolfgang, 42, 171, 179
Neo-Romanticism, 30, 193
Nervenkunst, 25, 44
Nestroy, Johann Nepomuk, 36, 141, 156, 185, 252
Nestroy, Johann Nepomuk, works by: *Zu ebener Erde und erster Stock,* 36
Neue Deutsche Beiträge, 111
Neue Freie Presse (Vienna), 37–38, 137, 154, 178. *See also Die Presse*
Neue Subjektivität, 30
New Historicism, 30
Nietzsche, Friedrich, 26, 30, 44, 251
Nijinsky, Vaslav, 183
Nordau, Max, 30, 39
Nordau, Max, works by: *Entartung,* 30

Novalis (real name: Friedrich von Hardenberg), 60, 144

Obenauer, Karl Justus, 235
Offenbach, Jacques, 28, 130, 195
Opera buffa, 121–22
Opera seria, 121–22
Otway, Thomas, 100–101, 166
Otway, Thomas, works by: *Venice Preserved,* 100, 166

Pallenberg, Max, 141–42
Pannwitz, Rudolf, 125, 137, 142, 144, 159, 161, 164, 167, 179, 234, 248
Paracelsus, 52, 74
Paris, 29, 31, 141, 178
Pater, Walter, xv, 6, 29, 183, 195–96
Perels, Christoph, 19
Perl, Walter, 246
Perrault, Charles, 26
Pestalozzi, Karl, 62, 115, 154, 156
Pfeiffer, Joachim, 222
Pirker, Max, 139
Platen, August von, 48
Pléiade, 3, 141
Plummer, Christopher, 36
Polheim, Karl Konrad, 154, 166
Politzer, Heinz, 35, 252
Pound, Ezra, 11–12
Poussin, Nicolas, 73
Präexistenz (Preexistence), 53, 75–76, 87
Prague, 40
Praz, Mario, 20
Pre-Raphaelites, xv, 6, 229
Presse, Die (Vienna), 243, 249. *See also Neue Freie Presse*
Prince, Morton, 71, 73, 84
Prossnitz, Gisela, 160, 179
Proust, Marcel, 239

Raimund, Ferdinand, 36, 183, 185, 188
Raimundtheater (Vienna), 139

Ránki, György, 224
Realism (movement), 230
Redlich, Josef, 149, 155
Reformation, 192
Reinhardt, Max, 39, 97–98, 100,
    113, 118, 121, 140, 144, 151,
    153–55, 159, 161, 165–67,
    177, 179–81, 188, 233–35
Remak, Henry, 222
Renaissance, 6, 147, 153, 191–92,
    199–200
Requadt, Paul, 238
Residenztheater (Munich), 139
Rey, William, 238
Rezeptionsästhetik, 240
Rieckmann, Jens, 8–10, 22, 164,
    179, 223
Rilke, Rainer Maria, 11, 13, 20,
    29, 54, 56, 63, 197–98, 251
Rilke, Rainer Maria, works by:
    Sonette an Orpheus, 56
Rimbaud, Arthur, 28–30
Ringstraße, 8, 32
Ritter, Ellen, 18, 201, 222
Robespierre, Maximilien, 148–49
Rococo, 27–28
Rodaun, 4–5, 242
Rodin, Auguste, 197
Rölleke, Heinz, 19, 171, 179
Romanticism, 8, 20, 25, 30, 49,
    52, 60, 78, 83, 130–31, 144,
    183, 218, 233
Rome, 29, 125
Rorty, Richard, 205, 224
Rösch, Ewald, 154, 156
Rosegger, Peter, 185
Rosenberg, Alfred, 39, 44
Rückert, Friedrich, 48
Rüdgers, Hans, 153
Rühle, Günther, 152, 154, 156, 249

Sächsische Arbeiter-Zeitung, 233
Salten, Felix, 33, 151
Salzburg Festival, xvii, 5, 7, 10,
    18, 145, 149, 159–81, 183,
    188, 193, 202, 225, 247

Sandgruber, Roman, 42
Schaeder, Grete, 237
Schaeder, Heinrich, 237
Schalk, Franz, 161, 235
Schenk, Otto, 153
Scherer, Stefan, 43
Schiele, Egon, 34
Schilling, Max von, 236
Schlegel, Friedrich, 25, 44
Schmid, Martin E., 247–249
Schmujlow-Classen, Ria, 233
Schnitzler, Arthur, 2, 9, 20, 31,
    33, 35–36, 42, 44, 83, 140,
    142, 144, 153, 178, 180, 232,
    248, 252
Schnitzler, Arthur, works by:
    Liebelei, 33, 44; *Professor
    Bernhardi*, 9; *Reigen*, 33;
    Traumnovelle, 36; *Weg ins
    Freie, Der*, 9
Schoeller, Bernd, xiii, 19, 200–201
Schönberg, Arnold, 33–34
Schönbrunn, 4
Schönerer, Georg von, 9, 36
Schorske, Carl E., 2, 8, 22, 42
Schottenkirche (Vienna), 4
Schulmeister, Otto, 249
Schwarz, Egon, 35
Scott, Marilyn, 223
Second World War, 199, 237
Seeba, Hinrich, 18, 42, 252
Shakespeare, William, 5, 141, 183
Sheppard, Richard, 95
Silberer, Herbert, 76, 84
Sokel, Walter, 35
Sondrup, Steven P., 20, 22, 62
Sophocles, 97, 100–101, 110, 118
Sophocles, works by: *Electra*, 100–
    101, 118; *Oedipus at Colonnus*,
    110; *Oedipus the King*, 97, 110
Sösemann, Bernd, 241, 249
Sound of Music, The, 36
Sprengel, Peter, 222
St. Denis, Ruth, 197
St. Petersburg, 229
Staiger, Emil, 237

Stanzel, Franz K., 205–6, 225
Stauf von der March, Ottokar (real
    name: Ottokar F. Chalupka), 9,
    38, 44
Stein, Gerd, 214, 225
Steinberg, Michael P., 160–61,
    163, 178–79, 182, 202, 221,
    225, 239, 250
Steinboeck, Rudolf, 153
Steiner, Herbert, xiii, 18, 86, 238,
    248
Stemberger, Julia, 153
Stepanek, Lilly, 153
Stern, Martin, 154, 156, 201–2,
    238, 241
Stesichoros, 127
Stieler, Kurt, 139
Stöcklein, Paul, 240, 247, 250
Strauss, Johann, Jr., 32, 193
Strauss, Johann, Jr., works by:
    Fledermaus, Die, 32, 193
Strauss, Richard, 1, 4–5, 7, 18, 20,
    26, 36, 117–37, 159–61, 178–
    79, 234–36, 246–47, 249–51
Strauss, Richard, works by:
    Capriccio, 133; Intermezzo,
    125, 130; Schweigsame Frau,
    Die, 130
Strelka, Joseph P., 156, 222
Strindberg, August, 84
Strindberg, August, works by:
    Ghost Sonata, 84
Stuck, Franz, 183
Swinburne, Algernon, xv, 6, 29,
    194–95, 198–99
symbolism, 131, 134, 154–55
Symbolism (movement), 3, 7, 8,
    11–12, 16, 21–22, 28–29, 31,
    49, 62, 88, 95, 251
Szondi, Peter, 62

Taaffe, Eduard von, 36
Taxis, Princess Maria von, 71
Theater in der Josefstadt (Vienna),
    151, 153
Third Reich, 11, 37, 39

Thomasberger, Andreas, 18, 62,
    154, 156, 252
Toulmin, Stephen, 43
Träbing, Gerhard, 223
Trappmann, Wilhelm, 247

University of Munich, 145
Upstairs, Downstairs, 36

Valéry, Paul, 11
Van Gogh, Vincent, 73
Verlaine, Paul, 7, 29
Vielé-Griffin, Francis, xv
Vienna, 1–4, 8–9, 20–22, 26, 28–
    42, 68–70, 76, 95, 115, 119,
    128, 139–40, 153, 161–62,
    164, 172, 176, 178–79, 223,
    229, 231–33, 235, 243, 246,
    248, 252
Vilain, Robert, 20, 22, 176, 178–
    79
Volke, Werner, 2, 10, 22, 162,
    180, 230–31, 241, 250
Volkstheater (Vienna), 153, 183–
    84
Vormärz, 28

Wagner, Richard, 12, 22, 30, 37,
    44, 117, 205, 221, 251
Wagner, Richard, works by: Ring-
    Cycle (Ring des Nibelungen,
    Der), 205
Waldenfels, Bernhard, 221
Walk, Cynthia, 177, 180
Weber, Eugene, 43
Weber, Horst, 20, 237, 247, 250
Weck, Peter, 153
Weimar, 36, 90, 178, 188
Weiner, Marc, 12, 22, 221
Weininger, Otto, 37, 44, 214
Weininger, Otto, works by:
    Geschlecht und Charakter, 37, 44
Weiss, Walter, 166, 177, 180
Weizsäcker, Richard von, 243
Wiener Moderne, 9, 18, 25–44

Wilde, Oscar, xvi, 6, 16, 28, 30, 68, 71, 183–84, 196, 199, 208
Wilde, Oscar, works by: *De Profundis,* 71; *Picture of Dorian Gray, The,* 30, 208
Wildgans, Anton, 147, 247
Williams, Bernard, 205, 221
Wilson, Edmund, 8, 22
Wittgenstein, Ludwig, 40, 43, 89, 94
Wittgenstein, Ludwig, works by: *Tractatus logico-philosophicus,* 40
Woolf, Virginia, 70, 184
Worbs, Michael, 25, 44
Wunberg, Gotthart, 31–32, 38, 42, 44, 229, 231, 239–40, 245–46, 248, 250
Wuthenow, Ralph-Rainer, 154, 156

Yates, W. E., 18, 165, 178–80, 252
Yeats, W. B., 7, 11, 239

Zeiss, Karl, 150
Zeit, Die (Vienna), 232, 246
Zinn, Ernst, 19
Zionism, 37
Zohn, Harry, 35
Zola, Émile, 228
Zurich, 239, 247